27

ONE HUNDRED YEARS
OF
THE TOURIST TROPHY

SHOEI
10
RACING

TOURIST TROPHY

TT CENTURY

ONE HUNDRED YEARS OF THE TOURIST TROPHY

Stuart Barker

C
CENTURY

MCN
www.motorcyclenews.com

Published by Century 2007

10 9 8 7 6 5 4 3 2 1

First published in Great Britain in 2007 by
Century
Random House, 20 Vauxhall Bridge Road,
London SW1V 2SA

www.randomhouse.co.uk

Addresses for companies within The Random House Group Limited can be found at: www.randomhouse.co.uk

The Random House Group Limited Reg. No. 954009

A CIP catalogue record for this book is available from the British Library

ISBN 9781846052354

The Random House Group Limited makes every effort to ensure that the papers used in its books are made from trees that have been legally sourced from well-managed and credibly certified forests. Our paper procurement policy can be found at: www.randomhouse.co.uk/paper.htm

Designed by Peter Ward
Printed and bound by Firmengruppe APPL, aprinta druck, Wemding, Germany

Title-page photograph: No fear. John McGuinness ignores the stone walls at Handley's Corner

This page: Back on top. In 1995 Joey Dunlop won a big bike race – the Senior – for the first time since 1988

Pages 6–7: Out of the shadows. Phillip McCallen hammers through Kirkmichael in 1996 – his most successful year at the TT

Pages 8–9: The last win. Just weeks after completing his third TT treble with victory in the 125 race, the irreplaceable Joey Dunlop lost his life in Estonia.

Pages 10–11: Robert Holden takes the equisite Ducati Supermono to victory in the 1995 Singles race.

Arai
Castrol
3
MICHELIN
Arai
Arai
HONDA

This book is dedicated to Gus Scott and Colin Breeze, both of whom lost their lives pursuing their TT dreams.

And to John Crowe and David Oliver who liked nothing better than to sit at the 33rd Milestone and watch the greatest road racers in the world.

It is written with respect and admiration for every single man and woman who has had the courage to face the challenge of the TT over the last 100 years.

ACKNOWLEDGEMENTS

Thanks to the following riders (in alphabetical order) for consenting to give interviews for this book:

Giacomo Agostini, Geoff Duke OBE, Mick Grant, Ron Haslam, Ian Lougher, Guy Martin, Phillip McCallen, Rob McElnea, John McGuinness, Jim Moodie, Chas Mortimer, Phil Read MBE, Ian Simpson, John Surtees MBE, Charlie Williams.

Thanks also to the following for their assistance in compiling this book:

Timothy Andrews at Century, Peter Ward for his design work, Jacqueline Harris and James Doherty at EMAP archives, Tom Parker, Marc Potter, Ben Purvis and Alison Silcox at *Motor Cycle News*, John Noble, Howard Boylan and Dave Collister for taking some awesome photographs, Bill Snelling at FoTTofinders, Pauline Hailwood, Alan Seeley, Brian 'Badger' Crichton, Paul Warburton, Donna Costello, Shannon Greenwood, and finally my parents, Jim and Josie Barker, for taking me to the TT when I was just a wee laddie and for all their help and support since. Cheers folks.

Extra special thanks must go to Ally Cubbon for proof reading the book and compiling the results pages. A huge thank you must also go to Steve 'Morty' Mort for his invaluable 'contribution' in helping put this book together. Good on ya mate!

Photographs supplied by EMAP Archive, FoTTofinder Bikesport Archives and www.photocycles.com.

Results compiled by Ally Cubbon.

CONTENTS

DUKE

TOURIST TROPHY
CENTURY

FOREWORDS

GEOFF DUKE OBE

'When I was young, most budding racers felt the TT was the be-all and end-all of racing and I, for one, never lost that feeling. Winning a TT almost meant more than being world champion. It's so different; it's a very demanding race which required the utmost concentration from a rider and the bigger the challenge, the better I preferred it. There have been times, like when the TT lost its world championship status in 1976, that I thought it was the beginning of the end, but it didn't happen. The TT kept going because of the enthusiasm of the young people who wanted to ride in it and because of the spectators who came over on a regular basis to watch. This is what has kept the event going over the years. There is always the danger that, if the TT has a really bad year in the way of fatalities, then that could have serious consequences for its future. But otherwise, it seems to go from strength to strength – and long may it continue to do so.'

Geoff Duke was motorcycle racing's first mainstream superstar and household name. A six-times world champion and six-times TT winner in the 1950s, he was, for many, the most stylish rider ever to grace the Mountain circuit.

JOHN SURTEES MBE

John Surtees won six TTs and seven motorcycle world championships before switching to car racing in 1961. In winning the 1964 Formula 1 World Championship, he became the only man in history to win world titles on two wheels and four.

'I think in Grand Prix racing in the 1950s and 1960s, the TT was the optimum challenge which was there to be, if possible, conquered. If you succeeded there it gave you immense satisfaction because you were on the world stage competing against the world's best riders. The future of the TT of course, does not hold that, nor does the present. What the present riders do around the Isle of Man is quite fantastic but it has developed into a specialist one-off type of event. As such, I wonder – with the way the Isle of Man is developing – whether the TT has a future. The important thing is to remember what has passed, and particularly the good parts. It would be sad to see the opportunities that still arise from the Isle of Man authorities' willingness to work and cooperate with the world of motorsport, lost to us. I would think that there's more potential in turning the TT into more of a festival, not only of yesteryear, but also of motorcycle racing today – rather like Goodwood where the latest F1 cars and Grand Prix bikes mix with machines from bygone years. Perhaps there could be one feature race at the TT with the rest of the fortnight being centred around the past, and maybe not just for two wheels either. It may be that there could be a hill climb and a race on a shorter circuit – perhaps on the Clypse course – and possibly a historic race on the main course. If you bring that festival factor in you would widen the interest and make it more commercially viable. But, of course, against that is probably the fact that if you did create a big commercial interest, there probably isn't the hotel capacity to take advantage of it.'

PHIL READ MBE

'The TT course is the greatest challenge of man and machine – ever. So to conquer that course and lap at reasonable speeds for six laps gives great satisfaction. There's fantastic camaraderie and spirit amongst riders at the TT. It's almost like flying in a Spitfire squadron in wartime – you all make the most of the moment because you know you might be dead the next day. The difference between a good TT rider and a great TT rider is in his determination to win, his focus, and his ability to set up a bike. You also need to learn the course well and be able to drum up enough courage to go through corners at higher speeds than you know is sensible. And you can only pray that you don't have any mechanical problems; that your gear-box doesn't seize, or the frame doesn't break, or whatever. Hopefully, because of my actions in boycotting the TT in 1972, the riders since then have been much better paid and enjoy better safety features and more consideration from the organisers. I wouldn't like to say what will happen to the TT in the future – circumstances may cause it to be stopped. It affects businesses which in turn affects the Isle of Man's economy and now all the boarding houses are closed and the camping sites are not particularly good so they don't get the crowds over and the money being spent on the Island like before.'

Phil Read is one of the most controversial competitors in TT history. After winning six races between 1961 and 1972, he boycotted the event before returning to win two more races in 1977. His views today are as forthright as ever.

GIACOMO AGOSTINI

Giacomo Agostini has won more world championships than any other rider in the history of motorcycling. As well as his 15 world titles and 122 Grand Prix wins, he won 10 TT races between 1965 and 1972.

'I have three very important memories of the TT: one when I crashed at Sarah's Cottage in the 1965 Senior race, another when I won for the first time in 1966 in the Junior and another when I didn't win against Mike Hailwood in the Senior in 1967. When I ride parade laps now it brings back memories for me but sometimes they are not so happy – because I remember when I was younger and I could go faster and win races! But I like to come back to the TT and see old friends and say hello to everybody. I think the future of the TT must be to build a short circuit. I suggested this to the Isle of Man government – to keep the traditional grandstand and the traditional paddock, but to build a safe circuit. There is a lot of space on the Isle of Man to make a circuit of maybe 9-10 kilometres and I'm sure everybody would be happy to come back to the Isle of Man – even MotoGP riders. But we need to make a safe track. I don't understand why it's not been done because I think it's possible.'

CHAS MORTIMER

Chas Mortimer was one of the biggest stars of the TT in the 1970s, taking seven wins between 1970 and 1978. He retired from racing following a bad crash in 1980 but still rides at many classic events.

'I used to like riding in the Isle of Man and always found it a challenge. I like the Manx people and the money was a big pull as I always used to go over there and earn lots of cash! A TT win was something special – there was no comparison even to a Grand Prix win. I won three or four Grands Prix but the satisfaction of winning a TT was completely different. It was much more of a challenge. To me as a rider, taking the world championship status away from the TT in 1976 made no difference whatsoever. The challenge was still there, irrespective of whether it was a world championship race or not – the challenge of the circuit was always there.'

MICK GRANT

A seven-times TT winner between 1974 and 1985, Mick Grant will always be remembered for his awesome lap records on the Kawasaki KR750 'Green Meanie' in 1975 and 1977.

'The TT was the highlight of the racing year for me. I would have been as bored as hell just doing short circuits every weekend so it was nice to go to the TT and do something different. But it frightened me, there's no question about that. I was always anxious because I knew that even if you didn't make a mistake yourself, you could always have a mechanical problem. But at the same time, what a buzz! To go round there and come out of certain corners, like the 32nd Milestone, absolutely right, and see an extra 200 or 300rpm on your rev counter was just something special. Some of those big, fast corners, you'd just find yourself taking a deep breath and as you came out of the corner it was like winning the lottery. It was just like "Yes, I did it!" On the boat on the way to the Isle of Man I would always tell myself to just be careful, and in a way I was glad when it was finished, but at the end of the day I enjoyed every minute of it.'

CHARLIE WILLIAMS

'I may have got great pleasure from winning other big races but for actual riding satisfaction nothing came close to the TT. One of the most satisfying things in racing was to do a near-perfect lap of the TT course. And while I enjoyed racing on other road circuits, nowhere else was as technical as the Isle of Man. You can make a mistake on the TT course and still be paying for it two miles farther down the road.

'When I retired from the TT it left a huge gap in my life. I've never replaced the buzz I got from riding round the Mountain circuit. I was tempted to make a comeback just to get that rush again because I got terrible withdrawal symptoms for years after I stopped. I knew one former TT racer who tried skydiving and umpteen parachute jumps but said he still couldn't replace the buzz of racing at the TT. Sadly, he missed it so much that he made a comeback and was killed.

'I wouldn't begin to try and predict the future of the event because I did that in the 1970s and was completely wrong! But all we can hope for is that it carries on and doesn't claim too many more lives because that is the big issue. I've lost a lot of friends and colleagues at the TT but I would never dream of suggesting that it should be stopped on those grounds. It's always been a trade-off: you get such a fantastic buzz from the place but you also know that you might not come home. Maybe for some people, that's what the attraction is.'

As well as being an eight times TT winner in the 1970s and 1980s, Charlie Williams has been a lifelong supporter of the event and is now a well-known radio commentator during TT fortnight.

PHILLIP McCALLEN

Phillip McCallen is the only man to have won four TT races in one week, which he did in 1996. His total tally of 11 victories ranks him amongst the greatest TT riders of all time.

'On the world calendar, the TT was *the* race. Coming from Ireland, if you wanted to be a proper road racer and really earn the name you had to conquer the TT. Our races at home were really just junior races compared to the TT – it was the toughest, meanest road race in the world. It was *hours* of flat-out riding, as fast as you wanted to go, not just a 20-minute jaunt. As a rider, you know that the adrenaline rush, the buzz of racing at the TT, will never be replaced once you retire. It's such a high and such a feeling of satisfaction to stand on the top of the rostrum at the TT and it's hard to come to terms with not having that feeling. When I first went and watched the races after I'd retired, I'd still think, "I could go faster than that – maybe I should do it again", but eventually you just have to accept that it's over, however hard that may be.'

JIM MOODIE

'When I was a kid, even going to the TT to *watch* the races seemed unachievable. For me, to compete there would have been a dream, but I could never even have dared to dream that I would one day win a TT – it would have been beyond my wildest expectations. I think the way forward for the TT is to build a Spa-Francorchamps-type short circuit, incorporating part of the TT course – maybe from Kate's Cottage down towards Creg-ny-Baa and then back onto a short circuit. It could be used for the Manx GP, the Manx Rally and the TT, as well as hosting corporate events and track days. The Isle of Man is a very nice place and it's not the most difficult place in the world to get to, so if a short circuit was marketed properly, I don't see why it wouldn't work.'

Jim Moodie won eight TT races before a leg injury forced him to miss the event in 2004. Unable to stay away, he used his vast Island experience to guide John McGuinness to a record-breaking hat-trick of victories.

Ian Lougher is the most experienced top TT rider still racing. He has ridden in 87 TTs and had six wins since his debut in 1984.

IAN LOUGHER

'The TT is the most important race of the year for me. I always had to work really hard to be fast on short circuits but I found it easy to ride fast round the Isle of Man. Because the TT is so different, even the mental preparation for it is different to any other race. Each year I'll think about what sort of machine support I'm going to get, who's going to help me in the pits, how I'm going to gain a little bit of time here and there, how to improve my fuel stops, whatever. It's totally different thinking and it still gets my blood racing just thinking about it now. The TT is dangerous and you have to respect it, but I suppose you've also got to shut the dangers out or you'd never race there. My racing motto has always been "expect the unexpected", and maybe that's why I'm still racing!'

JOHN McGUINNESS

'The TT is 100 years old because it's special – it's not just another piece of road. It's like the Holy Grail of motorcycle racing – it's part of history and for me it's great to be part of that. It's really been dragged out of the shit in recent years and is back in the limelight. The "blue coat brigade" has gone and the riders can deal with real people now – not accountants and solicitors who all thought we were idiots anyway. I think people are putting more pressure on themselves for the centennial races but I'm going to treat TT2007 like every other year. Just because it's the 100th anniversary doesn't mean the walls will be made of rubber and the trees made of cheese. There's still some horrendous obstacles out there that are gonna have your pants down if you get it wrong. So you've still got to be in control and do it exactly the same as you always do. I think the TT has a safe future because there will always be people who want to do it. It's always been a magnet for bike racers and I'm sure it will carry on, but I don't know if it'll be around in another hundred years – unless they race it on space bikes and wear suits that inflate when you crash!'

The current master of the Mountain course, John McGuiness, has 11 TT wins to his credit as well as the outright lap record (129.45mph) going into the centennial races.

TOURIST TROPHY

CENTURY

CHAPTER 1

1907-14

11
5

A VIKING HERITAGE

The location of the startline for the first ever TT race could not have been more appropriate. As the 25 entrants lined up on a dusty road in the village of St John's on May 28, 1907, they were quite literally under the shadow of Tynwald Hill – the seat of the Isle of Man's ancient parliament. And without that hill, used as an assembly by Viking settlers as far back as the year 979, the Isle of Man TT races would never have existed.

Although Tynwald considers British legislation, it is free to make its own decisions and create its own laws and in 1904, the Manx authorities spotted an opportunity in the still embryonic world of motorsport. At the time, British roads were covered by a blanket speed limit of 20mph and the British Government refused to sanction the closure of roads for racing. The secretary of the Automobile Club of Great Britain (now known as the RAC), Julian Orde, was keen to stage a car race somewhere within the British Isles. Fortunately, he happened to be a cousin of the Governor of the Isle of Man, Lord Raglan. Raglan was a fan of the motorsport events being held on the Continent and he quickly persuaded the Manx authorities of the potential benefits of staging similar events on the Island. The Manx Parliament agreed to allow its roads to be used for racing and, with the decision having been made in principle, the matter was passed over to Tynwald to make it legal. At a special public sitting on May 5, Tynwald made the 1904 Road Closure Act law. Thanks to a parliament founded by the Vikings, the legislation which would eventually allow for the Isle of Man TT races to take place was ratified.

With the first motorcycle having only recently been invented, bike racing in the early 1900s was still in its infancy. While some steam-powered motorcycles were built in the late 19th Century, it was German engineer Gottlieb Daimler who is credited with producing the first motorcycle powered by an internal combustion engine in 1885. The first known bike (and car) race took place in 1895 and ran from Paris to Madrid. It attracted over three million spectators along the route but eventually had to be abandoned when too many of them were killed by out of control cars. From the very outset, it was clear that motor racing was a dangerous sport – a fact which haunts the TT to this day.

The first motorsport event to take place on the Isle of Man was a time trial for car drivers hoping to represent Britain in the Coupe International (or International Cup) in France. On Tuesday, May 10 at 9am, a host of huge seven-litre, one-ton cars lined up directly in front of the Quarterbridge Hotel in Douglas to begin the Island's long history of motorsport.

Despite several crashes and incidents with cars exploding, the race was deemed a success and when the Automobile Club expressed an interest in returning to the

Before the TT – Riders, entrants and machines at the weigh-in for the 1905 International Cup trials.

The original TT course: The St John's circuit linked the villages of St John's and Kirkmichael with the old Manx capital of Peel. It was also known as the 'short course.'

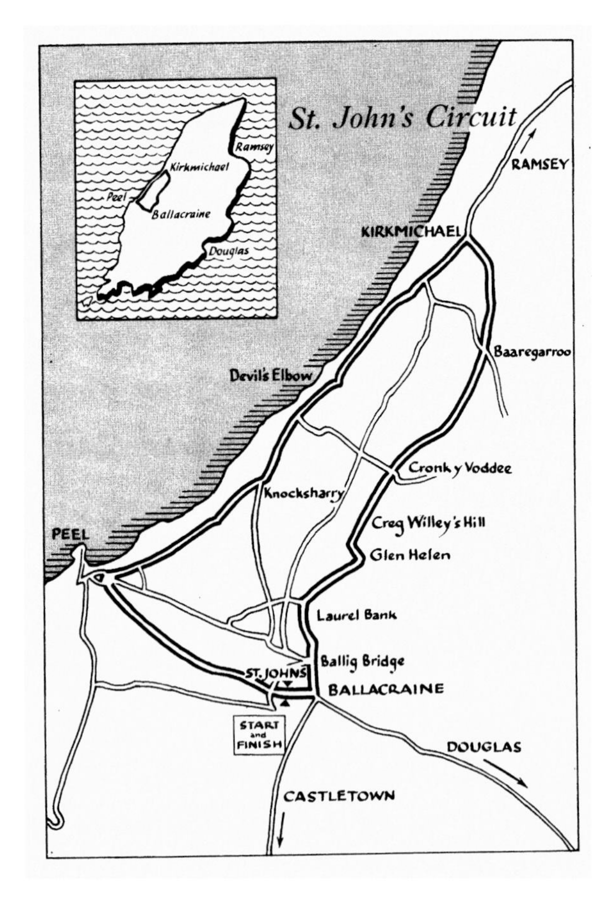

Isle of Man in 1905, the Manx authorities were happy to oblige. They were also accommodating to the wishes of the Auto-Cycle Club (later to become the Auto Cycle Union or ACU) who wanted to stage time trials for motorcycles the day after the car trials. The purpose of both events was again to select British teams to compete in the International Cup, so the first motorcycle 'race' to be held on the Isle of Man was actually an eliminating trial for the 1905 International Cup. It was scheduled to take place in May over the same 52-mile course used by the cars. But problems encountered by riders in practice soon eliminated that idea. Despite the fact that the motorcycles were pedal-assisted, coaxing them up a 1,400 foot-high mountain course – and one which had been so deeply rutted by the car trials the day before – proved impossible, and when one of the favoured British riders, J.F. Crundall, crashed and broke his arm at Ramsey, the decision was taken to run the bikes over a shorter, less arduous course.

A 25-mile route was chosen which excluded the mountain section altogether but included the section of the modern TT course from Ballacraine to Douglas, albeit running in the opposite direction. The event would be over five laps, a total of 125 miles and, while 18 entries were received, only 11 machines made it to the Island, and even fewer made it to the startline. Some failed to meet the maximum weight limit of 50kg (110lbs) when weighed in at Quiggin's Rope Works in Douglas and others did not make it through practice. One of the machines at the weigh-in – a 9hp Roc to be ridden by Thomas Tessier – was entered by the celebrated author, Sir Arthur Conan Doyle, creator of Sherlock Holmes. It would not finish the race.

The race was due to begin at 3am to minimise disruption to the Manx people and spectators were already taking up vantage points at 2.30am. In an era before licensing laws, the Quarterbridge Hotel made the most of its new-found trade by serving up pints of ale and hot breakfasts all through the night. The race was postponed by half an hour due to mist lingering on parts of the course but by 3.30am on the morning of May 31, 1905, the six riders who had made it to the startline were waved off at one minute intervals.

There may not have been many starters for the Island's first bike race but it still provided many of the traits that would later become synonymous with the TT: crashes, breakdowns, drama, daring and determination. When Freddy Barnes's Zenith failed to fire up on the line, for example, he pushed until out of sight of the gathered crowd. His determination went unrewarded however as he failed to complete a lap.

The honour of being the first man to do so fell to Harry Collier, who got round the 25-mile course in 37m 51s. Collier's brother, Charlie, was thrown from his Matchless-JAP 4 at Braddan Bridge but was relatively unscathed despite a complete lack of protective clothing – cloth caps and tweed trousers were the accepted riding apparel in 1905. Having damaged his front wheel in the crash, Collier pushed his bike back to the startline to make adjustments. He fitted a new wheel and set off again but rode his Matchless so hard to make up time that it suffered a broken con rod on the second lap and Collier's race was over. Collier could not, however, blame his mechanics or the bike he rode for his early demise – he and his brother were, after all, the co-owners of Matchless.

There was further drama during the pit stops when J.S. Campbell's Ariel burst into flames. Undeterred, the Scotsman simply beat out the fire and continued on his way. But while there may have been excitement in the pits, there was precious little of it for the spectators out on the course. With bikes only coming past every forty minutes or so, many wearied of the event and returned to their boarding-house beds.

Campbell eventually won the trial in a time of 4h 9m 36s at an average speed of just under 30mph. He took the historic victory from Harry Collier who was the only other man to finish the race. Long time race leader Charles Franklin's machine had broken a con rod on the last lap but he was awarded third place even though he never made it to the flag.

It was also in 1905 that the name of what would become the world's most famous motorcycle race was first coined – somewhat ironically from the world of car racing. With growing disinterest in the International Cup amongst the car racing fraternity, the Automobile Club approached the Manx authorities and proposed holding their own race for road-going touring cars. The authorities agreed and the meeting, which took place in September, 1905, was called the Tourist Trophy Race. It quickly gained the acronym 'TT' and would eventually come to be associated purely with motorcycles.

MAKING PLANS

The 1906 International Cup for motorcycles was a complete fiasco. Held in Austria, there was widespread outrage at the advantages enjoyed by the home-grown Puch team. Puch mechanics followed their riders round the course on a sidecar loaded with spare parts for the bikes and fixed them on the spot if they broke down, while other riders had to push their way back to the pits or retire from the race. Naturally, the Austrian machines came first and second while the unassisted Charlie Collier finished in third place. And it wasn't the first time local enthusiasts had interfered to assure a home team victory; in France, local fans had scattered tin tacks on the track in a pattern known only to French riders who could therefore avoid the menace. This blatant home favouritism spelt the end for the once popular International Cup but it also paved the way for the first TT race for motorcycles.

The idea of running a bike TT can be credited to four men; Charlie and Harry Collier, Freddie Straight and the Marquis de Mouzilly de St Mars. The Collier brothers were both riders and manufacturers of Matchless machines while Straight was secretary of the Auto-Cycle Club. The Marquis was a keen motor-sport fan who was a prominent figure in both the Automobile Club and the Auto-Cycle Club. As the four travelled back by train from the 1906 International Cup, they discussed the notion of having a Tourist Trophy race on the Isle of Man along similar lines to the car TT. Only at home, Charlie Collier felt, could 'fair play be assured'.

His brother Harry voiced the need to have a race for genuine road-going motorcycles rather than for the 'freak' machines which were being raced on the Continent. These machines, designed only for outright speed, bore very little resemblance to production road-going machines. Teams simply slotted the biggest engines they could fit into skinny, lightweight frames and went racing. Collier thought an annual TT race would be the best way to develop real world 'touring' machines and he found the Marquis to be in agreement. Enthused by the idea, the Marquis promised to supply a magnificent trophy for the winner. The 2 foot, 10 inch high silver statuette of Mercury – the Roman messenger of the gods – poised on a winged wheel, was based on the Montagu Trophy which was presented to the winner of the car TT. It would be presented to the rider who won the 1907 motorcycle TT on a single-cylinder machine. One hundred years later, it is still presented to the winner of the Senior TT.

Once the Marquis had convinced the ACC that a motorcycle meeting could work, even with limited funding, the ACC announced that it would be held on May 28, 1907 and Freddie Straight set about drawing up the technical regulations which would govern the race. They were refreshingly free of restrictions; there would be no engine capacity or weight limits, and riders would be allowed to use pedals to assist them round the course. But the rules did state that effective silencers had to be fitted along with a proper saddle and mud-guards, and all bikes would be required to have two-inch diameter tyres. The only real restriction was on fuel. Single-cylinder machines were to be allowed a gallon for every 90 miles covered while Twins were allocated a gallon for every 75 miles. Singles and Twins would run in the same race but the results would be quite separate, thus creating a race within a race.

Prize money was the same for both classes with £25 going to the winners and £15 and £10 for second and third places respectively. The Auto-Cycle Club agreed to pay the Manx authorities £250 for the use of their roads and ever since, the TT has provided a crucial source of income for the Isle of Man.

1907 THE FIRST TT

Thursday, May 28, 1907 dawned grey, windy and cold. Competitors, officials and spectators milled around the Tynwald Green and the area next to the Tynwald Inn which formed the first TT paddock. The makeshift scoreboard positioned there was actually a blackboard borrowed from the local school and journalist Laurie Cade later recalled that, 'It was a queer-looking crowd on the village green. The grandstand, if my memory serves me, consisted of a couple of beer crates on which the officials stood.'

Frank Applebee, who would go on to finish eighth in that historic first race, echoed Cade's sentiments, saying, 'We must have looked a motley crowd. We found on our arrival that the field close by Tynwald Hill, St. John's, had been divided into sections and, having located our respective positions, the entire space quickly became a dumping ground for motor-cycles, cans of petrol and oil, and personal belongings. Anything more unlike the pits as we know them today cannot be imagined.'

Practice for the first ever TT race was held on the morning of race day, on roads which were still open to everyday traffic. The official session ended at 8am and there were severe financial penalties for any rider caught doing 'racing speeds' after that time. The session threw up several unexpected problems for the competitors. Chief amongst them was that the road surface on the 15.8-mile St John's course was plain Macadam (untarred) and the dust thrown up by riders made visibility a serious problem as Rembrandt 'Rem' Fowler discovered. 'One of the main hazards was overtaking other riders,' he recalled almost fifty years

later. 'They were obscured in thick clouds of dust and it was very difficult to judge where they were.'

The race organisers sprayed an acid solution on the roads in a bid to suppress the dust but this was thrown up by the bikes' wheels and sprayed onto following riders. As a result, one of the unexpected hazards of an already dangerous event became acid burns. Riders found the acid was soon burning through their clothing, inadequate as it was, and leaving it in tatters. In an era long before one-piece leather suits and crash helmets, the nearest anyone got to 'proper' riding gear was a long leather jacket, a raincoat or a rubber poncho. Aviation goggles offered at least some protection from the dust clouds and acid.

Race distance was to be 10 laps – 158 miles. The top speed of motorcycles in 1907 may only have been around 60mph, but the dangers of racing were just as great as today. Minimal suspension, skinny tyres, almost non-existent brakes, lack of protective clothing or helmets, deeply rutted and dusty roads which were strewn with nails from horses' shoes, and an absolute lack of roadside protection, meant the pioneers of TT racing faced an undeniably dangerous challenge. Rem Fowler was concerned about all these issues but he also remembered having a more pressing problem as he prepared to set off and write the first page in TT history. 'I had an abscess in my neck lanced two days before the race – in photographs the bandages could be seen flapping in the wind! I was in no fit state to ride for I was in a very run-down and nervous condition. Twenty minutes before the race, however, a friend of mine fetched me a glassful of neat brandy tempered with a little milk. This had the desired effect and I set off full of hope and Dutch Courage.'

The honour of being the first men to set off in a TT race went to Frank Hulbert and Jack Marshall, both on Triumphs. One minute later they were followed by the Collier brothers, Harry and Charlie, mounted on their own 3.5hp Matchless Singles. Around 25 minutes after the flag had first dropped, Jack Marshall on his single-cylinder Triumph became the first man in history to complete a lap of a TT race. Rem Fowler on his Peugeot-engined Norton was the first to complete a lap on a twin.

Machine reliability soon became a key issue as virtually every rider broke down, stopped to make adjustments, or crashed at several points during the race. With so many stops – and at a time before pit signals became standard practice – it was difficult for riders to know exactly where they were in the overall standings. Rem Fowler stopped so many times he was convinced his race was over and was about to call it a

The beginning of it all. Frank Hulbert (number 1 on right of picture) and Jack Marshall pictured just seconds before the 10am start of the first TT race on May 28, 1907.

Winner of the twin-cylinder class in the first TT, Rem Fowler, pictured in 1911 on an Ariel. He retired in the Senior.

day when a keen timekeeping spectator told him he was actually in the lead. Fowler is acknowledged as being the first TT rider to receive a pit signal of sorts when 'Pa' Norton, founder of Norton Motorcycles, held out a cardboard sign at the end of lap two with 'Oil' written on it to remind Rem to pump oil into his engine. This had to be done manually by all riders every few miles to prevent their engines from seizing. Other riders received their information more directly as Jack Marshall remembered. 'As I came up Creg Willey's Hill, my chap ran alongside and just shouted.' Such was the lowly speed the single-gear machines could manage up the steepest climb on the course.

The race was interrupted by a compulsory ten minute lunch break which gave the riders time to grab some refreshments and to refuel their machines. After some four hours, Charlie Collier eventually crossed the finish line to win the Singles class by more than 11 minutes from Jack Marshall. Many wondered if Collier would have won without the assistance of pedals – a luxury Marshall wasn't afforded – and this controversy would lead to pedals being banned from the TT the following year.

Rem Fowler won the twin-cylinder class but lost out to Collier as the overall winner as his time for the race was 13 minutes slower than Collier's. In turn, Fowler won his class by over half an hour from Billy Wells (still the largest race-winning gap in TT history) and also had the honour of setting the first ever outright lap record at a speed of 42.91mph. Fowler always remembered that first TT race as the most eventful he ever took part in. He told *The TT Special*: 'My most exciting moment was when I had to make up my mind whether to stop and maybe lose the race, or to plunge blind through a wall of fire which stretched right across the road at the Devil's Elbow. It was caused by a bike which had crashed there. Owing to the density of the smoke and flames I had no idea where the wrecked machine was. I decided to risk it, and luckily came through okay. I shall never forget the hot blast of those flames. I think that the 1907 TT was the most hectic I have had in all my riding years.'

Incredibly, Fowler stopped no less than ten times during the race for a variety of reasons. 'In eight laps,' he recalled, 'I had ten stops. I had a punctured front tyre, which meant changing the inner-tube. I had to change two plugs. I came off at two corners and had to strap up a mudguard which broke when I hit the kerb. Apart from that, I wired up the advance spark rod and, travelling at high speed, had to return to pick up the pump which had dropped off the machine.'

After more than four hours of racing, 12 riders from the 25 who started (18 Singles and seven Twins) made it to the finish line. There had been thrills, spills, controversy and displays of dogged determination from the first men to ever take on the challenge of the TT. But none who took part could have realised the significance of what they had been part of and none could ever have imagined that other riders would still be taking up the same challenge 100 years later on 200mph missiles. The TT had begun.

1908 NO MORE PEDALLING

The controversy over pedals was swiftly nipped in the bud by banning them after the inaugural TT. As a direct result of the new ruling, development work on the motorcycles which would take part in the 1908 TT was stepped up and in the space of just one year, considerable technical advances were made. During practice for the second TT, riders found the latest machines had no problems climbing Creg Willey's Hill, the steep stretch which had caused so many problems the previous year.

In 1908, the Auto Cycle Club renamed itself the Auto Cycle Union (ACU) and established its identity in its own right. Even so, the organisation still worked closely with the Automobile Club and since the 1908 car TT was scheduled to take place in September, the ACU decided it would make life easier to share facilities and stage the motorcycle TT during the same week.

A long-standing Island tradition was instigated in 1908 – the use of marshals around the TT course. Lessons had been learned from the previous year when sheep had strayed onto the track, and local traffic had caused further problems (although there were estimated to be only 40 vehicles on the Island's roads at the time), so the Manx authorities decided that volunteer marshals would be given the powers of special constables for the duration of the practice and race period. The same system is still in place today.

After the success of the first TT, entries had risen to 36 and the event gained a more international flavour with both foreign riders and machines included in the line-up. Two German NSU's had provided the first foreign entries in 1907 but amongst the 1908 line-up were both German and Swiss riders and two Belgian-built four-cylinder FNs as well as the returning NSUs.

Race fans, who had paid the Isle of Man Steam Packet six shillings for a round trip to attend the event, were expecting a renewed battle between the Matchless-mounted Charlie Collier and Jack Marshall on his Triumph. The return of Rem Fowler on the Norton gave the twin-cylinder competitors a target to aim for. In the event, both winners from the previous year's TT (Collier and Fowler) were to be disappointed. In the single-cylinder class it was Jack Marshall who put in a late charge, after falling off at Kirkmichael, to beat Charlie Collier and set a new fastest lap for Singles at 42.48mph. He also had the satisfaction of setting the first 40mph-plus race average with a time of 40.49mph for the ten lap race. Marshall's determination to win, despite having had to change a valve after his crash, had impressed many, but the local Manx paper – the *Isle of Man Examiner* – believed it had an explanation for Marshall's tenacity and reported that, 'A charming lady, so it was freely rumoured, had promised to make him a happy man, provided he was acclaimed first in his class.' It is uncertain whether Marshall ever claimed – or was indeed offered – his just reward.

Early motorcycle racers came from a wide variety of backgrounds, a fact which was clearly demonstrated by the third place finisher in the single-cylinder event. Captain Sir Robert K. Arbuthnot, Bt, RN had taken special leave to be able to compete at the TT on his Triumph and was rewarded with a podium finish. Promoted to Admiral just a few years later, Arbuthnot sadly lost his life along with all 903 crew members when his ship, HMS *Defence*, was sunk during the

Battle of Jutland in World War I. His beloved Triumph was on board and went down with him.

With Rem Fowler being forced to retire from the race while leading, it fell to newcomer Harry Reed to take the twin-cylinder honours but Fowler at least had the satisfaction of keeping his outright lap record which he had set the year before.

1909 FROM TOURISTS TO RACERS

Speeds at the 1909 TT, again held in September, took a huge leap forward thanks to a change in the ACU regulations governing the event. The original idea of holding a Tourist Trophy race was to put more emphasis on real world motorcycles rather than copying the specials raced on the Continent. But in 1909, the gap between the two was bridged as fuel restrictions and the need to run silencers were lifted. The immediate result was a 10mph increase in lap times from the year before. Speeds rose from Jack Marshall's 1908 lap of 42.48mph to the 52.27mph lap recorded by Harry Collier in 1909. Prize money was up too, from £25 to £40 for the winners of both the Single and twin-cylinder events.

Despite the racier nature of the motorcycles, saddles and mudguards were still compulsory in keeping with the 'Tourist' moniker of the race. Further changes to the regulations included new capacity limits to allow Singles and Twins to compete together in a straight race, rather than as separate classes. There was now a 500cc limit for Singles and a 750cc limit for Twins.

Yet some things in racing never change. When bikes are tuned for more top speed, reliability tends to suffer and this was clearly demonstrated when only 19 bikes from 54 starters managed to complete the race. In fact, 20 of the entrants failed to even make the half-way point, including one of the pre-race favourites, Charlie Collier, whose Matchless suffered a broken belt fastener. His brother Harry, now riding a Twin, upheld family honour by winning his first TT and setting a new outright lap record at 52.27mph. Collier's overall race time was a massive 52 minutes faster than the previous year's winner in the twin-cylinder class.

Harry Collier's task was made somewhat easier by the demise of Jack Marshall's Triumph which suffered terminal valve problems while he was holding second place. American rider Lee Evans took an impressive second spot on the American-built Indian while third-placed finisher Billy Newsome limped home with a broken throttle cable to reveal that he had been operating the carburettor by hand for the remaining part of the race! Newsome was the first single-cylinder rider home.

Newsome wasn't the only hero in the race. As is normal at the TT, there are always plenty of lower-placed finishers who deserve much more credit than they ever receive. In this instance, it was Bert Sproston on a Rex who finished 18th out of 19 finishers. Sproston had crashed into the wall at Ballacraine just after the start and broke his ankle. He rejoined the race and, clearly in considerable pain, stopped to remove his boot at the end of the first lap. He started off again – by pushing off with his right foot only – and held on to complete the 158-mile race in his stocking sole. When he reached the finish line, Sproston had to be lifted off his machine by two policemen and was carried to the local police station where he was treated for acute exhaustion. But he had done what he set out to do – he had finished his TT race.

A TT tradition which remains to this day began in 1909 – the prize-giving ceremony. The very first ceremony was held in the Palace Ballroom in Douglas which, at the time, was claimed to be the biggest ballroom in the world. After being held in various locations over the last 100 years, the ceremony is currently held at the Villa Marina on Douglas Promenade.

1910 LOCAL RESISTANCE

It usually takes a national crisis like a world war or an outbreak of foot and mouth disease to stop a TT race but in 1910, an irate local farmer tried it all by himself.

Winner of the first single-cylinder TT in 1907, Charlie Collier is pictured here on the Matchless Twin in 1910 after becoming the first man to win two TTs. He also set the first 50mph lap in the same year.

Tired of bikes and cars racing round the roads close to his farm, Arthur Mathews demonstrated his disapproval by riding his horse and cart along the startline just minutes before the race was due to start. Spectators hurled verbal abuse at Mathews before physically assaulting him. The farmer then pulled out a whip and lashed out at one of his assailants who caught the end of it and pulled it free. Mathews then used his horse's reigns as a weapon but was overcome as the crowd managed to separate his horse from its cart. When someone in the crowd then fired a cap gun, the already frightened horse bolted and smashed into one of the parked-up race bikes before being caught and subdued. The police tried to intervene but their efforts were in vain and it was only when TT official Freddie Straight got involved that a riot was averted. Straight was one of the four men who had dreamed up the idea of running the TT and he was not about to see his creation being foiled by a local farmer. Showing a great deal of diplomacy, Straight managed to placate the farmer, not with threats, but by honouring him with a committee members' armband, thereby making him an official of the meeting. Mathews was satisfied, the crowd cheered their approval, and the 1910 TT races were ready to roll.

There were more changes on the cards in 1910 and a great deal of improvements were made in the running of the event. The blackboard from the local school was replaced by the first purpose-built scoreboard and *The Motor Cycle* magazine had arranged for special wire transmissions to be made to many parts of Britain to keep enthusiasts updated with what was happening in the race. From garages in Glasgow to Harrods in London, motorcycle fans eagerly awaited news on the latest lap positions.

The Boy Scouts became involved with the TT for the first time in 1910 and were appointed various tasks to assist in the smooth running of the event. From signalling the approach of oncoming riders in Morse code using flags, to cleaning riders' number plates and keeping livestock off the course, their contributions were highly valued and continue to be so to this day.

A record 83 entries prepared themselves on Tynwald Green to begin the fourth TT race, and what would prove to be the last ever round the St John's circuit. The race turned out to be a benefit for the Collier brothers, who finished first and second, but it was not without its drama. Harry Barshall's BAT twin burst into flames when he stopped to refuel and Harold Bowen, also on a BAT, set a new lap record at 53.15mph before crashing into the new wooden boarding at Ballacraine which had, ironically, been designed to help riders get safely round the corner. German rider Alfred Oberlander was chasing the leaders on his NSU until he developed engine trouble and was so disgusted at his machine that he threw it into a ditch.

At the flag, it was Charlie Collier who secured victory by five minutes from his brother Harry and, in doing so, became the first rider in history to win two TT races.

1911 NO TEA PARTY

During the winter of 1910-1911, motorcycle manufacturers turned their attentions to building machines with gears. The ACU had decided that the TT should be more of a challenge and felt that motorcycles were now capable of tackling the Mountain Course used by the cars. Known as the 'Four-Inch' course because of the stipulation on piston length for the 1908 car TT, it included an eight-mile uphill climb from Ramsey to the highest point of 1,400 feet at Brandywell. Manufacturers immediately realised that if a motorcycle was going to repeatedly climb to such heights up a mountainside, it would need to have variable gears. Naturally, in such an experimental age, there were various ways in which to achieve this; Matchless opted for a six-speed belt system while AJS built a three-speed gearbox. Still, despite the demands of the Mountain climb, one third of the machines entered for the 1911 races still only had a single gear.

Nevertheless, the development of variable gears amongst most manufacturers was a classic example of the TT races directly affecting motorcycle development and design. There remains no better test bed for real world motorcycles than the bumpy, demanding, and punishing TT course.

The new course was 37.5 miles long (about a quarter mile shorter than today's course) with the start-line located on the level section of Quarterbridge Road

Competitors line up on Quarterbridge Road, just after Bray Hill, for the start of the first TT to be held over the Mountain Course. 1911.

between the bottom of Bray Hill and Quarterbridge corner. Riders followed the same route as today's racers with one main exception; the course turned right at Cronk-ny-Mona before turning left onto Ballanard Road and right again at St Ninian's cross-roads where riders then plunged down Bray Hill and back to the startline. Only the 7-mile section from Douglas to Ballacraine was tarred and the Mountain section was little more than a deeply-rutted cart track. Because the course was so much longer, refuelling depots were set up at Braddan and Ramsey.

While the biggest change to the 1911 TT was undoubtedly the move to the Mountain Course, another institution began that year when the ACU – who had now taken over complete control of running the TT – announced the introduction of the Junior TT. This race, initially for 300cc Singles and 340cc Twins, most of which made around 2.5hp, is still run today and has encompassed many different capacities over the years including 250cc two-strokes and the current formula of 600cc four-strokes. The introduction of the Junior TT meant there were two separate races for the first time.

Sadly, practice for the 1911 event saw the first fatality at the TT when Victor Surridge was killed on the Glen Helen section after crashing his Rudge, directly in front of his horrified team manager. It would be the first of many deaths on the course and no other issue has so persistently threatened the continuation of the TT. Since Victor Surridge's sad demise, more than 200 fellow riders have lost their lives on what is now widely regarded as the most dangerous race course in the world – although it must be pointed out that some of these fatalities occurred during the Manx Grand Prix which would be staged in later years.

Surridge may have paid the ultimate price for participating in the sport he loved, but every other rider was finding new meanings for the words stamina, fatigue and exhaustion, thanks to the gruelling new course. After sampling the circuit for the first time, famous American board-track racer, Jack de Rosier (who was one of three riders mounted on the American-made Indian machines which posed such a threat to British dominance) quipped, 'Tell you what boys, I guess this ain't no tea party.'

It certainly wasn't a tea party over the new Mountain section where the first rider in practice had to stop and open three different gates for his fast-approaching colleagues – or make arrangements with a local shepherd to do the job for him. The gates were to help control livestock but wandering sheep and cows still presented a constant hazard to the riders, as did the road surface. Rutted and dusty in dry weather or rutted and muddy when wet, the only constant was the endless potholes which remained whatever the conditions.

Of the 104 riders entered for both races, 34 of them lined up on the Quarterbridge Road to start the first ever Junior TT which was to be held over four laps, one less than the larger capacity Senior machines would tackle. The honour of completing the first racing lap over the Four-Inch Mountain course went to Hugh Gibson in a time of 55m 26s. But it was the Collier brothers on their new Matchless Twins who fought it out with Percy Evans on his single-geared Humber Twin for the win. Evans eventually became the first man to win the Junior TT and his five other Humber-mounted colleagues were amongst the 25 finishers.

The Senior race was being built up as a classic match race between the Americans and the British. The American-built Indians took the initial advantage with Jack De Rosier leading by half a minute before crashing on the approach to Ramsey and bending his machine too badly to continue. It was his seventh crash of the meeting, having already parted company with his machine six times during practice. Charlie Collier's inherited lead was lost during fuel stops leaving another Indian rider, Oliver Godfrey, to take the victory – the first for a foreign machine at the TT. Godfrey later lost his life in World War I while serving with the Royal Flying Corps. When Collier was later disqualified for taking on fuel outside of the official depots, the Indians took a clean sweep of the top three places. This did not go down well with the British manufacturers and would have repercussions for the 1912 TT. British honour was only upheld by Frank Phillip who set the fastest lap of the race at 50.11mph on his pioneering two-stroke Scott twin. It was the first ever 50mph lap of the Mountain course.

1912 BOYCOTT

In its one hundred year history, the TT has never been short of controversy or crisis and the 1912 races were the first to be threatened. Complaints came chiefly from two groups – Island residents and British motorcycle manufacturers. The formers' patience was being sorely tried by having to put up with road closures which many felt made them prisoners in their own homes. For their part, the British motorcycle manufacturers complained that the new course was too demanding and the roads were unfit to race on. How much of this can be traced to their defeat at the hands of the Indians the year before is open to question. Sour grapes or not, when the manufacturers threatened to find an alternative venue in Belgium for racing, the Manx authorities had some serious decisions to make.

Frank Applebee, winner of the 1912 Senior, rounds Kate's Cottage. Note the gate being held open for him.

Despite the local complaints, the authorities once again agreed to close their roads and the TT races went ahead, albeit with a much depleted field of just 74 (30 less than the previous year), due to many manufacturers boycotting the event. The bikes which did arrive for the Junior and Senior TTs were mostly private entries, although some privateers had still managed to get hold of 'official' factory machines. Technical regulations could not have been simpler, with both Single and twin-cylinder machines limited to 350cc for the Junior race and 500cc for the Senior.

After two weeks of practice, the Junior race got underway in wet conditions for the first, but by no means last, time. Belt-driven bikes suffered greatly in the wet due to the belts becoming slippery and this gave chain-driven bikes a clear advantage. The chain-driven Douglas machines took full advantage and scored a one-two with Harry Bashall taking the win from Eddie Kickham, both of whom were listed as private owners. Kickham had the satisfaction of setting the fastest lap of the race at 41.76mph.

The Senior was another privateer affair with 49 starters but it was notable as being the first win for the two-stroke Scott in the hands of Frank Applebee. No TT during this period would have been complete without a Collier on the rostrum and Harry duly obliged with a third place behind Triumph-mounted Jack Haswell. Charlie Collier finished fourth on another family-made Matchless. A second Scott, in the hands of Frank Phillip, had been lying in second place on the last lap before a burst tyre at Ballaugh put paid to any hopes of a Scott 1-2.

1913
SUFFRAGETTE CITY

If the future of the TT had looked bleak in 1912, it made its first sensational comeback in 1913 with entries up to 147 – more than double that of the year before. Despite all the grumblings of 1912, the TT had shown its ability to bounce back from adversity, a trait it would display many more times over the following century.

The manufacturers had overcome their earlier concerns, or pettiness, and rejoined battle, with new names like Veloce (later to become Velocette) and Levis appearing for the first time. In all, there were 16 different makes of machine represented in the Junior race and 32 in the Senior.

Once again, the format of the races was changed, largely due to one Major Tommy Loughborough who had taken over from Freddie Straight as secretary of the ACU. Although class capacities would remain unchanged, Loughborough decided to make both the Junior and Senior races even tougher by upping the number of laps and holding both events over two different stages. The Junior race would cover six laps in all with a two-lap race held on the first race day being followed by a four-lap race two days later. Competitors in the Senior would start with a three-lap event to be followed by another four laps along with the Juniors. To distinguish competitors in the mixed race, Junior riders would wear blue waistcoats while Senior competitors wore red. In a further bid to help spectators tell exactly who was who, a TT programme was produced for the first time to replace the simple scorecards which had previously been used.

During practice for the 1913 TT, Manx suffragettes had strewn broken glass all over the Mountain circuit. While the Isle of Man had become the first country in the world to grant the vote to women in 1881, it was only to those who owned real estate to the value of £4 or more, so there were still plenty of embittered women on the Island. A team of road sweepers had to be formed to clear up the potentially lethal mess and many claimed they were picking up shards of glass 'by the bucket-load'. The team worked until 4am on the morning of the first race day to reduce the risk to the competitors who were not told of the debacle.

With the glass cleared away, racing finally got underway with the first laps of the Junior event which was won overall by Hugh Mason, showing an early example of the grit which makes great TT riders. Mason had signed himself out of hospital following a practice crash to win on his oddly named NUT. The initials actually stood for 'Newcastle-upon-Tyne' where the bikes were made.

In the headlining Senior race Tim Wood took the victory for Scott, giving the manufacturer its second Senior TT win in a row. He also set a new lap record at 51.12mph but the end result could have been very different had tragedy not struck the TT for the second time in two years. The 1913 event was marred by the first fatality during an actual race. While Victor Surridge had been killed on his Rudge in 1911, it had been during practice and not during a race. Frederick Richard Bateman had also been riding a Rudge and had been leading the second part of the Senior when he crashed on the fast descent from Keppel Gate after suffering a puncture. He had just turned 23 years old.

1914 THE ROAD TO WAR

With speeds rising and two deaths already having occurred at the TT, crash helmets became compulsory for the 1914 event. Sadly, the move was not enough to avoid another tragedy.

The major change in 1914 saw the startline moved yet again, this time to the top of Bray Hill. The finish line was at the end of Ballanard Road where it intersected with Bray Hill. The move was made to allow for more paddock space and a proper pits area was constructed at the top of Bray Hill. It was also hoped that, by starting at the top of a hill, riders would find it easier to fire up their machines. But with front brakes still a rarity at this time, the prospect of plunging down Bray Hill remained daunting. For the first time, the Junior and Senior races were held on separate days, allowing riders to compete in both events should they wish to.

The five-lap Junior race was held in atrocious wet and misty conditions but that didn't stop the lead riders from having a monumental scrap. It was, however, to end in tragedy. Frank Walker on a Royal Enfield had been leading on the second lap when he crashed and handed the battle for the lead over to the two AJS machines being ridden by Eric and Cyril Williams (no relation). Determined to get back in on the action, Walker remounted and gave it everything he had – and a little bit more – for the remainder of the race. He crashed two more times but still got back on his Enfield and, incredibly, was lying in third place as he raced along Ballanard Road to the chequered flag. The TT organisers had allowed for a run-off area after riders crossed the finish line but they couldn't have foreseen that excited spectators would mob that area after the first and second men came through. As Walker approached the flag at speed, he realised he was going to crash into spectators. Showing the utmost bravery and concern for the safety of others, Walker veered his bike to try and avoid hitting anyone but crashed straight into a wooden barrier and suffered what would prove to be fatal injuries. He was taken, unconscious, to hospital and hung on to life for five days before finally succumbing to his injuries. Despite crashing three times during the race, Walker finished in third place then gave his life so that no one else would be injured. In just a few months his country would be in dire need of men such as he.

Eric Williams won the race by 4m 44s from Cyril Williams, making it a one-two for AJS. It was the first time a single-cylinder machine had won the Junior TT. But no one felt like celebrating when one of their own was lying in hospital fighting for his life. After Frank Walker's crash, the TT organisers started roping off areas to keep spectators out of harm's way – a system which is still in use today. The Bray Hill/Ballanard Road start and finish line was never used again.

The Senior race saw no less than 30 factory teams entered and it would prove to be the Collier brothers' last TT. It wasn't a fairy-tale ending however, as Charlie broke down on the first lap with hub-gear problems and Harry crashed at 70mph, shattering his knee. But Charlie Collier had already established himself as the first real star of the TT by not only winning the first ever race, but also by co-creating the bike he won it on, and by setting the first TT lap record in the single-cylinder class. He maintained his passion and involvement with bikes right up until his death in 1954.

Tim Wood set a new lap record of 53.50mph on his Scott before suffering a burnt magneto. His misfortune allowed Cyril Pullin to take the victory for Rudge – the first win for a single-cylinder machine over the Mountain. But it was the scrap for second place which was to go down in history. Experienced TT rider Oliver Godfrey rode the wheels off his Indian in a bid to see off newcomer Howard Davies and his Sunbeam. With today's electronic timing, the race organisers could have split the duo at the flag but to the naked eye in 1914 there was nothing in it, and the first ever dead heat was announced at the TT. When positions were usually decided by minutes rather than seconds (just seven years before, the winning margin had been over half an hour), this result caused a great deal of excitement and proved how competitive the TT was becoming.

As dangerous as motorcycle racing was, it was nothing compared to the danger that now faced an entire generation of young men throughout the world – including many of those who raced at the TT. Just 55 days after the chequered flag dropped on that Senior race, the First World War broke out and the largely irrelevant pastime of TT racing was brought to a halt. But both directly and indirectly, the breakthroughs in technology achieved by factories and engineers who had tackled the TT for the last eight years would prove invaluable in military terms. The TT, in its own small way, contributed to the Allied victory in the Great War. Sadly, many of its pioneering riders would never set foot on their beloved Mona's Isle again.

G.W. WALKER. 2ND 1923.

CHAPTER 2

1920-29

1920

AFTERMATH

Although the exact figures are still debated, it is certain that at least 15 million people were killed in the horror that was World War I. Many countries had lost practically an entire generation of young men – the same kind of brave, spirited young men who were drawn to the thrills of racing at the Isle of Man TT. Many pre-war TT racers had been killed in the five years of bloodshed including one of the event's biggest stars, Oliver Godfrey, who was reputedly killed in an aerial dogfight with the famous Red Baron's squadron. With Britain still recovering from its appalling losses there were naturally no TT races in 1919, but by the following year there was sufficient interest to try and pick up where the event had left off before the Great War.

Organising the 1920 TT was no easy task. The Steam Packet Company was unsure if it could secure enough ships to carry competitors and spectators across the Irish Sea due to all the shipping losses it had endured in the war. The British Government was also considering imposing a duty on petrol (which didn't actually happen) and good old-fashioned personal greed also played its part in trying to halt the races. When Manx politician Hugo Teare bought property in Ramsey which included part of the TT course, he refused to allow racing on it unless he was paid. The TT organisers decided instead to alter the route through Ramsey and it wasn't until 1922 that the original course was used again after the ACU agreed to pay for improvements to Teare's stretch of road – including his private driveway.

The ACU had demanded a minimum entry of 30 bikes for each race before agreeing to stage the TT once more. This was only just achieved and the fact that more than half the field were newcomers showed just how grave a toll the war had taken on Britain's male population. To avoid the Ballanard Road/Bray Hill start and finish line which had inadvertently caused the death of Frank Walker in 1914, riders would now continue past Cronk-ny-Mona and take in Signpost corner, Bedstead, the Nook and Governor's Bridge before turning onto Glencrutchery Road where the new startline was situated, just a few yards down the road from the present one. The additional loop took the circuit from 37.5 miles up to 37.74 miles and, with the reinstatement of the original Ramsey section in 1922, the course has remained unchanged ever since – excluding, of course, continual improvements to the roads.

A new addition for the 1920 event was a race for 250cc machines to be run concurrently with the 350cc Junior. It was to be called the Lightweight TT. It had been six years since the last TT but the bikes which lined up to contest the 1920 event were not much more advanced than those used before the war. While the internal combustion engine had been much improved in aviation circles during the conflict, motorcycle design had not enjoyed the same attentions. The Manx

A rare shot of a rider on the coastal section of the original TT course.
Note the complete lack of protective riding gear.

roads had not been improved to any great degree either and the only tarred sections were from Douglas to Ballacraine and a short stretch in Ramsey. Elsewhere the circuit was either rolled earth and stones or, in the case of the Mountain section, still the same old cart track. But after the dangers and horrors of war, racing round the TT course must have seemed like a walk in the park.

Another new addition for the first post-war TT was the laying of a telephone line all the way round the circuit to allow more accurate reporting of riders' positions in the races. One rider who was not monitored closely enough in practice was Duggie Alexander who created a sensation by slashing more than five minutes off the lap record. However, just as the press were falling over themselves to report the sensational story back to the mainland, Alexander admitted to his prank – he had slipped off the course and taken a detour which was eight miles shorter. Just for laughs.

Two familiar faces from the 1914 event returned to the fray in 1920; Eric and Cyril Williams were once again AJS-mounted for the Junior 350cc event and there was to be no shortage of drama during the five-lap race. Eric Williams – winner of the 1914 Junior – established the first lap record for the new Mountain course of 53.16mph but failed to finish the race due to mechanical problems. This left Cyril Williams in the lead on the last lap but then he too suffered problems and was reported coasting at Keppel Gate, around four miles from the finish line. But Williams wasn't finished. Even though he had been racing for over four hours, he still found the stamina and determination to push his bike home, freewheeling where he could in the downhill sections but relying on sheer grit to reach the flag. When he did push over the line totally exhausted, it was to find out that he had won the race by 9m 10s from Jack Watson-Bourne on a Blackburne. But Williams' efforts had taken their toll and he collapsed in the pits and had to be given 'stimulants' to bring him round. It was his first and last TT win.

Not so exhausted but suitably content was tenth-placed finisher Sidney Haden who reportedly pulled in to the pits at the end of every lap for a snack! One R. Clark (his Christian name has been omitted from the official results) finished top of the 250cc Lightweight runners in fourth place overall.

Compared to the 1914 event which saw 30 factory entries, the 1920 Senior race was a poor showing with only four factory teams – Sunbeam, Indian, AJS and Norton. But the fact that a 500cc race was run at all was a victory as some parties had been calling for a 350cc limit at the TT due to the big bikes becoming too fast – and this at a time when top speeds were just 70-75mph.

Fortunately, the calls fell on deaf ears and the Senior race got underway as planned. Newcomer George Dance set a lap record of 55.62mph as he led in the early stages on his Sunbeam but, as so often happened in the early days of the TT, he succumbed to mechanical gremlins and was forced out of the race. His exit allowed Tommy de la Hay on another Sunbeam to take the victory and the honour of being the first man to average over 50mph for a whole race.

1921
GIANT KILLER

As the effects of WW1 began to slowly recede, interest in the TT races burgeoned and no fewer than 133 riders entered the 1921 event with 12 works teams contesting the Senior race. Most were to leave with egg on their faces as Howard Davies humbled the larger machines by winning the Senior race on his Junior 350cc machine. It remains the only time a Junior bike has won the Senior race.

Davies, like many TT riders, had endured a hectic war. Initially serving as a despatch rider, he later joined the Royal Flying Corps. Having already been shot down once, he was downed again in 1917 and spent the remainder of the war in a German POW camp – unbeknown to *Motor Cycling* magazine which published a report stating that Davies had been killed in action. When he miraculously reappeared, Davies wryly commented on the report saying that 'The facts are all correct save the central one – I am not dead.' All the same, Davies kept a copy of his obituary in his wallet from that point on and admitted that, 'On reading that notice, I was tickled to death at being alive.'

Due to a puncture, Davies could only manage

Alec Bennett was the first man to win five TT races. He is pictured here at Ramsey hairpin during the 1921 Senior in which he finished fourth.

second place in the Junior race against bikes of equal capacity. He would have to wait until the big race to show what his little 350 was truly capable of. The Junior was won by his AJS team-mate Eric Williams with Manxman Tom Sheard completing an AJS clean sweep of the rostrum. As a measure of how much the AJS machines had improved in 12 months, Eric Williams – in similar weather conditions – slashed a whole hour off the previous year's race-winning time set by Cyril Williams.

The 1921 Senior ranks as one of the great races from the early TT years with the lead changing constantly between Freddie Dixon, Irish-Canadian Alec Bennett, and Freddy Edmond. Lurking in second place throughout was Howard Davies on his 350cc AJS. By the final circuit, Davies took the lead from Bennett and beat him to the flag by just over two minutes after more than four hours of racing. With Edmond establishing a new lap record at 56.40mph, the event was hailed as a classic.

But while the top men received all the adulation, there were then – as there are now – many less publicised battles going on further down the field. For these men there are no cash rewards, trophies or media attention, just the huge personal satisfaction of finishing a TT race. One such rider, George Strange, later recalled his own race in the 1921 Senior TT in a 1939 edition of *The TT Special*. His memories offer a unique insight into what it was like to be a competitor in a 1920s TT race:

"*This was my first TT and, being excited, I did not sleep at all the night before the race. However, my number was 21, and off we started without incident. Down Bray Hill, Quarter Bridge and then, approaching Braddan, I realised my vision was nil, owing to steamed goggles. A dive into the grass verge after the second bend resulted in a fearful wobble that took as far as Union Mills to correct. Goggles clearing, I began really moving towards Ballacraine, when the rear plug packed up. A quick change of plug, and off again, leaving gloves on the road.*

'Safely round on lap one (although eight machines had passed during my stop), I had covered about five miles of the second lap when the front plug packed up. A rapid change carried out with no gloves brought about severe burns on both hands but I got going again until Laurel Bank when, whilst watching the oil pump, I ran into the ditch at speed, bent the oil plunger, lost a footrest, bent the forks and hurt both legs and elbows. Owing to the crash, I forgot the second lap fill-up and consequently suffered mental agony until the lap was safely completed

'Fourth lap. Met George Dance on the corner above Keppel Gate, tried to take the same corner at impossible speed and crashed into a heap of stones across the road, taking about three somersaults at 60mph. Practically stunned, I remounted, against advice, and found I had lost nearly all the petrol. A fill-up at the pits and then I made up quite some time until the last lap, when only a few were left in the race. I did not know where I stood by position, but I was doing my utmost to make up for all my delays when, near the Bungalow, bang went the back tyre. Past Windy Corner, Keppel Gate and so on, I carried on to the finish and I am certain that I rode at the speed the bike would do in spite of the burst tyre. At any rate, I got to the finish. There were no cheers for me; Howard Davies had won.

'I was sore, tired, and fully realised how right was Jake de Rosier when he said "The TT ain't no tea party." Anyhow, I finished 20th out of twenty four finishers in the toughest ride I ever had. Still, I did better in after years, but, nevertheless, I would not go through that 1921 Senior experience again for much money.

The 1921 TT gets underway on Glencrutchery Road. The present-day startline is just a few yards farther back up the road.

A.C.U.
16
20
24
19
OH 6926

Watching that Senior race at Hillberry corner was a 16-year-old Irishman who was so transfixed by what he saw that he was determined to experience it first hand the following year. He was to become the TT's first real superstar and one of the most successful TT riders of all time. His name was Stanley Woods. As he watched the race, he turned to his friend and said, 'I could do that.' He could. And he did.

A TT winner in the 1922 Lightweight and later biking journalist, author and publisher of *The TT Special*, Geoff Davison pits at his 'cage' for fuel. Note the boy scout cleaning his number plate so spectators can identify the rider.

1922
A YEAR OF FIRSTS

The 1922 TT was to be a year of firsts, from the debuts of three future stars – Stanley Woods, Jimmy Simpson and Wal Handley – to the first win for a Manxman and the first sub-four hour lap. The 1922 TT was a classic in every sense.

Handley's debut during practice on the Mountain course proved to be rather embarrassing. He would later recall that, 'I had never seen the TT course and when I arrived (at the startline) on Wednesday morning there was heavy mist. I pushed onto the road on my machine, half pointing to Governor's Bridge and was then told that I could go. I did. At full speed – the wrong way of the course! There was a lot of excitement over that but by the time I reached Governor's Bridge I realised what was the matter and turned round.'

The 1922 Lightweight TT would, for the first time, count as a race in its own right. The winner was Geoff Davison who would later achieve fame as a biking journalist, publisher of *The TT Special*, and as the author of many books on racing. In the same race, Wal Handley became the first man to lap the course at over 50mph on a 250cc machine.

Another first was to follow in the Junior race when local AJS rider Tommy Sheard became the first Manxman to win a TT. Further down the field was a 17-year-old Stanley Woods who was making his debut on a Cotton. He would later explain just how treacherous the Mountain circuit was in its infancy. 'The Mountain road from Ramsey as far as Creg-ny-Baa was sand and gravel. On the upper reaches it was sand only

It's always been a dangerous game. By the 1920s, when this picture was taken, several riders had already lost their lives round the TT course.

– rutted, with grass growing on the top of the ruts. And there was no fencing. The road was hardly more than ten feet wide. If two cars met, it was a job to pass.'

The manner in which Woods secured bikes for the TT has become the stuff of legend. He wrote to several manufacturers and informed them that he had a mount for the Junior TT and asked if they would be interested in supplying a machine for the Senior race. At the same time, he wrote to several other manufacturers explaining that he was riding in the Senior and was looking for a bike to race in the Junior. His double bluff worked and Cotton agreed to supply Woods with a Junior machine – but only on the condition that he could supply a favourable reference. No problem. Woods obtained one from the Cotton agent in Dublin, who just happened to be his good friend Paddy Johnston who had visited the TT with him the year before. Johnston would himself go on to become a TT winner taking the 1926 Lightweight race.

Woods' debut was, quite literally, a baptism of fire. During his refuelling stop, two gallons of petrol suddenly ignited engulfing Woods in flames. He was later complimented for the quick thinking which saw him drop to the ground and roll the flames out but later admitted he had panicked and tripped and was not worthy of the compliments. 'It was purely automatic,' he said. 'I jumped off the bicycle then I tripped over my own feet and rolled on the ground. Then we picked ourselves up and straightened the handlebars and we went off again.'

Woods managed a heroic fifth place finish before revealing the secret behind his turn of speed – he had ridden half of the race with no brakes! 'I found I could get round the corners a lot faster than I'd ever thought possible,' he admitted. 'I still had my two feet (for brakes) so I carried on.'

Yet more new ground was broken in the Senior race, this time by Alec Bennett who became the first rider to lead a TT race from start to finish. Bennett, who had learned his riding skills as a despatch rider in WWI before flying Bristol fighters in the Royal Flying Corps, came agonisingly close to setting the first 60mph lap but in the end he lost out by just one second. There was to be some consolation in the fact that Bennett and his Sunbeam became the first pairing to finish a six-lap race over the Mountain course in less than four hours. Coming home in a respectable fifth position was one Graham Walker, father of future motorsport commentating legend, Murray.

The 1922 event saw the introduction of the now familiar silver TT replicas. Initially they were awarded to the first six finishers in each race but this later changed when they were given to riders who had finished within a fraction or percentage of the winner's time. Bronze replicas were introduced in later years to give more competitors the chance of winning a trophy and, for many riders, they remain the hardest prizes they ever won.

Graham Walker, father of legendary commentator Murray, on his way to second place in the 1923 Sidecar event. His only TT win came in the 1931 Lightweight after 12 years of trying.

1923
THE CHAIRS

The idea of running a Sidecar TT had been around since 1920 but the manufacturers of the machines were not susceptive to the idea in case such a race should prove to be too dangerous and would therefore reflect badly on their family-oriented products. By 1923, most had been persuaded that it was a risk worth taking as a successful Sidecar TT would have the opposite effect on showroom sales and trade would increase. Unlike today, Sidecars were a popular mode of transport in the 1920s and most of the 14 outfits entered were the same as customers of the day could buy. The antics of the passengers in particular, as they leaned completely out of their chairs to try and keep the third wheel on the ground – even though it sometimes lifted several feet into the air – thrilled the crowd to such an extent that the Sidecar race looked like becoming a permanent fixture on the TT calendar. Sadly, things didn't quite work out that way.

Overall entries for the 1923 TT broke all records with 177 in total being received. Amongst them was a newcomer who, like Stanley Woods, would soon become a TT legend. But Jimmy Guthrie's debut showed no signs of his later greatness. He competed in the Junior race but retired and would have to wait another seven years before scoring his first victory.

During practice, Walter Brandish crashed and broke his leg on the sharp left-hand corner between Creg-ny-Baa and Hillberry. Ever since, it has been known as Brandish Corner making Walter Brandish the first man to have a corner named after him on the TT course.

The first race of the week was the Junior which had received a record entry of 72 riders. Jimmy Simpson set a new lap record of 59.59mph on his AJS before retiring from the race, leaving Stanley Woods to claim his first TT win on a Cotton. It was to be the first of many.

The following day Scotsman Jock Porter won the six-lap Lightweight on his New Gerrard after Wal Handley was forced out of the race. Handley had the consolation of setting the fastest lap, but the small stuffed monkey he always tied to his rear mudguard for luck had failed him on this occasion.

The first Sidecar TT provided plenty of thrills, spills and breakdowns, not to mention some strange-looking machinery. Chief amongst the latter was Freddie Dixon's unique 'banking' Douglas outfit which his passenger, Walter Perry, could lean into bends by means of a manually-operated lever. Dixon was already an established solo racer with a second place finish in the 1921 Senior race under his belt. He started the

22
22

Sidecar race as favourite and didn't disappoint, setting an impressive average speed of 53.15mph – only 2mph slower than the fastest average lap in that year's Senior race. Reports from Ramsey Hairpin had him casually smoking a cigarette as he slid his outfit round the bend, complete with his favoured socks and shoes instead of riding boots. Dixon's win in the Sidecar race set him on his way to achieving a unique record of winning TTs on two, three and four wheels. After winning the Sidecar event, he would go on to win the 1927 Junior solo race and would later win the 1935 car TT which was, by then, held on the Ards course near Belfast.

The Senior race was run in appalling conditions with thick mist over the Mountain section and it was marred by the death of J. H. Veasey when his handlebar clipped the wall at Greeba Bridge, causing him to crash. Local knowledge must have helped Douglas-mounted Tommy Sheard to win his second TT in such poor visibility, but the bikes Douglas brought over to the TT were in themselves rather special. The RA model featured an early form of disc brake, dual balanced carburettors and a twist-grip throttle rather than a lever-type. They were an early sign of things to come.

The weather was so bad that by the time tenth-placed finisher, Alec Bennett, arrived at the grandstand he found it deserted. 'On crossing the finish line I was surprised to find nobody about to flag me in,' he later said. 'Not a soul to be seen, not even a pit attendant. I proceeded to the marquee, where even the bar attendant was missing. I set about climbing over the bar in search of something good to drink. Just as I got on top of the counter, the attendant popped out from behind some cases and said "Caught you! Who are you and what do you want?" Not realising that my face was covered with mud and grit, I was a bit surprised at this, as he knew me quite well. However I eventually received the very much needed whisky, and as I was soaked to the skin and very cold I naturally drank quite a lot of the good stuff.'

Freddie Dixon and the incredible banking Sidecar! Note passenger, Walter Perry, pushing a lever forward to 'bank' the outfit into Ramsey Hairpin. The duo won this first ever Sidecar TT in 1923.

1924

A MILE A MINUTE

Getting ready for a 17-rider massed start at the TT in the 1924 Ultra-Lightweight race. The experiment was not repeated until 1948.

With the introduction of the Ultra-Lightweight class for 175cc machines, the TT now offered a full programme of five races: Seniors, Juniors, Lightweights, Ultra-Lightweights and Sidecars. But what really set the 1924 TT alight was the achievement of the long-awaited 60mph lap. To travel at an average speed of a mile a minute would have been unthinkable when the TT started in 1907, but all three riders in the first race of the 1924 event – the Junior – achieved this landmark. The honour of being the first went to Jimmy Simpson on his AJS. Wal Handley and Len Horton became the next two men to add their names to the record books. Somewhat ironically, it wasn't the big Senior machines which set the outright fastest lap that week, but rather Jimmy Simpson on his 350cc Junior mount at 64.54mph.

Simpson's lap times, in 1924 and beyond, were simply incredible. He was the first man to break the 60mph lap and would eventually follow that up with the first 70mph and then 80mph laps. But his overall win tally didn't reflect his blinding speed thanks to a string of mechanical breakdowns. Out of the 26 TT races he entered, Simpson only finished 11 of them, yet he set the fastest lap no less than eight times. He might have resented the tag he earned as the 'record *and* machine breaker', but Simpson would surely be proud to know that even today, the trophy awarded for the fastest lap of any TT week is a statuette of himself.

All three riders who completed the first lap of the 1924 Junior at over 60mph (Simpson, Handley and Horton) eventually retired from the race leaving little-known Kenneth Twemlow on his New Imperial to take a surprise victory at a race average of 55.67mph.

The first ever Ultra-Lightweight race also saw the first massed start at the TT with 17 riders hurtling down the fearsome Bray Hill together. Wal Handley, like Jimmy Simpson, had a habit of leading races then being forced to retire with mechanical gremlins and he repeated the pattern once again in the Ultra-Lightweight handing the win to Jock Porter on his New Gerrard.

T. T. START. 1924
FIRST MASS START TO BE HELD.

Later on the same day, the four-lap Sidecar race was flagged away, this year attracting only ten entries. Freddie Dixon was once again the hot favourite but, like Handley before him, he led the race but never made it to the finish line, leaving George Tucker to become only the second ever winner of a Sidecar TT race. After the race, Tucker revealed that he had sawn two inches off his handlebars to allow him to take Brandish Corner faster than anyone else! A hugely disappointed George Grinton had been leading the race until receiving a pit signal which simply read '3'. Taking this to mean that he had a lead of three minutes, he slackened his pace and lost the three-second lead that he actually had. Cursing his pit signaller, he had to be content with third place.

Walter Handley led in the Lightweight class before succumbing to mechanical problems and once again it looked like Jock Porter would inherit the race win, but a last lap crash put paid to his winning a third TT. Instead, Eddie Twemlow took the chequered flag to ensure a major celebration in the Twemlow household that night – his brother Ken had already won the Junior TT that week.

In the Senior class, Freddie Dixon led for four laps before his Indian started to lose power allowing Alec Bennett to take over the running. Bennett had been more than two seconds adrift at one stage but by averaging over 60mph for the entire six laps (making him the first man to do so), he managed to claw his way back and take his second Senior TT race win in three years. Dixon eventually finished in third and, along with second placed finisher Harry Langman, also averaged more than 60mph for the race.

1925 THE FIRST DOUBLE

There were no major changes to the race programme for 1925 and it appeared the TT had settled into a tried and tested pattern. The week's racing turned out to be all about one man – Wal Handley. After having led so many races only to have broken down, Handley's persistence and talents were rewarded when he became the first man to win two TTs in a week.

Ongoing technical developments and improvements to the TT course saw Handley win the Junior TT at an average speed of 8mph up on the previous

year. Much credit for this dramatic increase in speed must go to the Manx authorities who had spent considerable sums of money in finally laying down Tarmac on the full length of the TT course. Now even the Mountain section was properly surfaced and fencing was erected over the same section to contain livestock.

Handley's race average on a 350cc Rex-Acme was an incredible 65.02mph – just one year after the first 60mph lap had been achieved – and, as well as taking

The stuff of dreams: Howard R. Davies wins the 1925 Senior TT on a bike he built himself. His initials (H.R.D.) were displayed on the fuel tank.

a well-deserved win, he also bagged new lap and race records. Jimmy Simpson also made it onto the podium in third place and Howard Davies on his own home-built HRD slotted into second spot. From Davies, however, there was better to come.

Although he failed to finish the Junior race, Stanley Woods showed some of the spirit and determination which would later make his name legend. When the handlebars on his Royal Enfield snapped off, Woods continued the race, using what little was left of the bars to steer his machine. In the process however, his throttle had broken, but Woods carried on using his air lever to control his speed! He was eventually ordered to stop but had proved his determination beyond doubt.

Sixth-placed finisher, Len Horton, had an equally interesting race which ended with a most bizarre request. After running straight on at Sulby Bridge, he crashed into a cart full of oranges and managed to knock several spectators over in the process. He rejoined the race but several days later received a letter from a woman he had knocked down in the mêlée. Her clothes, she complained, were ruined and she would be very pleased if Horton and/or his team could buy her a new frock, a new pair of stockings, a pair of knickers and a corset. Horton said 'She was very sporting and said that if supplying these would get the marvellous rider who had joined them at Sulby into trouble, she would not claim them. Naturally, the things were sent along, the managing director's typist going out and buying them.'

The mass start for the Ultra-Lightweight class was abandoned for 1925 but it wouldn't have made much difference anyway with only seven entrants taking to the grid. The low numbers were a direct result of the organisers insisting on a new 68kg (150lb) weight limit for Ultra-Lightweights which most manufacturers felt was dangerous and practically impossible to achieve. In the event itself, Wal Handley hustled his Rex-Acme to the flag in first place and once again he set new lap and race records ahead of the five other men who made it to the finish.

Handley then looked set to achieve the near unthinkable in an era of such poor machine reliability. He was leading the Lightweight race by two minutes after two of the scheduled six laps and looked odds-on to become the first man to win three races in a week. But Lady Luck was not prepared to be over-generous and Handley crashed out at Signpost Corner thanks to a flat rear tyre. But he couldn't complain; he had won two races, set new lap and race records in both the Junior and Ultra-Lightweight classes and cemented his triumphant week with the first ever 60mph lap in the Lightweight class. Eddie Twemlow won the Lightweight race for the second year running.

Howard Davies had already made TT history by being the only man to win the 500cc Senior race on a 350cc Junior machine back in 1921. Despairing at the amount of technical problems he had suffered in other races however, he took the bold step of building his own bike for 1925 – the JAP-engined HRD. His Senior race victory against all the factory teams and five previous TT winners on his home-built machine was straight out of a Hollywood movie – and a not very believable one at that. Winning first time out, on a bike he had made himself, in the most important motorcycle race on earth, was a simply astounding feat. To this day, Davies remains the only man to have won a TT on a motorcycle which featured his own name (or rather, initials) on the tank.

While filling that very tank at his pit stop, Davies took on a rather unorthodox (at least by today's standards) form of refreshment – champagne! In an era long before drinking and driving was viewed as a social evil, many riders fortified themselves with alcoholic beverages mid-race. For Davies, it was only the best stuff and a contemporary race report states that he 'had a hurried drink of champagne and went off again feeling quite refreshed.'

In his TT debut, Tommy Bullus finished a fine fourth and later revealed just how exhausting these early motorcycles were to ride for 226 miles. 'I did finish the race feeling very, very tired. My hands – I was almost unable to use them anymore – they were so swollen with the vibration.'

The third Sidecar TT attracted 18 outfits, almost double that of the previous year but the class was living on borrowed time with the manufacturers still not convinced it showed their products in the best light. And 18 entries was still considered a poor showing against the 52 for the Junior TT, especially since there were only five finishers in the 1924 race. Unknown to those enthusiastic entrants as they lined up on the Glencrutchery Road, it would be the last Sidecar TT for many years. The honour of winning it went to Len Parker on his Douglas outfit after previous winner Freddie Dixon had set the early pace. But there was a price to pay – Parker could not be interviewed for sometime after the race because he had been temporarily deafened by his roaring Douglas engine. There wouldn't be another Sidecar TT until 1954.

1926 LESS IS MORE

The TT race programme underwent big changes for the 1926 event with the abolition of the Ultra-Lightweight and Sidecar classes due to lack of entries. In both cases, there were those who mourned the demise of a particular class but, on the whole, the decision was taken to ensure full, competitive grids for the benefit of spectators. Watching five Sidecars circulate on a 37-mile course means a lot of empty road.

The race programme was trimmed down to a classic format which would remain until after World War II – the Lightweight, Junior and Senior TTs. All races were now over seven laps, an incredible endurance challenge of 264.11 miles.

The continuing success of the TT saw its fame spreading all over Europe and the positive publicity it provided for British bikes was not lost on other manufacturers. In 1926, three Italian manufacturers entered bikes – Moto Guzzi, Garelli and Bianchi, with Moto Guzzi very nearly winning at its first attempt.

One machine which attracted much attention during practice was the new Velocette which produced 20bhp and was capable of 90mph. In the hands of Alec Bennett in the Junior TT it was untouchable and he became the first man to chalk up three TT wins.

The Lightweight TT was marred by controversy. Italian rider Pietro Ghersi had shown great form in practice on his Moto Guzzi and went on to lead for six laps of the race – enough to win in any previous year – but the new addition of a seventh lap was to prove his downfall. Having to stop to refuel for the last lap, he was overtaken by Paddy Johnston who went on to win by 20 seconds. It had still been a brilliant debut showing by the Italian factory and by Ghersi but it was all to end in controversy at the prize-giving ceremony when it was announced that the Italian had been excluded from the race results for using a different make of spark plug to the one he had declared. There were howls of protest but the ACU held firm although it did still credit Ghersi with the fastest lap of the race because he had been 'excluded from the results' rather than disqualified outright.

Stanley Woods had signed a full-time contract with Norton for 1926, but only after turning the firm down initially because he felt he had better prospects in his toffee-selling job! Woods was paid £500 a year by Norton but, together with retainers from spark plug companies, tyre companies and other personal deals, he earned a total of £1,631.16 in that year alone – a relative fortune at the time. But Woods was able to justify Norton's faith in him by winning the big event of the week, the Senior TT. He had his hands full fending off Wal Handley during the first lap but when Handley had to change a spark plug and lost seven minutes in doing so, the race went to the Irishman by four minutes. In one of the most impressive rides ever witnessed round the TT course, Handley rode his heart out to come back from 22nd place and finish second. Also making history was Jimmy Simpson who, characteristically, led the race and set the fastest lap before breaking down yet again. His lap was an astonishing 70.43mph – and that just two years after he posted the first 60mph lap.

1927 OPEN PRACTICE

Hard as it is to imagine now, in 1927 TT practice sessions were still taking place on roads which were open to everyday traffic. While the idea was to disrupt local citizens as little as possible, the downside was that it made things incredibly dangerous for TT competitors. Even though the sessions were run as early as 5am to avoid traffic, there was still the occasional vehicle out on the course as Archie Birkin was to find to his dreadful cost. Exiting Kirkmichael village, he was forced to swerve to avoid colliding with a fish delivery van but crashed into a wall and was killed. As a mark of respect, the section was named Birkin's Bend but Birkin's death was also to inspire a more drastic measure and one which has undoubtedly saved many lives over the years. For the following year, the Manx Parliament amended the Roads Closure Act to enable roads to be closed to ordinary traffic during practice sessions so the TT riders could go about their business in a much safer environment.

A gloomy practice over, Wal Handley must have been cursing the change to seven lap races. Having led the Junior for six full laps, he was forced to retire on the seventh when his Rex-Acme developed mechanical problems. This left Freddie Dixon to take his first – and only – solo win to add to his Sidecar victory while Handley had to console himself with a new lap record. Jimmy Simpson brought his AJS home in third place, but only after he'd survived a high-speed encounter with a dog in Kirkmichael village. He later remembered that, 'Right in the middle of the village there was a woman on one side of the road and a greyhound on the other. And just as I approached, the daft creature called the dog across to her. I hit it for six into a brick wall. I didn't fall off, but it slowed me a bit and affected the steering.'

The beauty of the TT has long been that riders get more than one chance at victory. After his disappointment in the Junior, Handley went on to win the Lightweight TT held two days later on the Wednesday of race week. Moto Guzzi placed second with its rider, Luigi Archangeli, becoming the first Italian rider to figure in the results at the TT.

Throughout the 1927 meeting, all eyes had been focused on the mighty Norton team with its new single-cylinder ohc 500cc machines which were to become the benchmark bikes at the TT for years to come. The factory's rider line-up was impressive too; Stanley Woods was joined by three-times TT winner Alec Bennett and Joe Craig, who was later to manage the Norton team to great success.

Spectators at the grandstand were treated to the first ever commentary on a TT race, though it proved disastrous; the commentator apparently found the job impossible and abandoned his post halfway through the race. To fill the silence between bikes passing, the resident band struck up mournful dirges which were barely more pleasing than the commentary had been.

Pre-race favourite for the Senior, Stanley Woods, took control over the first four laps and posted a new lap record of 70.90mph which helped him build a four minute lead over his team-mate Alec Bennett. Woods' record lap was also the first sub-32-minute lap of the course and he was timed over a one-mile stretch of the Sulby Straight at 93.7mph. By the fifth lap, however, Woods started slowing with a slipping clutch and Bennett took control of the race to eventually rack up his fourth TT win. But it was another rider who stole the crowd's attention by scything his way through the field towards the end of the seven-lap race. Jimmy Guthrie had returned to the TT and this time he meant business, fighting his way up to second place at the chequered flag on his New Hudson. There would be more magic to come from Guthrie.

1928 CHANGING GEARS

The sensation of the 1928 TT was the 350cc Velocette ridden by Alec Bennett. Until this year, riders had changed gear by hand with a lever mounted either on the side of the fuel tank or down by the gearbox itself. Not only was this awkward and time-consuming for the rider, it was also dangerous as it meant he had to take one hand off the handlebars every time a gear change was required. The Velocette pioneered the foot gear change which is still in use today and which all modern riders take for granted. But when it first appeared at the TT in 1928 it was a real novelty. Designed by Harold Willis, it proved extremely effective as Alec Bennett won the Junior TT using the new system and Willis himself came second, also mounted on a Velocette.

The very rare occurrence of melting tar on the Isle of Man didn't stop Alec Bennett lapping at over 70mph in the Junior race for the first time and taking his fifth win which made him the most successful TT rider to date.

The Lightweight and Senior TTs were both won by riders new to the top step of the rostrum. In the Lightweight, Frank Longman took the honours on his OK-Supreme, eventually finishing 17 minutes ahead of the second-placed man. Longman had enjoyed two podiums in the past and also finished fourth in the 1925 Sidecar TT but the 1928 Lightweight was his maiden victory.

After a week of scorching sunshine, the heavens opened for the Senior TT making conditions extremely difficult. Many of the fancied runners retired early in the race leaving Jimmy Simpson to lead the way before retiring yet again with mechanical gremlins. Incredibly, despite the amount of times he had led races and set lap records, Simpson had yet to win a TT.

Little-known Charlie Dodson had first ridden at the TT in the Ultra-Lightweight class in 1925 and he could hardly have been considered a race favourite for the Senior on a bike nearly three times the size of that first mount. But showing tremendous race craft, not to mention bravery, in the swirling Manx mists and torrential rain, he brought his Sunbeam home in first place, soaked through and freezing cold. Dodson must still have considered himself lucky however, as his machine had slowed on the final lap allowing Graham Walker to build a three-minute lead. It was only when Walker was then forced to retire that Dodson claimed his well-earned victory.

If there has been one constant at the TT in its 100 year history it's the spirit of the riders who have taken part in it. No matter how much the bikes have changed, how much faster they have become and how many safety improvements have been made over the decades, the determination and spirit shown by TT riders has always remained the same. Despite any number of injuries or hardships, they seem determined to do whatever it takes to get back to the chequered flag on Glencrutchery Road. Third-placed finisher in the 1929 Senior race, Henry Tyrell-Smith, typified that spirit as his later recollection of the race proves:

"I had a lead of about three minutes when I came to Glen Helen on the fourth lap. It was a pretty tricky bend in those days and I took it a shade too fast. The exhaust pipe touched the road and spun me round. I crashed into the bank, was winded and tore my leathers badly. They carried me into the hotel and pinned my clothes together. After a bit I got my breath back but had a nasty pain in my chest. However, I came out of the hotel to see what was doing and found that someone was holding my machine up with the engine running and the clutch out – strictly contrary to regulations – all ready to move off. They sat me on it and, still very muzzy, I let in the clutch and carried on. I believe that the officials had more than half a mind to stop me and they would certainly have been quite justified in doing so, for it was discovered later on that I had cracked three ribs. I was very glad that they didn't, however, for I was just able to carry on and I was very glad to finish third.

In finishing first in the same race, Charlie Dodson proved his wet Senior win the previous year had been no fluke. He also became the first man to average above 70mph for a whole race and he set a new outright lap record at 73.55mph.

Despite Dodson's victory, the Senior TT was marred by four riders coming to grief at Greeba Bridge with one of their number, Douglas Lamb, being killed. Wal Handley's courageous efforts to clear the bikes from the track, attend the injured riders, and ride off to seek medical assistance resulted in him receiving a formal letter of praise from the ACU.

Heroic as he was, Handley could do nothing with the relatively unknown Freddie Hicks in the Junior TT which had opened race week. Hicks had made a name for himself on the Brooklands circuit in England but as yet had only managed a sixth place at the TT. That was all to change as he set new lap and race records en route to winning the Junior race. It was Velocette's third Junior victory in four years.

The Lightweight race saw the return of Italy's Pietro Ghersi for the first time since his exclusion in 1926. Ghersi led the race for five-and-a-half laps before retiring with spark plug trouble – somewhat ironically, considering plugs had been the cause of his problems three years earlier. After once again setting the fastest lap of the race, Ghersi must have been cursing his luck. The Italian never would win a TT race but his countrymen would soon come to dominate the event like no other foreign nation had done before.

Ghersi's retirement left the way open for Syd Crabtree to take a maiden TT win for both himself and Excelsior. Sadly, he, like so many other great TT riders, would eventually pay the ultimate price for his brief moments of glory on the world's most unforgiving racetrack.

Ten times winner, Stanley Woods, negotiates Governor's Bridge in 1934 on a DKW. His win tally would not be bettered until the era of Mike Hailwood in the late 1960s.

TOURIST TROPHY

CENTURY

CHAPTER 3

1930-39

OF 141
Velocette

1930

AN INTERNATIONAL EVENT

The TT underwent various improvements in time for the 1930 event and, as a result, became a much more professional and international event.

One of the most welcome changes was the Manx government's donation of a £5,000 grant to assist the ACU with prize money. Anyone winning a TT would now pocket £200. The introduction of travelling expenses for competitors also ensured a much more international field with entries being received from as far afield as Australia, South Africa, Japan, Iraq and even Egypt. In total, 19 countries were represented in 1930 and as a result of its increasing popularity, the BBC made its first broadcast from the event during Friday's Senior race.

As was now the norm, the week kicked off with the Junior TT which proved to be a clean sweep for the new experimental and highly secret 350cc Rudges. With Henry Tyrell-Smith having shaved 26 seconds off the lap record in practice, he started the race as favourite and his scintillating practice lap proved to be an accurate predictor of what was to come as he won the race from his team-mates Ernie Nott and Graham Walker. With Tyrell-Smith setting a new race record and Nott establishing a new lap record, things could not have gone any better for the Rudge team. The factory's achievements were even more remarkable given that it was the first time the firm had ever competed in the Junior event. In 15th place was the first Japanese rider to compete in the TT. Kenzo Tada soon became known as the 'India Rubber Man' thanks to his ability to survive numerous crashes without hurting himself. He would later sing the praises of the TT to a fellow countryman and encourage him to enter his own machines in the event. His name was Soichiro Honda.

The Lightweight 250 race saw Jimmy Guthrie take his first ever TT win but the Scotsman was forced to fight for it all the way. Having been down in sixth place at the end of the first lap on his AJS, Guthrie battled through to fourth on the second circuit and finally took the lead on lap three. During the final four laps he fought off challenges from the OK-Supremes of Paddy Johnston and Cecil Barrow and held on to win the first of the six TT victories which would eventually come his way.

Two-time TT winner Wal Handley pulled off an incredible result in the Senior race to create another piece of TT history. Originally down to ride an FN machine, Handley looked to be in trouble when the bike failed to materialise during practice week. He was then given special permission to ride a privately entered Rudge belonging to Jim Whalley, a Bristol-based agent for the firm. Handley shocked spectators and officials alike when he knocked 40 seconds off the Senior lap record during practice! He maintained a similar pace come race day and, despite the latter part of the race being dogged by rain, he set new lap and race records to become the first man to win all three classic TT classes – the Lightweight, Junior and Senior.

Kenzo Tada became known as the 'India Rubber Man' thanks to his ability to survive numerous crashes without hurting himself.

Handley also became the first man to lap the Mountain circuit in under 30 minutes with a lap time of 29m 41s. In a statement which must have further demoralised his rivals, Handley admitted after the race that he'd seldom had his throttle more than three-quarters open!

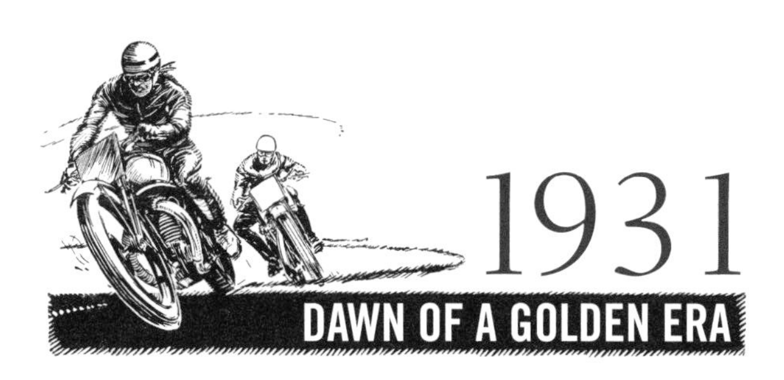

1931

DAWN OF A GOLDEN ERA

By 1931 the British bike industry was the envy of the world with marques such as Rudge, Norton, Velocette, Sunbeam, AJS, Raleigh and the Jap and Blackburne-engined Rex-Acmes and OK-Supremes. In an era when cars were still too expensive for the man in the street, motorcycles provided a relatively cheap mode of transport and success at the TT transferred directly to bike sales. But foreign competition was growing and there were no less than eight foreign factories represented at the 1931 TT including NSU, Moto Guzzi, Husqvarna and FN.

After Rudge had dominated the 1930 Junior with a 1-2-3 and finished first and second in the Senior, Norton had worked long and hard in the intervening year to make sure its bikes were capable of beating its Coventry-based rivals. Norton's four-man rider line-up was impressive: Stanley Woods, Jimmy Guthrie, Jimmy Simpson and Manxman Percy 'Tim' Hunt. But in an early example of team orders, Norton team boss Bill Mansell decided that the race winner would be decided at the end of the first lap as Simpson later explained. 'Mr Mansell laid it down that whoever led at the end of the first lap was to keep that position and the other three would be signalled to keep in their respective places. In other words, it was to be an open race between us for one lap and we were then to be controlled.'

Mansell's thinking was that there was no point in any Norton teamsters risking non-finishes by blowing bikes up in a flat-out race against other Nortons. But plans have a habit of going wrong as Simpson found to his cost. He led at the end of the first lap and received the signal to hold station only for his team-mate Tim Hunt to overtake him on the fifth lap. When Simpson's bike developed problems as he gave chase, Hunt was clear to take the win and he did so in style, knocking more than eight minutes off the race record and setting a new lap record at 75.27mph. His team-mate Jimmy Guthrie was three minutes behind him at the flag.

The Lightweight race provided a just result. After 12 years of trying and several podium positions both on solo machines and in Sidecars, Graham Walker just couldn't seem to win a TT. A heavily-built man, Walker had always opted for the bigger 350 and 500cc machines, believing the power-to-weight ratio would not suffer so much on larger machines. But with Rudge having built a new 250, he bit the bullet and squeezed his sizeable frame around the smaller machine, prompting *The Motor Cycle* to comment that, 'The age of miracles would not be past if a 250 engine could carry Graham Walker's fourteen-and-a-half stone to victory.'

The age of miracles clearly was not past as, against all expectations, burly Walker and the little 250 proved to be the winning combination. Walker not only won the race from his team-mate Tyrell-Smith, he also became the first man to complete seven laps of the TT course on a 250cc machine in under four hours. It was to be Graham Walker's one and only TT win.

In the Senior, Norton's four riders picked up every accolade possible in a single race; a clean sweep of the podium and a new lap record to boot. Tim Hunt completed a remarkable Junior/Senior double and knocked ten minutes off Wal Handley's race time from the previous year, while Jimmy Guthrie came home second in his first year as a Norton rider. Stanley Woods took the final podium place. Jimmy Simpson had been the first man to lap the TT at 60mph back in 1924 and the first to lap at 70mph in 1926. He now added to this unique record by becoming the first man to lap at 80mph – before breaking down yet again.

Dream team.
The 1932 Norton squad featured Stanley Woods (27), Jimmy Guthrie (22) and Jimmy Simpson (15). They finished first, second and third respectively in the Senior race.

Jimmy Simpson on the Norton was fastest in practice for both the Junior and Senior classes in 1932 but, with his history of breakdowns during actual racing, his rivals were probably not over-concerned. Sure enough, in the week's opening race, the Junior, Simpson was charging hard in third place before succumbing once more to technical gremlins. His team-mate Stanley Woods was in scintillating form and raised the lap record to 77.16mph as he led Wal Handley over the line by over two minutes.

The Lightweight race produced a real surprise which proved you didn't need to be in the all-powerful Norton or Rudge teams to win a TT. Little-known New Imperial rider, Leo Davenport, started his race fairly quietly in fifth place before clawing his way through the field to second place on the fourth lap. After overtaking the vastly experienced Wal Handley, who was on lap record-breaking pace, Davenport led the race for a short time before being passed by Ernie Nott. Nott, however, failed to reach Ramsey on the last lap and Davenport was rewarded with a surprise victory from Graham Walker with Wal Handley in third.

Just two days later, Handley – who was known as 'the man who couldn't be frightened', was to have what he later called the worst accident of his career. With HRH Prince George (the future King George VI) watching the Senior race, first from the Grandstand and then Creg-ny-Baa, Handley had been splitting the Nortons of Stanley Woods and Jimmy Guthrie for three exciting laps when his brakes locked at an

The 1932 Senior race continued however, and Jimmy Simpson set another new lap record at 81.50mph. The only surprise this time around was that he actually managed to finish the race, albeit in third position. Ahead of him the battle raged between the great TT rivals and team-mates Woods and Guthrie. The verdict eventually went to Woods – giving him his first Junior/Senior double – with Guthrie and Simpson making it another 1-2-3 for Norton.

Wal Handley's expression here in 1933 shows him for the hard man he was. After winning four TTs and having a corner on the course named after him, he was killed in a plane crash in WWII.

S-bend known then as Alma's corner. Handley was thrown spectacularly from his Rudge at 85mph and landed briefly in a bed of nettles before bouncing back into the middle of the road. His bike was lying in the track just inches away with its engine still running and fuel pouring out from the tank, soaking both Handley and the bike. With his back badly hurt, Handley was effectively paralysed and could not get himself off the track to safety. While other bikes swerved to get past both him and his wrecked machine, Handley's greatest fear was that the bike would catch fire and enshroud him in flames. Handley was eventually carried to safety and made a full recovery but his name is still known to modern TT fans because the corner where he came to grief was renamed Handley's Corner in memory of his crash. Handley returned to the TT but in 1935 he lost part of his thumb while trying to adjust his rear brake along the Sulby Straight. This ended the bike racing career of a man who had won all four solo TT trophies. Sadly, Handley was killed in an aeroplane crash near Carlisle in the early part of World War II while serving as a Captain in the Air Transport Auxiliary.

1933 UNAPPROACHABLE

By the end of the 1933 TT, Stanley Woods had established himself as the greatest TT star to date. His second consecutive Junior/Senior double took his tally of wins to six, more than any other rider in the event's history – and there was still more to come.

The Nortons truly were 'unapproachable' in 1933 as the firm's long-running slogan proclaimed. Nortons filled all three podium positions in the Junior and Senior races – the first time any manufacturer had achieved this. Woods led the Junior from start to finish and posted lap and race records for good measure. Even so, his team-mate Tim Hunt was only seven seconds behind at the flag while Jimmy Guthrie completed the Norton clean sweep. As an advert for machine reliability however, Velocette could not have wished for more; after the Norton 1-2-3, their machines filled the rest of the top ten.

The Lightweight proved to be a much more open affair with Excelsiors, Cottons, Rudges and New Imperials all contesting the leader board positions. Wal Handley, now Excelsior-mounted (his exquisitely complex machine was dubbed 'the mechanical marvel' and would later evolve into the famous Excelsior Manxman), led the first laps but was overtaken on lap two by team-mate Sid Gleave who went on to take the win. Sadly, the race was marred by the death of Gleave's team-mate, 1928 Lightweight winner Frank Longman, after he crashed on the approach to Ramsey. Longman's forks had broken on the plunge down Bray Hill but, rather than retire, he fixed them up as best he could in order to cruise round to the finish. It was a fatal error. The forks collapsed between Sulby and Ramsey and Longman was thrown from his bike and killed.

It was only by sheer good luck that there were no more fatalities when the organisers opened the roads to the public at Creg-ny-Baa while there were still competitors racing. Thankfully no one was hurt by this dangerous oversight.

In the Senior race, Stanley Woods became the first man to record a race average at over 80mph when he clocked 81.04mph over the seven laps. The Irishman led from start to finish to take his second consecutive Senior win and his fourth win in just two years. Jimmy Simpson made it to the end of the race, finishing in second place ahead of Paul Hunt and Jimmy Guthrie, all of whom were Norton-mounted.

1934
LUCKY THIRTEEN

Portrait of a winner. Jimmy Guthrie on his 1934 Junior-winning Norton. The Scot won six TTs before losing his life at the German Grand Prix in 1937.

The 1934 TT produced what was, arguably, the most popular win in the event's 27-year history. After thirteen years of trying to win a race, Jimmy Simpson had set eight lap records, finished second four times and third four times but – primarily down to machine failure – had never managed to cross the finishing line in first place. In the 1934 Lightweight race Simpson changed all of that and there wasn't anyone on the Isle of Man who begrudged him his long overdue win. At the sold-out prize-giving ceremony, Simpson was carried shoulder-high around the grounds of the Villa Marina. After saying the previous year that he would 'give his life' to win a TT, Simpson's dream finally came true – and thankfully, he didn't have to give his life in the pursuit of it.

Before the event got underway, Simpson had already decided that this would be his last TT so it was even more fitting that he should end such a fine career with a flourish. Like Graham Walker before him, Simpson's maiden, and only, victory came in a class he had never contested before, the Lightweight TT. 'It was a coincidence that I won a TT race on my last year's racing,' he later said. 'I didn't just go on until I won, as some people seem to think. And it was a coincidence that it was the luckiest year I ever had.'

It wasn't lucky for every competitor however. Unbeknown to those celebrating Simpson's victory, a tragedy had unfolded on the mist-shrouded Mountain section of the course. Syd Crabtree had been killed after crashing his Excelsior in mist which was so dense that no one saw or even heard the accident. In an age before travelling marshals, Crabtree's body lay undiscovered for 40 minutes before a search party came across it. Crabtree's sad demise was responsible for the introduction of travelling marshals the following year. These bike-mounted marshals could search the course for any missing riders and deliver first-aid supplies while racing continued. It's a valuable practice which continues to this day. But as is too often the case in motorcycle racing, someone had to die before positive action was taken.

Stanley Woods had announced that for the 1934

Record-breaker: Jimmy Simpson set the first 60, 70 and 80mph laps round the TT course but broke as many machines as he did records. His only win came in the 1934 Lightweight. He is pictured rounding Hillberry in the Junior race that same year.

BP ETHYL
DUNLOP
PRATTS HIGH TEST

The legendary Jimmy Guthrie rounds Creg-ny-Baa in 1934. The view remains largely unchanged today.

TT he would be riding a Swedish-built Husqvarna in the Senior race and an Italian Moto Guzzi in the Lightweight. Woods's decision to leave the all-conquering Norton team was at least partly motivated by money as he explained many years later. 'It created quite a stir because I was really at the height of my career with Nortons and Nortons were virtually unbeatable. But to tell the whole truth, I was making no money and I was getting older every year – I was already long past what I thought was a reasonable age for a racing motorcyclist – and the opportunity came to ride these Husqvarnas.'

He may have been well paid to ride for Husqvarna, but Woods had also become disillusioned by Norton's team orders, particularly when he was told not to win his home race – the Ulster Grand Prix, in 1933 – in order that his team-mates may have their share of glory. When his team-mates all broke down, Woods went on to win the race anyway then left Norton to its own devices.

As was becoming a habit, Norton – with or without its star rider Woods – blitzed the Junior race with Jimmy Guthrie setting new lap and race records to lead his team-mate Jimmy Simpson home by just nine seconds. Stanley Woods's Husqvarna team-mate Ernie Notts finished a fine third on the twin-cylinder machine, albeit a full six minutes in arrears.

The big race of the week saw Woods locked in a fierce battle with his arch rival Jimmy Guthrie. Woods set the fastest lap of the race in an attempt to get ahead of the Scotsman but ran out of fuel with just ten miles to go while lying in second place. Guthrie's

Junior/Senior double gave Norton its fourth double in as many years but Stanley Woods was not going to let his former employers get away with it for much longer.

Jimmy Simpson finished his final TT race, the Senior, in second place, but he clearly still had the pace to impress spectators and marshals around the course. While he was watching practice at the 13th Milestone the following year along with Wal Handley and Tim Hunt, a marshal turned to Simpson and said, 'You think the riders look dangerous this morning? You should have been here and seen last year's Senior. That man Simpson frightened the life out of us. He was terrifying. You weren't here by any chance were you?'

'I suppose I must have been,' replied Jimmy. 'Seeing as I'm that man Simpson.'

George Formby was the biggest music hall star in the country in 1935 and in the summer of that year, he arrived on the Isle of Man to make one of his most famous films – the classic *No Limit*. The movie stars Formby as chimney sweep George Shuttleworth who builds his own 'Shuttleworth Snap' for an assault on the TT races. It became one of Formby's most famous movies and for the best part of 60 years, was shown in Manx cinemas during TT week.

A General Strike on the Island meant that early arrivals for the races had no gas, electricity or public transport at their disposal. The strike very nearly caused the cancellation of the TT but fortunately, matters were settled for the beginning of practice.

Stanley Woods was entered in the Lightweight and Senior on Moto Guzzis and took half a minute off the Senior lap record in practice. With no bike for the Junior race, Woods was forced to watch Jimmy Guthrie rack up his third consecutive TT win and his fourth in total. Further down the field, Scotsman Jock West had enjoyed a fairly drunken race. In a bid to shake off the flu, West had arranged to have a glass of Scotch prepared for him at his pit stop. He explained the full story in Geoff Davison's 1948 book *Racing Reminiscences*. 'I pulled into the pits for machine and personal refuelling. Everything functioned as arranged and while attending to the quick filler with my left hand I found no difficulty in disposing of the contents of the glass that had been thrust into my right. As I knocked the liquid back I thought that it seemed unusually potent and by the time I arrived at the top of Bray Hill a very definite internal glow was becoming apparent, and it dawned on me that my request for a "short" had received such conscientious attention that I had been given a treble brandy! By Quarter Bridge I was feeling fine and by Braddann I had a job deciding which road to take. From Union Mills to Ballacraine the road seemed extremely narrow and I remember hoping against hope that the motor would keep going, as I was certain that

I was for the Gaol House if for any reason at all I stopped.'

West brought his NSU home in a respectable 15th place, having been sensible enough to refuse the second helping of brandy which was offered up at his next pit stop!

Stanley Woods made history by becoming the first man to win the Lightweight TT on a foreign machine but the race best remembered from 1935 was the Senior which is still regarded as one of the finest ever. It was the first TT to be postponed to the Saturday (due to the perennial Manx mist) and special permission from Tynwald was required to close the roads. With all the bureaucracy finally sorted, the race got underway at 11.30am on Saturday with Jimmy Guthrie setting off at number one. Woods, starting at number 30, had to wait a full 15 minutes before being set loose to give chase to his nemesis. His job was made somewhat easier by the fact that his bike was the first to feature rear suspension, a major handling advantage over the Island's notoriously bumpy roads.

Even so, it was Guthrie who held the upper hand throughout most of the race and as he flashed past the Grandstand to begin his last lap, he held a seemingly unapproachable 26 second lead. The more astute fan however, would have realised that Woods had cut Guthrie's previous lead down from a massive 52 seconds and was still pushing hard. Woods's pit was a hive of activity as the Guzzi team prepared for a second and final pit stop. But Woods had other ideas. Years later, he explained how he had out-foxed the Norton team by organising a dummy pit stop. 'I had my stop at the end of three laps and had my pit man prepare for another stop at the end of six which I didn't intend to take – it wasn't necessary. I started the last lap still 26 seconds behind and as I crossed the finishing line and got the chequered flag, the press plane took off with the press pictures of the winner – Jimmy Guthrie. He'd been declared the winner, I couldn't catch him.'

But catch him he did – and pass him too. As well as the press plane leaving, the BBC commentator at the Grandstand also declared Guthrie the winner and he was interviewed as such. Even the organisers joined in the celebrations. But they had seriously underestimated the talent of Woods. When the final calculations were made, it emerged that the Irishman had won by just four seconds – the closest race in the TT's history to date. To do so, Woods had been forced to up his previous lap record by 4mph to take the new record to 86.53mph – an astonishing speed on such primitive machinery and the fastest Senior race time ever recorded. 'I turned on everything I had on the last lap,' said Woods, 'I over-revved and I beat him by four seconds and put the lap record up about 3 or 4mph. And that, I think, gave me more satisfaction and more joy – the fact that I'd beaten Norton. It's what I set out to do. It was very, very satisfactory.'

Jimmy Guthrie was out for revenge in the 1936 Senior TT but first he had some drama to contend with in the Junior. He was leading the race on the fifth lap when he was forced to halt his Norton at Hillberry to replace its chain. After setting off again, officials claimed he had received outside assistance from a marshal and was to be disqualified. Flagged in at Ramsey on the following lap, Guthrie grabbed the telephone which connected to the Grandstand and vehemently denied having had any help. He remounted and finished the race in fifth place despite his two enforced stops but was still officially disqualified. The crowd went wild with the injustice and a menacing mood prevailed at the prize-giving ceremony held later. It was only at the ceremony that the ACU admitted it had been wrong and that Guthrie had *not* received outside assistance. He was to be awarded the prize money for second place (where, it was calculated, he would most likely have finished had he not been forced to stop at Ramsey) but, bizarrely, was only classified as a finisher, not as being the second-placed finisher. The race was won by Freddie Frith, on another Norton, at his first attempt. Frith had previously won the Manx Grand Prix – an amateur race held over the same Mountain course each year in September as a stepping-stone to the TT – but to win the TT proper first time out was a tremendous achievement. With 'Crasher' White being officially credited with second place on yet another Norton, the Birmingham-based

Jimmy Guthrie rounds Quarterbridge in the 1936 Junior. He was controversially awarded prize money for second place but excluded from the official results.

firm took the team award but Guthrie was angered and even more determined to win the Senior.

Due to Mussolini's invasion of Abyssinia, Moto Guzzi did not contest the 1936 TT, forcing Stanley Woods to ride Velocettes in the Junior and Senior and a German-built DKW in the Lightweight race. After breaking down in the Junior, he was leading the Lightweight on the two-stroke DKW, the bike which is widely regarded as being the loudest bike ever to race on the Isle of Man. Some reports said it could be heard as far away as the British mainland! By the sixth lap, however, the German machine fell silent allowing Bob Foster to take the win on a New Imperial. It was to be the last Lightweight win for a British-built machine.

Then came the headline event: the Senior race. Although there was never more than 27 seconds between Guthrie and Woods, it was always the Scotsman who held the upper hand this time around. Both riders broke the lap record on their sixth circuit with Guthrie circulating in 26m 05s and Woods in 26m 02s on his Velocette. It was not enough for Woods however, and Guthrie came home to win by 18 seconds to put the disappointment of the previous year behind him – and to prove to the organisers that he didn't need outside assistance to win the world's greatest motorcycle race.

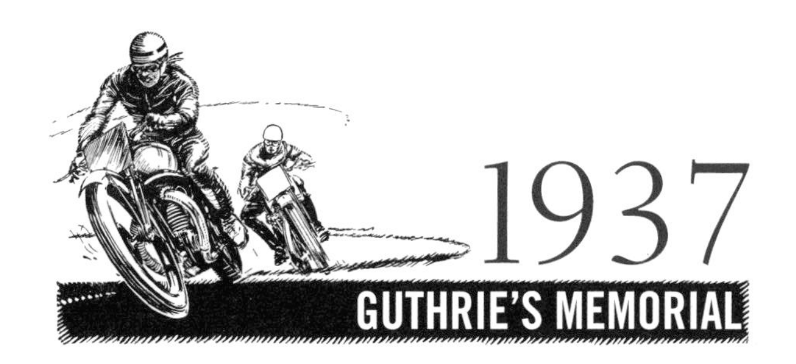

1937 GUTHRIE'S MEMORIAL

As expected, Norton ran away with the Junior TT yet again in 1937 with Jimmy Guthrie leading from start to finish to collect his sixth TT win. It was to be his last. Just two months later, Guthrie was killed while leading the German Grand Prix on the now defunct Sachsenring circuit. He was within one mile of the finish line when his rear wheel locked up and caused him to crash. He died later from his injuries. No satisfactory explanation has ever been given for the cause of the crash and this has led to all sorts of theories, one of the wildest being that he was shot by a nationalistic German sniper. The closest we can probably come to the truth was published in the book *Motor Cycle Racing at the Sachsenring.* It read:

At the start of the final lap, Guthrie crossed the line amid a sea of humanity and had to check himself twice in an effort to pass a back-marker – the German, Mansfeld. Then, less than 2 km from the end of the race, his Norton began to twitch from right to left. He slammed into a tree, the rear wheel was torn off and the rider and his machine became airborne. The stray wheel stayed to the left of the track, with one of Guthrie's boots and the bike's chain; the rider was stretched out on the verge, 20 metres beyond the point of contact with the tree. Stanley Woods, heading slowly towards the finish with a stricken motorcycle, witnessed the carnage. He dropped his bike and ran to Guthrie's aid, but found him unconscious. The atmosphere was heavy at the finish. Winner Karl Gall was in no mood to celebrate and Kommandant Huhnlein chose to dedicate the main prize to the fastest man of the day, James Guthrie. A first diagnosis of his condition disclosed severe head and ankle injuries. Several hours later, however, the sad truth was confirmed: the best rider in the world had died that evening as a consequence of his injuries. What had happened? Although some pointed a finger at Mansfeld, and others believed a seized engine was to blame, a detailed inquest appeared to prove a sheared axle caused the accident. Specialists at the time even went so far as to suggest that Norton had gone too far in its efforts to save weight.

Whatever the cause of the accident, the TT – and motorcycle racing in general – had been robbed of one of its greatest stars. The esteem in which the Scotsman was held on the Isle of Man is proven by the fact that he remains one of the few riders to have a memorial on the TT course. Formerly known as the Cutting and now as Guthrie's Memorial, the site is marked by a simple cairn of stones with a plaque in memory of the great man. It is one of the most picturesque parts of the TT course and, on a clear day, offers stunning views of Guthrie's native Scotland.

While British machines still dominated the Junior TT (Freddie Frith and Crasher White had completed another Norton clean-sweep of the event), things were markedly different in the Lightweight division. With more foreign bikes and foreign riders setting the pace in practice, a British win – for machine or rider – looked unlikely. And so it proved to be in the race with Italian Omobono Tenni becoming the first foreign rider to win the Lightweight TT ahead of Stanley Woods on an Excelsior and Ernie Thomas on the DKW. Such was the significance of this Italian win, in light of the growing Fascist movement in that country, that the news of it was cabled straight to Benito Mussolini.

Jimmy Guthrie had been leading his last ever TT race until the fateful breakdown at the Cutting on the fifth lap which would later give rise to the Guthrie Memorial. This gave his great friend and rival, Stanley Woods, the lead on his Velocette until Norton's Freddie Frith posted an identical time to Woods on the sixth lap. It was all to play for on the seventh and final circuit. When Woods recorded his fastest ever lap round the TT course (25m 20s) and clocked an average speed of 122.49mph over a one-mile section of the Sulby Straight, it looked like the Dubliner was on for yet another famous victory but Frith amazed everyone by going even faster. His time of 25m 05s equated to the first ever 90mph lap of the Mountain circuit (90.27mph to be precise) and it was enough to secure Frith his first Senior TT win. It no doubt also contributed to his later becoming the first motorcycle racer to be awarded the OBE for services to the sport.

1938 FREAKS

When Harold Daniell replaced the late Jimmy Guthrie in the factory Norton team for the 1938 TT, he couldn't have imagined that the lap record he would set in the Senior race would stand for twelve years. He could also not have known that, despite this mercurial feat, the army would refuse his application just one year later on the basis that his eyesight was too poor!

By now, the manufacturers were making no attempt to keep their racing machines similar to their road-going 'tourist' models. The 'freak' machines used for racing now featured exotica like overhead camshafts, telescopic front forks, rear suspension and superchargers which ordinary road riders could only dream about. The original ideals of the Tourist Trophy were rapidly being eroded.

Stanley Woods returned to his winning ways for the first time in three years when he won the Junior by nearly four minutes on a Velocette and set a new lap record in the process. It was to be his only success of the week. As the chequered flag was brought down for Woods, the man waving it failed to bestow the same honour on second-placed Ernie Mellors. Not realising the race was over, Mellors started an eighth lap and made it all the way to Creg-ny-Baa (some 34 miles into the course) before being flagged off the circuit.

DKW dominated the Lightweight race with Ewald Kluge winning by over 11 minutes from Stanley Woods on an Excelsior. Kluge also set the first ever lap at over 80mph in the Lightweight class.

If the opening two events of the week were relatively dull at the top of the leaderboard, the Senior TT was anything but. After four laps and 150.92 miles of racing, there was only one second between Stanley Woods on his Velocette and Freddie Frith on the Norton. Frith's team-mate, Harold Daniell was only seven seconds behind in third but, after setting the first ever sub-25-minute lap of the course, he took the lead from Woods and Frith who could not be separated on time. On the final circuit, Daniell raised the bar

Celebrations for the top three in the 1938 Senior race. Winner Harold Daniell is flanked by second-placed Stanley Woods and Norton team-mate Freddie Frith.

Unlikely hero. Harold Daniell set a record lap of 91mph in 1938 en route to winning the Senior race. The army still refused his application due to poor eyesight.

even higher and posted a lap at exactly 91mph – a time which would not be bettered for 12 years. It was enough to secure the race win by 15 seconds from Woods who himself had seen Frith off by just 1.6 seconds after almost 265 miles of racing.

1939 THE GATHERING STORM

As the riders lined up for the start of the 1939 TT, a boy scout walked alongside them on Glencrutchery Road carrying a huge flag emblazoned with the Nazi Swastika. It had not yet, of course, become the universal symbol of evil it is seen as today, but it must still rank as one of the most bizarre sights in the TT's long history.

World War II was still some weeks away when the 1939 TT was held but it had a direct effect on the races nonetheless. After supporting the event since its inception in 1907, Norton did not enter new factory machines in 1939 as it was too busy building production bikes for the armed forces in anticipation of war. Instead, Freddie Frith and Harold Daniell had to make do with the machines they had raced the previous year.

The state-supported German motorcycle manufacturers took a completely different approach. With Adolf Hitler determined to show Germany's superiority in every field in the run up to war, the country's presence at the TT had never been greater and the machinery shipped over had never been more magnificent. All of BMW's entries featured supercharged engines as did DKW's, while NSU fielded exotic blown, ohc twins. Against all this, the Norton riders on year-old machines did not even enjoy the assistance of a solitary factory mechanic.

Even so, Freddie Frith on his old Norton led the early stages of the Junior from Germany's Heiner Fleischmann on the supercharged DKW with Stanley Woods chasing hard in third place. By the fourth lap, Woods had taken the lead and when Frith retired from the race, it looked like it would be a straight battle between the Irishman on the Velocette and Fleischmann on the DKW. Then out of nowhere, Harold Daniell forced his way into the action and, on the last lap, posted the fastest lap of the race to take second place. That last lap had been 15 seconds quicker than Woods's, but not quite enough to steal victory from the by-now legendary Irishman.

Woods had now won an incredible ten TT races, four more than his late friend, Jimmy Guthrie, who stood second best in the list of winners. That 1939 Junior victory was to be Woods's last TT win. His TT career had started in 1923 and since then he had started in 37 races on nine different makes of machinery and finished in 21 of them. Of the races he finished, he was never placed lower than sixth. He set 11 fastest or record laps along the way and became the first man to win two races in a week on three different occasions. His tally of ten TT victories would not be bettered until the late 1960s and only then by the great Mike Hailwood. Stanley Woods died of natural causes at home in his beloved Ireland on July 28, 1993 aged 90. The clock on the TT scoreboard opposite the Grandstand, bears an enlarged copy of Woods's signature as if to remind today's competitors that he is still keeping an eye on their times.

Despite the financial backing enjoyed by the Italian and German teams, reliability eluded them in the Lightweight race. Omobono Tenni and Stanley Woods's Guzzis both failed to make the finish and Fleischmann's DKW also gave up the ghost. This left

Germany victorious. BMW team-mates Georg Meier (right) and Jock West after their one-two in the 1939 Senior. Note the Swastika on victorious Meier's leathers. Within weeks, the pair would be at war for real.

Ted Mellors to take a first win for Benelli from Ewald Kluge on the other DKW, with Tyrell-Smith at least getting his Excelsior on the rostrum in what was to be his last TT appearance.

The supercharged BMWs had been timed at 135mph on Sulby Straight in practice – a full 10mph faster than the Nortons – and looked odds-on to take the Senior win. BMW had come to the Island with three riders: Georg Meier, Jock West and Karl Gall, but Gall had died after crashing in practice at Ballaugh Bridge. This tragedy left just Meier and the more experienced West to line up for the Senior race. It would not be the last time that men would line up on Glencrutchery Road to honour a recently deceased team-mate. In 2004, when he was 95 years old, Jock West spoke to *MCN Sport* about the dangers of the TT. 'How dangerous was it? I don't know what standard you'd use. I can remember 1935 when there were five killed in the Isle of Man. It just happened. I think it's been a relatively equal danger all the way, the only difference today is that the circuits allow you to run off, whereas there were so many places with no run-off at all. The Isle of Man was bad, but most places took their fair percentage. Jimmy Guthrie was killed in Germany, and we used to say about the Belgian Grand Prix that if they get any more memorials around there they'll have a fence. It didn't ever make me think I should stop. It was always the other chap's fault. I was sure I would make my own luck. If you couldn't do it without falling off you shouldn't be there.'

As expected, the BMWs had things all their own way against the older British singles. Meier led by almost a minute at the end of the first lap while Stanley Woods put up a brave battle on his Velocette to tie with West in second place. The German bikes continued to pull away from the rest of the field and Meier eventually brought his home two minutes ahead of his team-mate West. In his last TT, Woods was overhauled by Freddie Frith on the Norton for the final podium position.

Germany had gained its great propaganda victory by beating the previously all-conquering British bikes in the world's greatest motorcycle race. Within three months, an infinitely more serious battle would erupt between the two countries. It would last for six years, claim the lives of countless millions and change the world forever. The trivial pursuit of motorcycle racing would have to be put on hold while Britain fought for its very existence. The dangers of the TT suddenly paled in comparison to the horrors which awaited many of its competitors. Yet the bravery they had displayed whilst racing round the world's most dangerous circuit would stand them in good stead for the battle that lay ahead. After finishing the 1939 Senior race in second place on his BMW, Jock West adapted his skills to flying a Spitfire and took the fight to his former employers.

TOURIST TT TROPHY CENTURY

CHAPTER 4
1947-59

A determined Freddie Frith at the bottom of Bray Hill during 1947 practice on a Moto Guzzi. He later crashed and missed the races.

Velocette

1947

AN END TO WAR

While Britain was finally at peace in the summer of 1946, the country was still licking its wounds after six long years of war. Rationing, petrol shortages, steel and manpower shortages – and the fact that British motorcycle manufacturers had been completely focused on building bikes for the armed forces in recent years rather than developing new racers – all combined to scupper any notion of holding a TT in 1946.

The first post-war TT was not held until 1947 and even then, shortages were still evident. Many had doubted the TT's ability to revive itself but more than 100 riders posted entries, amongst them several pre-war TT stars including Harold Daniell, Freddie Frith and Jock West. But there were notable absentees too – men who had given their lives in defence of their country. Wal Handley, Walter Rusk and Sid Gleave were just a few former TT heroes who would never get to challenge their beloved course again.

While the well established three-race programme continued as before, spectators could now enjoy the added bonus of the all-new Clubman's TT which featured three races within one (250 Lightweight, 350 Junior and 1000cc Senior) for standard production machines.

For some, the productions bikes seemed just a little too slow. Eric Briggs recounted an episode during practice for that first Clubman's TT. 'Approaching Ramsey at a fair speed, two dogs appeared from nowhere and, for what seemed quite a long time, ran alongside me. After various remarks made by people as to the capabilities of Clubmen and their steeds, this incident seemed the final blow to our pride! However, it was some consolation that there was no one about to witness and recount this "race", which I am glad to say I won, the dogs eventually retiring, apparently to wait for the next Clubman.'

Slow or not, Briggs went on to win the Senior Clubman's race ahead of one Allan Jefferies – grandfather of future TT legend David Jefferies.

The quality of machinery, as well as that of the petrol, for the main TT races was down on the pre-war years. Supercharging was banned and all riders had to use the same low grade fuel. The result was that the 1947 Nortons were making just 40bhp – ten less than they had in 1939.

While Velocette was now without its star rider, Stanley Woods, it didn't stop the British firm from completing a clean sweep of the first post-war TT. Bob Foster led the Junior throughout, and when most of the top Norton runners broke down, it left the way clear for David Whitworth and Jock Weddell to fill out the podium places with Velocettes.

The Lightweight race saw the only serious challenge from foreign machinery all week as Moto Guzzi returned to the TT, this time fielding Maurice Cann and

War is over. Bob Foster won the first post-war TT, the 1947 Junior, on his Velocette. His son looks unimpressed with all the fuss.

Manliff Barrington rounds Quarterbridge en route to winning the 1947 Lightweight 250 race on his Moto Guzzi.

Team-mates. Manliff Barrington (left) and Maurice Cann finished first and second in the first post-war Lightweight 250 race on their Italian Moto Guzzis.

Maurice Cann is congratulated on setting the fastest lap of the race on his way to second place in the 1947 Lightweight 250 race. He won the event the following year.

Manliff Barrington. Apart from the two Italian bikes, the rest of the field was made up of British machines, all of which were between eight and ten years old and didn't stand a chance against the newer Guzzis. Cann and Barrington dominated the race but Barrington's win proved to be a controversial one after there were doubts over the accuracy of the official timekeeping.

Of the 33 entries for the Senior race, 26 were Nortons and all had changed little since the 1930s. Jock West and Les Graham – who had been a bomber pilot in WWII – at least had new machines in the form of AJS 'Porcupine' twins, so called because of their spiky cylinder-head fins. But a slipping clutch put paid to West's chances and Graham crashed out of the race at Glen Helen. He was unhurt and remounted but was well out of contention.

That left the Nortons to dominate with Ulsterman Artie Bell leading Harold Daniell and Ken Bills at the end of the first lap with only nine seconds covering the top three. It was Bell's first TT and no one expected him to beat his team-mate and current lap-record holder, Daniell, but by the start of the last lap Bell held a one second lead and looked like pulling off a shock victory. On that final circuit however, Daniell put all his experience and course knowledge to good use and came out the victor by 22 seconds to win his second TT.

The fastest lap of the race was shared by Bell and Peter Goodman at 84.07mph – a full 5mph slower than Harold Daniell's 1938 lap record. But it hardly mattered; the TT had survived its second world war and as Britain slowly found its feet again, the event would go from strength to strength. It would not be cancelled again for over half a century.

1948 GATHERING MOMENTUM

If there were any lingering doubts about the popularity and relevance of the TT after WWII, they were completely dispelled in 1948 when the Junior race attracted 100 entries. It was the highest number of riders ever to

Artie Bell pulls off an unexpected win for Norton in the 1948 Senior after most of the fancied runners struck trouble.

enter a TT and it proved the event was more popular than ever. The Junior race wasn't exactly a thriller however, with Freddie Frith winning by over five minutes from his Velocette team-mate, Bob Foster.

So famous had the TT become worldwide, that Australian rider Eric McPherson decided to enter the 1948 event, though he probably later wished he hadn't bothered. After spending four weeks on a steamer and travelling a total of 13,000 miles, he crashed at Governor's Bridge during practice, fractured his pelvis, and didn't even get to race.

In the Senior, Moto Guzzi was the only firm to run factory bikes and Omobono Tenni led the race for the first four laps on one of the Italian works machines. Behind him many of the fancied runners dropped out of the race, then Tenni stopped to make adjustments on the fifth lap, Artie Bell took advantage to lead home an unexpected Norton 1-2-3 with Bill Doran and Jock Weddell filling out the podium.

For the first time since 1924, it was decided to hold a massed start for the Lightweight race. But it was hardly a massed pack which crossed the finish line – only six bikes finished the race from 26 starters, with Maurice Cann winning by a massive margin of ten minutes.

At the end of the week, Omobono Tenni became the very first recipient of the Jimmy Simpson trophy for setting the fastest lap of the meeting. Sadly, he would never get the chance to win another. Tenni was killed during practice for the Swiss Grand Prix later in the year.

In 1949, motorcycle racing changed forever. Prior to that year, there had been several Grands Prix held annually but they had never been linked together into a meaningful championship. It had been planned in 1939 but WWII put paid to the idea. Now, ten years later, the FIM (Federation Internationale de Motocyclisme) organised the first ever world championship for racing motorcycles.

The FIM, as its name suggests, was made up of various national motorcycle federations (the ACU represented Britain) and to this day it is the governing body of world motorcycle sport. The six-round World Motor Cycle Racing Championships would kick off at the TT and would be followed with races in Switzerland, the Netherlands, Belgium, Northern Ireland and Italy. There would be five classes: 125s, 250s, 350s, 500s and Sidecars but only the premier class, the 500s, would race at all six rounds. The first five men home in each race would score points (from ten down to five) and at the end of the season riders would choose their three best results to arrive at a final championship score. This system not only allowed for the mechanical breakdowns which were so prevalent at the time, but it also meant riders did not have to travel to every round in an age when foreign travel was hugely expensive and beset with difficulties.

So after already being established for some 42 years, the Isle of Man TT was given a huge boost by having the honour of staging the first ever world championship motorcycle race – the direct ancestor of today's MotoGP championship. It would continue to host the event for the next 27 years.

For the first time at the TT, riders lining up for the 1949 Junior started in pairs at 20 second intervals. By the end of lap one, Les Graham led by 19 seconds but on the second lap his clutch expired and Bill Doran inherited the lead. He soon suffered a similar fate when his gearbox broke at the Gooseneck and the previous year's winner, Freddie Frith, took over at the front on his Velocette and held his lead to the flag to become the first ever winner of a world championship motorcycle race. By the end of the season, he would also be the world's first 350cc champion, having won every round in the series. He went out on top by retiring at the end of the year.

The Junior was marred by the death of TT stalwart Ben Drinkwater. Riding in what he had announced would be his last TT, he was killed after crashing near the 11th Milestone. The fast right/left combination is now called Drinkwater's Bends in his honour.

The Clubman's race was held on the Wednesday and it marked the TT debut of one of the greatest racing motorcyclists of all time – Geoff Duke. Lancashire-born Duke had already taken part in the previous year's Manx Grand Prix and had shown

Freddie Frith on the 350cc Velocette at the 1949 TT. He would go on to become the first ever 350cc world champion that same year.

glimpses of his future genius by leading the race (his first ever road race) only to retire with a split oil tank. In the Clubman's race Duke rode a standard production Norton so hard that he posted a lap time which was only eight seconds outside the outright lap record held by Harold Daniell on the factory Norton. It was enough to give Duke victory by over two minutes. Some 57 years after that race, Geoff Duke is still at a loss to describe the joy he felt riding in his first TT. 'I've never been able to describe the feeling of elation and absolute wonder of going down Bray Hill for the first time,' he says. 'I could have wept for joy.'

A few months after the TT, Duke returned to the Manx GP to settle an old score: he won the Senior and placed second in the Junior. In the space of four months, Duke had registered two wins and a second place round the Mountain circuit. It was enough to persuade Norton to sign him up for the TT proper and, in 1950, his legend would truly begin.

The Lightweight TT was once again a massed start and was eagerly watched by the Duke of Edinburgh in his capacity as patron of the ACU. Twenty-nine riders blasted down Bray Hill and Dickie Dale and Tommy Wood had the joint distinction of becoming the first riders to break a pre-war lap record when they both circulated at an identical 80.44mph – and that on low grade fuel. Magneto trouble halted Dale's charge but Wood managed a second place on his Moto Guzzi behind team-mate Manliff Barrington. Once again the Italian machines had dominated the Lightweight race and would go on to win the first 250cc world championship, but with a rider who didn't yet feature in the TT – Bruno Ruffo.

The Senior TT was flagged off by the Duke of Edinburgh and it proved to be a classic. After the first lap, the timekeepers could not split AJS team-mates Les Graham and Ted Frend but after two circuits Bob Foster also joined the party on his Guzzi and, for the first time in TT history, three riders shared the lead. Frend's challenge ended abruptly when he crashed out at Glen Helen on the fourth lap leaving Foster to lead for a lap before his clutch expired. Les Graham

Dario Ambrosini (Benelli) heading for the closest finish in history to date. He won the 1950 massed start Lightweight race by just 0.2 seconds from Maurice Cann (Moto Guzzi).

entered the final lap with a 90 second advantage over Harold Daniell but by Hillberry his AJS could take no more – its magneto shaft had sheared.

After his clutch had let him down while leading the Junior, Graham had been desperate to salvage something from the week but had been foiled again. The TT can be a cruel mistress. Showing the grit that had seen him through countless bombing missions in WWII, Graham refused to give up and, after completing over 260 miles of gruelling racing, he began pushing his AJS the three miles – some of it uphill – to the finish line. Exhausted, but gaining strength from the hundreds of spectators who urged him on, he slumped over the line to take tenth place. It was the hardest-earned tenth place in TT history.

For Graham, the 1949 TT had been nothing short of a disaster but his eventual reward for his monumental efforts was fitting. By the end of the year he would become the first ever 500cc world champion, his name to live forever in the annals of motorcycling history. After his display of stamina and determination at the TT, there could have been no more worthy champion.

1950 THE DUKE

Improvements to the TT course, higher octane fuel and significant new developments in machinery saw speeds rise dramatically at the 1950 TT. In practice, Artie Bell slashed 32 seconds off Freddie Frith's lap record from the year before. Bill Doran didn't have such a successful time of it in practice, crashing as he did near Ballig Bridge and breaking his leg. He was forced to sit out the races but at least enjoyed the honour of having a corner named after him – Doran's Bend.

Geoff Duke made his debut in the TT proper riding for the factory Norton team. The team's new 'Featherbed' frame (the nickname was given by Harold Daniell when describing what it felt like to ride) had been designed by Cromie and Rex McCandless and it proved a revelation around the bumpy TT course. Simple yet effective, it featured a twin-loop, all-welded

96

As close as it gets.
Geoff Duke tries hard to impress an elderly spectator in Kirkmichael. He won his first TT in 1950 wearing the first ever one-piece leather race suit.

Motorcycle racing's first superstar, Geoff Duke, pictured in 1951 with some of his TT silverware. Note the Jimmy Simpson fastest lap trophy in the centre.

design complete with a swinging arm and twin rear shock absorbers. Not only did the design help save weight, it also improved handling immeasurably. The frame was so effective that it would allow the single-cylinder Nortons to remain competitive against multi-cylinder opposition for far longer than they should have.

Duke debuted his own innovation at the 1950 TT – the first ever one-piece leather race suit. Although standard issue for bike racers and many road riders now, before Duke, every racer wore a leather jacket and leather trousers, often with a wide, body belt around the middle to combat the effects of jarring on the spine caused by the rough roads. It also helped to support the kidneys, another part of the anatomy which the TT is hard on. Sidecar racer Mick Boddice once admitted that he urinated blood for two weeks after every TT thanks to the battering his kidneys took on the Mountain course.

Duke had discovered the benefits of a tighter-fitting suit when he taped back baggy parts of his leather jacket and trousers while speed testing and knocked almost half a second off his times. Knowing that this improved streamlining would be equally beneficial in racing, he asked his local tailor, Frank Barker, to make up a tight-fitting one-piece suit and it became so popular with other riders that Barker turned to making them full-time. Not so popular was the undersuit which Duke had made up by a firm which specialised in ballet dancing costumes! Of the leather suit Duke now says, 'It was so light that it didn't offer much protection in a crash, but it was aerodynamically effective and comfortable. And my thinking was that you're not supposed to fall off anyway so I didn't worry about the suit's protective qualities.'

As the 1950 Junior race got underway, the leading riders were all aiming to beat the class lap record which was still held by Stanley Woods from 1938. The race record, belonging to Jimmy Guthrie, was one year older. Bob Foster was the first to break the fastest lap at a speed of 86.22mph before retiring at Quarterbridge. Artie Bell then upped the pace to 87.31mph on his way to victory over Duke who finished second in his first proper TT race. Harold Daniell brought his Norton home in third place in what was to be his last TT podium. He retired at the end of the season.

The Lightweight race was another massed start affair and once again it looked like being an Italian benefit – but for which firm? Moto Guzzi was pinning its hopes on Maurice Cann and Tommy Wood while Benelli fielded Dario Ambrosini who would go on to become the 1950 250cc world champion. The race turned into a terrific battle between Cann and

Ambrosini after Wood had developed a technical problem. By the end of lap four, Cann had a 37-second advantage but with one lap to go, Ambrosini had whittled this back to just 15 seconds and the race was truly on. Halfway over the Mountain section, Ambrosini had Cann in his sights and on the downhill run he overhauled him to win by 0.2 of a second – the closest finish anyone had ever seen round the TT course.

After an impressive debut in the Junior race, Geoff Duke was on fire come the Senior. He broke Harold Daniell's lap record from a standing start with Daniell himself in hot pursuit. His fifth lap speed of 93.33mph was a new outright lap record and helped him to win the race by a huge margin of 2m 40s from team-mates Artie Bell and Johnnie Lockett. Duke had won the biggest motorcycle race in the world at his first attempt. From his home on the Isle of Man, Duke recalls, 'To say I was impressed is to put it very lightly. It was strange to have my name up there with all the TT legends who had gone before.'

The Nortons, with their new frames, had claimed every podium place in both the Junior and Senior TTs and Geoff Duke had become the only man in history to win three 500cc races over the Mountain course in the space of 12 months; the 1949 Senior Clubman's, the 1949 Senior Manx and the 1950 Senior TT.

1951 SUPERSTAR

Geoff Duke's immaculate appearance and professional approach to the business of motorcycle racing was fast turning him into the sport's first household name and mainstream star. In a similar way in which Barry Sheene transcended the boundaries of the sport in the 1970s, Duke was doing it in the early Fifties, and the thousands of glossy black and white promotional shots of him handed out at each TT also made him the sport's first pin-up. His mainstream appeal was such that, at the end of 1951, he won the Sportsman of the Year award (voted for by the general public) and he also became the first motorcyclist ever to win the coveted Segrave Trophy for outstanding achievements on land, at sea, or in the air (and he would also be awarded an OBE in 1953). For the first time, the most famous sportsman in Britain was a motorcyclist – and a modest one at that. So what was it like to be biking's first superstar? 'I suppose I did become a household name,' Duke admits, 'but I was only interested in the sheer delight of racing. My parents were both quiet people and I was a little bit the same way. People were making a fuss of me and I loved that but I didn't get

Cromie McCandless (left) after winning the 1951 Lightweight 125 race from team-mate Carlo Ubialli. Cromie's brother, Rex, is second from the right. The pair designed Norton's famous 'Featherbed' frame.

carried away with it. I think all the attention helped make motorcycling more acceptable to the public in general so that was a good thing.'

There were some major changes to the TT race programme in 1951, chief amongst them being the introduction of a race for 125cc machines. Officially termed the 'Lightweight race, 125cc class', the two-lap sprint became more popularly known as the Ultra-Lightweight race. The 250cc Lightweight event would no longer feature a massed start and would be reduced from seven laps to four, and the 250cc and 1000cc Clubman's races were scrapped due to a lack of entries.

Geoff Duke's first Junior victory was a dominant one. Having set the fastest lap in practice, he led the race from start to finish and beat second-placed man Johnny Locket (also on a Norton) by over three minutes. Duke also set new lap and race records with his fastest lap making him the first man to average more than 90mph on a Junior machine. He simply could not have bettered his performance. And three more wins in the 350cc class in Belgium, Holland and Ireland would see him crowned world champion by the end of the season.

The Lightweight race was another all-Italian battle, at least for the podium places. After years of absence from the TT, Fergus Anderson proved he still knew his way around by setting a new lap record at 83.70mph before his Moto Guzzi cried enough on the third circuit of the scheduled four. Going into the last lap, Dario Ambrosini had clawed back Tommy Wood's lead from nine to just three seconds and he looked like being able to repeat his dramatic last lap victory of 1950. As he crossed the line, the crowd – and the time-keepers – had to wait 1m 50s for Wood to take the chequered flag. When he did, corrected time gave Wood the victory by eight seconds. Ambrosini would never get another chance to win a TT as he was killed at the French Grand Prix just a few months later.

The inaugural 125cc TT attracted only 18 entrants but still provided a good race with Cromie McCandless (Mondial) averaging an impressive 74.85mph on his way to victory ahead of team-mates, Carlo Ubbiali and Gianni Leoni.

Another Italian firm, MV Agusta, made its first appearance at the TT in 1951, having persuaded former AJS rider Les Graham to race its machines in the Ultra-Lightweight and Senior events. The marque would soon become legendary around the TT circuit but not before it had sorted out the handling problems which plagued its machines in their early TT appearances. Reliability proved another issue in MV's debut with Les Graham getting no farther than Bray Hill on the fickle little 125.

Geoff Duke's dominance of the Senior race mirrored his performance in the Junior. Fastest in practice (and three seconds under his own lap record), he led every lap of the seven-lap race and set new lap and race records in the process. In doing so, he became the first man to lap the course at over 95mph. At least part of the reason for his blinding speed was a cock-up with the Norton team's pit signalling as Duke later explained. 'I had a clear road ahead of me as the first man away in the Senior TT. I made my usual big effort on the opening lap so it was a shock when my first signal at Ramsey Hairpin on lap two read "3 -1" (third place and one second down on the second-placed rider). In error, I had been shown the board intended for my team-mate Jack Brett. This spurred me on to what was probably my greatest effort ever over the Mountain section, only to be given the correct first lap position as I passed the pits: "1 + 42".'

Duke maintained the devastating form he displayed at the TT for the remainder of the season and added the 500cc world title to his 350 crown by the end of the year.

1952
FRIDAY THE 13TH

The opening race of the 1952 TT saw Geoff Duke continuing his devastating form. Once again he controlled the Junior from the front and held a comfortable lead of one-and-a-half minutes at the chequered flag. Although he didn't quite beat his own lap record, his consistent pace saw him better his own race record from the previous year. It was Duke's fourth consecutive TT win and there was no reason to think his run of form wouldn't continue. For various reasons, however, it would prove to be Duke's last TT win for three years.

Geoff Duke literally flying in the 1952 Junior which he won for Norton. He is pictured on the jump before the Highlander.

Luck of the Irish:
Reg Armstrong crosses the line to win the 1952 Senior TT just as his chain breaks.
It can be seen hanging from his Norton.

Another name, soon to become legendary on the Isle of Man first appeared in the 1952 Junior Clubman's race. Bob McIntyre finished second and set a new lap record at 80.09mph on his BSA. He went on to win the Junior Manx GP in September and finished second in the Senior but would have to wait four years before figuring in the TT proper.

The Lightweight race was yet again won by a Moto Guzzi meaning that an Italian motorcycle had won every 250cc TT since 1939. This time it was Fergus Anderson's turn to pilot the winning machine and set a new race record while reigning 250cc world champion, Bruno Ruffo, set a new lap record before striking mechanical problems on the final lap and touring in to finish sixth. Eventual world champion Enrico Lorenzetti finished in second place.

The 125cc race had been increased from two to three laps for 1952 and it was to give MV Agusta its first TT win. Cecil Sandford was the man who opened MV's account and he also became the first man to clock a sub-30-minute lap on a 125. Mondials filled the remaining rostrum places in the hands of Carlo Ubbiali and Len Parry.

The Senior was held on Friday the 13th and would certainly prove unlucky for Geoff Duke. Fastest in practice at 94.04mph, 'the Duke' was aiming to win his fifth TT in a row and was going about it in the usual manner when drama struck. With a lead of one-and-a-

Fergus Anderson tips his Moto Guzzi into Governor's Bridge during his victorious ride in the 1952 Lightweight 250 race.

half minutes over Les Graham at the end of lap four, Duke pulled into the pits and retired his Norton with severe clutch trouble. His race was over and Duke could only look on from the pit lane as Les Graham on the MV Agusta and Reg Armstrong on the Norton tussled for the lead. It proved to be a titanic scrap with the lead constantly changing and the riders sometimes being inseparable on corrected times. If Friday the 13th proved unlucky for Duke, it was kinder to his team-mate Armstrong. As he crossed the line to take the chequered flag after nearly 265 miles of racing, his primary chain snapped and fell off his bike. He wouldn't have made another mile.

1953 THE SHOW MUST GO ON

Geoff Duke shocked the motorcycle world with his switch to the Italian Gilera company for the 1953 season. In today's international environment, it may seem difficult to understand the fuss about riding a foreign motorcycle, but in the patriotic fervour of 1953

Ray Amm sweeps through Hillberry on his Senior Norton to complete a Junior/Senior double in 1953. He would also win the Senior the following year, but in controversial circumstances.

– less than ten years after WWII – it was tantamount to treason to try and beat British bikes on foreign ones. 'British riders switching to foreign bikes was very unpopular with a lot of the public,' says Duke. 'Even some of my good friends took a very poor view when I moved.'

But Duke's hand was forced by Norton. Despite the growing dominance of foreign multi-cylinder machines like the Gileras, Moto Guzzis and MV Agustas, Norton continually stalled development of a multi despite Duke's persistent pleas. The Gileras were producing 68bhp while the Nortons made 54bhp and it was only the combination of the Featherbed frame and Duke's talent that kept Norton competitive at the TT.

But there was another issue: Duke was not making as much money from racing as he should have been as the sport's first superstar and, when Norton refused to match the financial offer from Gilera, Duke felt he had no choice but to sign up for the Italian manufacturer. His Norton team-mate, Reg Armstrong, joined him.

With Les Graham's MV breaking down on the first lap of the Junior, Rod Coleman led the race until hard-riding Rhodesian Ray Amm (Norton) caught him. When Coleman then dropped out, Norton's Ken Kavanagh took over the lead by one second from Amm. At the start of the seventh and final lap, only seven seconds separated the two and it was anyone's guess who would take the honours. At the flag, Ray Amm took the race by 9.2 seconds from his Australian rival to claim his first TT win, setting new lap and race records in the process.

The Lightweight 250cc race yet again reverted to being a massed start but this time, while Fergus Anderson managed to win his second consecutive Lightweight on a Moto Guzzi, there were fresh challenges from other foreign marques, namely NSU and DKW. The German machines finished second and third respectively in the hands of Werner Haas and Siegfried Wunsche.

The 125 race provided one of the most popular winners ever when Les Graham finally managed to win a TT: he had been trying since 1938. The race was again a massed start and Graham, mounted on an MV Agusta, stamped his authority on the three-lapper from Ramsey on lap one. From a standing start, the first four over the line (Graham, Cecil Sandford, Werner Haas and Carlo Ubbiali) all broke the existing lap record and a fierce battle ensued for second spot while Graham controlled the race from the front. Haas, who would go on to become both 125 and 250cc world champion that year, pipped Sandford to the line by just two seconds to score second place but the spectators could not have been happier with the winner and Les Graham's long overdue victory was toasted all over the Island. One day later he would be dead.

Tragedy struck just seconds into the second lap of the Senior TT when Les Graham crashed after the fearsome dip at the bottom of Bray Hill. He was killed instantly in what was the worst TT to date for fatalities: four men had lost their lives over the fortnight. Incredibly, Graham remains the only 500cc world champion to have been killed while racing a motorcycle. He was 42 years old. Proving the overwhelming hold the TT has on its followers despite its dangers, Graham's son Stuart would later travel to the Island to follow in his father's wheel tracks and win a TT.

The 1953 Senior race, however, continued and Geoff Duke, having smashed the lap record from a standing start, was just one of the top runners to pass the carnage at the bottom of Bray Hill. 'I realised that someone had crashed there and it was obviously serious but I didn't know it was Les and I didn't know he had been killed until after the race. It may seem harsh but when you're racing, you're busy thinking about what you're doing yourself. You only have time to be sad after the race. I suppose, rather stupidly, we all just think "it'll never happen to me".'

Les Graham had been lying in second place before his fatal accident and with his demise, Ray Amm took up the chase on his Norton. The duel everyone had been expecting between Amm and Duke was on. Duke later recalled, 'I was *so* anxious to win – perhaps too anxious! After I had caught and passed Ray Amm on the Norton, he re-passed me at Ballaugh when I missed a gear-change. Then there was the frightening experience of following him to the end of that lap, the third. Ray could be pretty lurid when he was really trying! So when he pulled into the pits to refuel, I was relieved and glad that my pit stop was to be at the end of the fourth lap, only to crash at Quarterbridge when a combination of wet tar and over-exuberance on my part caused an uncontrollable slide.'

Duke was unhurt but his petrol tank had split open meaning he was unable to continue the race. Amm had broken the lap record in pursuit of Duke and set an incredible average speed of 97.41mph to build a comfortable lead over Reg Armstrong on the other Gilera. But nothing is ever a foregone conclusion at the TT and, on the last lap, Amm crashed at Sarah's Cottage. Unhurt, he remounted and continued, despite having broken a footrest off his Norton, but his spill had given Armstrong time to close the gap. Then the Manx Fairies decided to curse Armstrong and he was reported to be stopped and replacing his chain at Ramsey Hairpin. The duel was finally over and Ray Amm became only the fifth man in TT history to complete a Junior/Senior double.

1954
THE LADY AND THE CLYPSE

The issue of women racing on the Isle of Man had been contested for many years and in the male-chauvinistic Fifties, there were few, other than women themselves, who supported the idea. Female racers had tried to gain entries to the 1947 TT only to be refused and Laurie Cade (writing of the matter in his 1957 book *TT Thrills*) summed up the typical male viewpoint of the time when he said, 'One or two girl riders who had done well in trials and other competitions, sought the right to race. Wisely they were turned down by the Auto Cycle Union. TT racing is definitely a he-man's

Controversial conditions. Ray Amm won the 1954 Senior when the race was stopped short due to rain. Geoff Duke had been leading but pulled in to refuel, thinking the race was over full distance. Amm did not refuel and was granted the win when the race was stopped after four laps.

game, and I tremble to think what would have been said of the promoters had they permitted the fair sex to ride and one of them had met with disaster.'

In 1954, the 'promoters' did allow a woman to compete in the TT – in the newly resurrected Sidecar race. Sidecar racing hadn't been seen on the Isle of Man since 1925 and their return was warmly welcomed by most. For their comeback however, they would be racing on the new 10.79-mile Clypse Course. The Clypse was brought into use as a less-demanding alternative to the Mountain course for the Sidecars and smaller solo classes. The startline was the same as for any other TT but when riders got to St Ninian's crossroads at the top of Bray Hill, they turned right and eventually joined the Mountain course at Cronk-ny-Mona, albeit in the opposite direction. At Creg-ny-Baa, the riders veered right and followed the road down to Onchan before rejoining the Mountain circuit at Signpost Corner. From there they followed the usual route to the finish line with the exception of the dip at Governor's Bridge which was omitted.

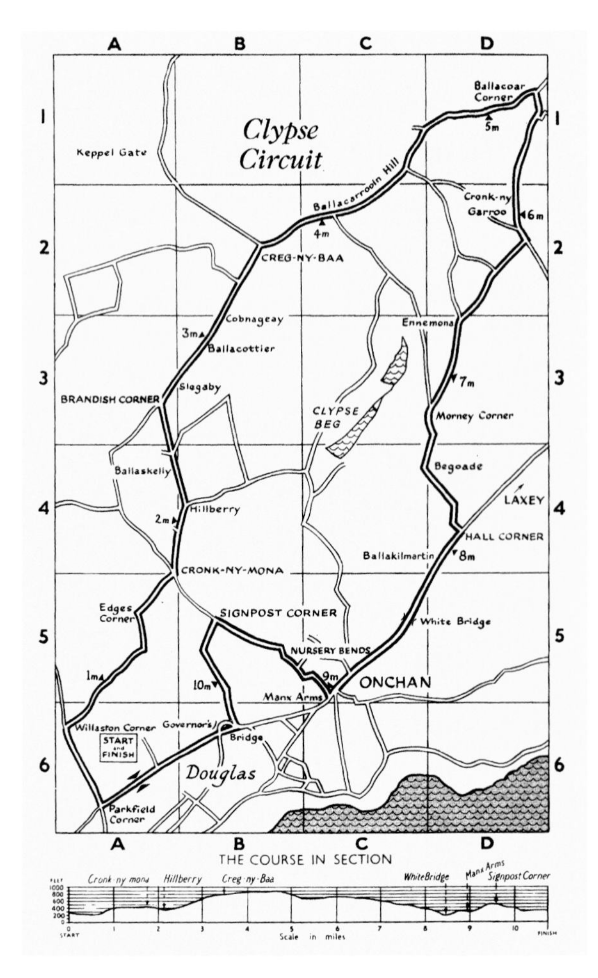

The 10.79-mile Clypse Course was used between 1954 and 1959 for Lightweight, Ultra-Lightweight, and Sidecar races as a less-gruelling alternative to the full Mountain circuit.

WELLWORTHY
76

Eric Oliver was already a four times world champion when the Sidecar class returned to the TT in 1954. He is pictured here on the Clypse Course that same year taking his only TT win.

As Laurie Cade rightly mentioned, female competitors had taken part in trials and speedway events but never in a TT, and it may have been down to a simple typo in the race regulations which eventually allowed Switzerland's Inge Stoll-Laforge to become the TT's first ever female competitor, as passenger to Jacques Drion in the Sidecar race. The regulations for solo entrants at the TT stipulated that they had to be 'male persons between 18 and 55 years of age' but the rules for Sidecar passengers only stated that they had to be 'persons' over 18 years of age. Whether this wording was intended to allow for female passengers or whether it was simply an oversight may never be known but the result was that Inge Stoll-Laforge – who was already an experienced passenger in Continental races – became the first woman to compete in a TT.

In the race itself, Eric Oliver, with Les Nutt in the chair, sped off into an early lead and never looked back, eventually winning by almost two minutes from former Luftwaffe fighter pilot, Fritz Hillebrand. Inge Stoll-Laforge finished in a fine fifth place on her Island debut, thanks in no small measure to her riding style – and apparent likeness to Fifties screen icon Marilyn Monroe. Laurie Cade, who had been so against women racing at the TT, described Stoll-Laforge's style: 'She was energetic enough on the corners, and really threw her Marilyn-like weight about.'

Stoll-Laforge returned to the TT in 1957 but retired after just four laps. It would be her last TT. She was killed in a Sidecar race in Czechoslovakia shortly afterwards.

The Clubman's TT races lost their TT title in 1954 and were subsequently called the Clubman's Trophy races. Declining prestige and lack of interest eventually saw them wiped from the programme completely in 1957.

The first race of the 1954 TT had been the Junior which took place on the full Mountain circuit, even though the race was reduced from its traditional seven laps to five. It produced a surprise winner in Rod Coleman after most of the fancied runners dropped out with mechanical problems. Among them were Fergus Anderson and Ken Kavanagh on Moto Guzzis and Ray Amm on a Norton. Before his demise however, Amm once again showed his turn of speed by setting the first sub-24 minute lap in the Junior class. Proving that 'to finish first, first you have to finish', Rod Coleman brought his AJS home to claim victory from his team-mate Derek Farrant and Bob Keeler on a Norton.

Like the Junior, the 250cc Lightweight was also reduced in length, this time from four laps to three and in it Werner Haas showed his class by breaking the lap record from a standing start, claiming the first ever 90mph lap for a 250cc machine, and becoming the first German to win a TT since Georg Meier in 1939.

The first ever race on the Clypse course was the ten-lap/107.9 mile 125cc Ultra-Lightweight TT and the notion that the shorter circuit would be easier on machines proved unfounded: only nine bikes made it to the finish line. Even so, the massed start race turned into a terrific, short circuit-style tussle between Hollaus and Italy's Carlo Ubbiali. The pair were so evenly matched that by the end of the sixth lap the timekeepers could not separate them. Two laps later, Hollaus pulled out a meagre one-second lead and eventually stretched it to four seconds at the flag.

Between changes of course and reduction of laps in every other race category, the sacred Senior class was the only one unchanged in any way for 1954. Foul weather had delayed the start from 10.30am until 12 noon but even then conditions were far from ideal.

Geoff Duke, back again on his factory Gilera, led Ray Amm by 14 seconds after the first lap but speeds were well down – Duke's second lap being more than 10mph down on Amm's record from the previous year. When Duke stopped for his scheduled pit stop after the third lap he could have had no idea that it would cost him the race. Ray Amm went straight through and established a lead of 28 seconds, then, at 1.48pm, as the sun was shining down on the grandstand came the announcement that the race was to be stopped at the end of the fourth lap. There was no warning given to riders or teams that the race was to be shortened and with Duke having lost time taking on fuel, he lost the race to Ray Amm by well over a minute. Could Duke have won the race if he'd been told it was only four laps? 'I still think that the Norton people knew that the race was going to be stopped at the end of the fourth lap,' Duke says now. 'We certainly didn't know that and so at the end of the third lap I stopped to take on fuel. The Gilera was quite capable of going for four laps without refuelling so, had we known, I'd have just carried on for another lap. I was very, very upset by that, I must admit, and Gilera was convinced it was a big fiddle.'

Fiddle or not, Duke would have his revenge in spectacular fashion: in an unprecedented run, he won the next six Grands Prix to take the world title on his Gilera. In the process, he scored twice the points of his arch rival Ray Amm. He had proved his point.

1955 TALK OF THE TON

The TT was missing one of its greats in 1955 after Ray Amm was killed at Imola early in the season. He had been making his debut for MV Agusta when he crashed and collided with an iron fence post. He was taken to hospital but died 20 minutes after arrival. Amm had enjoyed an incredible, if brief, career at the TT, entering eight races, winning three of them and setting three fastest laps. There seems no doubt that, had he lived longer, he would have gone on to become one of the TT greats. As things turned out, he never saw his 28th birthday.

Practice week for the 1955 TT races was dominated by talk of the first ever 100mph lap. Geoff Duke had taken his Gilera round at a speed of 97.14mph in practice and would 'only' have to find another 41 seconds under race conditions to break the magical 'ton'.

While British bikes were notably absent from the leaderboard in 1955 (it would be the first time in the event's history that a British bike failed to win a race), British riders were not, and two names which would soon become legendary first came to prominence in that year's Junior TT – John Surtees and Bob McIntyre.

Surtees had first entered the TT in 1953 but had to sit out the races after crashing his 125 in practice and breaking his wrist. In 1954, he could only manage 11th place in the Junior and 15th in the Senior but in 1955, he finally showed what he was capable of. McIntyre's TT pedigree was similarly deceptive. He had retired in 1953 and could only manage a 14th place the following year but he too would show his true potential in 1955.

Carlo Ubialli with the fully-faired MV Agusta in 1955. He won nine world titles as well as five TTs in the smaller classes.

Burying himself under the streamlining of his Moto Guzzi, Bill Lomas speeds to victory in the 1955 Junior. He completed a double with victory in the Lightweight 250 race on an MV Agusta.

With the Junior race back up to seven laps, it was Surtees and McIntyre who shared the lead after one circuit with identical average speeds of 91.38mph. While McIntyre held onto the lead on his Joe Potts-prepared Norton, Surtees dropped back slightly allowing Cecil Sandford on the Moto Guzzi to take up the challenge. It was not until lap five that McIntyre relinquished his lead to Bill Lomas on another Guzzi. After posting the fastest lap of the race on lap six, Lomas was untroubled on his final circuit and had the distinction of being the first rider to win the Junior TT on a non-British bike. He also became the first man to win on both the Mountain course and the Clypse course in the same week, and the first to finish four TTs in a week.

The Lightweight was held on the Clypse course for the first time in 1955 and it turned out to be a classic short circuit-style confrontation between Lomas on his MV Agusta and Cecil Sandford on the Guzzi. Sandford led for seven of the ten laps before Lomas overtook him and, in a desperate attempt to regain the lead, Sandford crashed at Creg-ny-Baa and threw away any chance of victory. Unhurt, he still managed to remount and finish second, such was the lead the pair had over the pursuing field.

The 125cc race produced a classic battle between Carlo Ubbiali and Swiss newcomer, Luigi Taveri. Ubbiali had been runner-up in three TT races already and was desperate to go one better, but it was Taveri who controlled the race in the early stages. Ubbiali eventually caught and passed Taveri on the sixth lap of nine and led by one second until Taveri retook the lead. Ubbiali made the decisive move of the race at Creg-ny-Baa on the final lap and held on to win his first TT race by two seconds.

The Sidecar race was to be another Norton versus BMW battle but one of the pre-race favourites, Cyril Smith, was forced to retire on the first lap after losing his passenger – not an uncommon occurrence in Sidecar racing. After leading on several occasions, Eric Oliver retired on lap four leaving BMWs filling the top three positions. With the retirements of Willi Noll and Willy Faust however, British pride was somewhat saved by Bill Boddice (father of future 9-times Sidecar winner Mick) taking second place, though more than three minutes behind BMW's Walter Schneider.

The 1955 Senior race is still talked about today as the one in which Geoff Duke could have, should have, or maybe even *did* set the first ever 100mph lap. After

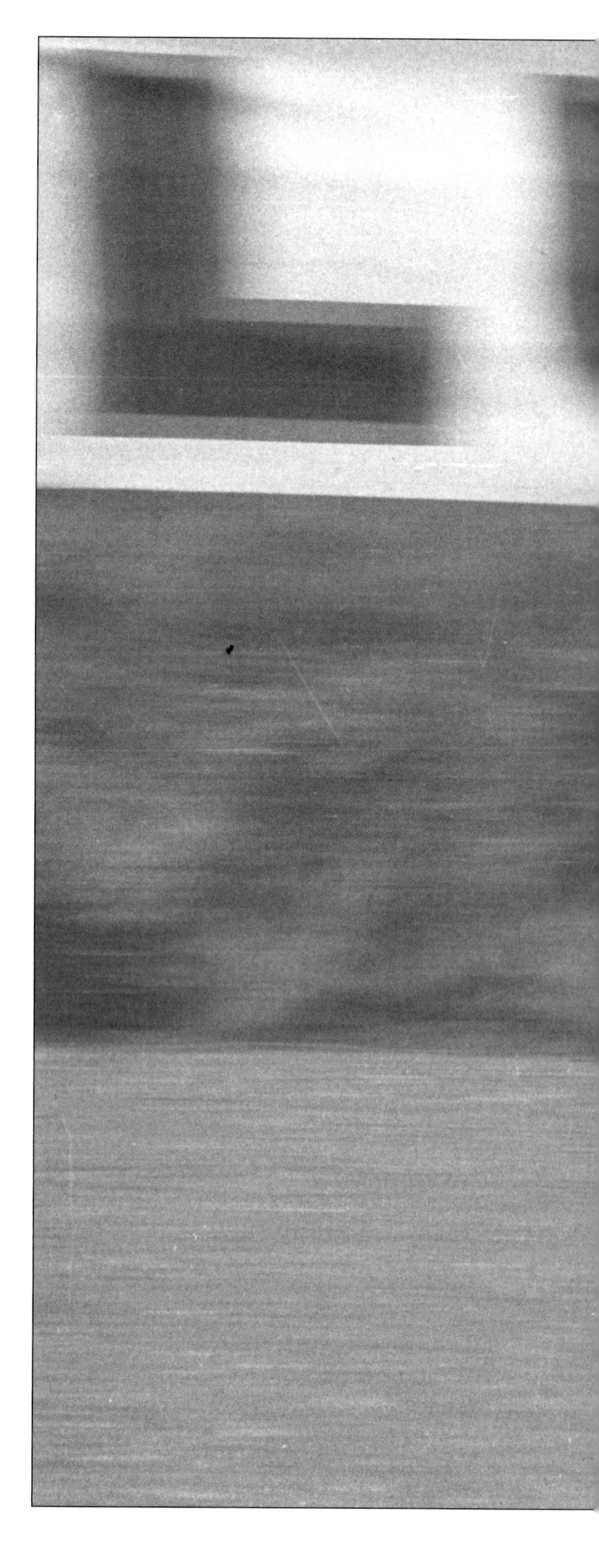

ICA
72

Ken Kavanagh (Moto Guzzi) on the way to winning his first TT despite only being in sixth place on the opening lap of the 1956 Junior.

setting a new lap record from a standing start at 98.37mph, his first flying lap on the Gilera came even closer at 99.04mph – just nine seconds outside of the magic and elusive barrier. At the end of lap three, the grandstand erupted at the commentator's announcement that Geoffrey Duke had finally done it – he had lapped in 22m 39s, exactly 100mph. It was a figure which no one involved in the early days of the TT would ever have thought possible – an incredible achievement, but one which was to be short-lived. Soon after the initial announcement came another from the clerk of the course which downgraded Duke's seemingly historic lap. It read: 'The chief timekeeper reports that the time recorded by Geoff Duke on his third lap is 22m 39s which equals a speed of 99.97mph.'

The timing had not been wrong, only the conversion from lap time into average lap speed. According to the chief timekeeper's revised arithmetic, Duke had missed out on the first 100mph lap by less than a second. For many, Duke did post the first 'moral' 100mph lap, their argument being that fine decimal places on stopwatches are all well and good if the *precise* length of the course is known, but the precise length of the TT course has always varied from year to year with ongoing road improvements. The efficiency of handheld stopwatches and the effects of human reaction times have also caused some to claim that Duke, to all extents and purposes, did achieve that milestone in TT history.

Whatever the case, official records are official records and Duke and his army of fans were denied the privilege of the first ton-up lap. It hardly mattered as far as Gilera was concerned. The Italian factory was far more interested in claiming its first TT win, and with Duke having more than two minutes in hand over Reg Armstrong, it would have been foolish to throw away a debut victory – and what would be Duke's first Senior

With Geoff Duke banned from the 1956 TT, 22-year-old John Surtees gave MV Agusta its first Senior win. He is the only man in history to win world titles on two and four wheels.

win since 1951 – by trying too hard to set a record lap and falling off. 'I can't say that I wouldn't have been delighted to have done the first 100mph lap,' Duke admits, 'and I'm pretty sure that, had I known how close I was, I could have gone a bit quicker. But that wasn't of fantastic importance to me at the time – it was winning the race which mattered. Mr Gilera wanted to win a TT above everything else – even the world championship. I was just very, very happy to have done that for him.'

Duke duly handed Gilera its first TT win (which also proved to be Duke's last) and Reg Armstrong added the icing to the cake by making it a 1-2 for the firm. The duo would go on to finish first and second in the 500cc world championship that year but it would prove to be Duke's last world title, because in 1956, he was banned from riding in the Isle of Man TT.

Although they had nothing personally to gain from their actions, Geoff Duke and 13 other top riders had agreed to strike at the 1955 Dutch TT in support of privateer competitors who were desperately in need of more start money. Duke's reward was to be banned from taking part in the first half of the 1956 season, including the TT. 'I was shocked at being suspended,' Duke says. 'It seemed to be very unfair – overdone, shall we say. But I think the powers that be were wanting to make an example to make sure that it didn't happen again.'

Although Duke would enjoy further success in bike racing, he would never again win a world title and he still cites his 1956 ban as the beginning of his downfall. 'I always looked upon that suspension as being the beginning of the end as far as I was concerned. I was still riding quite well and the Gilera was still a very competitive machine but nothing seemed to go right from then on.'

But there were further-reaching consequences of the penalties handed out by the FIM. Many of the leading manufacturers were so furious with the decision that Duke believes it led to them to withdraw permanently from Grand Prix racing. 'Really it was crazy to deny race fans the chance to see the world's top riders and thankfully, I don't think it could happen in this day and age. It really was a very bad time for motorcycle racing. It had so much effect. The loss of top-flight riders and the competition that involved, and the total supremacy of MV Agusta subsequently which really didn't mean very much. I think the combination of these factors very nearly put an end to motorcycle racing.'

Gilera, Moto Guzzi, Mondial and MV Agusta all agreed to withdraw from racing after the 1957 season but MV later had a change of heart (much to the chagrin of the other factories) and, in the absence of any serious competition, went on to dominate the world championship scene for years to come. 'The withdrawal of the other factories left a huge vacuum for MV Agusta to dominate in,' says Duke. 'What shook a lot of people was that MV had in fact agreed with the others to stop racing at the end of 1957 and then they reneged on the deal. And of course, they had a clear run from then onwards, especially with a rider like John Surtees on board. But, quite honestly, I don't really think it did them any good – I think the majority of enthusiastic motorcyclists weren't very impressed by a lot of MV's success.'

The first of those major successes came in the 1956 Senior TT when 22-year-old short circuit star, John Surtees, led the race from start to finish. More impressive still was the fact that Surtees was forced to ride his number two bike after hitting a cow in practice and destroying his number one machine. 'I think the bike came off worse – the cow got up and went off,' Surtees recalls. 'How it suffered afterwards I'm not quite sure. But I understand it had been taken away from its calf rather too quickly and this meant that it jumped over one or two hedges and ended up on the road at Creg Willey's Hill. I jammed everything on but still hit it and I lost my race bike. I got away unhurt apart from hurt feelings – and concern for the cow as well!'

With less than perfect weather conditions, Surtees never looked like cracking the 100mph lap barrier, his best being a circuit at 97.79mph. But he had notched up his first TT win nonetheless and had discovered the importance of the 'TT rhythm' which he felt was the key to success on the Island. 'The TT is something that one needs to have very, very special respect for. It needed a different style of riding and you needed to switch on to a slightly different mentality. You had to get the TT rhythm, and the TT rhythm is all about being in the right place on the road at the right time. Whereas you scratch here and you scratch there on a short circuit, what you do at any one point on the TT course controls what you do for the next mile or so up the road. I didn't have a vast surplus of power so I had to carry speed through corners and to do that you had to be very much on the right line. By scratching through corners, you would actually scrub off speed.'

The Junior race had kicked off the week and it proved to be a dramatic affair. Despite its being June, riders were pelted with hailstones up on the Mountain but the pace was still frantic and would take its toll on many of the favourites. First to retire was Bob McIntyre who pulled out on the second lap. Bill Lomas held a 50-second lead by lap five before he too retired with engine trouble. This left Surtees in the lead on his MV Agusta but when he too was forced to stop in the dying stages of the race, Australian Ken Kavanagh brought his Guzzi home for an unexpected win.

Any expectations of a repeat of the previous year's battle between Carlo Ubbiali and Luigi Taveri in the Lightweight 250 race were thwarted when Taveri crashed out at Governor's Bridge. Sammy Miller on an NSU would instead give Ubbiali a good run for his money but when he retired at Creg-ny-Baa, the Italian cruised home to claim his second TT victory.

With Taveri ruled out of the 125 race thanks to his earlier 250 crash, Ubbiali made it two wins in a week when he crossed the line almost four minutes ahead of his nearest challenger, Marcel Cama.

Once again BMWs dominated the Sidecar race but, after 1955 winner Walter Schneider retired at the Creg, it was down to Fritz Hillebrand to carry the flag for the German firm ahead of the Norton outfits of Pip Harris and Bill Boddice.

Cecil Sandford guns his Mondial round the Clypse course in the 1957 Lightweight 250 event. He won after race leader Sammy Miller crashed within sight of the finish line.

1957
THE TON

In 1957 the Isle of Man TT celebrated its 50th anniversary and the week would belong to one man alone – Bob McIntyre.

Robert McGregor McIntyre had signed for Gilera in 1957 after Geoff Duke crashed at an Easter race meeting at Imola and was again ruled out of the TT. McIntyre immediately showed his potential on a factory bike by setting the fastest lap in practice in the Junior class. Come Junior race day, Bob Mac broke the lap record from a standing start but after a slow second circuit due to a misfire, he was down to third place behind the Moto Guzzi of Dickie Dale and the Norton of rising star John Hartle. When both men later crashed out on oil, McIntyre went on to take his first TT victory with lap and race records to boot.

Famous trials rider Sammy Miller came so close to winning a TT race in the 1957 250cc Lightweight after taking the lead on the last of the ten laps round the Clypse Course. Then, practically within sight of the chequered flag, he dropped his works Mondial and allowed his team-mate Cecil Sandford through to take the win. Miller pushed in to finish fifth.

Tarquinio Provini had to fight hard to claim his first TT win in the 125cc class. After a race-long battle with two-time winner, Carlo Ubbiali, and his MV team-mate, Luigi Taveri, Provini kept his cool while Taveri crashed out of second place and held on to take the win.

For the third year in a row, a BMW outfit won the Sidecar TT with Fritz Hillebrand claiming his second consecutive win and smashing lap and race records along the way. Better still for the German manufacturer, BMWs filled the top three places with Walter Schneider and Florian Camathias chasing Hillebrand home. But in racing, celebrations tend to

78
78

be short-lived. Hillebrand and his passenger, Manfred Grunwald were later crowned world champions but seven weeks later, Hillebrand lost his life in a practice crash for an insignificant race in Bilbao, Spain. Grunwald escaped with his life but could not escape further tragedy: he married female passenger, Inge Stoll-Laforge, who then also lost her life to the sport which she, Hillebrand and Grunwald had loved so much.

The Senior race had been lengthened to eight laps (301.84 miles) to mark the TT's Golden Jubilee and with weather conditions being perfect, expectations were high for the first official 100mph lap. Bob McIntyre took a gamble and opted to run the full 'dustbin' fairing on his Gilera for the big race. It meant he could coax more speed from his bike but the pay-off was the adverse handling the bodywork could cause, especially in windy conditions. But after recording a lap of 99.99mph from a standing start in calm weather, it looked as if McIntyre's gamble had paid off. Then, on his second circuit, Bob Mac made TT history; his time of 22m 24.4s equated to an average speed of 101.03mph. This time there were no retractions from the timekeepers and Bob McIntyre was officially credited as being the first man in history to lap the TT circuit at 100mph. From Bray Hill to Ramsey and back again spectators went wild when the news was announced; they realised they were witnessing history in the making.

As if to prove it was no fluke, McIntyre then posted another three 100mph+ laps to win the race by over two minutes from John Surtees on the lone MV Agusta. Surtees had decided not to run the full dustbin fairing on the MV for reasons he now explains. 'It was strange, considering the amount of time we spent in the wind tunnel with the bike and the fairing – and the fact that Agusta was an aeronautical company – but the dustbin fairing just didn't work on the MV. We had cooling problems with the engine. At the TT, I played for safety just to get a finish. We probably wouldn't have finished that race if we'd ran the full fairing on the 500. It was worth a good 10mph but it wasn't worth the risk.'

Surtees attempted to make up his top speed deficit with sheer hard riding and his aggression impressed a young spectator that year by the name of Phil Read. A future TT great, Read was watching the 1957 Senior at the bottom of Barregarrow with a group of friends. He later recalled that, 'John steamed into Barregarrow on the MV Agusta four-cylinder, scaring the pants off us. He came in so fast that I thought he

The most famous lap in TT history? Bob McIntyre finally cracked the 100mph barrier in the 1957 Senior and repeated it three more times during the race.

The ton at last! John Surtees (left) congratulates Bob McIntyre on winning the 1957 Senior TT – and on setting the first ever 100mph lap of the course. Note the cut on McIntyre's forehead caused by a stone being thrown up from another bike.

was out of control, with a series of shakes, wobbles and tank-slappers. Half the spectators sitting on the bank, only a few feet away, fell backwards in sheer fright.'

Bob McIntyre had some lurid moments too. Pictures of him post-race show a scar on his forehead, the cause of which could have been disastrous. 'A stone hit me, thrown up by the wheels of another rider I was about to lap,' he explained after the race. 'It was probably no bigger than a pea, but at 100mph it felt like a brick. It caught me between my goggles and my crash helmet and cut my left temple. I felt dazed and sick, it brought tears to my eyes and I felt blood running. But fortunately, the rush of cold air coagulated the blood above my goggles.'

A raw cure for a hard man. But with that lap Bob Mac had become a TT legend and he himself was elated at being elevated to the ranks of the all-time greats, not least of which was a certain fellow countryman. 'I was a happy man that night,' he said. 'Not so much because of the 100mph laps that were to be so publicised, but because I was the only other Scot apart from Jimmy Guthrie to bring off the Junior and Senior double.'

1958 THE UNTOUCHABLES

With most major manufacturers, including Moto Guzzi, Gilera and Mondial, having pulled out of world championship racing after 1957, and Norton, AJS, DKW and NSU having already withdrawn, MV Agusta was the only factory team to contest the 1958 TT. And with a rider of the calibre of John Surtees onboard, the combination looked untouchable for the Junior and Senior races. In fact, MV Agusta went on to win every solo class at the TT – the first manufacturer to do so.

John Surtees had succeeded Geoff Duke as 500cc world champion in 1956 at the age of 22, giving MV Agusta its first 500 title in the process. In the same year he also won his first TT and by 1958, he was ready

No 69 S.L. Lewis (Match) halts for machine inspection at R. Hairpin S. No.23 Norman J. Price (Norton) follows.

to dominate the event on the blood red 'fire engines' which were, by now, far superior to the competition. Not that Surtees needed a machinery advantage to win races; riding a 250cc NSU as well as private and factory Nortons in 1955, he had won 65 out of the 72 races he entered. Surtees was an exceptional talent who brought an almost scientific approach to motorcycle racing. In his preparation and technical skills, he was decades ahead of his time. Born of a motorcycling father – and mother – Surtees was literally brought up on bikes and began racing, underage, at just 15.

At the sharp end of the 1958 TT, no one else would get a look-in, but making his debut in that same year was another giant of a talent who would not only surpass Surtees's eventual win total, but would also come to be regarded as the greatest motorcycle racer of all time. His name was Stanley Michael Bailey Hailwood.

As expected, Surtees dominated the Junior TT, leading from start to finish and setting a new race record; proof that, even though he wasn't being pushed, he was still the fastest man in the history of the class.

The MV domination continued in the Lightweight race with Tarquinio Provini and Carlo Ubbiali providing a terrific tussle round the Clypse Course on their Italian machines. Provini eventually took the win and established new lap and race records but, of

Mike Hailwood (18) racing his NSU towards his first ever TT podium position in the 1958 250 race held on the Clypse course. He is seen here chasing Bob Brown on another NSU.

18
18

The confidence of youth. John Surtees pictured in 1958 when he scored a Junior/Senior double for MV Agusta.

even more significance was the third placed finisher, 18-year-old Mike Hailwood. Having finished a steady 12th in the Junior on his TT debut, Mike was clearly a quick learner and was awarded the Westover best newcomer trophy for his performance on the 250cc NSU.

Ducati riders Romolo Ferri and Dave Chadwick gave MV Agusta a slightly harder time in the Ultra-Lightweight race, finishing second and third respectively, but Carlo Ubbiali clocked up the third win of the week for MV while Hailwood gained more vital experience on the Clypse Course by finishing seventh.

The Sidecar race was once again a BMW benefit, this time for Walter Schneider. A curiosity of the class was that, while British outfits had their chairs on the left of the bike, Continental outfits had theirs on the right. When Schneider and his passenger Hans Strauss came up to lap British pair Ernie Walker and Don Roberts on the narrow Clypse Course, Strauss was forced to grab Roberts's leg and shake it to let the slower pair know they needed to pass! Former multiple world champion, Eric Oliver, put in a heroic performance on a completely standard Norton Dominator to take tenth place – and all with the redoubtable Mrs Pat Wise in the chair.

The only question in the Senior race was how much John Surtees would win it by. His team-mate, John Hartle, had retired in the Junior and was to have no better luck this time round. After running in second

John Hartle walks away in disgust as firemen try to extinguish his burning MV Agusta during the 1958 Senior. Ironically, the blood red MVs were nicknamed 'fire engines'.

place, his machine caught fire coming out of Governor's Dip when a fuel leak ignited and, while he escaped uninjured, his MV 'fire engine' needed the full attention of the real fire brigade.

Bob McIntyre hounded Surtees valiantly on his Norton but the Scot proved faster than his mount and by lap three it had foundered. Still without competitive machinery, Geoff Duke battled bravely on an under-funded BMW only to retire with brake problems. In the absence of such worthy adversaries, John Surtees romped home to win by over five minutes, and secure his first Junior/Senior double. He had led every lap of both races and won them with military precision.

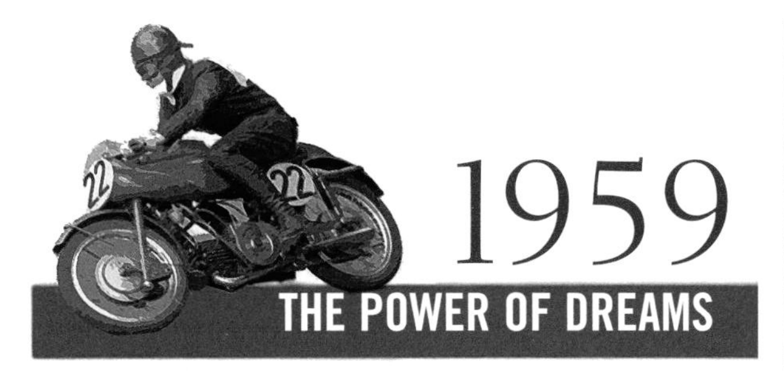

1959

THE POWER OF DREAMS

How it all began.
Honda's first year at the TT and Naomi Tanaguchi (pictured) takes sixth place with his team-mates 7th and 8th. It was enough to win the team prize for Honda. The rest is history.

'I here avow my intention that I will participate in the TT race and I proclaim with my fellow employees that I will pour all my energy and creative powers into winning.'

So spoke Soichiro Honda – founder of what is now the largest motorcycle manufacturer on earth – in March, 1954. The press release which contained these words has become part of motorcycling legend, but in the 1950s, few took the thought of Japanese machines contesting TT races seriously. They would soon be forced to change their minds.

Honda became the first Japanese manufacturer to participate in the TT races when it made camp at the Nursery Hotel in Onchan in 1959. Armed with beautifully crafted, twin-cylinder 125cc machines to contest the Ultra-Lightweight race, Honda's aim, according to American team manager Bill Hunt, was to 'give a high speed demonstration of reliability with an eye to an all-out effort next year.'

Hunt was the only non-Japanese rider in the five-man team and also the only one to crash out of the Ultra-Lightweight race. The remaining four riders finished in sixth, seventh and eleventh places to claim the Manufacturer's Award for Honda at the first attempt. The race was won by Tarquinio Provini on the MV Agusta but it was Honda's achievement which would prove the more significant – even if no one yet realised it.

Provini also won the Lightweight 250 race and in doing so became the first man to lap the Clypse Course at 80mph. But Mike Hailwood had led the race at times and was challenging for victory before his Mondial developed engine trouble three-quarters of the way through the race. The writing here too, was on the wall.

The opening race of the week had been new to the TT calendar but was doomed to be a one-off due to lack of interest. The Formula 1 TT (with separate classes for 500 and 350cc machines) was open only to production bikes which anyone could buy over the

8
HONDA
8

Tarquinio Provini scored a 125/250 double in 1959. Here he rounds the corner at the Manx Arms on a 125cc MV Agusta.

counter and was largely aimed at giving British bikes a chance of winning without the interference of Italian factory exotica. Scotsmen won both classes with Bob McIntyre taking the 500 honours and Alistair King the 350. Although the race was not repeated the following year, the F1 title would later return to save the TT in its darkest hour.

The Junior saw Geoff Duke back on a British bike for what would prove to be his last TT race. He finished a hugely popular fourth on a private Norton but bowed out of racing at the end of the season having poured too much of his own money into developing the machine. John Surtees's victory was his third consecutive TT win and his team-mate, John Hartle, followed him home to give MV Agusta a Junior one-two.

The 1959 Sidecar TT was the last race ever held on the Clypse Course and it handed a third win to Walter Schneider, again BMW-mounted. From 1960 onwards, all TT races would be held on the Mountain circuit.

Appalling weather conditions forced the postponement of the Senior race until Saturday but it made little difference – after the first lap they were every bit as bad again. Surtees had shattered Bob McIntyre's lap record from a standing start in the dry conditions which prevailed during the opening lap and his speed of 101.18mph was enough to place him ahead of John Hartle with McIntyre himself doggedly chasing the superior MVs on his Norton before the heavens opened. And how they opened.

Torrential rain battered the riders and a heavy mist fell on parts of the course. Worse still, the wind became so strong that one rider, Alan Trow, was literally blown off the road at Alpine Cottage. Many riders pulled out and no one blamed them, but John Surtees gritted his teeth and pushed on through the cold and the wind and the mist and the rain to record another Junior/Senior double in what many consider to be his most gutsy performance. At the end of the race, Surtees was frozen so stiff that he had to be lifted off his bike. His mechanics furiously rubbed at his hands in an attempt to restore circulation. Surtees remembers those hideous conditions to this day. 'The 1959 Senior TT was probably the worst conditions I ever rode in. You didn't only have the rain but also sleet

Rain, hailstones, wind and mist combined to make John Surtees's 1959 Senior victory a miserable one. He was so frozen he had to be lifted off his bike at the end.

which was as big as marbles. It actually damaged the fairing on the MV – took the paint off. I wasn't able to use my fingers, I could only keep them clasped together and pull them in, en masse, to operate the clutch and brake levers. All I had on was my normal race leathers. There were no one-piece undersuits like today – I just wore my vest and pants underneath! I never thought about giving up though. I just struggled on and hoped the others weren't doing any better and were finding it just as difficult.'

Surtees himself rates that victory as one of his finest, if only because it proved that he didn't need the MV's power advantage to win races. His determination to finish the race led to Surtees becoming only the second rider to record Junior/Senior doubles two years running – Stanley Woods being the only other man to achieve the distinction. Never one to belittle the efforts of other, less talented riders, Surtees declared that every man who had had the guts to finish that race should have been awarded a silver replica. His own performance had so impressed the Japanese that they presented Surtees with a Samurai helmet to honour his courage. Proud as they are of their warrior heritage, the Japanese do not bestow such honours lightly. In their eyes, as in the eyes of so many others, John Surtees had proved himself a true fighter.

CHAPTER 5

1960-69

5

1960

SURTEES'S SWANSONG

As promised, Honda returned to the Isle of Man in 1960 and, also as promised, it returned with better bikes – a twin-cylinder 125 and a four-cylinder 250. Honda had also signed up promising Australian rider Tom Phillis to join Bob Brown and its own Japanese riders. In the 125 race, Hondas filled out the complete second half of the top ten but failed to win the team award as MV Agusta made a clean sweep of the podium with Carlo Ubbiali winning the three-lap race from new signings Gary Hocking, and Luigi Taveri. Finishing in 16th, 17th and 18th positions were three other Japanese bikes new to TT racing – Suzukis.

While Suzuki's debut results were not sensational, the firm's determination to succeed at the TT was not in doubt. Back in February, Suzuki team boss, Jimmy Matsuyima, had spent ten days lying across the bonnet of a borrowed Morris Minor photographing every corner on the TT course so his riders could learn it off by heart. Together with notes from a helpful Geoff Duke – who had already tested the Suzuki Colleda twin during a trip to Japan – this formed the basis of the team's preparation for its first TT. The Suzukis may have been relatively slow but all three finished the race and lessons had been learned.

Gary Hocking won the Lightweight 250 race in what was only his second year at the TT. The Rhodesian led throughout the five-lapper to beat team-mate Ubbiali and Tarquinio Provini on the Morini. Hondas, led by Bob Brown in fourth, filled the next three places.

Although the lap record posted in the first Sidecar TT to be held over the Mountain course since 1925 was 27mph faster than Freddie Dixon's old record, the race itself was something of a disappointment. Bad weather, a small entry, and numerous breakdowns took some of the shine off Helmut Fath's victory on a BMW.

John Surtees almost broke the 100mph barrier in the Junior with a circuit at 99.2mph but had to settle for second spot after his MV developed gearbox problems. His misfortune allowed his team-mate, John Hartle, to take a well deserved win after the catalogue of misfortune he had endured in the past. As ever, Bob McIntyre pursued the MVs with all he knew on his outdated single-cylinder AJS to take a hard-fought third place.

As Surtees set off in the 1960 Senior, no one knew that it was to be his last TT. Few riders have retired from the sport while still at the top of their game but Surtees was becoming increasingly frustrated with MV owner, Count Domenico Agusta's, insistence that he would only supply bikes for Grands Prix races. Worse still, Surtees was forbidden to enter his own private machines in lesser events and was exasperated by the lack of planning on MV Agusta's part – a situation which was severely affecting Surtees' occasional forays into car racing. He admits now that he was also

Gary Hocking (MV Agusta) speeds to his first TT victory in the 1960 Lightweight. He won two world titles and two TTs before being killed in a car race in 1962.

Bob McIntyre spent years bravely chasing the factory MVs on outdated British singles. Here he heads for third place on an AJS in the 1960 Junior behind the MVs of John Hartle and John Surtees.

frustrated at not being allowed to race in the 250cc class at the TT. 'I wish I'd had a 250 MV to ride at the TT but unfortunately there was a man called Ubbiali who had quite a lot of sway with the factory and Count Agusta sort of ruled that I couldn't ride the 250s. He wanted that to be the domain of the Italians. I was sad about that, particularly when they built the little twins. And I would have loved to have had a go on the full-blown 250 triple but, no, they wouldn't let me.'

It was business as usual for Surtees in his last TT. He led every lap, set a new lap record at 104.9mph, became the first man to achieve a race average of over 100mph, and also the first man in history to win three Senior TTs in a row – and all this in just a few years of Island racing. 'There are some riders nowadays who are quick at the TT because they spend so much time on the circuit,' he says. 'They do so many races on the circuit. In our time we did one or two races each year and I ended up having only done seven or eight TTs in total and that was it. It was only *part* of the world championship programme. But nowadays you have almost full-time TT riders: in recent years Joey Dunlop was the best example of that.

John Hartle finished in second place, some two-and-a-half minutes behind Surtees and behind Hartle was Mike Hailwood, finishing on the podium in the Senior TT for the first time. In his spirited ride to third place, Hailwood had lapped the course at over 100mph on a single-cylinder Norton but just missed out on being the first man to do so. Although his millionaire father Stan had put up £100 for anyone who could accomplish this feat, Derek Minter beat Hailwood to it by posting his time just before Mike – though he failed to finish the race.

When Surtees announced his retirement from bike racing at the end of 1960, he was able to look back on one of the most successful careers in motorcycle racing: six TT wins, seven world championships and 38 Grand Prix victories, and he was still just 26 years old. But he wasn't finished yet. After making the switch to full-time car racing, he went on to win the F1 world championship in 1964. To this day he remains the only man to ever have won world championships on both two and four wheels. It is unlikely the feat will ever be repeated.

Hailwood and Honda – a devastating combination. Mike is pictured in 1961, the year he became the first man to win three TTs in a week.

Hailwood 250: A lesson in style. Mike Hailwood is as one with the 250 Honda exiting Governor's Dip in 1961. Needless to say, he won the race.

1961

MIKE THE BIKE

As the son of a millionaire, Mike Hailwood had access to top quality machinery from the outset of his career, a fact which could easily have alienated him in the paddock from jealous rivals. Two things prevented that from happening; his prodigious talent on any kind of racing motorcycle, and his natural charm and sense of humour which combined to ensure that he won over everyone he met. 'Once they had got used to the idea that I was not Mr Moneybags and that I could hold my own,' Mike once explained, 'I was accepted for what I was – a motorcycle racer.'

But behind the happy-go-lucky exterior beat the heart of a man who could not accept defeat – the heart of a champion. Alan Baker, a former flatmate of Hailwood's once said of Mike, 'It didn't matter if it was go-karts or table tennis, he just couldn't stand being beaten. He was a lovely bloke, but a real tough bastard too.'

Hailwood, although not part of the official Honda team, was down to ride Hondas in the 125 and 250cc Lightweight races in what was the Japanese manufacturer's third attempt at the TT. With reliability already well established, Honda now had the outright speed to challenge for TT glory and, by the end of the first lap of the 125 race, there were five Hondas in the top six. Leading them was Hailwood who had posted a new lap record on that first circuit. After a determined charge from Luigi Taveri – which saw him reduce Hailwood's lead from 11 to just 2 seconds – Mike just held on to win his first TT. It was also a first win for Honda and the firm's bikes, in the hands of Taveri, Tom Phillis, Jim Redman and Sadao Shimazaki, rounded out the top five. It was an incredible achievement for Honda but there was still more to come later in the day.

Since his debut in 1958, Mike Hailwood had

No-one was more surprised than Phil Read when he won a TT at the first attempt in 1961. He only realised he was the victor of the Junior race when he got back to the paddock.

feared the 'dark and dangerous' side to the TT course and, despite close counselling from Geoff Duke on the matter, he had failed to exorcise his demons even by the end of practice week in 1961. But after his debut win, Mike felt he had conquered his fears and was ready to tame the Mountain course.

His Honda 'team-mate', Bob McIntyre, led the first lap of the Lightweight 250 race from Gary Hocking on the MV before retiring at Sulby Bridge. It was then a straight scrap between what are now two of the biggest names in the history of TT racing – McIntyre and Hailwood. Entering the last lap, Bob Mac led Mike the Bike by 34 seconds only for his Honda to uncharacteristically break down, leaving Mike clear to clock up his second TT win in a day. Hondas filled the first five places at the end of the race but few people noticed the sixth-placed finisher, Fumio Ito, who was riding yet another Japanese machine – a Yamaha. The Japanese invasion had truly begun.

The Sidecar race was won by Max Deubel on a BMW and the German firm took all the podium positions in a race which was marred by the death of female passenger Marie Lambert in an accident just after Creg-ny-Baa. Her husband Claude had been the driver.

Although MV Agusta had officially withdrawn from racing in 1961 due to falling sales of road bikes, the firm still supplied 'privateer' Gary Hocking with a full garage of bikes and mechanics for the TT. He started as hot favourite for the Junior but was beaten into second place by a new name for TT fans – Phil Read.

Read had won the 1960 Senior Manx Grand Prix at just 21 years of age but had retired his Bultaco from his first TT race – the Ultra-Lightweight – earlier in the week. Now on a Norton, Read was challenging riders of the calibre of Hailwood and Hocking. Destined to become one of the most controversial figures in TT history, Read still has fond memories of those early years learning the course. 'I took it easy and was told to learn the circuit and get to know where I was going. It was impressed upon you that it was bloody dangerous and if you crashed you were dead. I remember once the chief marshal came to see me at the Manx Grand Prix and told me I was riding over my limits and looked dangerous and I thought "Oh, really?" I didn't think so. I went out and won the race at record speed.'

Read also won a TT at his first attempt. By lap five of the 1961 Junior, Hailwood had pulled out a lead of two minutes and, when Gary Hocking dropped back with engine problems and a lengthy pit stop, Mike looked like becoming the first rider in history to win three TTs in a week. Then, with just 14 miles to go, a gudgeon pin broke on Hailwood's AJS and Read took his first TT win by over a minute from Hocking – even though he wasn't aware of the fact until he came into the paddock. 'I suppose I was surprised to be running in the company of Mike Hailwood and Gary Hocking at my first TT,' he admits. 'I didn't go there with the intention of winning – just doing as well as possible. My mechanic and I worked hard on the bike and made sure everything was wired up and checked over and, as it happened, I kept going and won the race. It was unbelievable and, actually, coming down the Mountain I didn't know I was in the lead. All the people were waving and I was occasionally waving back – though I don't really like to wave until I've crossed the finishing line. But it was only when I came into the paddock that someone said "You've won. Hailwood retired and Hocking came in second – you've won it." I went nuts. It was unbelievable.'

Mike Hailwood had one race left to make history. If he could win the Senior on his Norton, he would have achieved what no man before had ever done before – won three TTs in a week. When more races were added to the programme in later years, this feat became more achievable, but with just four solo races being held in 1961, to win three was a true measure of greatness.

Gary Hocking held the advantage in the early stages on his multi-cylinder MV but Hailwood and Bob McIntyre hung on grimly on their Norton singles. Another long pit stop, this time to rectify a sticking throttle, dropped Hocking down to fifth by the fifth lap and Hailwood took up the running to lead Bob Mac by almost two minutes. His speed was such that he became the first man to win a TT on a single-cylinder machine at over 100mph as well as being the first to achieve a hat-trick of victories. It was an outstanding performance and would not be equalled until a certain Joey Dunlop repeated the feat in 1985, almost a quarter of a century later. Had it not been for that gudgeon pin failing him in the Junior, Hailwood could well have made it four in a week. The pin was worth ten pence.

1962
DEFECTION

East German rider, Ernst Degner, had been leading the 1961 125cc world championship on his two-stroke MZ when he defected to the West immediately after the Swedish Grand Prix. He not only brought his wife and child with him, but also many of the secrets of MZ's two-stroke design genius, Walter Kaaden. Some rumours even have him bringing a complete MZ engine with him. Whatever the case, when Degner joined Suzuki for the 1962 season, his input paved the way for the Japanese to dominate two-stroke racing into the foreseeable future.

Degner began his new life by entering the all-new 50cc TT on a Suzuki. If some of the other machinery raced on the Isle of Man over the years had been considered 'freaks' because they bore no resemblance to road-going models, then the 50cc racers were super-freaks. Degner's single-cylinder Suzuki produced just 10bhp but was capable of more than 80mph on tyres barely wider than a bicycle's. Revving to 12,000rpm, Degner had to continually dance on the eight-speed gearbox to keep the tiny engine on the boil.

For the first time, the Sidecars had the honour of kicking off TT week. Max Deubel broke the lap record from a standing start and became the first man to lap the course at over 90mph in a Sidecar. He looked like a certain winner until his BMW broke down on the last lap allowing Chris Vincent (father of future solo racer Jay Vincent) to take an unexpected first on a British-built BSA. It was BSA's first TT win and the first time in eight years that a BMW had failed to win.

The 250cc race was upped to six laps in 1962 and Bob McIntyre took up the early running only to suffer another retirement. This put another all-time TT great into the lead – Jim Redman. The English-born Rhodesian was now Honda's leading rider in the 250 and 350cc Grands Prix and was proving every bit as fast round the TT course. When a loose fuel cap lost him time however, Derek Minter went on to win the race and helped give Honda a 1-2-3. Minter, however, was

not a member of the Honda works team and Japanese bosses were less than thrilled to have their official riders, Redman and Tom Phillis, beaten by a privateer.

Because Mike Hailwood had signed to ride for MV Agusta in the major classes, Honda would not give him a bike for the 125 and 250 events, forcing him to seek other mounts. The Benelli he rode in the 250 Lightweight expired on the last lap while he had been in contention, and he fared no better in the 125 race. After leading at one stage, Hailwood again retired on the last lap leaving Luigi Taveri, Tommy Robb and Tom Phillis to take another clean sweep for Honda. Taveri also posted the first ever 90mph lap by a 125.

The Junior was marred by the death of reigning 125cc world champion, Tom Phillis. Although he had never won a TT, Phillis was a class act and would surely have scored many wins had he lived longer. He had been lying in third place before his fatal crash at Laurel Bank.

Just five years after Bob McIntyre's 100mph lap in the 1957 Senior, Gary Hocking became the first man to break the ton mark in the 350cc class – and he did so from a standing start. His blistering opening lap had given him an 11 second lead over Mike Hailwood but Mike eventually clawed it back to lead Hocking over the line by five seconds.

The first woman to ever ride in a solo TT race lined up on the grid for the inaugural 50cc race. Beryl Swain had taken advantage of the FIM's new rules which finally allowed women to compete, but there were still many against the idea and even after she managed to finish 22nd out of 25 finishers, the

East meets West. East German rider Ernst Degner defected to the West and brought the secrets of MZ two-stroke technology with him. He won the 1962 50cc TT for Suzuki.

Chris Vincent gave BSA its first TT win in 1962. It was also the first all-British Sidecar win for eight years.

governing body reversed its decision and women were once again barred from riding at the TT.

If there were some parties who sniggered at the prospect of 50cc machines taking on the rigours of the Mountain course, they were quickly silenced by Ernst Degner's incredible lap speed of 75.52mph. The East German defector's brilliant performance handed Suzuki its first TT victory and one which must have been doubly satisfying since the Japanese firm had beaten two Honda riders, Luigi Taveri and Tommy Robb, in the process.

The much anticipated clash between MV Agusta team-mates, Mike Hailwood and Gary Hocking, in the Senior race did not fully materialise. Hailwood was in the running until he lost bottom gear and then spent 13 minutes in the pits having his clutch plates changed. Behind Hocking, Phil Read battled hard with another new name, Mike Duff. A hard-charging Canadian, Duff would not only make his name as a great rider in the 1960s but would also become famous as the only top TT and GP rider to undergo a sex change. In 1984, Mike Duff took the name Michelle Ann Duff and underwent a four-year process to become a woman.

After having been dead level with Read on corrected time, Duff then retired on lap four and when Read also went out on the last lap, Gary Hocking cruised home to win by a huge margin from Ellis Boyce and Fred Stevens. But Hocking didn't feel like celebrating. He had been a close friend of Tom Phillis and was so shocked at his death that he decided to retire from bike racing at the end of the season as he felt it had simply become too dangerous – though the dangers didn't stop Hocking winning 12 Grands Prix in his final season en route to becoming both 500cc and 350cc world champion. But in a supreme irony, 25-year-old Hocking then turned to the 'safer' sport of car racing, only to be killed in a car race in South Africa in December.

In what was a black year for motorcycle racing, Bob McIntyre also lost his life in a crash at Oulton Park, three months after the TT. Having survived the most dangerous circuit in the world so many times, the man who had set the first ever 100mph lap of the TT course was killed on a supposedly 'safe' short circuit. Without McIntyre, Hocking and Phillis, the sport of motorcycle racing was an infinitely poorer one. Yet it seemed no punishment short of death itself would deter young riders coming through to take the places of the fallen.

1963

THE BULAWAYO BANDIT

Few motorcycle racers have had tougher upbringings than London-born Rhodesian Jim Redman who won his first TT in 1963. He survived the Blitz only to be devastated when his father committed suicide by laying his head on a railway track and waiting for a train. Just weeks afterwards, when Jim was still only 17, his mother died from a cerebral haemorrhage (although Jim claims it was from the shock of discovering the full details of her husband's suicide in the newspaper), leaving Jim as the breadwinner for his three siblings. When the army then demanded Redman carry out National Service – which would have meant his younger brother and sister being sent to an orphanage – Redman refused and emigrated to Rhodesia where he worked his heart out to make enough money to be able to send for his brother and sisters. When Jim Redman transferred this kind of resolve and determination to the sport of motorcycle racing, it was little wonder that he became a six-times world champion.

But Redman's racing career almost ended before it had properly begun. When his great friend and Honda team-mate, Tom Phillis, was killed in the 1962 TT, Redman seriously considered quitting the sport, but after much thought and encouragement from friends, he decided to continue and in 1963, everything came together and the 'Bulawayo Bandit' not only won two TTs, but the 250 and 350cc world championships as well.

Redman's debut TT win came in the Lightweight 250 race where, for the first time, Honda had serious opposition from Yamaha. The latter had sat out the 1962 event in order to develop its bikes and was now back with a much stronger package. So strong in fact, that Japanese Yamaha rider Fumio Ito led the early stages of the race with Tony Godfrey – also Yamaha-mounted – running second and Redman chasing hard in third. On the startline, Godfrey had cheerily called out to his rivals, 'Last man home's a cissy!' He was lucky to make it home at all: in his eagerness not to lose his own dare, Godfrey crashed out heavily at Milntown and fractured

his skull. He was air-lifted to hospital – a first at the TT – where he eventually recovered.

Redman then took up the running and eventually saved Honda pride by beating Ito and the Yamaha to take his first TT win after years of trying. 'That was one of my most thrilling moments,' Redman admitted in his autobiography *Wheels of Fortune*. 'I had been racing there since 1958 and had never really shone on the circuit. It had become an obsession with me to win there. But I had to overcome my intense dislike of the course. And that took some doing.'

Redman had an even stronger ride in the Junior race, leading as he did from start to finish ahead of such luminaries as Mike Hailwood, John Hartle and Phil Read. Read and Hartle were both riding for a new team which had attracted a lot of attention in the

Above: Mitsuo Itoh's win in the 1963 50cc race on a Suzuki remains the only TT victory by a Japanese rider.

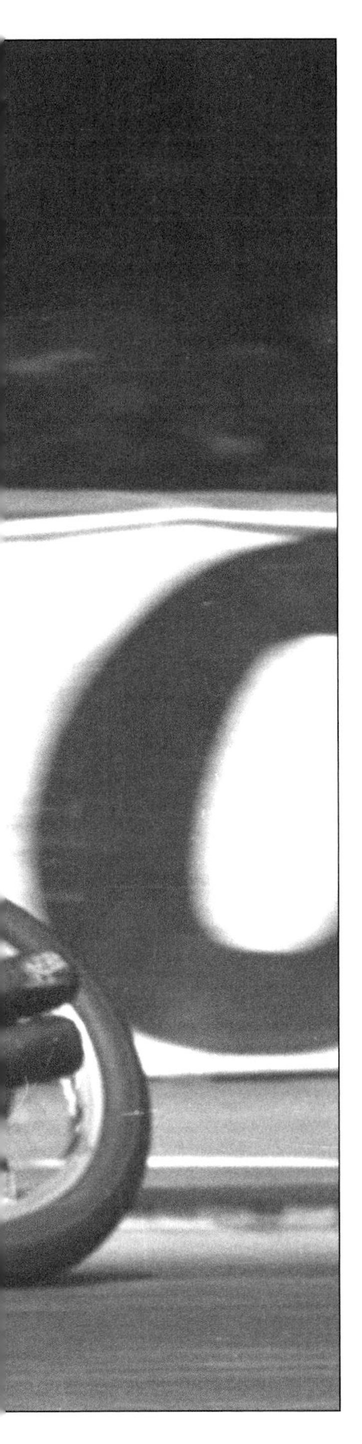

Left: The Bulawayo Bandit, Jim Redman, winning the 1963 Junior race. He won the Lightweight 250 the same week and repeated the double for the next two years.

run-up to the TT – Team Scuderia Duke. Geoff Duke had persuaded Gilera to loan him its 1957 works 350 and 500 machines in the belief that they could be rebuilt, upgraded and remain competitive. When the bikes posted encouragingly fast times in shakedown tests at Monza, it seemed he was correct. One of Duke's riders, Phil Read, wasn't so impressed with the Gilera effort but didn't find out the real reason for the bike's poor handling until it was too late. 'The bike wasn't handling well,' he recalls, 'and it transpired that Geoff Duke didn't know that the Gilera factory had moved the engine back four inches to compensate for the weight that the dustbin fairing had put over the front of the bike back in 1957. They were wearing out front tyres too quickly so they moved the engine back. The factory only told Geoff Duke at the end of the 1963 season. I said all along that they were too light at the front and didn't handle. But I was only a rider – it didn't seem to matter what I said.'

Read pushed his 350 Gilera so hard in the Junior race that it broke down while he was in a leader-board position, but Hartle did well to finish second behind runaway winner Jim Redman who led the race from start to finish on the factory Honda. Redman was thrilled almost beyond words with his TT double. 'It will be a long time before I forget that week,' he later said. 'To win one TT is a great achievement – to win two is a near miracle. It's impossible to express my feelings.'

Yet even an unchallenged victory is not easy at the TT and Redman's description of the course in his autobiography clearly shows why. 'On some parts of the TT course, at speeds of around 140mph, the road feels like a corrugated roof. The bike bounces and bucks wildly, making your wrists ache; and you yearn for a rest. It's like a concrete Grand National. A marathon, danger-filled race that you think is never going to end. You ache. Every bone, every muscle and sinew is buffeted every inch of the way. But you forget the nagging pains. You dismiss the cramp, the crick in the neck, and the needle-sharp rain on cheeks that are slapped out of shape by the wind. You have to forget all this. You are too busy keeping one eye on the rev counter and one on the wriggling ribbon of road.'

While Honda took the honours in both middleweight classes, Suzuki, completely dominated the 50cc and 125cc events. The 50cc race had been increased from two to three laps and Ernst Degner looked like becoming a two-time winner before his Suzuki broke down on the last lap allowing his team-mate, Mitsuo Itoh, to take the win. Itoh, like every other Japanese rider of the time, had learned his trade racing on volcanoes in his native country. More used to rubble and ash than Tarmac, the Mountain circuit was the first fully surfaced track he had ever raced on. Itoh remains the only Japanese rider ever to win a TT.

The 125cc race was a battle between the two-stroke Suzukis and the four-stroke Hondas with the two-strokes coming out clear winners. New Zealander Hugh Anderson led home a Suzuki 1-2-3 and set a new lap record at 91.32mph.

The Sidecar race attracted a record entry of 45 outfits and it was business as usual for BMW with the German firm taking the first three positions, Florian Camathias being the first man home.

Mike Hailwood started the Senior TT as reigning 500cc world champion, a title he held for four straight years through to 1965. On the superior MV, he was untouchable and led the race from start to finish, setting new lap and race records in the process. Hartle and Read did well to finish second and third on their Scuderia Dukes but the race appeared to be a walk-over for Hailwood. It was anything but. Gear selector problems were already making his MV buck and weave dangerously when matters became worse and he lost all but two gears. Reaching down and using his hand to shift the gear lever, Hailwood won at an average of 104.64mph. His lap record of 106.41mph would stand for three years – and only he and the fearsome Honda-4 would beat it.

1964

WITHDRAWALS, ATTRITION AND SICKBEDS

Lack of funding meant the Scuderia Duke team was disbanded after 1963. Geoff Duke decided he could no longer afford to fund the project himself and so MV Agusta looked like being untouchable in the big races yet again – except for one problem: its star rider, Mike Hailwood, had contracted a bout of tonsillitis and was forced to miss much of practice week.

While Gilera was not represented by Duke's team in the solo classes, Florian Camathias had managed to persuade the firm to loan him one of its four-cylinder engines to slot into his Sidecar outfit. He had been lying in second place behind the BMW of Max Deubel before mechanical problems dropped him down to 15th. Deubel led from start to finish to win his second TT.

The rate of attrition in the 250cc race was reminiscent of the early days of TT racing. Of the 64 men and machines that started the race, only eight made it to the finish line – and only two of those with a respectable enough time to win a silver replica. Jim Redman managed to keep his Honda running to win his second 250 TT from Alan Shepherd on an MZ and Alberto Pagani on a Paton.

The Ultra-Lightweight served up a much more enthralling scrap between the Hondas of Redman and Luigi Taveri after every works Suzuki dropped out of the race. When Redman crossed the line to start his last lap he had a healthy 12-second lead over Taveri but the diminutive Swiss rider posted an incredible final lap at a record-breaking 93.53mph to take the win by three seconds from his team leader. Ralph Bryans made it a Honda clean sweep by taking third spot.

Having spent four days confined to his bed, Mike Hailwood reluctantly pulled out of the Junior TT leaving Jim Redman with limited opposition. Only Alan Shepherd on the MV put up any sort of challenge but when that faded, Redman went onto auto-pilot to bring his Honda home ahead of AJS riders Phil Read and Mike Duff. For Redman it was a 'double double',

Home James. Jim Redman and his fly-splattered Honda after winning the 1964 Lightweight 250 race. Alan Shepherd (right) brought his MZ home in second spot.

having now secured the Lightweight and Junior titles for two years running.

Redman had a complex relationship with the Isle of Man. While admitting that his wins there were amongst the greatest of his career, he also had an intense dislike of the TT course itself. In his autobiography he wrote: 'I don't like the course. There are too many wicked-looking walls and too few escape routes if you come adrift. You know that usually your first mistake there is your last. All the time you are racing there you are running a treacherous gauntlet of solid houses, garden walls and rock-faces. Too many good racers have been killed there to ignore its threat.'

Yet the thrill of racing on the Mountain circuit, for Redman as well as countless others, cannot be denied, and this he also acknowledged. 'I have heard riders from every corner of the world say it is the most terrifying circuit they have ever clapped eyes on, and in the same breath have said they would not have missed racing on it for all the tea in China.'

The 50cc race was won by Kiwi Hugh Anderson on a Suzuki – a bike he also had a hand in developing. And as with all classes in the 1960s, development was intense as Anderson explained many years after his final TT win. 'We started off with the 50cc as a single-cylinder which was very good but, as the Japanese did, they went to more cylinders and we ended up with a twin which did 18,000 revs and had a 14-speed gearbox. They did actually move onto a three-cylinder with 18 gears. They were capable of 118mph which is not bad for a 50cc.'

Finally rising from his sickbed, Mike Hailwood was passed fit to race in the Senior TT, even though he had lost a stone in weight and still felt far short of perfect. Had there been stronger competition in the race Hailwood might have struggled, but as it was he coasted round to win by over three minutes from Derek Minter on a Norton and Fred Stevens on a Matchless. It was the slowest Senior since Mike's Norton days four years previously but, under the circumstances, a well-earned win.

An unusual shot of riders entering Kirkmichael during the 1965 Ultra-Lightweight TT. The race was won by Phil Read.

'My first time, I am very surprised because it's completely different than any other circuit. I think the Isle of Man excited everyone who raced there. It's a very difficult circuit and very emotional to ride there. Of course, it's one of the most dangerous circuits in the world because it has everything; it's a normal road and it's very fast and you don't have any space when you crash – you've got trees, houses, everything.'

Even now, more than 40 years later, Giacomo Agostini oozes enthusiasm as he remembers his first experience of the TT as a 23-year-old Italian champion who had just signed for MV Agusta. As the son of a millionaire with movie-star looks, Ago could have lived a playboy lifestyle on his family's money. Instead he chose to race motorcycles, against his father's wishes (his father offered to buy him a sports car if he *stopped* racing bikes), and he proved to be a natural.

A measure of how serious Agostini was about winning at the TT can be gleaned from the way in which he learned the course. Driving alone to the Island from Italy, he hired a bike and spent the next

Hailwood off: A smashed fairing, squashed exhaust, bent bike and a bloody nose. Mike Hailwood didn't care: he rode like a demon to win the 65 Senior for MV Agusta.

12 days learning the course on open roads. In his biography *Fifteen Times*, Ago said: 'I would set off at nine and come back at midday. Then I'd go back out at two and return at 4.30. On a good day I'd complete the circuit five times: that's 350 kilometres. It was such a complex circuit that I had a book where I jotted everything down: the gears, the revs, the braking points . . .'

Agostini's exhaustive preparation worked: he mounted the rostrum in his first TT, the 1965 Junior. MV Agusta had signed Ago as Hailwood's team-mate at the beginning of the season after he had won the 250cc Italian championship on a Morini. Although he personally got on well with Mike, Ago's golden boy status in the all-Italian team would eventually lead to Mike switching camps.

Another new name at the TT in 1965 was one of the most colourful characters ever seen in bike racing – the diminutive Londoner, Bill Ivy. More like a rock star than a motorcycle racer, Ivy had long hair and trendy clothes, and a penchant for Ferraris, Maseratis, rock music and beautiful women. It is hardly surprising that he was the idol and inspiration for a then 15-year-old fellow Cockney who would also prove himself a racing genius and ardent playboy – Barry Sheene.

Like Jim Redman, Bill Ivy was no lover of the TT course and openly admitted that, 'It scares the bloody pants off me.' But he knew that, in the 1960s, if you wanted to be a successful motorcycle racer, you had to master the TT course, so Ivy set about doing just that. Having just been offered a place in the factory Yamaha team which also included Phil Read and Mike Duff, Ivy rode superbly in his first TT – the 250cc Lightweight – lapping just off record pace and holding second place before crashing out – his utter lack of track knowledge eventually being his undoing. With Read also out, Jim Redman won the race for the third year in succession.

Spectators enjoyed a whole new dimension to TT racing in 1965 as Manx Radio broadcast live coverage of the event for the first time. And a running commentary was most definitely needed in the opening race of the week, the Sidecars, such was the closeness of the racing. Max Deubel and Fritz Scheidegger, both BMW-mounted, enjoyed a terrific game of cat and mouse as they smashed the lap record in turn before Deubel managed to pull clear and become the first man to win at an average speed of over 90mph.

Phil Read gave Yamaha its first TT win in the

Battered, broken, bloody but unbowed. The great Mike Hailwood crashed his MV Agusta, picked it up, kicked it straight and went on to win the 1965 Senior. The man was unstoppable.

Lightweight 125 race after a hectic scrap with teammate Mike Duff and Honda's Luigi Taveri. With Duff finishing third and Bill Ivy recording his only finish of the week in seventh place, Yamaha also took the manufacturer's team award.

Interest in the 50cc class was now waning and the 1965 race wasn't particularly great PR for the little screamers. Postponed, then run in poor weather, Luigi Taveri won by a less-than-exciting margin of 53 seconds from Hugh Anderson and only five other men made it to the finish line.

Jim Redman set a unique record when he won the Junior to become the first man to win both the 250 Lightweight and Junior races three years running. But it had been no straightforward cruise to victory. Mike Hailwood set a new lap record from a standing start to lead Redman by 20 seconds, a gap which he increased to 28 next time around. Had it not been for a lengthy pit stop, Hailwood may well have won the race but his delay allowed the Bulawayo Bandit to steal the lead and hold it to the flag. Agostini inherited third place on the last lap when Derek Woodman was forced to retire.

Intermittent heavy rain made for tricky conditions in the Senior race – conditions which caught out the inexperienced Agostini at Sarah's Cottage on the second lap. He had been lying in an impressive second place behind Hailwood before the tumble damaged his machine too badly to continue. Incredibly, Hailwood crashed at exactly the same spot on the following lap. After kicking, pulling and beating his bike straight, Mike pushed the battered MV down Creg-Willey's Hill to get it started then turned round and set off in determined mood. The bike's screen was smashed to pieces, its exhaust was flattened, the handlebars bent, and Hailwood's nose was streaming blood. Yet he rode like a demon back to the pits where he spent over a minute straightening the bars before rejoining the race. Such was his advantage before falling, Mike was still in the lead when he commenced battle and he went on to win his third consecutive Senior race in what was one of his finest ever performances.

Later that year Hailwood won his fourth consecutive world title for MV but, with Agostini enjoying preferential treatment within the team, Mike looked elsewhere for a ride in 1966. He found it with Honda and the combination of the world's greatest rider on the most fearsome motorcycle ever assembled – the 500cc four-cylinder RC181 – would prove explosive.

1966

HELP ME HONDA

'It'll be the death of me, that big Honda. It won't go in straight lines and it's like a concertina, it flexes so much. And when you're having to go like I'm having to go, it's bloody terrifying.'

So spoke Mike Hailwood of the RC181 which was Honda's first attempt at building a bike for the premier racing class, the 500s. Speed, the bike had in abundance, but getting it to go round corners – or as Mike pointed out, to even behave itself in a straight line – proved a terrifying task, even for a rider as skilled as he.

The development of the 500 now fell solely to Mike since Jim Redman had been forced to retire from racing following a heavy crash at the Belgian Grand Prix earlier in the year. He bowed out with a record to be proud of: six TT wins, six world championships and

'You talkin' to me?' Agostini and his crew look menacing as they huddle round the MV in 1966.

Little Bill Ivy had the heart of a lion. Two years after this victory in the 1966 Ultra-Lightweight race, he lapped the TT at over 100mph on a 125cc machine. It shouldn't have been possible.

an MBE for his services to the sport. The latter was, according to Jim 'the crowning moment of my career'.

Given his concerns over the big Honda, maybe Mike Hailwood would have been happier if the 1966 TT *hadn't* gone ahead, and it very nearly didn't, thanks to a national seamen's strike. Forced to cancel the traditional May/June slot, the organisers arranged for the TT to be run at the end of August, just before the Manx GP.

With time being of the essence, the Sidecar became the first TT race to be held on a Sunday and it dished up both close racing and long-standing controversy. Fritz Scheidegger with his English passenger, John Robinson, won the race on his BMW by just four-fifths of a second from Max Deubel but was then disqualified on a fuel irregularity and Deubel was declared the winner. After two separate protests to the FIM however, Scheidegger was eventually reinstated as the rightful winner.

Mike Hailwood already had seven TT wins to his credit as he lined up for the 1966 Lightweight 250 race. After breaking the lap record from a standing start, Hailwood's lead was never really challenged and he cruised home to win the race by almost six minutes from a rider with a familiar surname – Stuart Graham. The son of the first ever 500cc world champion, Les Graham, Stuart had not been put off the TT by the fact that his father had been killed there in 1953. Now, 13 years later, he was bidding to join his late father on the winners' list.

It may be all smiles from Yamaha team-mates Bill Ivy (left) and Phil Read after the 1966 Lightweight 125 but their later rivalry became the stuff of legend.

Bill Ivy's debut TT win in the 125 race came under the most unusual, and dangerous, circumstances. Struggling with the lingering effects of concussion from a Brands Hatch spill, he was determined to rise from his sickbed and pay back Yamaha's faith in him. In a 1966 interview with Mick Woollett of *The Motor Cycle*, he explained: 'I missed the first two days of practice, but finally they let me out on the Wednesday morning on a 125. I was getting headaches and could hardly see, but things improved. When I started in the race I still must have been concussed, otherwise I'd never have gone so fast. It was sheer luck that I didn't crash! I clouted the straw bales coming out of Schoolhouse Bend at Ramsey. Then I got on the loose surface at the Gooseneck and clanged against an advertisement hoarding on the bank. The second lap was a series of slides, the third was enjoyable – things were back in focus again. No slides, no trouble, and just as fast. Lovely.'

In his semi-deranged state, Ivy set new lap and race records and beat his Yamaha team leader Phil Read to the winner's post. But the real grudge match between those two riders had yet to begin.

Giacomo Agostini notched up his first TT win in the 1966 Junior, his task being made easier when Mike Hailwood's Honda expired halfway round the first lap. But Ago's class was clearly apparent; he led Peter Williams by almost two minutes after just one lap, smashed Hailwood's lap record, and won the race comfortably to become the first Italian to win the Junior.

16

Giacomo Agostini: Movie star looks and the talent to match. After winning 10 TTs he would later play a large part in having the event stripped of its world championship status.

Left: Giacomo Agostini taking the first of 10 TT wins in the 1966 Junior. He has won more world titles (15) than anyone in the history of motorcycle racing.

Today he still has fond memories of that maiden win. 'To win on the Isle of Man was like winning the world championship because it's so difficult. And when you win a TT the emotion is more and you are more happy than with any other victory because every lap is so long so you must remember everything. And when you start, maybe it's sunshine, then halfway round it's rain – and then on the Mountain it's foggy. It's very difficult.'

Although the 50cc race provided some close action between Honda riders Ralph Bryans and Luigi Taveri, interest in the class continued to decline, a fact borne out by the poor field of 17 riders who screamed off at the massed start. Bryans eventually secured his first TT victory from just 12 other finishers and set a lap record at 85.66mph which stands to this day.

Because the TT had been delayed until late August, the 500cc world championship had already been decided by the time the riders lined up for the Senior TT. Agostini had stolen the crown which had been held by Mike Hailwood for the last four years, though Mike had ridden admirably on the fearsome Honda-four to take second place. A TT win over Ago and the dominant MV would go some way to making up for losing the world championship, but Hailwood was aware that the Honda's instability would only be exaggerated over the Mountain course.

The first few miles, as described by Mike, were a predictor of what was to come: 'I thought I would have a go at taking Bray Hill flat out. I hit the bottom with such a bump, the next thing I was heading for the wall on the far side and I had to stand up to pull it back.'

Despite his handling woes, Hailwood still managed to break the lap record and, while Agostini did the same, Mike's time of 107.07mph was faster. Rain in the later stages of the race prevented any new race records but Hailwood retained his lead over Agostini to win his ninth TT in what was one of his most impressive displays of riding. Still, the Italian was only in his second year of Island racing and everyone knew that with a little more experience, Ago would be capable of pushing Hailwood all the way. The scene was set for an epic showdown in 1967, the TT's Diamond Jubilee year.

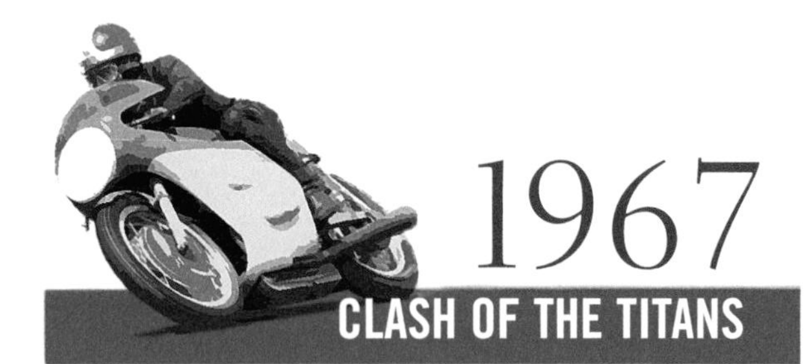

By the time he retired from racing at the end of 1977, Gicacomo Agostini had won 15 world championships. To date, no motorcycle racer in history has won more. Yet he still remembers the 1967 Senior TT as the most important in his glittering career. In his unconventional autobiography *Fifteen Times*, he says: 'There have been plenty of important races in my career. But there is one into which I put body and soul, one where I performed to the limit. Even now, I sometimes dream about it. It was one of the most difficult circuits against one of the toughest opponents in the world. It was the 1967 Tourist Trophy.'

If the 50th anniversary of the TT races had thrown up that historic 100mph lap by Bob McIntyre, then the event's 60th birthday provided one of the greatest and most talked about motorcycle races in history. But that was scheduled as the climax of the week and there was plenty to whet spectators' appetites before the main

Giacomo Agostini prepares to lead the field off in the 1967 Junior. He would relinquish his number one plate to Mike Hailwood by the end of the race.

NLOP
JOE FRANCIS

John Hartle winning the 1967 Production 750 race on a Triumph after a brief retirement from the TT.

event, not least the all-new production race which kicked off proceedings.

With three classes for 250, 500 and 750cc machines, the three-lap Production race would feature a massed start for each class and it would give British machines a chance to shine again without having to take on any factory MVs or Hondas. And so it proved, at least in the larger capacity events. John Hartle enjoyed a triumphant return to the Island after a brief retirement by winning the 750 class on a Triumph – his first TT win since 1960 – while Manxman Neil Kelly also had a start-to-finish victory on his 500cc Velocette. It would be the last TT victory for the famous British marque. Tommy Robb and Bill Smith, both Bultaco-mounted, could not be separated on the road throughout the 250 race but as they approached the finish line together Smith just pipped his friend by four-tenths of a second.

The Sidecar TT saw BMW continue its amazing dominance (only one race had been won by anything other than a BMW since 1954) but this time threw up a new winner in the shape of Siegfried Schauzu. In only his second TT, 'Sideways Sid' took the first of many victories, but only after his passenger had fallen out of the chair at Governor's Bridge then jumped back on board to make it to the finish line ahead of Klaus Enders.

Riding the exquisite six-cylinder Honda 250, Mike Hailwood led after the first lap of the Lightweight 250, but only just from the dynamic Yamaha pairing of Phil Read and Bill Ivy. Hailwood set a new lap record at 104.50mph to increase his lead and when Ivy went out on lap four, Read settled in second and Ralph Bryans was promoted to third. Mike held on to the flag to equal Stanley Woods's long-standing TT record of ten wins and Woods, who had been watching the race from the grandstand, was amongst the first to congratulate him.

Since Honda had pulled out of the 50cc and 125cc classes, the Ultra-Lightweight race turned into a fierce battle between Phil Read on a Yamaha and Stuart Graham on his Suzuki. With Bill Ivy having retired on the second lap and Graham having just taken the lead by one-fifth of a second, it went down to the wire with Read finally getting the verdict. Graham went on to score a well-deserved win in the 50cc race.

Hailwood's performance in the Junior was astonishing. From a standing start, he not only broke the class lap record, but the outright course record – on a 350cc machine! Admittedly, the six-cylinder RC174 was a special motorcycle – in fact, Hailwood said it was the best racing bike he ever rode. But to post a lap of 107.73mph – faster than he had managed on the 500cc Honda the previous year – was incredible. Not

Phil Read (right) listens in as Bill Ivy discusses business with a Yamaha team member in 1967. The battle between the team-mates in the 1968 world championships is amongst the most famous of all time.

even Agostini could offer any sort of a challenge when Hailwood was on such form and the Italian had to settle for a comfortable second place. He had one more chance to beat his friendly Nemesis round the TT course and that would come in the Senior TT.

Still widely regarded as the greatest TT race of all time, the 1967 Senior had every ingredient imaginable. It was to be a head-to-head between the two greatest riders of their time (and arguably of all time) held in perfect conditions with so much at stake. Hailwood's Honda was fast but frightening, handling as it did, like a nitrous-powered shopping trolley. Ago's tried and tested MV handled sublimely but was not quite so fast. With Honda and Hailwood both withdrawing from motorcycle racing at the end of the season, it would be the last chance Ago would ever have to beat the acknowledged master round the TT course. It was his third year of competing on the Island and Ago finally had the course knowledge to take the fight to Hailwood who was in his tenth year of TT racing. If all that were not enough, both riders were battling for the 500cc championship of the world, Agostini having taken Mike's long-held crown the previous year. Ago had also won the first round of the 1967 championship while Mike's Honda broke a crankshaft. Mike desperately wanted to win the title for Honda, Ago felt he had to beat Hailwood round the TT in order to be seen as a worthy champion. It was all to play for. And race day just happened to be Agostini's twenty-fifth birthday. The build-up was perfect and everyone knew it. The clash of the Titans could begin.

With Hailwood starting at number four, Ago's race started 30 seconds later at number nine. *Motor Cycle News* reporter Robin Miller witnessed the race and later summed up the excitement:

“The tension was indescribable. It was as if everybody knew something special was about to happen. Plus there was the knowledge that two men were putting their lives on the line.

Eight miles out at Ballacraine, Agostini was five seconds ahead of Hailwood on time. At Ramsey it was nine seconds. At the Bungalow 11 seconds and at the end of one fantastic lap he was 11.8 seconds in the lead. Agostini pulverised the lap record from a standing start and broke the 21-minute barrier with a speed of 108.38mph. The grandstand crowds gasped as the speeds were announced. Obviously not happy with the handling of his Honda, Mike Hailwood gave a 'thumbs down' as he screamed through to start his second lap. His pit signal had told him what he had feared, that his opening lap of 107.37mph was not good enough and he would have to try even harder.

They thundered into the second lap glued together. Hailwood had got the message and was inching away from Agostini. It was his supreme effort. Spectators lining the road on the Ballacraine to Ramsey section will never forget the sight of Hailwood's heart-stopping progress. The Honda literally bounced from bump to bump as he wrestled it through a series of 150mph swoops, just managing to keep it between the walls and trees. His second lap speed was a new record at 108.77mph but still Agostini led the race by 8.6 seconds. What a duel!

After three laps, both were averaging over 108mph and the grandstand seethed with excitement as first Agostini and then Hailwood came in for their pit stops. Hailwood had cut the lead down to two seconds but he toured into the pits slowly. 'Get me a hammer' he shouted as the mechanics started to refuel. Something was indeed wrong. His twistgrip had been slipping off the handlebar. Furiously he battered it back into place before pulling down his goggles and roaring off again. The stop, lasting 47.8 seconds, cost Hailwood ten seconds because his opponent's pitwork had been that much faster, and at the start of the fourth lap Agostini led by 15 seconds. The fight was really on.

Having to hold the loose throttle in place and use sheer brute strength to keep the bike on the road, Hailwood still managed once again to pull back Agostini's lead. At the start of the fifth lap – with two laps to go – it was 11.6 seconds.

At Ramsey, it was reported that Hailwood led by one second, although he still got a '-6' from his board signalling station there. By now, Agostini was aware that he was in danger and he threw everything into it: timing at the Bungalow had him 2.5 seconds in the lead. Then sensation! As Hailwood screamed through the start for his last lap, Agostini's light had not come on to indicate he had passed Signpost Corner. Finally the news reached the grandstand. He had stopped on the Mountain with a broken chain. A groan went up from the crowd – the race was over.

Mike Hailwood runs it wide at Governor's Bridge in his epic 1967 Senior battle with Giacomo Agostini. Both riders finished the race with scraped leathers from brushing stone walls and cottages.

It was the cruellest of cruel luck. For the spectators, for Mike Hailwood – who never wanted to win a race in that way – and especially for the gallant Agostini who had proven himself every bit Hailwood's equal round the TT. 'I remember crying from the Mountain to the finish line,' he would later say. 'I cried because to win in the Isle of Man, to beat Mike Hailwood, is not easy. I was very disappointed.'

Agostini's pace and the evil-handling Honda which Mike would forever call 'the camel' had taken its toll

CAS
GIRLING
CASTROL
4

Above: Giacomo Agostini put his 'heart and soul' into the 1967 Senior to try and beat Mike Hailwood. He was leading when his chain snapped. It is still regarded as the greatest TT race of them all.

Above right: Mike Hailwood and the fearsome Honda-4 he called 'the camel' in the 1967 Senior. Only he could have lapped as fast as he did on a bike so brutal.

on Hailwood. He confessed to journalist and friend Ted Macauley: 'What a race that was! I wouldn't want to go through another like that – I was scared all the way. Ago's MV obviously handled that much better than the Honda and I was fighting it on every lap. I knew Ago would give it his all and I knew I had to make sure he didn't get away and, if possible, stay in front. But even though I expected it to be pretty bad, I didn't expect it to be a nightmare. There's not enough money in the world to make me go through that again. If Ago hadn't broken down, I doubt that I would have beaten him, he was brilliant.'

For his part, Agostini recalled: 'It had been a record-breaking race that had everyone on the edge of their seats. When we arrived (at the finish), the shoulders on our black leathers had turned white – we'd scraped along the chalk walls.' He added, 'I knew Mike would not surrender anything. He would not know how to give up. It was always the same and to beat him, ever, if only once, is a memory you could live on for the rest of your life.'

Looking back now, Ago believes the broken chain, which robbed him of any chance of victory, could have been avoided. 'My chain broke because it was not good enough. I think my technical people make a mistake – or some people from Regina (chains) make a mistake – because we had a special chain for the race and maybe some people make a mistake and don't put the special chain on. Maybe they put the normal one on.

'I regret that I never got a chance to race again with Mike Hailwood at the TT. In 1967 I was very, very happy to stay in front of Mike because nobody can beat Mike in the Isle of Man – very difficult. So that time I was leading by about eight seconds so I dreamed the victory. But I remember Mike at the end of the race when we went to the prize-giving he said to me "You are the winner" and he took me for dinner and we had a big party. He was very nice to me because he understood if he had a problem, I win, so he appreciated my efforts.'

Four months later at Monza in Italy, it was Hailwood's Honda which broke down and handed the 500cc world title to Agostini. It seemed a fair trade. Hailwood won the TT battle, Agostini the world championship war.

With that victory, Mike Hailwood had completed his second hat-trick of wins at the TT. When Honda withdrew from racing at the end of the season because of moves to limit 125 and 250cc machines to having two-cylinders and six gears, Hailwood also decided to quit bike racing. He was awarded the MBE in January of 1968 for his contribution to motorcycling. It seemed the fans had seen the last of the TT's favourite son and that his 1967 hat-trick would stand forever as his greatest racing achievement round the Mountain course. It wasn't. Mike Hailwood, champion that he was, saved the very best for last.

1968

TEAM ORDERS

If 1967 had been all about Mike Hailwood and Giacomo Agostini then 1968 belonged to Phil Read and Bill Ivy. Seldom has there been such a bitter battle over any world title than that between the Yamaha team-mates. It has become the stuff of legend.

On signing with Yamaha for the 1968 season, Read and Ivy had made gentlemen's agreements that Read should win the 125 title and Ivy the 250 championship. To this end, each rider was expected to back up the other in his respective class and allow him to win without making things look too obvious. Things had gone to plan (largely due to mechanical breakdowns) in the opening two Grands Prix of the season but at the TT, Read told Ivy that he wasn't going to hang around in the 250 class waiting for him. Incensed by Read's remark, Ivy set a scorching pace in the Lightweight race and shattered Mike Hailwood's lap record from a standing start to record a speed of 105.51mph. It was enough to give him a 14-second lead over Read but then Ivy got his foot caught under the footrest at the flat-out Milntown section and wrenched his ankle as well as ripping a gaping hole in his foot. Gritting his teeth, he rode on through the pain and was eventually rewarded by a signal that told him Read was out of the race with a puncture. Ivy nursed his bike, and himself, home, but was in such pain he had to be carried onto the podium. It was a price he was more than willing to pay to beat Phil Read.

Following Read's earlier comments, Ivy planned to give him a taste of his own medicine in the 125 race. Although he had no intention of reneging on his agreement with Yamaha, little Bill determined that he would ride as hard as it took to lead Read to make him think he was going for the win. Only when he had proved his point would Ivy throttle off and hand the victory to his team-mate.

By the end of lap one Ivy's plan was working and he held a four-second lead over Read. Then he really turned up the wick. His next lap is still considered one of the most outstanding in the long history of the TT.

Phil Read tips his Yamaha into Quarterbridge in 1968, the year of his infamous rivalry with team-mate Bill Ivy. Read won the 125 TT while Ivy took the 250. Then it all went wrong . . .

It had been just over ten years since the first 100mph lap had been posted by a 500cc machine but on his second circuit, Bill Ivy thrashed his tiny 125cc Yamaha round at 100.32mph. It was nothing short of sensational and news of the achievement sent a wave of excitement and disbelief through the packed spectator areas. It also sent a wave of concern through the Yamaha pit. Wondering if Ivy was going to break the (unwritten)

Shell
SHELL
Shell

Bill Ivy rounds Quarterbridge on the 250 Yamaha in 1968. He was 'the last of the great racing characters' according to his friend Mike Hailwood.

team orders, the Yamaha team sent a mechanic up to Governor's Bridge with instructions to stop Ivy, if he was still leading in the last mile, to allow Read through. They needn't have bothered. With an 11-second lead, Ivy coasted to a halt at Creg-ny-Baa on the last lap and cheerfully asked a spectator who was winning. He eventually cruised home allowing Read to win by over a minute and when asked if he'd thrown the race, Ivy claimed – with a wide grin – that his engine had gone off song. He fooled no one but, since team orders were against FIM regulations and he couldn't admit to riding to orders, his little demonstration at the Creg was as close as Ivy could come to showing the crowd that he could have won the race.

The rest of the 125 and 250 seasons continued in the same vein with the long-running feud sparking huge interest in the media. After Ivy had helped Read secure the 125 title as agreed, the Luton rider then announced that he was bucking team orders and going for the 250 crown as well. Read suspected that Yamaha was going to pull out of racing at the end of the season so felt he had nothing to lose by disobeying team orders. It was a devastating knife in the back for Ivy after he had upheld his end of the bargain, but he fought with everything he had to claw back the points he had given away to Read. It was all decided in a final showdown at Monza where an oiled plug scuppered Ivy's chances of winning the title that should have been his. Read completed the 125/250cc world championship double.

Even today, Read defends his actions on the basis that Yamaha refused to tell him of its plans and that Ivy simply failed to beat him in a straight fight. He says, 'I was saying to Yamaha "What's going to happen next year? Do I get a chance to win the championship again? What are your plans?" They were saying nothing. After I won the Czechoslovakian Grand Prix in 1968 Bill Ivy pulled up and shouted, "You bastard, you should have ridden to team orders and let me win." But everyone knew if I'd slowed down to let him win there would have been no glory in it for him because I was *letting* him win. If Bill had won at the last round with me *not* riding to team orders then it would have been fantastic for him. But he didn't. It obviously upset the Japanese the way things worked out and it upset me as well.'

Whatever one makes of Read's defence, it remains a fact that he never again raced a factory Yamaha.

Yamaha did withdraw from racing at the end of

1968 (though only for one season) and Bill Ivy was so disillusioned with bike racing that he tried his hand at car racing. In 1969 he returned to two wheels riding a Jawa but, tragically, was killed at the Sachsenring in East Germany on July 12. Paying tribute to his great friend, Mike Hailwood said that 'motorcycle sport suffered an immeasurable loss for Bill Ivy, in my view, was the last of the great racing characters.'

The Sidecars gained an extra class in 1968 to cater for big 750cc machines which would run concurrently with the traditional 500cc outfits. While BMW again dominated the latter class with a clean sweep of the podium led by Siegfried Schauzu, the 750 class was a BSA benefit with Terry Vinicombe leading home two more British outfits, one of which included a woman passenger. Rose Arnold partnered Tom Hanks on his BSA to second place and became the first woman in history to stand on a TT podium.

The honour of winning the last ever 50cc race went to Australia's Barrie Smith on a Derbi. With Suzuki having followed Honda's lead in pulling out of racing, the class lost even more prestige and was finally consigned to the TT history books.

There was no Mike Hailwood, no Hondas and so practically no opposition for Giacomo Agostini and MV Agusta in the Junior and Senior races, as well as in the world championship Grands Prix. In the four years following Hailwood and Honda's withdrawal, Agostini won *every* race he finished in the 350 and 500cc classes.

John Hartle had been signed up as team-mate to the Italian but his crash in the earlier Production race ruled him out of the Junior. It fell to another Italian rider, Renzo Pasolini on a Benelli, to mount the closest thing to a challenge that Ago was likely to see, but it was all over by the end of the first lap as Ago crossed the line with a 46 second lead. Despite having no strong competition, Agostini set a new race record at 104.78mph to win comfortably from Pasolini with TT stalwart Bill Smith a fine third.

The Senior TT was a far less exciting affair than the year before as Agostini cruised to an untroubled win to notch up his first Junior/Senior double. John Hartle's nightmare continued when he crashed out at Cronk-ny-Mona leaving little-known riders, Brian Ball (Seeley) and Barry Randle (Petty Norton) to trail him home in second and third places. Sadly, it was to be Hartle's last TT: he was killed at Oliver's Mount in Scarborough later in the year.

1969

FILLING THE VOID

After the most exciting decade in the history of motorcycle racing, both in terms of machinery and star riders, the last year of the 1960s proved rather disappointing. With Honda, Yamaha and Suzuki all having withdrawn from competition, there was a dire lack of cutting-edge machinery both at the TT and in world championship racing in general. In this void, MV Agusta enjoyed complete supremacy just as it had in the late 1950s when the other Italian marques pulled out of racing. Everyone except Giacomo Agostini had to make do with production 'specials' which were hopelessly outpaced. The yawning chasm between the MV/Ago combination and the rest of the world championship field was clearly demonstrated at the West German Grand Prix. Karl Hoppe on a Metisse got as close as anyone to beating Agostini all year by crossing the finish line just a few seconds behind the Italian; but Hoppe, like the rest of the field, was already a full lap behind Ago.

At the TT, attention quite naturally turned to the Production classes as they produced closer racing and allowed raw talent to shine through. With the demise of the 50cc TT, there was room in the programme to stage two separate Sidecar races with the 750 outfits opening proceedings on the Saturday evening prior to race week. Siegfried Schauzu made history by becoming the first man to win three Sidecar TTs with victory in the larger capacity class and followed up his success with a second place in the 500cc event which was won by Klaus Enders.

There was at least one official factory contesting the Lightweight 250 TT – Benelli had signed Phil Read and Australia's Kel Carruthers to pilot their four-cylinder machines. A Benelli 1-2 was widely expected but when Read retired at the pits at the end of lap five it was left to Carruthers to do the honours which he did with a start-to-finish win. Frank Perris rode a Suzuki to second place ahead of rising Spanish star Santiago Herrero on a single-cylinder Ossa.

Welshman Malcolm Uphill caused a sensation in

the 750 Production race by setting the first ever 100mph lap of the TT course on a production machine. He also won the race – which had a Le Mans-style start – on his 750 Triumph Bonneville ahead of rising star, Paul Smart, on a Norton.

As well as giving a much needed publicity platform for British motorcycles, the Production classes showcased some talented new riders. Besides Smart in the 750cc class, Charles 'Chas' Mortimer led the 250cc category before relinquishing the lead to John Williams who then also dropped back. Both men would go on to have fantastic TT careers. The 250 class was eventually won by Tony Rogers (Mortimer finished third with Williams in tenth), while Bill Penny took the 500cc class.

As expected, the Junior TT was a walkover for Agostini. Phil Read's challenge on a production Yamaha ended on lap two when he went out at the 33rd Milestone, while Kel Carruthers (Aermacchi) lasted a little longer before going out on the last lap. The other Aermacchi team-mates, Brian Steenson and Jack Findlay, were left to have a great scrap for the remaining podium places with Irishman Steenson eventually getting the better of his Australian rival. Agostini won at a relatively sedate pace without establishing any new records. There was simply no need.

The withdrawal of Yamaha was felt particularly keenly in the 125cc TT and without the devastating combination of Bill Ivy, Phil Read and the screaming little Yams, top speeds were noticeably down. Dave Simmonds gave Kawasaki its first ever TT win but his fastest lap was over 8mph slower than Ivy's record.

Agostini's winning margin in the Senior TT was a fairly ridiculous seven minutes. But while he may have made his victories look easy, Ago is still quick to point out that there was no such thing as an easy TT win. 'Winning TTs, if you have opposition like Mike Hailwood or Phil Read, is more important, but every time when you race on the Isle of Man you must always forget about everything else and be completely concentrated because there is always a chance to make a mistake.'

With a new decade looming, the TT – and all world championship motorcycle racing – looked to be in trouble, with little or no interest being shown by the manufacturers. But there was worse, much worse, to come as far as the Isle of Man was concerned. Within three years, most of the world's top riders would refuse to race at the TT altogether. It looked as though the world's oldest and greatest motorcycle race was about to become extinct.

Above: Australian Kel Carruthers taking a start-to-finish win on his Benelli in the 1969 Lightweight 250.

Below: With Hailwood and Honda gone, Giacomo Agostini was unchallenged at the TT from 1968 to 1972. Here he rounds Quarterbridge in the 69 Senior. He won the race by seven minutes.

TOURIST TROPHY
CENTURY
CHAPTER 6
1970-79

GOV
OLD ROAD

1970

DARK BEGINNINGS

The 1970s got off to a terrible start at the TT with six riders being killed during practice and racing in what was the worst year in the history of the races for fatalities.

Amongst those who lost their lives in 1970 were two extremely promising riders: Spain's Santiago Hererro and Ireland's Brian Steenson. Hererro, runner-up in the 250cc world championship in 1969, had finished third in the Lightweight TT in the same year. In 1970, he lost control of his 250 Ossa at the 13th Milestone in the Lightweight race and brought down Stan Woods in the process. Woods escaped with a broken leg, ankle and collarbone, but Hererro sadly passed away two days later.

Brian Steenson had also figured on the TT rostrum for the first time in 1969 by taking second place in the Junior TT. He crashed near the Mountain Box in the 1970 Senior race and died six days later. Dennis Blower, Mick Collins, Les Isles and John Weatherall also lost their lives in that tragic fortnight.

Not surprisingly, the high death toll prompted many to call for the TT to be banned and many national newspapers printed anti-TT articles. This was nothing new for the races but the sheer number of riders killed meant the protests grew louder and, although the racing carried on as normal in the short term, lasting damage had been done and it would only be a matter of time before drastic measures were taken.

Ducati-mounted Chas Mortimer scored his first TT win in the 250 Production race after a fierce battle with John Williams. He now recalls that production machines at the dawn of the 1970s were far removed from today's race replicas. 'They were very agricultural – they used to vibrate like crazy and they weren't stable. They were so primitive you can't even compare them to modern bikes. They were a real struggle to ride round the TT course.'

Malcolm Uphill again won the 750 class on his Triumph but only after fighting off the close attentions of another Williams who was soon to become famous. Peter Williams, a development engineer for Norton Villiers, hounded Uphill all the way and set a new lap record on the final circuit to finish just 1.6 seconds behind after five hectic laps. Frank Whiteway enjoyed a much easier flag-to-flag win in the 500 class on his T500 Suzuki.

Siggi Schauzu became the first man to win four Sidecar TTs when he stormed the 750cc race after Klaus Enders retired. In the same event, Ernie Leece became the highest placed Manxman in a Sidecar race with third place. Enders won the 500cc world championship race on his BMW with Schauzu this time taking second.

The Lightweight race was the first of many in which the new twin-cylinder production Yamaha was the only bike to have. Kel Carruthers used one to devastating effect to take his second consecutive Lightweight win and Rodney Gould followed him home on an identical machine. Paul Smart, Stan Woods and Alex George, were also mounted on the super-fast private Yamahas. Smart retired and Woods was taken out by Hererro in the fatal accident which marred the race. The only non-Yamaha

Giacomo Agostini in 1971 when the unthinkable happened – his normally ultra-reliable MV Agusta broke down.

on the podium was the MZ of Gunter Bartusch. In all, there were 16 Yamahas in the top 20.

When Benelli riders, Renzo Pasolini and Kel Carruthers, both dropped out of the Junior race, it only became a question of how much Giacomo Agostini would win by. The answer was five minutes, from Alan Barnett on an Aermacchi and Paul Smart on a Yamaha. Tony Rutter, the father of future TT and BSB star Michael Rutter, was fifth.

In an exceptionally rare occurrence, the 125cc Lightweight race was won by a newcomer to the TT: German rider, Dieter Braun. His TT win would help him capture the 125cc world championship later in the year. Incredibly, the second and third placed men, Borje Jansson and Gunter Bartusch, were also making their TT debuts.

In the Senior race, Peter Williams and Alan Barnett provided the crowd with a tremendous tussle for the first three laps, though unfortunately it was only for second place. Riding British Singles which had hardly changed since the 1950s, they had no hope of catching Agostini's state-of-the-art factory MV and when Barnett retired on lap four, Williams was left to claim second place comfortably from Bill Smith on a Kawasaki.

With that win, Agostini had become the first man to do the Junior/Senior double in three consecutive years. But the 1970 TT will sadly be more remembered for the number of men who paid the ultimate price for chasing their Mountain dreams.

1971

THE WRATHE OF SHEENE

A small incident which occurred during the 1971 Lightweight 125 race would prove to have far-reaching consequences for the TT.

The as-yet relatively unknown Barry Sheene had been lying in second place to Chas Mortimer in the appallingly wet race when he slipped off at Quarterbridge on the second lap. Sheene had only decided to race at the TT because he needed points for his 125 world championship campaign and, from the first practice session, he hated the course which he considered far too long and dangerous to be included in the world championships. And racing against the clock was not to Sheene's liking either. 'The Mountain circuit did not frighten me in any way,' he would later say. 'No circuit frightens me. I just couldn't see the sense of riding around in the pissing rain completely on your own against a clock. It wasn't racing to my mind.'

After a torrid week of practice, Sheene had pulled out of the Production 250 race after just one lap. He had suffered a tank-slapper so severe that several parts of his Suzuki had worked themselves loose. He had then led the 125 race briefly before his fall at Quarterbridge. It was enough. Sheene vowed never to race at the TT again.

Chas Mortimer, winner of that 125 race, had

Agostini has no trouble lifting the massive Senior trophy in 1971. He is flanked by Peter Williams (left) and third-placed Frank Perris.

known Sheene for some years at that point. He remembers that, 'Barry criticised the place right from the start. Why he went to the TT I don't know, apart from the fact that he was in that battle with Angel Nieto for the 125 world championship and he thought it would be easy points – but it wasn't. He may have been running in second place before falling off, but when you consider the bikes he was up against – I think mine was the only other works bike – the rest were all little Maicos or Hondas, so if he hadn't been lying second there would have been something wrong.'

That might have been the end of it as far as Sheene and the TT were concerned. But when Sheene had an opinion, he made it known, and over the next few years he wasted no opportunity to knock the TT and launched a crusade to have it struck off the world championship calendar. Contrary to popular belief, however, Sheene never wanted to see the TT being stopped altogether. He had, after all, enjoyed many happy summer holidays as a child there when his father Franco raced in the Clubman's events. 'I never suggested that the TT should be banned,' he said in defence of his stance. 'If people want to race there, let them, but don't force riders to go there to get championship points.'

That 125 race may have been the last time Sheene was seen in person at the TT, but his presence would be strongly felt on the Island in the years to come as the press readily turned to him each year for anti-TT quotes. Charlie Williams, who would become one of the most successful TT riders of the 1970s, still wonders what might have happened had Sheene stayed upright and actually won the race. 'It's all supposition,' he says now, 'but if Barry Sheene hadn't crashed out and had actually won the race, then maybe the whole future of the TT would have been different. But he did crash out and decided to attack the TT from then on – and he and I used to fall out over that quite a lot!'

The 1971 races saw the introduction of yet another new race taking the total to a rather over-crowded eight in a week. Fortunately, the new Formula 750 event proved to be beneficial to the TT, allowing, as it did, the very first Superbikes to race there. In doing so, it set the foundations for modern TT racing with its emphasis on production-based Superbikes.

Tony Jefferies, father of the late, great David Jefferies, led the race from start to finish on his Triumph and lapped at over 100mph from a standing start. He was followed home by Ray Pickrell on a BSA and Peter Williams on a Norton.

German Sidecar driver Georg Auerbacher finally won a TT after ten years of trying when he took victory in the 750cc class. His good fortune only came at the expense of others however, as Siggi Schauzu, Roy Hanks and Chris Vincent all fell by the wayside while in leader-board positions.

The Junior TT produced an almost unthinkable result – Giacomo Agostini's MV Agusta broke down! While Agostini remained popular with TT fans, it was a measure of how bored they were of non-races when cheers broke out at the news of his retirement. It meant no disrespect to the Italian but the fans had become desperate to see a close race with an unpredictable outcome, and with Ago's demise, that's exactly what they got.

When it became known that a race win, rather than another second place was up for grabs, a mad scramble took place at the top of the leader board. Phil Read led for a time before his production Yamaha suffered engine problems. Rod Gould crashed at Quarterbridge but remounted to continue, and Alan Barnett also came to grief at Glen Helen. With one lap to go, little-known Dudley Robinson led from Tony Jefferies who had already won the Formula 750 class. When Robinson too crashed out at Rhen Cullen, Jefferies went on to score an unexpected TT double from debutant Gordon Pantall and regular racer Bill Smith.

Siggi Schauzu made no mistakes in the 500cc Sidecar race and claimed his fifth win after a titanic tussle with 750 winner Georg Auerbacher. After three close laps, the BMW riders were separated by just five seconds.

Phil Read had yet to win a 250 TT but he started the 1971 event as firm favourite, even though Peter Williams was expected to put up a respectable fight on the factory MZ. When Williams's challenge ended in the pits after just one lap and Chas Mortimer's Yamaha refused to restart, Read had it all his own way and finally scored the Lightweight win which had for so long eluded him. His win helped him land the 250cc world title later in the year on his private Yamaha.

Tony Jefferies almost scored a TT hat-trick but had to be content with second place in the 750 Production class which went to Ray Pickrell (Triumph) who became the first man to average 100mph for a Production race. Pickrell had been pushed hard by Peter Williams until his Norton stopped on the third of four laps. Bob Heath completed a clean-sweep of the podium for British manufacturers when he took third on a BSA. There was to be no glory for British makes in the 500 and 250cc classes which were both won by Hondas. John Williams did the honours in the larger class while Bill Smith convincingly won the 250 event from Charlie Williams.

Poor weather forced the postponement of the Senior until the Saturday but there was still little doubt about the outcome. Such was the Italian's dominance, even a two minute pit stop to rectify carburation problems couldn't halt his charge. Ago won by almost six minutes from Peter Williams on a Matchless and Frank Perris on a Suzuki.

1972 TURNING POINT

The death of Italian rider Gilberto Parlotti in the 1972 TT would prove to be the most significant turning point in the history of the event. Like Barry Sheene the previous year, Parlotti had only gone to the TT hoping to gain crucial 125cc world championship points. He was leading the title chase on his Morbidelli after four rounds and needed every point available to have any hope of winning the title.

Parlotti had never been to the Isle of Man before but his close friend, Giacomo Agostini, was more than happy to help him learn the course – even if he was not

The beginning of the end. Ago (8) pushes off in his last TT, the 1972 Senior.

too happy about Parlotti being there in the first place. He said: 'Gilberto was involved in a battle with Angel Nieto and the Derbi factory right from the start of the season and saw the TT as a chance of getting an advantage over his Spanish rivals who had elected to give that round a miss. I still wish I had persuaded him not to go either.'

Race week got underway with a start-to-finish victory for Ray Pickrell on a Triumph in the 750cc Production class while Stan Woods (Suzuki) took the 500 category and John Williams (Honda) the 250.

Siggi Schauzu did the double in the Sidecar races, winning both the 750 and 500cc events. He was the first man to do so. The German's TT victory tally now stood at seven, making him easily the most successful Sidecar racer ever seen on the Isle of Man.

Phil Read had joined Giacomo Agostini in the MV Agusta squad for the Junior TT but dropped out with engine trouble on lap two. Read had been hired as a team-mate in a bid to keep Ago from becoming complacent after so many years of dominance. A name which would soon become legendary round the Mountain circuit then inherited Read's second place – Mick Grant. A former art student from Wakefield in Yorkshire, Grant had not enjoyed the best of debuts on the Mountain course – he finished dead last in the 1969 Manx Grand Prix! Now, riding a production Yamaha, he was finally starting to show the potential that would make him one of the greatest riders of the decade, but he would ultimately lose his hard-earned second place when he ran out of petrol approaching the finish line and was pipped by Tony Rutter. Agostini had no repeat of the problems he suffered the previous year and led from start to finish to record his ninth TT victory.

Phil Read had more luck in the Lightweight 250 race which he led throughout on his production Yamaha. Rod Gould and John Williams rounded out the podium places on similar machines.

The John Player Nortons proved a major disappointment in the Formula 750 race. Despite having such talented riders as Phil Read and John 'Moon Eyes' Cooper aboard them, both retired from the race with gearbox problems. In their absence, Ray Pickrell and Tony Jefferies fought for the top honours with Pickrell eventually winning the scrap to lift his second victory of the week.

And then there was the fateful Lightweight 125 race. Parlotti had every intention of winning the TT at his first attempt and was leading the race in atrocious conditions when he crashed on the Verandah, high up on the Mountain, on the second of the scheduled three laps. Eventual race winner, Chas Mortimer remembers the race as though it were yesterday.

“*The conditions were as bad as I'd ever known them in the Isle of Man. Very, very poor indeed. Visibility must have been about 20 yards on the Mountain. But I remember believing I was going to win that race right from the start, then I got my first signal and it was minus seven or eight so I thought, "Well, I'll try a bit harder." I knew it could only be Parlotti. By the time he crashed he had pulled out a 30- or 35-second lead and I was trying as hard as I could. I nearly fell off at Sarah's cottage. I lost the back end big style and really thought I was down. I was trying so hard and Parlotti was still pulling away – and that was his first TT.*

Giacomo Agostini was beside himself at the loss of his friend. He had taken him round the course in a car the night before the race as a final tutorial. Since the 125 race had been run on the Friday morning before the Senior, Agostini was already preparing for his big race when he learned of the tragedy. News of Parlotti's death was enough to convince Ago that his TT days were over. 'When you are younger you don't think about the dangers,' he says now. 'But after many years I see my friends killed too often on the Isle of Man and I decided, with some other riders, that we must stop. Of course, I wasn't happy to stop because racing on the Isle of Man was the best in the world. But if you think about the safety we must say "No, we don't race anymore." Some English people were not happy with my decision but, for our sport, I think it was important because it was very negative publicity – for motorcycle factories and for people who like to buy motorbikes – if they see very bad accidents. It's not a good promotion for motorcycling.'

Neat, stylish and pratcically unbeatable. Ago tips the MV into Signpost en route to winning the 1972 Junior.

Agostini was the TT's biggest star and the biggest name in world motorcycling. As such, his word carried a lot of clout as Chas Mortimer explains.

“*You've got to remember that Ago was very, very powerful in those days and he started the movement about the TT being finished. Barry Sheene jumped on the bandwagon and so did Phil Read. But Parlotti's crash was definitely the death knell of the TT as we knew it. I wouldn't say there was a feeling in the paddock that week that the TT was finished as a world championship round, but the press started to blow things up after the TT and things started snowballing. The head of the FIM at the time was very anti-TT anyway and his mob had enough power to finish the job.*

Agostini's decision to turn his back on the TT would affect the event forever. Yet he was expected to race in just a few minutes' time. For the sake of MV Agusta, the TT organisers and the fans, Ago forced himself to strap on his helmet and to tackle the treacherous Mountain course – which had just killed his friend – one last time. 'I knew there was nothing I could do to get out of it,' he later said. 'The organisation was under way, we knew it was dangerous, we knew that we might die – but we just had to race.'

And race Agostini did, after a lengthy delay because of the weather. Somehow managing to block earlier events from his mind, he sped home to win by more than six minutes from his MV team-mate Alberto Pagani. In what would be his last TT, Ago equalled Hailwood's record of winning the Senior five years in succession. His total tally of wins was 10, which put him second equal with Stanley Woods in the all-time winners list headed by Mike Hailwood with 12.

Then it was all over: Agostini left the Isle of Man never to return in anger and his employers, MV Agusta, also vowed never to return. They were not alone in feeling that the TT was now just too dangerous for world championship racing; Phil Read and Rodney Gould also decided to boycott the following year's event and Barry Sheene continued to voice his disapproval. The writing was on the wall for the Tourist Trophy.

Agostini's last TT win came in the 1972 Senior. Hours earlier his friend, Gilberto Parlotti, had been killed in the 125 race. It would be Ago's last TT.

Heading for home. Agostini heads onto the finish straight in his last TT, the 1972 Senior.

1973

NEW ORDER

Missing three of its biggest stars, the 1973 TT threw up a mixture of new faces and old hands, all eager to fill the gaps left by the superstars. And for one old hand, this would be the year that his lifelong dream finally came true. Like Jimmy Simpson and Graham Walker before him, Tommy Robb had been a great TT competitor with strings of podium finishes to his name but after 15 years of trying, he still hadn't registered a win – until the 1973 Lightweight 125 race.

Robb had retired from the world championship trail but continued to race at the TT simply because he loved it so much – even though it had been a cruel mistress to him on occasion. Thirteen years earlier he had broken his neck by riding straight into the wall at Windy Corner when it was obscured by mist.

It wasn't until a few days before the race that Robb got the go-ahead to ride the 125 Yamaha which the injured Chas Mortimer had vacated. With pre-race favourite, Charlie Williams, suffering engine problems and never really mounting a challenge, Robb led from start-to-finish to realise his dream. He even slowed the pace in the latter stages of the race to make sure as many riders as possible got replicas. Current Honda team boss, Neil Tuxworth finished third on another Yamaha behind Dutchman Jan Kostwinder.

To this day, Robb is a staunch supporter of the TT and has served as president of the TT Riders' Association. He believes it offers a unique challenge.

“*Having ridden round the TT, having broken my neck at the TT and lain in hospital for a while, and come back to race on it many years again, it is something which I think will always be there. And I personally feel sorry for those great riders in the world who have never ridden in the TT. The frights, the scares, the adrenaline flow is something you cannot match anywhere else in the world.*

Robb had also enjoyed a good run in the Production 250 race which had kicked off the week's proceedings. He took third place in the race which saw Charlie Williams take his first TT win. Weather conditions were so bad however, that the leader of the 500 class, Stan Woods, actually stopped at the Bungalow on the last lap. He eventually continued to take second spot but his stop had allowed Bill Smith through to win. Peter Williams had been calling all the shots on his John Player Norton in the 750 class before breaking down on the last lap and handing Tony Jefferies another Production win. It would be his last: Jefferies was later paralysed after crashing out of the Race of the Year at Mallory Park.

Siggi Schauzu had to settle for unfamiliar second places in both Sidecar races as Klaus Enders did the double on his BMW. Enders was in scintillating form, taking flag-to-flag wins at record speeds in both events.

The Junior was to see another first-time winner to add to Tommy Robb and Charlie Williams. Tony Rutter had finished the first lap 26 seconds down on Mick Grant but when the Yorkshireman lost 12 minutes in the pits fixing a fairing bracket, Rutter saw his chance and took it. In what was another Yamaha benefit, Ken Huggett and John Williams rounded out the podium. Over the next 20 years, Yamaha would win every Junior race but two.

Charlie Williams chalked up his second win of the week in the Lightweight 250 race after leading throughout from his namesake and good friend, John Williams.

The fastest lap of the week – and the second fastest lap ever – was set not in the blue riband Senior race, but in the Formula 750TT. Peter Williams, long overdue a win after finishing second so many times, recorded a blistering 107.27mph lap compared to the fastest Senior lap set by Mick Grant at 104.41mph on a Yamaha. The only man to have lapped quicker than Williams was Mike Hailwood in the classic 1967 Diamond Senior against Giacomo Agostini when he set the outright record at 108.77mph.

With such a blinding turn of speed, it was no wonder that Williams won the race and gave Norton its first TT victory in 12 years. Australian Jack Findlay on a Suzuki triple had pushed him hard but his challenge ended with gearbox trouble on the last lap, leaving Mick Grant to complete a John Player Norton 1-2.

Grant had an amazing ride for the first three laps of the Senior race, leading as he did on a bored-out 352cc Yamaha. But instead of pulling off a sensational victory, he crashed out on oil in Parliament Square halfway through the race. His misfortune allowed Jack Findlay to take the lead on his Suzuki twin and, despite a strong challenge from Matchless-mounted Peter Williams, he was able to pull away and give Suzuki its first Senior TT win.

Tony Rutter rounds Signpost on his way to winning the 1974 Junior. He claimed seven TT wins in all.

1974
UNDER THE WEATHER

Bad weather caused a rescheduling of the 1974 races which meant the Junior was the first event of the week. Fast becoming something of a Lightweight specialist, Charlie Williams set the pace on the opening laps but was forced out with technical problems on the third circuit. Former public schoolboy and top world championship contender, Chas Mortimer, was another fancied runner who fell by the wayside leaving the door wide open for Tony Rutter to take his second consecutive Junior win from Mick Grant.

In the 750cc Sidecar race, Siggi Schauzu was back to his winning ways, taking his eighth victory and setting a new race record in the process. But the result could have been very different. Rolf Steinhausen shattered the lap record with an incredible circuit at 98.18mph and was leading Schauzu right up until the last lap when the pace finally told on his Konig outfit and it spluttered to a halt on the last lap. Both Schauzu and Steinhausen hit problems in the 500cc race which dropped them out of contention and allowed BMW's Heinz Luthringshauser to take his one and only TT win.

Mick Grant, took his first win in the 1974 Production race (which now had an upper limit of 1000cc) riding one of the most famous bikes ever to compete in the TT – Slippery Sam. So named because a malfunctioning oil pump had covered its riders in oil at the 1970 Bol D'Or, the Triumph Trident had won its first Production TT in 1971 with Ray Pickrell at the helm. Pickrell won again on the same machine in '72 then Tony Jefferies rode it to victory the following year.

Grant's win took Sam's TT victories to four but there was still more to come – Alex George and Dave Croxford rode the bike to a fifth and final victory in 1975. Grant explains why an apparently ordinary production bike should have such a long lifespan.

“*The technical inspection back then was not as good as today so Slippery Sam was about as straight as Adolf Hitler. Apparently it had the same engine as was used for the Transatlantic Match Races – a full factory job. It had a lightweight frame which was made to look the same as a standard one and the exhaust system also looked the same but was all made of lightweight material – it was more like a full-on Superbike. The reason it was raced for five years was because it was so expensive to make it would have cost a fortune to build one every year.*

Grant had been threatening a TT win for some time and finally showed his class by dominating the Production race, despite having his wrist in plaster.

“*I had broken the scaphoid in my right hand'* he says *'so I was riding with my right wrist in a full plaster. I was having to roll the throttle with my hand which wasn't easy over the bumps. The guy to beat was Peter Williams on the Norton but my Triumph had more horsepower so I knew if I could get to the Mountain ahead of Peter on the first lap I'd have him beat, and that's what I did. It was a hot day and there were lots of flies around so I couldn't see where I was going. Normally you'd stay tucked in behind the fairing and avoid them, but because I had to work the throttle without my wrist bending, I spent more time above the fairing than beneath it. On the last lap I couldn't see a damned thing.*

When Darryl Pendlebury and Peter Williams both retired, the BMW pairing of Hans-Otto Butenuth and Helmut Dahne took an unexpected second and third on their Boxer twins.

Keith Martin gave Kawasaki a start-to-finish win in the 500cc class but Martin Sharpe had to fight tooth and claw for his 250cc victory. After a race-long battle, Sharpe finally out-braked Eddie Roberts just two miles from home to win the race.

Mick Grant and Chas Mortimer disputed second place until the final lap of the Junior race when Mortimer ran out of petrol and had to push his bike over the line for third place. Neither man had had an answer to Charlie Williams who led the race from start to finish for the second year running. All three men were Yamaha mounted.

For the first time in the history of the TT, the Senior was moved from its traditional prime time slot on the Friday. The Formula 750 bikes were now faster than the Senior machines and it was they who would provide the curtain-closer at the end of the week. The Senior was held on a wet and blustery Thursday and, because of the weather, was reduced from six laps to five. When Chas Mortimer dropped out and Charlie Williams slowed because of the conditions, Phil Carpenter went on to win his first, and only, TT.

Tom Herron took his first TT rostrum in the Ultra-Lightweight 125 race which was to be scrapped in 1975. It would eventually be reinstated in 1989 before being scrapped once again in 2004. Hot favourite, Chas Mortimer, retired on the first lap to allow Clive Horton through to take a debut win ahead of Ivan Hodgkinson and Herron.

It had been an unlucky week for Chas Mortimer but he made amends in the final race of the week, the Formula 750. Like many of the top runners, Mortimer had opted to ride an overbored 350 Yamaha, a decision which seemed to defeat the purpose of staging a Formula 750 event. It proved a wise decision however, as most of the 750s retired with problems leaving the bored-out Yamaha boys to take a clean sweep of the rostrum. Mortimer led home Charlie Williams and Tony Rutter to close a wet, windy and much rearranged TT.

1975

THE LONGEST DAY

With the demise of the Ultra-Lightweight class there was space in the TT programme to be filled so the organisers plugged the gap by hosting the longest TT in history. The 1975 Production race was held over ten laps of the Mountain circuit – a distance of 377.73 miles. Mercifully for the riders, duties were to be shared, Endurance-style, with teams of two riders taking turns on the same bike. There were still 500cc and 250cc classes within the race but the two larger classes were handicapped as the 250s had to complete 'only' nine laps.

If there were any fears – and there were – that such a long race would prove to be boring, they were mostly dispelled. Lap records and close racing ensured the new formula was a success. Dave 'Crasher'

Croxford teamed up with Scotsman Alex George to ride Slippery Sam in the big class. After early race leaders, Helmut Dahne and Werner Dieringer retired their BMW Boxer on lap four, Croxford and George ensured Slippery Sam a place in the record books; it became the only bike to win five TTs in consecutive years. Given the rate of progress in modern racing, it's a record which will probably never be beaten.

Only on the penultimate lap did the eventual 500cc winners, Charlie Williams and Eddie Roberts, push their way to the front of the field. Chas Mortimer and Billy Guthrie were more dominant on the 250c, leading on every lap but one. Mortimer was amongst those who thought the race was perhaps too long. 'It was a good race – or at least, I enjoyed it. But I think it was pretty boring for the spectators. Ten laps of production bikes was maybe just too much.'

Charlie Williams broke Tony Rutter's recent stranglehold on the Junior crown but no one could break Yamaha's stranglehold on the class. Indeed, it may as well have been a one-make race: of the 38 finishers, only two were not mounted on TZ350 Yamaha twins. The race itself was entertaining however, with Alex George, Chas Mortimer, Tom Herron, John Williams and Derek Chatterton all in contention. When Alex George crashed at the flat-out 33rd Milestone, the win was Williams's for the taking. Incredibly, George was relatively unhurt and was back in the saddle later in the week.

With Siggi Schauzu retiring on the first lap of the 500cc Sidecar event, the race was thrown wide open and it became a classic duel between Rolf Steinhausen on his Busch-Konig and Mac Hobson on a Yamaha. Hobson's machine had refused to fire up at the start of the race and that most probably cost him the win as he lost out to Steinhausen by just four seconds at the finish after both men had smashed the existing lap record.

Schauzu was back in command in the 1000cc Sidecar race and won after a barnstorming last lap at 99.31mph – less than seconds off the 'ton'. His pace proved too much for Rolf Steinhausen's Busch-Konig which expired on the Verandah on the final circuit. It was Schauzu's last TT win and confirmed him as the most successful Sidecar racer ever round the Mountain circuit. His tally of nine wins would not be bettered until 2002 when Rob Fisher eclipsed him.

The Senior TT was still relegated to playing a mid-week supporting role and was postponed for 25 hours due to bad weather. When it finally got underway, Chas Mortimer took up the running for the first two laps but lost his lead after a lengthy pit stop. John Williams then took his turn to lead but was being hunted down by Mick Grant on the big Kawasaki. Yet Grant had almost given up on the race during the first lap for reasons he now explains.

Mick Grant in 1975, the year he finally beat Mike Hailwood's long-standing outright lap record.

> “*We all had water-cooled bikes by that point but the ACU – who were always behind the times – made us shut our engines off half an hour before the start of the race. So I started with a cold engine and when I rolled off the throttle at Quarterbridge it just locked solid. I dropped the clutch and got it going on two-and-a-half cylinders and then just plodded round thinking it was better than walking back to the paddock. Then at the end of the lap I realised I was actually on the leader board and thought "Hell – I better keep going now." Basically, I ran the bike in for five laps and on the last lap I gave it hell. I really caned it and gave it massive revs and the bike lasted and I won the race.*

Alex George was back on a bike for the 250cc Lightweight race on Friday morning and had a gutsy ride to fifth place. But there was never any doubt about the winner – Chas Mortimer led from start to finish in perfect conditions. It may have been different if Tom Herron's plan to complete all three laps on one oversize tank had worked out but he retired at

Safely landed from the humpback bridge, Alex George speeds out of Ballaugh village.

Milntown on the last lap leaving Derek Chatterton to take second spot and John Williams third.

The Formula 750 race had been replaced by the new Classic TT which was now considered the big race of the week (and not to be confused with today's understanding of the word 'classic' to denote races for older bikes). And it provided *the* talking point of the entire meeting. Mike Hailwood was an interested spectator in the grandstand as Mick Grant set off on his three-cylinder 'Green Meanie' Kawasaki. From a standing start, Grant muscled the big Kwacker round the course at a speed of 107.85mph, just fractions outside Hailwood's long-standing outright lap record. It looked like history was about to be made.

Sure enough, as the Kawasaki team filled Grant's tank after the second lap, it was announced: Hailwood's lap record of 108.77mph, set way back in the 1967 Senior, had finally been broken – Grant had lapped at an average speed of 109.82mph. It had taken eight years to beat Hailwood's awesome lap but Grant had not set out to do it. 'I don't think I've ever tried to set a lap record – it just doesn't work like that,' Grant says. 'I always just tried to win races and lap records were simply by-products of that. I didn't think I'd have any bother at all winning the Classic but the bloody chain broke on the third lap. The Isle of Man is just one of those unpredictable places.'

With Grant out, Tony Rutter inherited his lead, thanks to setting the fastest ever lap on a 350cc machine at 107.88mph but he then suffered a similar fate to Grant when his chain came off at Ballaugh Bridge. John Williams then led Percy Tait home by four minutes to claim the biggest prize in the history of the races – £1,500. It was a gesture on behalf of the organisers which many felt was too little too late. Until as recently as 1971, the ACU had been paying the same prize money for Junior and Senior race wins (£200) as they had in the 1940s.

1976

END OF AN ERA

The Isle of Man had hosted the British round of the world motorcycling championships every year since their inception in 1949. But 1976 would prove to be the TT's last year as part of the series as the FIM announced that the TT was to be stripped of its world championship status, after the 1976 event, because the Mountain circuit was now considered too dangerous.

Most of the top Grand Prix riders had long since deserted Mona's Isle; the main protagonists in the 1976 500cc title battle were Barry Sheene, Marco Lucchinelli and Phil Read, all of whom gave the TT a wide berth. But the event was still attracting huge crowds and the racing was every bit as thrilling as it had been, even if it had lost some of its importance. And not every Grand Prix rider had abandoned the TT; Tom Herron, John Williams and Chas Mortimer were all regular top ten GP finishers and all enjoyed extremely successful TTs in 1976. Some riders, Charlie Williams included, even thought that removing world championship status was a good thing. 'I've always been a staunch TT supporter but to take world championship status away from it was the best thing that could happen. It was unfair to have a world championship race on such a circuit and it cost the lives of a few riders.'

Yet, while some riders were determined not to set foot on the Isle of Man, Williams all but moved heaven and earth to get there in time for the Junior race. On the Thursday of practice week, Williams flew out to Italy to contest the World Endurance Champion-ship as he was contractually obliged to do. After crashing out of the race, he left the medical centre to fly back to the Island in a light aircraft. En route from Liverpool to the Isle of Man, Williams noticed an oil pressure gauge on the aeroplane had dropped to zero. He alerted the pilot who shut down the affected engine and headed back to Liverpool. After changing planes and making it to the Island, Williams was picked up at the airport by his racing friend John Williams. As Charlie struggled into his leathers in the back seat, John drove at breakneck speed to the Grandstand as Charlie was due to be first away in the race. Running to the startline, Charlie was dismayed to hear bikes already setting off – he was five minutes late. Fortunately, the clerk of the course was aware of the epic trip and allowed Charlie to start at the back of the grid. Riding like a man possessed, Williams had slotted into second place behind eventual race winner, Chas Mortimer, at the end of the first lap. But his super-human efforts were all in vain: his bike lost all its water on lap two and his race was over.

Tom Herron proved equally determined. Having held second place for much of the race, the Irishman's chain jumped off on the last lap but rather than retire, Herron pushed his machine home to take 26th out of 44 finishers. He would be amply rewarded for his determination later in the week.

Rolf Steinhausen and Josef Huber enjoyed a start-to-finish victory in the 500cc Sidecar event after Siggi Schauzu made a slow first lap. He regrouped to set a new lap record at 97.50mph but had to be content with fourth place at the flag. In the 1000cc event, Dick Greasley looked odds-on to win on one of the two-stroke Yamahas which were now dominating the class, but with victory in sight his outfit faltered and he could only limp home in third place, allowing Mac Hobson to take the win.

Few people would have put money on a 250cc machine winning the ten-lap Production race against 500cc and 1000cc machines – unless they realised that the smaller bikes only had to cover nine laps instead of 10. It was a strange handicapping system but one that worked in favour of Chas Mortimer and his Scottish team-mate, Bill Simpson – father of future TT winner and British champion, Ian Simpson. The first 500cc machine home was that of Frank Rutter and Mick Poxon in third place while the best 1000cc runner was the BMW of Helmut Dahne and Hans-Otto Butenuth.

The 500cc Senior race provided drama in generous amounts and a stunning new outright lap record. John Williams broke the existing record from a standing start at a speed of 110.71mph. It was the first ever 110mph lap of the Island but Williams was only warm-ing up. Despite clutch problems and the fact that he was riding on intermediate tyres following a rain warn-ing, he scorched his factory two-stroke RG500 Suzuki round at an incredible 112.27mph on his first flying lap to build a 4.5 minute lead over Tom Herron. Going into the last lap, Williams had a three-minute lead over the

Irishman but then started slowing dramatically. His Suzuki team believed the RG500 would manage six laps with just one fuel stop. But then, no one had allowed for Williams's fantastic pace – even the man himself. At such speeds, he reported finding huge bumps on the course which had not been apparent at lesser speeds; Williams had to fight a 170mph wheelie for several hundred yards along Sulby Straight. The result of Suzuki's pit-stop strategy and Williams's furious pace was that the RG500 ran out of fuel a few miles from home on the last lap. Williams, like so many other TT heroes before him, refused to be beaten by the Mountain course and pushed his machine along the Glencrutchery Road for home. Utterly exhausted and close to collapse, Williams was urged on by a standing ovation from the crowds in the Grandstand. He only just made it to the line in seventh place before collapsing.

With Williams having to push in, Tom Herron eventually beat Ian Richards by just 3.4 seconds to win his first TT. He also became the last winner of a 500cc world championship round to be held on the Isle of Man.

The Lightweight and Classic races were postponed to the Saturday due to poor weather and Tom Herron proved his class by scoring a Senior/Lightweight double.

John Williams rounded the week off with a start-to-finish victory in the Classic to the delight of the fans who had felt so sorry about his cruel luck in the Senior. Once again he set a new lap record of more than 110mph (110.21mph) to head home Alex George and Tony Rutter.

The 1976 TT was significant for another reason; it marked the Island debut of the greatest pure road racer of all time. Two retirements, an 18th place in the Senior and 16th in the Junior were not results indicative of what was to come from William Joseph Dunlop of Ballymoney, Northern Ireland, but then Joey had never even been round the TT course before his first practice session. 'It was wet and I rode a 250,' he later remembered of that first practice. 'And I'd never been round it before even in a car and I didn't know where to go to. I remember coming up to Ballacraine and didn't know whether to turn right, left, or straight ahead.'

He would soon learn.

1977 JUBILEE

The budget for the 1977 TT was set at £150,000 making it the richest motorcycle meeting on the planet. But money can only achieve so much: what really kept the TT going and gave it a much-needed status boost after losing its Grand Prix world championship status, was the creation of a whole new kind of world championship. The Formula TT Championship was split into three classes, Formula 1 (for machines between 601cc and 1000cc), Formula 2 (401-600cc) and Formula 3 (250-400cc). All classes were officially recognised by the FIM despite the rather absurd notion that a rider could become a world champion after just one race. But desperate times called for desperate measures and, no matter how hollow the championships seemed, they still gave the TT a much needed shot of credibility.

The greatest sensation of the 1977 TT was the comeback of Phil Read. Read had been one of the most outspoken critics of the races back in 1972 and played a significant part in the TT being stripped of its world championship status. Yet now that had happened, he was lured back by the prospect of a big pay day. Thirty years later, Read explains his reasons for the boycott and his decision to return: 'I just felt the organisers weren't taking it seriously enough and weren't making any effort to protect certain parts of the circuit. There was little contact between marshals – and the money we were being paid was a pittance. Now they pay the top riders a lot of prize money; if you win three races in a week you can walk away with about £75,000. In 1972 I got £50 start money as a five-times world champion. When I won the Lightweight 250cc race I got £100. Thank you very much. In 1977 – just five years later – my appearance money had gone up from £50 to £12,000!'

But it wasn't just money that motivated Read – he also felt he had unfinished business at the TT. 'I felt I still had something more to achieve at the TT in 1977. I'd never won the Senior and there was the new Formula 1 race so I thought that with the proper bikes

I could come back and win *and* earn some money. And I did.'

But TT fans – both visitors and Island residents – had not forgiven Read for his part in the boycott as he found out when he arrived on the Isle of Man. 'When I arrived I parked my van outside the hotel on Douglas seafront. A policeman tapped on the door and said, "Mr Read, I advise you to move your van out of the way round the back because there's a bit of a feeling here." I also had a Rolls-Royce at the time and was going round the circuit with a friend. When we stopped for petrol they refused to serve me. The marshals threatened to go on strike too. I thought, "My God, I didn't think I was so important."'

Worse was to come. During the practice sessions, Read was actually pelted with stones by angry spectators. Whatever some people thought of Read's return, his presence at the TT attracted a lot of publicity – as did the team he was riding for. Honda had not competed at the TT since 1967 when Mike Hailwood had won that glorious Senior battle with Giacomo Agostini. Now the Japanese giant was back, under the moniker of Honda Britain. So while the event had lost its Grand Prix status, the organisers of the TT had still managed to create three new world championships, put up the biggest purse ever seen at a motorcycle meeting, attracted one of the TT's most famous and controversial sons out of retirement, and lured the biggest motorcycle manufacturer in the world back to the Isle of Man. The TT was a long way from being over.

With the Production race being dropped in favour of the new TT Formula races – which were all production-based anyway – the first event of the week was the Junior. It too had undergone some changes; not only was it reduced from five to three laps, but the capacity limit was dropped from the traditional 350cc down to 250cc. This also meant the end of the 250cc Lightweight race. Fifty of the 65 starters were on Yamahas and Charlie Williams dominated the race throughout. Bill Simpson had held second spot almost to the flag but dropped his Yamaha at the Nook on the last lap, less than a mile from home, allowing Ian Richards to take second spot and Tom Herron third.

The first TT Formula 1 race was held in increasingly bad weather conditions which would, ultimately, decide the race. In his first TT ride since 1972, Phil Read was leading Roger Nicholls by 46 seconds on the second lap. As the weather worsened however, this lead turned into a deficit of 22 seconds. When Nicholls pitted for fuel at the end of the third lap, he unwittingly lost the race. Read had gone straight through and, when the race was halted due to the weather at the end of lap four, he was declared the winner and the first TT Formula 1 world champion. Like the 1954 Senior when Geoff Duke lost out to Ray Amm because the race was stopped short in similar conditions, the decision to stop the Formula 1 race caused considerable controversy but the result stood and Phil Read claimed his eighth world title although, for many, if not Read himself, it was a hollow victory compared to the others he had earned over full racing seasons in Grands Prix.

If anyone felt Read's Formula 1 win was a little lucky, he truly proved his worth in the Senior race by leading from start-to-finish. The Senior was also shortened by one lap due to worsening weather but Read had led all the way and no one could deny his comeback double win was something quite special. If Read had not alienated himself with TT fans to such an extent, his performances in 1977 would have been much more celebrated. As things were, his victories were metaphorically swept under the carpet. As Read himself admitted, 'The reception at the prize-giving was mediocre, to say the least.'

In keeping with the general overhaul of the race programme in 1977, the Sidecars also got a shake-up. Gone were the separate 500cc and 1000cc races and in came a two-leg formula with an upper capacity limit of 1000cc in both legs. The new arrangement got off to the best possible start when Dick Greasley and Mick Skeels finally clocked the first 100mph lap (100.59mph) of the TT course in a Sidecar – from a standing start. George O'Dell and passenger Kenny Arthur bettered that with a speed of 102.80mph on their last lap to beat Greasley by 50 seconds. When O'Dell retired from the second leg, Mac Hobson was left to lead throughout and take the win but the overall win went to Rolf Steinhausen thanks to his two third places.

Phil Read was ruled out of the Classic TT after breaking a collarbone during an unofficial – and highly illegal – practice session. 'I left the Island with my arm in a sling,' he explains. 'I'd paid to have a mechanic flown in from France to look after my Yamaha at the TT and for the last practice I told him what had to be done: chains, brakes, tyres, all the things that had to be run-in ready for the race. He did bugger all to it so I sacked him then and there. That forced us to do the work and go up and test at Creg-ny-Baa. Freewheeling round Brandish I sort of lost it for some reason – I can't remember why, but I did – and I broke my collarbone and knocked myself out. I woke up in my van and a copper put his head in the window and said, "You're nicked." Some bloody Islander had followed us down into Douglas, called the police and I was fined £25 for riding a bike with bald (slick) tyres.'

The Manx, it seems, had finally got their own back on Read the Rebel.

With his departure, it was left to Mick Grant and his 'Green Meanie' Kawasaki to rule the Classic TT and set yet another absolute course record, this time at 112.77mph on his second lap. Slotting into third place for a brief period before retiring at the Verandah was a young Grand Prix star and the first American rider to win a Grand Prix. His name was Pat Hennen and his star would shine brightly but all too briefly in motorcycle racing.

Grant's lead was never seriously challenged and, when John Williams crashed out at Creg-ny-Baa, Charlie Williams and Eddie Roberts brought their Yamahas home in second and third.

The Formula 2 and 3 races were run concurrently over four laps on the final race day. Alan Jackson won the former and John Kidson the latter to become the first F2 and F3 world champions. Neither title would be long-lived.

Joey Dunlop's second TT had been going better than his first attempt; he'd finished tenth in the Junior, seventh in the Classic and fourth in the Senior. But the final race of the 1979 TT was the one which finally made fans sit up and take notice.

Because 1977 was the Queen's Jubilee year (as well as being the TT's 70th birthday), an extra event was laid on – the Schweppes Jubilee Race. The entry was by invitation only and special rules meant that slick tyres were not permitted. Most of the top riders were absent too, an intentional omission to allow non-factory riders a shot at glory. Joey Dunlop didn't need a second invitation.

Riding John Rea's cobbled together Yamaha TZ750, Dunlop's opening lap of 110.80mph was just 20 seconds short of Mick Grant's new outright lap record – and that on a bike which didn't fire on all four cylinders until after Braddan Bridge. It was enough to give Dunlop a lead of 17 seconds over George Fogarty (father of future World Superbike legend Carl) and it was a lead Joey never relinquished. The future 'King of the Roads' had staked his claim on the track that was to become his own, but he later remembered having some etiquette concerns towards the end of the race. 'I remember coming down (the Mountain), and I knew that I could near enough freewheel to the line if anything went wrong. But I was that afraid of opening the bottle of champagne – I'd never opened one in my life before and I didn't know what you'd do with it. I remember thinking to myself, "Should I win this or should I breakdown?" But I kept her going anyway.'

As well as opening his first bottle of champagne, Joey also tasted serious prize money for the first time in his life. Until that debut TT win, the most he'd ever been awarded was £100 and 50 gallons of free petrol. Victory in the Scwheppes race netted him £1,000 and, more importantly, a desire to repeat his TT success. That wouldn't happen for another three years, but once it did, Joey Dunlop was unstoppable.

'He was bored,' Pauline Hailwood admits of her late husband Mike. 'We were living in New Zealand at the time and he was just bored. I think in many ways the TT was just a challenge to himself to see if he could still do it.'

When Mike Hailwood announced he was to make a comeback at the TT after an 11-year retirement from bike racing, he was middle-aged, partially crippled, overweight, and out of shape. What's more, he was financially sound and, with nine world titles and 12 TT victories to his credit, was already regarded as the greatest motorcycle racer the world had ever seen. He had nothing left to prove. What could possibly motivate him to return to the TT under so much pressure and media attention and risk his life racing against names he had never even heard of? Even Mike's most ardent admirers – and he could count them in the tens of thousands – thought it was an impossible dream and that the best 'the legend' could hope for was a few steady laps to allow spectators a

Hailwood hustles his 500cc Yamaha through Union Mills in the 1978 Senior. Machinery problems dropped him to a lowly 28th place.

chance to see the man who had once been king. He was, after all, a relic from an entirely different era. Mike had other ideas, as his biographer and the mastermind behind his comeback, Ted Macauley, noted. 'If nobody else believed it, Mike was set in deadly determination. Not only to do well – but to win. And win in some considerable style.'

Since Mike's last TT in 1967, the world of motorcycle racing had moved on immeasurably. Speeds had increased dramatically, tyre technology allowed riders to achieve near-impossible lean angles, knees scraping the tarmac in a style totally alien to Hailwood's. And chassis improvements meant bikes could be thrown around in a way Hailwood had never experienced. He had nothing going for him. Except, perhaps, the fact that he was the greatest bike racer on the planet.

News of Hailwood's sensational comeback attempt set the Island alight and interest in the TT races exploded. Ferry and hotel bookings rocketed and as practice week began, the Island was packed to capacity and beyond. Never before or since has there been more people at the TT. Just two years after losing its world championship status, the TT was stronger than ever.

In the build-up to the event, Hailwood had gotten himself in shape and arrived on the Island looking lean, tanned and healthy. But after 11 years away, he was still a little rusty and asked current TT star, Mick Grant, if he could ride round in practice with him. Grant remembers:

> *"Mike was struggling a little in practice and asked me to show him round the course during the Thursday session of practice week. I thought "Bloody hell! That's like God asking me to explain the Bible." I knew I was good from the start to Ramsey, absolutely awful from Ramsey to the Bungalow, and then exceptionally quick coming back down the Mountain to the startline. So the only place I didn't want him to follow me was up the Mountain. I followed him to Ramsey Hairpin and then, sure enough, he waved me past. I made an even bigger balls of going up the Mountain than I usually do – I just completely lost the plot. Afterwards Mike said, "Thank you very much, but how you get round like you do I just don't know!"*

Hailwood had arranged to ride a 900SS Ducati in the Formula 1 race and had secured Yamahas for the Senior, Junior and Classic. The privately-funded Sports Motorcycles Ducati, on paper at least, should have been no match for the factory Honda of Phil Read who had returned to the Island despite his unhappy experiences the previous year. But while the Honda had all the power, the Ducati handled better and Mike's later practice times (a best lap of 112.36mph compared to the course record of 112.77mph) showed he would be a major threat to Read. There could have been no better sparring partner for Hailwood. Not only was Read a worthy adversary from Hailwood's past, but with his current reputation on the Isle of Man, he provided a perfect 'baddie' for Mike the good guy to chase. Having both won their first TTs way back in 1961, Hailwood and Read now had 16 world titles and 128 Grand Prix wins between them. The duel was on.

Formula 1 race day did not start well for Hailwood; he fell off his 250 Yamaha at Braddan Bridge during the morning practice session. Unhurt, Mike made his way back to the paddock to ready himself for the greatest challenge of his life.

Fans had been packing every possible vantage point on the 37.73 mile TT course for seven hours before Hailwood's comeback race began. As Mike lined up alongside his new rivals, they were unaware that he had needed to be briefed as to who was likely to pose a threat as he hadn't heard of most of them! Such was the length of time Hailwood had been out of racing.

When the flag finally dropped, Hailwood, riding number 12, set off 50 seconds behind Phil Read who carried the number one plate. Mike's plan was to catch Read on the road. Tom Herron led the race for a brief period on lap one but after that, it was Hailwood all the way. After setting a new lap record at 110.62mph, by the third lap, to the utter joy of the record crowds, he had caught Read on the road and the two old rivals wound the clock back more than a decade as they fought it out neck and neck, giving a master class in TT riding.

By this point, Read knew he was beat but to this day he has fond memories of having the best seat in the house for Hailwood's comeback. 'For Mike to come back was brilliant,' he says. 'It was great. He rode really well and it was a fantastic race. For three-and-a-half laps we were together swapping places, we pitted together, we came out together, and it was just so inspiring to watch him through some of the corners. He was riding like he'd never been away.'

Read was forced to ride his Honda to destruction in a bid to better Hailwood. On the fifth lap, while ahead on the road but well behind on corrected time, his engine started smoking and by the 11th Milestone it was all over. Covered in oil and having suffered some dangerous slides, Read pulled in and became just another spectator of the fairy tale. Mike had only one more lap to go. His wife, Pauline, recalls the tension of that last lap even though she was hundreds of miles away in England looking after their children. Ted Macauley was keeping her informed by telephone. 'He was giving a running commentary,' she explains. 'When it came to the last lap he was screaming, "He's gonna do it! He's gonna do it!" There was so much excitement – everyone was going crazy during those final few miles.'

Crazy indeed. The biggest crowd in TT history responded as one when Hailwood passed, roaring its approval and flapping tens of thousand of rolled-up programmes. The commentary team was beside itself with excitement, the media was preparing to file fairy tales back to editors the world over and from Bray Hill to Governor's Bridge, grown men wept. Every father who had told his son that Mike the Bike was the greatest motorcycle racer who ever lived watched through welled-up eyes as the man himself proved it in front of a whole new generation. As Hailwood crossed the line to take victory it was, without doubt, the greatest moment in the TT's long history. It was also one of the finest moments in 20th Century sport. Hailwood himself wept tears of joy as he took the chequered flag marking his 13th – and greatest – TT victory. Yet they could so easily have been tears of another sort. No one knew it at the time, but as Mike crossed the line, his Ducati engine expired. It would not have gone another hundred yards.

It was not until Steve Wynne – who had bought the bike and prepared it for Hailwood – stripped the machine down that he discovered it had stripped the main bottom bevel gear which drove its camshafts and, in the process, bent the con-rods and valves. Phil Read still ponders how different things might have been. 'When Mike caught me up on the road I knew there was no way I could beat him unless his bike blew up or he fell off. But he didn't. If I'd kept running for an extra half a lap and been pushing him then maybe his

Dreams do come true. Mike Hailwood takes a fairy tale win in the 1978 F1 race after an 11-year lay-off.

Ducati might have blown up a mile from the finish line instead of 500 yards from it and he wouldn't have won the race. But then I'd have been the most unpopular winner on the Island!'

Read was such an admirer of Hailwood's talents that he took defeat graciously and went straight to Mike's hotel – still dressed in his Honda Britain leathers – to congratulate him and buy him a beer.

Pauline Hailwood remembers that Mike found his own fairy-tale comeback almost impossible to believe. She says: 'When Mike called me after the race it was as if he was saying he'd won but it was difficult for him to believe that he had actually done it. All the adulation he received was completely overpowering for him. It was something that surpassed anything that had gone before. He considered it his biggest challenge and his greatest ever achievement.'

After such a joyful opening to the week, things quickly turned sour, with the first shock coming in the Senior event. American GP star, Pat Hennen, was nothing short of sensational in only his second TT. Giving chase to race leader, Tom Herron, Hennen became the first man to lap the course in under 20 minutes when he posted a sensational lap at 113.83mph. With Mike Hailwood out of the race with a broken steering damper and John Williams retired at the pits, it was a straight battle between Herron and Hennen on the factory Suzukis. Hennen had closed the gap when, on the last lap, he crashed heavily at Bishopscourt and suffered serious brain damage. He would never race again.

There were no witnesses to Hennen's crash but feathers smeared over his helmet suggest he may have hit a bird at high speed. Today, almost 30 years after the accident, Hennen still suffers from its after-effects with impaired speech and mobility. Herron won the race but there was more tragedy to follow in the next race on the programme.

The first leg of the Sidecar double bill was only minutes old when three men lay dead. Mac Hobson and Kenny Birch died following a crash at the top of Bray Hill, a few hundred yards from the startline, and Swiss rider Ernst Trachsel was killed in a separate accident at the bottom of the same hill. His passenger escaped with a broken leg. It was the blackest day in TT history for Sidecar racers. Yet, as always, the race went on and, had it not been against a background of such tragedy, it would have been considered a classic. Rolf Biland broke the lap record from a standing start at an average speed of 103.07mph and continued to up his pace before retiring on the final lap. His demise gave the win to Dick Greasley with talented young Scottish rider, Jock Taylor, taking second place. Taylor backed this up with a third in the second leg to take the overall win though the wet second race was won by Rolf Steinhausen with another rising star, Mick Boddice, in second.

Chas Mortimer led the Junior from flag to flag while Charlie Williams and Tom Herron slugged it out for second spot, the honour finally going to Williams.

As if there hadn't been enough drama, triumph and tragedy in one week, Mick Grant decided to end the week with his own contribution – another absolute lap record. This time he upped the speed to 114.33mph to steal the record which Pat Hennen had held for only four days. John Williams held second place throughout but could do nothing with Grant on such form – and the Yorkshireman did it all without the help of the Manx Fairies. It has long been a tradition that everyone crossing the Fairy Bridge (between Castletown and Douglas) says hello to the Fairies for good luck. Grant decided to buck the trend. 'I've always been against superstition because it's a weakness,' he says. 'But when I started at the TT I was a little bit superstitious so I decided to fight against it and told the fairies to sod off as I drove up to the paddock from Castletown for the start of the 1978 Classic race. It just made me feel stronger.'

As a final snub to the Fairies, Grant won the race comfortably from John Williams while Alex George brought his Yamaha home in third place. Mike Hailwood suffered another disastrous ride on a Yamaha which failed him on the first lap. In 12 months time, Mike would be back and would discover first-hand just how good Alex George really was.

In 1979, the Isle of Man celebrated 1,000 years of its parliament, Tynwald, and TT fans joined in the celebrations. After all, without Tynwald's permission, there would never have been a TT.

To the delight of all, Mike Hailwood had decided to return once again with the only difference this time around being that everyone knew what he was capable of. This time, armed with Ducatis and Suzukis, he also had machinery to match his outrageous talents.

Outright lap record holder, Mick Grant, had suffered serious pelvic injuries at the North West 200 just a few weeks before the TT in a meeting which shook the road racing world to its very core. Tom Herron, Ireland's top Grand Prix and TT rider, was killed on the final lap of the 1000cc race. Herron's close friend, Joey Dunlop, had no idea of the carnage behind him as he won the biggest race of his career to date. Herron had helped Dunlop learn the TT course and, in a doubly devastating blow for Joey, the same meeting also claimed the life of another close friend, Frank Kennedy. It was under a dark cloud that the road racing fraternity set up camp on the Isle of Man.

Mick Grant would ride later in the week but for the opening race, the Formula 1, Honda handed his factory Honda to Alex George. It was a wise move on Honda's part as George broke the F1 lap record from a standing start and went on to win the race from Charlie Williams with debutant, Ron Haslam, in third place. Haslam had a baptism of fire by having to fight off a determined Mike Hailwood for most of the race before machinery problems saw Mike drop back and cruise home in fifth. One place ahead of Hailwood was another TT newcomer, New Zealander Graeme Crosby.

Alan Jackson won his third consecutive Formula 2 race – and world title – while, in the Formula 3 event, Australia's Barrie Smith took a remarkable victory after a 10 year absence from the TT.

Mike Hailwood's last Senior TT victory had been in 1967. In 1978, his Yamaha had proved unworthy of

His last win. Hailwood leads Grant through Ballacraine in the 1979 Senior. He went on to win his final TT while Grant succumbed to the pain of his broken pelvis and retired.

his talents but now, mounted on an RG500 Suzuki, he was determined to add to his comeback F1 win. Mick Grant gritted his teeth and was practically lifted onto his Honda to take up the challenge of racing against the legend who had become a friend. Grant was in such poor shape that he was allowed a pusher to get him off the line but once he got going, his grit and pace surprised everyone. Despite barely being able to clamber onto his machine, he led the race by four seconds at the end of the opening lap. By lap two however, the pain began to tell and the Yorkshireman dropped to third spot behind Alex George and the flying Hailwood, who had once again taken the lead in a TT race. On the third circuit, Hailwood set a new lap record of 114.02mph to lead George by 13 seconds. When Grant finally had to retire due to the pain he was suffering, and George was forced out with a coil problem, Mike the Bike screamed home to take his 14th TT win.

The first leg of the Sidecar double-header was a classic three-way battle between Trevor Ireson, Dick Greasley and Mick Boddice. There was nothing between the three until the third and final lap when each had their share of drama. Greasley slowed as his petrol tank dried up but he managed to hold onto second place from Boddice who had to stop at Cregny-Baa to refit his chain after it slipped off. Trevor Ireson's passenger, Clive Pollington, gashed his arm badly on a kerb but managed to hang on and help Ireson to a debut win, even though their outfit had no brakes for most of the race. The pairing made it a double later in the week by winning the second leg from Nigel Rollason and Dave Saville – but only after Pollington ripped out the stitches in his own arm to allow him full movement in it!

The Junior TT was back up to six laps for the first time since 1970 and Charlie Williams dominated every one of them on his Yamaha. He also smashed Giacomo

Legend: Geoff Duke negotiates Governor's Bridge on a Gilera during the 1979 lap of honour.

Agostini's eleven-year-old lap record with a circuit at 106.83mph and his pace ensured a new race record just for good measure. Australian Graeme McGregor brought his Yamaha home in second place just ahead of the similarly-mounted Ian Richards.

The six-lap Classic TT which rounded off the week was a classic in more than name as Mike Hailwood and Alex George provided one of the closest battles ever seen around the TT circuit. George, on the four-stroke Honda Britain machine set the early pace ahead of Hailwood, who rode the two-stroke ex-factory RG500 Suzuki. Riding at record pace, Hailwood had nosed ahead by just half a second at Ballacraine on lap five but by the Bungalow the pair could not be split on corrected time. Entering the final lap, Mike's lead was an impossibly slim 0.8 seconds. George tried everything he knew, and a little more, to get ahead as he later explained. 'I got the "-1 second to Mike" sign and it could not have come at a worse time. I was tired mentally and physically by then because the race was a tough one. I started to go to pieces and made a mess of the Creg, scattering the spectators, if my memory serves me right. It was the same at Signpost where I nearly clipped the bank.'

Of George's near-desperate riding, Hailwood said: 'I can't imagine how close to the edge he must have been. I was over the limit all around the place and I know it must have been the same for him. He was like a man possessed – but all credit to the chap. I couldn't, or rather, didn't want to, go any quicker.'

Hailwood crossed the finish line first and had to wait for George's arrival to learn who had won. The timekeepers announced George had taken victory by 3.4 seconds in what was dubbed as 'the richest race in the world' – and with a £30,000 prize fund, it was easy to see why. A start-to-finish winner would have collected £10,000 as opposed to the paltry £100 Phil Read had collected after winning the 1972 Lightweight race.

Mike Hailwood had finished second for the first, and last time, in his glorious TT career. Despite being balked by backmarkers, he set a new outright lap record of 114.18mph on his final circuit, but it wasn't enough to beat George. Yet George had mixed feelings about beating a man he admired so much. 'It was the happiest yet the saddest moment in my life at the end of that race,' he later said. 'I just wish Mike had stopped and that I had not beaten him in the way I did. Despite my win, Mike the Bike is still the maestro and he always will be as far as I am concerned.'

Mike Hailwood would never race on the Isle of Man again. He finally retired from the sport soon after that last, heroic TT performance and must have considered himself lucky to be alive after such a long career which had claimed the lives of so many close friends. Yet on March 21, 1981, the man widely considered to be the greatest motorcycle racer who had ever lived was killed in a road accident while taking his young son and daughter for fish and chips. David Hailwood was the sole survivor of the crash which was caused by a lorry driver making a sudden, and illegal, U-turn on the A435 dual carriageway near Birmingham. The driver of the uninsured lorry was found guilty of careless driving and fined £100. His actions left a little boy without a father and sister, a wife without a husband and daughter, and the world of motorcycling without its greatest hero.

19

CHAPTER 7

1980-89

Shell
37
REA RACING
31

1980

GIANT KILLERS

'The TT is different because you're riding on your own and I was always good at that. If I could get out on my own I could go as quick as any other rider that's there. Without any trouble, I could go as quick.'

Joey Dunlop proved in the 1980s that, not only could he go as quick as any other TT rider, he could go a hell of a lot quicker. After his debut victory in the 1977 Jubilee TT, Dunlop had not enjoyed much further success on the Island but in 1980 that would all change and the real legend of William Joseph Dunlop would begin.

Hailing from Ballymoney in Northern Ireland, Dunlop could not have been more dissimilar to the glamour boys of the sport like Giacomo Agostini and Barry Sheene. With his long, greasy hair and unshaven appearance, he looked more likely to ask you for spare change than to win a £10,000 TT race. But if ever looks belied a person's abilities, it was in the case of Joey Dunlop. The man was quite simply a genius on a motorcycle and in 1980, he truly proved it to an international TT audience.

But that was in the week-ending Classic event and there were many more races on the programme for TT 80. The organisers had finally brought the meeting into line with the real world by upping the total prize money to £200,000 in a bid to retain interest. Mike Hailwood had retired and Dunlop had yet to emerge as his natural successor so something had to be done in the meantime.

Practice was marred when Alex George sustained serious injuries in a crash at Ginger Hall. He recovered and raced at the TT again in 1987 and 1992 'just for fun' but the crash marked the end of his brief career as a TT winner.

The first TT of the Eighties, the Formula 1, was dogged by controversy after New Zealander, Graeme Crosby, took over Alex George's starting number. Instead of starting at his allocated '3', Crosby elected to start at 11 in order to keep tabs on his most likely rival, Mick Grant, who was number 12. The Kiwi had enjoyed a meteoric rise to the top of motorcycle racing and had been snapped up by Suzuki to replace Barry Sheene for the 1980 Grand Prix season. He had finished fourth on a Kawasaki in his TT debut in 1979 and now armed with factory Suzukis, looked every inch a potential race winner.

Honda protested that Crosby's number change gave him an unfair advantage because he could latch onto, and learn from, the more experienced Grant. The protest fell on deaf ears and the race unfolded as predicted: it became a straight battle between Crosby and Grant, both on the roads and on corrected time. After the lead had changed several times, Grant's experience showed in the end and he won the race by 11 seconds but it was clearly just a matter of time before 'Super Croz' won his first TT.

1980. The year in which Joey Dunlop established himself as a TT star by beating the might of the factory Honda team on a private Yamaha.

Reach for the sky: Mick Grant celebrates his 1980 F1 victory ahead of Graeme Crosby (left) and Sam McClements.

After the race it was Suzuki's turn to lodge a protest, this time about the size of Grant's fuel tank. When Honda demonstrated that the extra large tank had been filled with table tennis balls to limit its actual capacity, the organisers seemed satisfied and the protest was thrown out – but in 1981 there would be an altogether more infamous feud between Honda and Suzuki at the TT.

Renowned Sidecar builder and racer, Trevor Ireson, won his third TT in a row in the opening Sidecar leg but lost out to young Scotsman, Jock Taylor, in the second race. Taylor had a new passenger, Benga Johansson, and the combination proved hugely effective. The pair went on to win the Sidecar world championship later in the year.

As expected, Graeme Crosby opened his TT account sooner rather than later with a win in the Senior race. He was aided by the retirement of several front-runners including Charlie Williams and Dennis Ireland, but showed his class by clawing back race leader Ian Richards to lead by 1.6 seconds at the start of the last lap. When Richards retired with a seized gearbox, Crosby cruised home to win by 53 seconds from Ulsterman Steve Cull.

Charlie Williams emulated the great Mike Hailwood by winning two TTs in a single day when he took relatively easy wins in the Junior and Formula 2 events. And while it may sound like hard work, Williams didn't have any major problems. 'It wasn't too tiring doing both in a day as 250s were fairly easy to ride and the circuit, and the bike's suspension, had improved a lot from the early 1970s,' he says. 'You had to change braking points quite a bit when you rode different bikes but that was an accepted thing in those days – jumping off a 125 onto a 350 or even Formula 1 bike was quite normal.'

Barry Smith won the F2 race for the second year running.

Also for the second year in succession, the Classic TT lived up to its name. All the week's big winners – Mick Grant, Graeme Crosby and Charlie Williams – lined up to do battle in the unlimited race which would bring TT 1980 to an end. But ranged against the factory might of Honda and Suzuki was a privateer Irishman on a scruffy old Yamaha TZ750, fitted with the same motor he had raced two years before. Joey Dunlop looked every bit as rough and ready as his bike, but looks can be deceptive and the pairing would prove to be giant-killers – with the aid of a little Irish ingenuity.

On the night before the race, Dunlop decided the only way he could take the fight to the factory men was to run an oversized tank to ensure that he, like the factory Hondas, would need only one fuel stop. While this was completely within the rules, it wasn't the sure-fire solution it seemed to be as Joey explained. 'I decided I would try and do three laps. Sam McClements loaned me the tank and he had tried to do three laps on it and he said it wouldn't do it, so he loaned it to me. I went and got a wee bit welded – another inch-and-a-half – round it in the middle of the night, and went out on it the next morning and I did the three laps.'

The tank was huge and the diminutive Dunlop knew it would be a handful, especially since he couldn't find a screen big enough to cover the tank and his helmet. At Ballacraine on the opening lap, things got even worse as two of the straps holding the tank in place broke, leaving Joey to hold the eight-gallon monstrosity in place with his knees and chest for the rest of the race.

By the halfway point there had been a host of retirements, Graeme Crosby and Charlie Williams

Jock Taylor and Benga Johannson took first and second in the two Sidecar legs in 1980 and went on to win the world championship later in the year.

amongst them. This left Dunlop holding a lead of 22 seconds over Grant as the pair approached the pits for fuel. Grant had the advantage of a high-tech quick-filler while Dunlop had to rely on an old conventional gravity-fed system. Grant's Honda team boss, Barry Symmons, remembered that everyone's hearts went out to Joey as the struggling privateer came in for fuel. 'It was very close,' he said, 'and we had one of these high-tech refuelling rigs. Mick Grant came into the pits and we refuelled him in about six seconds and Joey came in and they were still using the hand filler. And I remember seeing my mechanics sort of . . . not quite cheering him (Dunlop) on, but urging him on, and wanting to dive in and help. We almost felt that we didn't deserve to win. Well, as it happened, we didn't – and Joey did.'

Dunlop's fuel stop was an agonisingly slow 53 seconds while Grant's factory back-up saw him in and out in just 12 seconds. As a result, Grant left the pits with a 19 second advantage over Dunlop. If Joey was to regain the lead, he would have to do it on talent alone. Fortunately, he had it in abundance.

By the end of the penultimate lap, Dunlop was just one-fifth of a second behind Grant and in no mood to be beaten. Still holding the huge fuel tank in place with his knees and terrified that it would pull the pipes off the carburettors, he rode like a man possessed on that final circuit and set an absolute course record at 115.22mph – the first ever lap over 115mph. It was enough to give him the win by 20.4 seconds over Grant and the factory Honda and it was a victory that, for the rest of his life, Joey cited as being the most satisfying – not least because he had outfoxed the biggest team in TT racing. 'It was the way I fooled Honda,' he later said, 'because they knew they had it (the race) because they could do three laps easy and they knew I couldn't do it – but I fooled them for once.'

There was an added poignancy to Dunlop's win: just a few weeks before the TT, Joey's brother-in-law and mentor, Mervyn Robinson, had lost his life at the North West 200. Dunlop had been distraught and was on the verge of quitting racing. He had cancelled all his racing entries apart from the TT, thinking that he might just give it one last shot. After dedicating his famous victory to Mervyn, Joey Dunlop went on to become the greatest pure road racer the world had ever seen. The legend had begun.

Men in black. Ron Haslam (11) and Alex George (9) clad in black as part of Honda's infamous 1981 protest against the organisers' ruling that Graeme Crosby was the rightful winner of the F1 race.

The Honda-Suzuki feud spilled over into the 1981 TT and led to one of the strangest sights in the event's history. In the opening race of the week, the Formula 1, Suzuki's Graeme Crosby was scheduled to start at number 16. But having decided to opt for a rear slick tyre at the last moment, he missed his starting position and was moved to the back of the grid. This would give him time to make the necessary adjustments but it would also mean the clock was ticking from when he *should* have started while he was still sat on the grid. Yet the organisers clearly stated that he would *not* be credited with any extra time to compensate for this and, with the clock already well under way, he finally took the plunge down Bray Hill to give pursuit.

Mick Grant had now signed for Suzuki and was Crosby's team-mate, while the Honda team consisted of Joey Dunlop and Ron Haslam. Grant was closing in on race leader Dunlop when his Suzuki expired on the third lap promoting Haslam into second place behind his Honda team-mate. When Dunlop opted for a wheel change during his fuel stop, Haslam took the lead and held it to the flag. Crosby had ridden superbly to carve his way through the field and take third place at the flag behind Dunlop. His exploits had resulted in a new lap record but, for Suzuki, it wasn't enough. The team protested and insisted that the clock should only have been started on Crosby when he left the startline – not when he was *supposed* to leave the startline before changing his wheel. After some debate, Crosby was granted the extra time and declared the winner, but the organisers failed to inform Ron Haslam or Honda – both of whom were to find out about the decision in the most galling manner. Ron Haslam takes up the story. 'That was the most excitement and disappointment in one hit that I've ever had. Neither me nor Honda had any inkling of it until the evening presentation. I got the champagne on the rostrum and all that stuff and then we went back to the hotel and got ready for the presentation. I was waiting at the side of the stage to be called up to receive the winner's trophy and they shouted me up for second place. I just thought they'd got it wrong so I went up on the stage and thanked them but said they'd got it wrong because I'd won the race. They said, "No, no, no. We're giving it to Graeme Crosby." I just couldn't believe it – and Honda couldn't either. That was the first time we'd been told we were second.'

Haslam and Honda naturally wanted to protest the decision but soon realised they were in a Catch-22 situation. 'Crosby had a problem changing his tyre and he missed his starting time so he went to the back of the grid. In the rule book for that year it said if you don't start in your position you'll get docked the time so we decided to protest the decision. But the rules also said you have to protest any decision within 30 minutes of the race finishing and since no one told us we had lost the race until hours later there was nothing we could do.'

Jock Taylor on his way to setting a new lap record of 198.2mph in the 1981 Sidecar first leg. The Super Scot also won the race and set a new race record.

What made the decision doubly hard for Haslam to swallow was knowing he could have gone faster if required. 'I'd backed off after the first lap because I had such a big lead' he says. 'I just rode round enjoying the hell out of the race at a nice pace. They awarded Graeme Crosby about a minute and, when we checked up, he only beat me by about five seconds which I could easily have made up had I known.'

As it was, Haslam was relegated to second place and Dunlop to third in what was one of the most controversial decisions in the history of the TT. For his part, Crosby defended the decision saying 'It just goes without saying that anybody that goes around here is against the clock – whenever you start and whenever you finish, that's the time. I went round, I think, two minutes faster than anybody else and got the lap record so I don't see how anybody can argue against a win like that.'

Reigning world Sidecar champion Jock Taylor could not have been more dominant in the opening Sidecar race, scoring, as he did, a start-to-finish win with lap and race records thrown in. A victory in the second leg made it three in a row for the Scotsman but poor weather conditions prevented any further record-breaking.

Bad weather also affected the Senior race which was called off after two laps and postponed to the following day. Chris Guy, riding his traditional number 13, had been leading comfortably before the flag came out. By the end of lap two in the rerun, the heavens opened once more and caught out both Guy and George Fogarty at Braddan Bridge. With Graeme Crosby and Charlie Williams already out of the race, Mick Grant cruised home to a comfortable victory in front of Ulsterman Donny Robinson and impressive TT debutant, John Newbold. Unfortunately, Newbold would never get the chance to improve on his position as he was killed at the 1982 North West 200, just weeks before the TT.

For the first time in a decade – when Giacomo Agostini won on an MV Agusta – a Yamaha failed to win the Junior TT. Breaking the Japanese firm's stranglehold was Steve Tonkin on a Randle Armstrong, but only after Kawasaki-mounted Australian Graeme McGregor retired while leading on the last lap. TT rookie Bob Jackson finished second ahead of old hand Charlie Williams.

Tony Rutter won the Formula 2 event on a Ducati Pantah road bike which had been written off the previous month and only just rebuilt. But there was

Graeme McGregor screams through Union Mills in the 1982 Junior. He led for two laps but then retired at the pits.

disappointment for Phil Mellor who had held second spot throughout only to be disqualified for a petrol tank infringement. Barry Smith made it a hat-trick in the F3 race and set a new lap record at 101.31mph.

Honda had been fuming all week at the perceived injustice of the Formula 1 result. But time had not proved a healer in this instance and it was in front of a bewildered paddock that the team rolled out its bikes. The machines, usually painted in Honda's corporate red, white and blue colour scheme, were sprayed black. Even the riders, Ron Haslam, Joey Dunlop and Alex George, turned up in plain black leathers in protest at the organisers' ruling.

Future Honda race boss, Bob McMillan, was a Honda rep at the time and felt the nature of the protest was misjudged. 'It didn't seem like the best decision in the world to have your riders wearing black at the TT,' he later said. 'I don't think a lot of thought was given to the feelings of the riders. It seemed a bit bitchy and political which is not what I expected at the TT.'

Ron Haslam, who the whole protest hinged on, felt it was the right thing to do. 'I was quite pleased to wear the black leathers because we had to show the people that we weren't happy with the organisers' decision but we didn't want to pull out of the meeting. It was a nice gesture from Honda to me really, with me having my first win taken away like that.'

If anything, Joey Dunlop went *too* fast to make amends. Lapping at over 115mph from a standing start, he upped his speed on every circuit until he ran out of fuel at Hillberry on the third lap. Team boss Barry Symmons admitted: 'We reckoned on 9.2 litres per lap . . . even our most pessimistic calculations gave him enough to complete three laps non-stop . . . but we didn't reckon on three 115mph laps.'

Dunlop pushed in to the pits, refuelled, and set off at the same record pace until the Honda's cam chain broke and finally ended his race.

Ron Haslam fared no better and retired from third place with ignition problems. This left Alex George as the sole Honda teamster in third place as the Suzukis of Graeme Crosby and Mick Grant ran away with the race. Crosby completed a memorable double in what was to be his last TT. In 1982, he concentrated on the 500cc Grand Prix world championships where he finished second to Franco Uncini. His TT career had lasted only three years.

STOP

1982
ROCKET MAN

'I went to the Island a week before my first race and borrowed a bike and a car and spent the whole week going round the course,' Ron Haslam recalls.

"At first I thought I'd never learn it – I'd had two days at it and was still completely lost. I can remember thinking, "I don't know how I'm going to cope with this. But it wasn't as dangerous as I'd thought – because I didn't know the course well enough, I was forced to take it easy. When you're not positive on what's coming up next, you automatically close the throttle. It got more frightening when I started to get to know it better – that's the dangerous time. It's so easy to make a wrong judgement when you think *you know what's coming up but you're still not 100 per cent sure. It wasn't until my third year that I really knew where I was going and knew all the drain covers, the hollows, the jumps – everything. Until then I was riding at about 8/10ths but after my third year I knew it like a short circuit and I rode it as hard as the bike would go. I was riding at 10/10ths by then.*

Ron Haslam as he looked in 1982 – about the same as he looks now! He would certainly have scored more than one TT victory if a career in Grands Prix hadn't beckoned.

Rocket Ron Haslam finally got his just reward in 1982 with a clear-cut victory in the Formula 1 race which kicked off the TT's 75th anniversary. His new Honda Britain team-mate, Mick Grant, had led the early stages and set a new lap record at 114.93mph from a standing start, but his furious pace eventually proved too much for his machine and he retired on lap five. Haslam then enjoyed a comfortable margin over Joey Dunlop to the finish line with New Zealander Dave Hiscock a fine third.

When Jock Taylor suffered mechanical problems in the opening Sidecar leg and Mick Boddice retired on the final lap with engine problems, Trevor Ireson picked up the pieces to record a fourth win. With his machine fully functional for the second leg it was back to business as usual for Taylor, but only after early leader Mick Boddice had once more broken down. On his way to victory, Taylor increased the lap record to 108.29mph – a speed which would not be bettered until 1989. In second place were husband and wife team, Dennis and Julia Bingham. Sadly, it was to be Jock Taylor's last TT as he was killed at the Finnish GP just 10 weeks later.

The Senior race included a class for 350cc machines for the first time and the honour of winning the category went to Tony Rutter on a Yamaha. In the main 500cc class, a new star introduced himself onto the TT stage – Norman Brown. It was the Ulsterman's first TT and, after Mick Grant crashed without injury at Ballig Bridge, Brown joined a very elite club by winning a TT at his first attempt. South Africa's Jon Ekerold, a former 350cc world champion, scored an impressive second-place finish and New Zealander Dennis Ireland made it a truly international podium by taking third place. But the fastest lap of the race went to Charlie Williams as he tried to make up time. Williams had coasted to a halt at Ginger Hall and looked like being a retirement before he traced his problem to a kinked fuel line. With the kink straightened out, he charged back through the field to take 13th place and a new lap record of 115.08mph.

Every starter from 1-10 retired in the six lap Junior race. Amongst the casualties were Charlie Williams, Steve Williams, Phil Mellor, Tony Rutter and Graeme McGregor. Irishman Con Law kept his Waddon-Ehrlich running to claim a debut win with Norman Brown continuing his impressive form by taking second from Pete Wild.

Veteran rider, Bill Smith, suffered a horrific crash at Ballaugh Bridge in the Formula 2 race. 'I had both legs very badly broken and my pelvis,' Smith explained. 'Both my elbows and forearms were broken and I had back injuries and my kidneys stopped working for a while so I was pretty badly knocked about.' Yet Smith would return to the Island to pursue his dream of winning 50 TT replicas. He would eventually go one better and win 51 of the prized trophies – more than any other rider has ever achieved.

The F2 race was won by Tony Rutter for the second year in succession while Gary Padgett led throughout the Formula 3 race to take his first TT win.

After the lengthy list of retirements in the Junior race, the Classic event fared no better with most of the fancied runners dropping out and leaving the way clear for little-known New Zealander Dennis Ireland to win his first TT. Amongst the early retirees were Mick Grant and Ron Haslam and Ireland was circulating in fourth place when two of the riders in front of him, Joey Dunlop and Charlie Williams also fell by the wayside. Despite this, Williams still considers the race as one of his best ever performances at the TT. 'It was a rare outing for me on a 500cc machine,' he says 'and when I left the pit stop to start the penultimate lap I was leading by nearly two minutes from Joey Dunlop, Ron Haslam, Mick Grant and all the boys. I was absolutely annihilating them and then the gearbox broke at Ballacrye on the fifth lap. I set a new 500cc lap record at 113.47mph but because I didn't figure in the results, people tend to forget that ride, but I consider it one of my best.'

Still with Jon Ekerold and Tony Rutter to deal with, Ireland kept his composure and brought his RG500 Suzuki home ahead of the two vastly experienced riders to record his only TT win.

1983

V-FOUR VICTORY

Joey Dunlop, with huge camera on his fuel tank, films his famous on-board lap during the 1983 Manx Grand Prix.

The Formula 1 world championship, introduced as a one-round championship at the TT in 1977 had grown to a three round series by 1983 with the other rounds being held at Assen and at Dundrod. Honda had signed Joey Dunlop for the 1982 season and, despite the fact that he did not win either of the two races which made up the series that year, he won his first F1 world championship with second places at the TT and Ulster GP.

As the championship gained momentum and prestige, Honda and Suzuki were both determined to win the 1983 title and Honda built a new RS850 V-four specifically for its title defence. Dunlop too was ready to begin a winning streak after an unhappy year with Honda. Being based in England and racing on short circuits hadn't suited him, and nor did the fact that he wasn't allowed to work on his own bikes. So Honda agreed to a unique arrangement: Dunlop could take all bikes bar his F1 mount back home to Ireland, work on them himself, and enter as many of his beloved local road races as he liked. Results were instant. A happy Dunlop was a fast Dunlop, as his rivals soon discovered.

In the blue corner, Suzuki had signed a young protégé to understudy the vastly experienced Mick Grant – Rob McElnea. Now better known as the manager of the Virgin Mobile Yamaha team in British Superbikes and as the founder of the Virgin Mobile Cup, McElnea was a devastatingly effective TT, and later, Grand Prix, rider in his own right. Over the next two seasons, he would be involved in some terrific scraps with Joey Dunlop.

Dunlop had a new team-mate too. With Haslam off contesting Grands Prix, he had been replaced by Roger Marshall, and he too would offer Dunlop some serious competition over the coming seasons, team-mate or not.

Battle commenced with the F1 race and Dunlop opened his account with a new lap record from a standing start to lead Grant by 18 seconds. On lap four, McElnea moved up into third spot ahead of Geoff Johnson but when Johnson retired, Roger Marshall stole fourth. Joey was never seriously challenged and, although Grant briefly took the lead after the pit stops, Dunlop went on to take his first ever Formula 1 TT victory by 53 seconds from the Yorkshireman.

With that win, Dunlop received the biggest cheque ever presented for a single TT win – £10,250. It was probably more money than the former turf-digger had seen in his lifetime and to cap the best year of his career to date, he went on to lift his first F1 world title with victory at the Ulster Grand Prix.

It takes an incredibly brave man – or woman – to agree to be a passenger in a Sidecar at the TT but it takes an even braver one to decide – on the night before a race which he was favourite to win – that the job was no longer for him. But that's exactly what Trevor Ireson's passenger, Ashley Wooler, announced before the first Sidecar leg in 1983. With no time to find a replacement, Ireson was forced into being a spectator and had to watch as Mick Boddice broke down and handed the win to Dick Greasley. Boddice made amends by winning the second leg after 14 years of trying. This time round it was Greasley's turn to break down.

Con Law (EMC) won the Junior for the second year in succession and, in doing so, became the first man to lap the Mountain circuit at 110mph on a 250cc machine. There were two Junior races in 1983 – one for 250s and one for 350s – and while Law won the former, Yorkshire's Phil 'Mez' Mellor took a popular win in the 350cc race after Law's machine broke down.

Tony Rutter continued his winning ways in the F2 event taking his third successive victory after passing Graeme McGregor, also Ducati-mounted.

Another change to the programme in 1983 was the merging of the Senior and Classic races to create the unimaginatively titled Senior Classic. Ulster's Norman Brown stunned spectators – and rivals alike – by setting the fastest lap ever recorded at the TT. After leading over the line at the end of lap one, Brown sped round at an average speed of 116.19mph, but his devastating pace took its toll and he ran out of fuel on the third lap. Rob McElnea seized the opportunity and went on to win his first TT win in only his second year of trying. He explains how he learned the notorious circuit so quickly. 'I really loved it from the start and I've always been quite handy at learning tracks – I suppose I just had a knack for it. I divided the course into sections and there were some sections you needed to focus on a lot more on than others and that's where you made the time up. You can't really learn the course on open roads because it's so different when you can use only one side of the road, so I learned it mostly during practice sessions.'

Irishman Con Law upped his game on the last lap to take second place from Joey Dunlop.

Brown's stunning pace marked him out as a new star at the TT and great things were predicted for his future. Tragically, he would never get to fulfil his potential – he was killed in a hideous accident at the British Grand Prix at Silverstone the following month. Brown had been cruising with his hand up when Swiss rider, Peter Huber, collided with him at full speed. Brown, only 23-years-old, was killed instantly, while Huber died later in hospital.

Rob McElnea hurtles through Kirkmichael village during the 1984 F1 race. He retired but went on to win the Senior and the Classic.

30
19

1984

RETURN OF THE MAC

Joey Dunlop always believed in winning races at the lowest possible speed. In the 1984 F1 race however, he was forced to ride beyond lap record pace to beat his Honda team-mate, Roger Marshall. The F1 world championship had now been increased to five rounds and Marshall, knowing how important it was to Honda, had his sights fixed firmly on the title.

A four-way battle between Dunlop, Marshall and the Suzuki riders, Mick Grant and Rob McElnea, was expected in the F1 TT but when both Suzuki men retired, it was left to the Honda teamsters to battle it out. Joey held a seemingly unassailable lead over Marshall by the third lap but was forced to stop when he noticed clouds of blue smoke pouring from his machine. 'I got off and parked her against the hedge,' he said. 'I thought the rear wheel had jammed, gave her a kick then noticed that the exhaust pipe was jamming against the tyre.'

Joey made on-the-spot repairs and rejoined the race, minus an exhaust pipe, but had seen his 50-second advantage become a 24-second deficit to Marshall. By now 'crabbit and angry', he was in no mood to lose out to his rival. Dunlop rode like a demon to claw back the precious seconds he had lost and by Ramsey on the last lap he was within 11 seconds of Marshall. By the Bungalow it was five. Marshall didn't stand a chance. Forced to ride out of his leathers to make up lost time, Joey had set a new lap record at 115.89mph to win his second F1 race by 20 seconds.

After waiting 14 years for his first Sidecar race win, Mick Boddice had clearly developed a taste for it and led throughout the first Sidecar leg of '84 to claim a second victory. Once again Dennis and Julia Bingham took second spot and Julia came so close to being the first woman to stand on the top spot of a TT rostrum but never quite made it despite being only two seconds behind Boddice on the last lap. The second leg was a race of attrition with Boddice, Bingham, Trevor Ireson and Dick Greasley all retiring and allowing Steve Abbott to claim a maiden victory.

For the first, and only, time at the TT, a historic (what would now be called 'classic') race was held over three laps of the Mountain circuit. And for the first and only time to date, an American rider won a TT. Dave Roper took his Matchless round at an impressive average of 96.11mph to win from future TT star Ian Lougher on a similar machine.

Once again the Senior TT had been shuffled around like unwanted baggage but at least it had its title back. The Senior and the Classic were now two entirely separate races and Rob McElnea dominated both of them. McElnea's TT career was brief but sensational. By 1984, he was Barry Sheene's Suzuki team-mate in Grands Prix and arrived at the TT from a front row qualifying position in Germany. McElnea was world class and one of the last GP riders prepared to tackle the dangers of the Mountain course. He was also one of the few riders who could challenge Joey Dunlop in his prime. He still believes that his short circuit experience made a difference at the TT. 'I was so much sharper than the average TT rider because I was running at the front in short circuit races in the UK and had done some Grands Prix. So I was obviously going to be faster than the guys who just did the TT and maybe a few other races each year. If a top MotoGP guy went to the TT now and only rode at 80 per cent of his ability you'd be amazed at how fast they could get round. They're just operating at a much higher level. Kevin Schwantz once did the Macau road race just for fun and blitzed everybody.'

The Senior race was a titanic to-and-fro battle between Dunlop and McElnea with the lead changing constantly. McElnea smashed the outright lap record on his second circuit with a speed of 118.23mph and took an eight second lead over Dunlop but by half distance Joey led by 19 seconds. On lap five, Dunlop raised the bar even higher with a lap at 118.48mph in his pursuit of McElnea. His astonishing lap gave him a 40-second lead and the race looked to be over when news came through that Dunlop had stopped on the Mountain on the last lap. There were suggestions at the time that Dunlop had run out of fuel but years later his manager, Davy Wood, admitted that 'The real problem was a broken oil seal along the gearbox. This caused the engine to seize, breaking the crankshaft. It was unfortunate to say the least for he had the race won.'

Rob McElnea remembers that Senior clearly. 'That was a hard race – the 500 was a real handful round the

Roger Marshall at Parliament Square in 1984, still chasing his first TT victory. It would forever elude him.

TT. It was much harder work than the big four-stroke, 1000cc Suzuki – it was just so much more intense. Every gear shift was crucial and once it started moving you really had to hang on. There are two things I'll always remember about that race; one was that the sun was going down and my visor was covered in flies but I still spotted Joey's bright yellow helmet by the side of the road and knew he was out. The other was the 32nd Milestone which you probably get correct about twice in a lifetime and on the last lap I got it absolutely inch-perfect. It was a beautiful day and the roads were bone dry, but as I came out of the 32nd there was a wet patch right on the white line. It must have seeped up from underground and I slid right across the road – I'll never forget it. I've no idea how I got away with it.'

McElnea recovered from his monster slide and held on to win the race while Roger Marshall inherited second spot, a placing he was to become all too familiar with at the TT.

Graeme McGregor became only the third man to win two TTs in a day when he took the Junior 250 (the Junior 350 had now been dropped) and F2 races. He also set new lap and race records in both events. The Australian had to fight hard to take his first ever TT win in the Junior, beating off quality names like Joey Dunlop, Charlie Williams and Brian Reid. When Dunlop suffered another retirement, Williams collected second spot in what was to be his last year of racing at the TT. He retired with an impressive tally of eight wins and 19 other rostrum positions, most of which were in the smaller bike classes, a fact which he now regrets. 'It was such a pity that I didn't get the chance to ride more big bikes at the TT,' he admits, 'but I got sort of typecast as a good rider on smaller bikes. It was ridiculous really because I'd been winning on big bikes in endurance racing since 1973. Maybe it was my fault a bit too though; when the Yamaha TZ700s came out in about 1974 we took one to the TT and I couldn't ride the damn thing. I'd recently broken my wrist – my first racing injury – and I was just very wary of the bike because it was so vicious and it put me off riding big bikes for a while. When I look back I'm quite annoyed that I didn't pursue the big bike thing more at the TT.'

Williams remains a staunch supporter of the TT and is now a famous radio commentator on the races as well as being president of the TT Supporters Club.

McGregor had things all his own way in the F2 race, leading as he did from flag to flag to round off his unique double. The winner of the race for the last three years, Tony Rutter, had to settle for second this time around.

Production racing was reintroduced to the TT for the first time since 1976 with classes being held for 1500cc, 750cc and 250cc machines. Geoff Johnson won his first TT in the big class on a Kawasaki while most of the excitement was seen in the battle between Trevor Nation and Helmut Dahne. Both riding Hondas, the pair were split by just fractions of seconds throughout the race with Nation eventually taking his first TT win by just 2.2 seconds. Phil Mellor won the 250 class after a close battle with Gary Padgett, Graham Cannell and *Motor Cycle News* road tester, Mat Oxley.

The Classic TT gave Dunlop, McElnea and Grant another chance for a battle royal and they all delivered. Dunlop led the first lap from Grant by six seconds but when the Yorkshireman posted his fastest ever TT lap at 116.71mph, he took the lead from Dunlop by one-fifth of a second. By lap three, McElnea took his turn at the front, then was ousted by Dunlop again and so it continued until McElnea took control of the race by setting a new lap record at 117.13mph and holding a ten-second advantage over the last lap. It was his third TT win in two years but it would also be his last as full-time Grand Prix duties beckoned. 'I loved doing the TT,' he says now 'but the law of averages stack up against you if you keep doing it. I decided in January of 1984 – without telling anyone else – that I wouldn't be doing the TT any more after that year. I told my team and my wife on the Friday night after winning the Classic that it would be my last TT. Then we flew over to France for the Grand Prix and the next morning I broke my bloody leg at Paul Ricard! The TT is such an awesome thing to do as a rider and I would never want to tell someone else not to do it.'

1985
THE CRUEL SEA

ITN news report, May 1985:

After recovering one bike during low tide, divers spent the afternoon preparing to lift seven others which they believe are still aboard the fishing boat, now 100 feet under water. As the first bike was brought ashore, two hours after the salvage operation had started, world champion Joey Dunlop was there to assess the damage. He'd been one of 12 people on the trawler who were eventually rescued by a local lifeboat crew.

Winning the last of seven TTs, Mick Grant leads the pack through Ginger Hall in the 1985 Production 750.

The 1985 TT almost claimed Joey Dunlop's life under the most bizarre circumstances. The grave danger he faced had nothing to do with racing 180mph motorcycles between stone walls, but rather was caused by the mode of transport he used to get to the Isle of Man – a fishing boat. When he first took the boat in 1980, Dunlop won the Classic TT and thereafter considered it a good luck omen. In 1985, it proved anything but. The boat crashed into rocks in rough conditions in Strangford Lough as it was leaving Northern Ireland for the Isle of Man and Dunlop and the other 11 people on board were lucky to escape with their lives. 'We'd almost geen up so we had,' Joey said after being rescued. 'Once we got off the rocks and got out a wee bit it was a bit calmer and kinda gave us a bit more spirit again. While it was on the rocks we'd no chance.'

While Dunlop himself was too modest to admit to any acts of heroism, his late manager, Davy Wood, left no doubt as to Joey's role in saving his fellow sailors. 'Joey was again an unsung hero because several of the boys were not swimmers of any good degree and Joey tied petrol cans around them and lowered them gently into the water and told them to sit still and be calm and cool and took command of the situation.'

All 12 people aboard were eventually rescued by lifeboats and an RAF helicopter but the racers – once back on dry land – were more concerned about their bikes. While Joey's factory Hondas had taken a more conventional route to the Isle of Man aboard a commercial ferry, eight bikes belonging to Joey's brother Robert, Brian Reid, Sam McClements and Noel

Hudson had to be salvaged from the bottom of Strangford Lough. Once they were, some serious work was needed to make them serviceable as Robert Dunlop explained. 'We had to strip every nut and bolt off and we seeped them in diesel oil then we washed them in petrol and started to reassemble the whole lot from scratch again.'

With no time to mull over the drama, Joey Dunlop flew to the Isle of Man to begin practice week while most other people would have been seeking therapy. Instead of allowing the fact that he came within minutes of drowning distract him, he went on to have the most successful TT week of his career.

His winning streak started in the Formula 1 race which he completely dominated after his main rivals, Roger Marshall and Mick Grant retired with mechanical problems and new Suzuki signing, Graeme McGregor, crashed out at Greeba Bridge. Dunlop set a new lap record at 116.42mph to lead home Tony Rutter by more than five minutes. Steve Parrish finished third but was later disqualified for using an oversized fuel tank.

Rutter went one better by winning the F2 race which had been extended to six laps. Ulsterman Brian Reid had set a new lap record (110.47mph) from a standing start but later retired from the race and when Gary Padgett dropped out of the lead with a lengthy pit stop, Rutter was clear to take his fourth F2 win in five years.

Mick Boddice and passenger Chas Birks had a heartbreaking end to the first leg of the Sidecar TT. With a ten-second lead and less than a quarter of a mile to go, the chain jumped off their outfit at Governor's Bridge and the pair had to watch Dave Hallam and John Gibbard take victory as they paddled over the finish line. Boddice made amends by taking a start-to-finish victory in the second leg.

Joey Dunlop and Brian Reid took turns leading the Junior with only their respective pit stops giving either any advantage. When both were fuelled up by the end of the fourth lap it was a straight two-lap fight to the flag – or at least it should have been. Reid smashed the lap record on the fifth lap to lead by 15 seconds but his EMC stopped at Hillberry just minutes from the finish line. Dunlop screamed past to claim his second victory of the week and his first ever in the Junior, though his heart went out to his fellow countryman.

Bill Simpson, father of future TT star Ian, came so close to winning the 1500cc Production race but was just pipped on the last lap by Geoff Johnson. Mick Grant took his final TT win in his last year of racing on the Island on Suzuki's all-new sports bike – the GSX-R750. His week would end on a slightly lower note however when he crashed out of the Senior and broke a thumb.

When Gary Padgett crashed out of the lead in the 250cc class, *MCN*'s Mat Oxley seized his chance and won the race from Manxman Graham Cannell. Oxley set a new class lap record of 96.40mph on his final circuit while Padgett remounted to finish third.

With Mick Grant and Germany's Klaus Klein both crashing out of the Senior, it was left to Roger Marshall to challenge Joey Dunlop but he couldn't match the pace of his team-mate and had to settle for second yet again. Grant felt his crash was one too many. 'I won the Production race on the Friday morning and then I crashed the 500 in the afternoon and broke my thumb. I just felt then that someone was trying to tell me something.' He never raced at the TT again but he would return as a team manager and suffer much worse heartache.

With his dominant victory, Joey became only the second man in history – Mike Hailwood being the first – to win three TTs in a week, and he was clearly pleased with his achievement, though exhausted and slightly shaken after witnessing several accidents. 'It's unbelievable – I just can't believe it yet,' he said. 'It was tight. I was tiring out pretty heavily and I knew Roger was catching up a bit. There was a hell of a lot of accidents around the course and it was detuning me a little bit.'

Dunlop's performance prompted his manager, Davy Wood, to suggest that sinking in a fishing boat may have to become an annual ritual. 'We ended up winning three races,' he said. 'I thought we should dump him in the water before every TT if this was gonna be the answer.'

The Senior race was marred by the death of 32-year-old Dover rider Rob Vine. His name lives on through the Rob Vine Fund, a charity which provides essential medical supplies and training for all doctors, paramedics and marshals involved in motorsport events on the Isle of Man.

Brian Reid won the Formula 2 race in 1986 before playing an unwitting part in the tragedy which followed in the Junior when Gene McDonnell collided with a horse.

1986

A BRIDGE TOO FAR

Gene McDonnell was a promising young Irish rider who looked to have a big future at the TT. That future never happened. His death in the 1986 Junior was the most horrific ever witnessed on a course which had already seen more than its fair share of tragedies.

When Brian Reid crashed at Ballaugh Bridge, the rescue helicopter was called to pick him up. As it approached, the helicopter spooked a horse in a nearby field causing it to bolt, leap several fences and hedges and eventually find itself trotting down the TT course. The section of the course, on the approach to Ballaugh Bridge, is one of the fastest and Junior riders would have been clocking speeds of up to 160mph as they rounded the blind right kink on the run up to the bridge. Gene McDonnell had no chance. He collided with the horse and his bike smashed into cars in the forecourt of a nearby garage, exploding into flames. McDonnell, just 24, was killed instantly and the whole Island was numbed as news filtered through.

Steve Cull, went on to win the race but was as devastated as everyone else when he was told the news afterwards. There were no celebrations that night.

There were other tragedies at the 1986 TT and by the time the final chequered flag had dropped, four men had lost their lives to the Mountain course. Sidecar passenger Alan Jarvis was killed in practice, Andy Cooper was killed in the Senior race and Ian Ogden was killed in a practice crash at Cronk-y-Voddy. A former Senior Newcomers winner at the Manx Grand Prix, Ogden was the first Manxman to be killed on the TT course. It was one of the bleakest fortnights in the event's history but still the racing went on. The TT has never been cancelled over the death of a rider.

Dreadful weather added to the gloomy feeling and caused the F1 race to be postponed for two days and reduced to four laps. Joey Dunlop, now an MBE, and the acknowledged master at the TT in tricky conditions, led the race from start to finish and crossed the line with a minute to spare over Geoff Johnson.

Roger Burnett was a surprise winner of the 1986 Senior. Here he speeds through Ballacraine on the way to his only TT victory.

Andy McGladdery was third while Roger Marshall retired, a TT win eluding him yet again.

When race favourites Mick Boddice and Chas Birks retired from the first leg of the Sidecar event, Lowry Burton became the first Irishman to win a Sidecar TT. Chas Birks fell out of Boddice's outfit at the fast Greeba Castle section to end any hopes of a win in the second leg. The race was won by Nigel Rollason on a British-built Barton Phoenix outfit using the engine from the 1980 bike racing movie *Silver Dream Racer*. Rollason, like all the other winners that week, sprayed his champagne over a new £420,000 grandstand which had been built to replace the 60-year-old wooden structure.

The F2 race was also reduced to four laps and saw Brian Reid win his first TT after leading throughout. The sixth-place finisher was a new name for TT fans but one they would soon hear a lot more about: Steve Hislop.

There were new lap and race records in every Production class in 1986 and Trevor Nation set the first sub-20-minute lap by a production bike to take victory in Class A on his Suzuki GSX-R1100. Phil Mellor rode the wheels off his Suzuki GSX-R750 to up the Production 750cc lap record by almost 5mph. His lap at 110.69mph assured him of a comfortable victory while another Suzuki, in the hands of Gary Padgett, won Class C. It was Padgett's second, and last, TT win. He was killed in a road accident shortly afterwards. *MCN*'s Mat Oxley set the first ever 100mph lap on a 250 production machine but slid off his Yamaha at Governor's Bridge leaving Barry Woodland to take the win.

Roger Marshall must have been hugely miffed with the result of the Senior TT. After running Joey Dunlop so close on so many occasions but never actually managing to win, his former mechanic, Roger Burnett, pulled off a surprise victory in only his fourth attempt at the TT. The race was flagged off by HRH the Duke of Kent and Marshall took early control from Trevor Nation. After setting the fastest lap of the race, Nation took the lead at the end of lap two but his pace was such that he eventually ran out of fuel. Marshall retook the lead, this time from Honda team-mate Burnett with Joey Dunlop in third place. When Marshall lost time in the pits with chain problems and Dunlop struggled with steering damper problems, Burnett held on to take an unexpected victory from Geoff Johnson and Barry Woodland.

Burnett would never win another TT. He finished third in the 1988 Formula 1 race but retired in both races at his last TT in 1990. He now runs a successful promotional/management company.

1987

A DREAM COME TRUE

The TT celebrated its 80th anniversary in 1987 and there were no fatal accidents to mar the occasion. The Manx weather, however, did try hard to impede proceedings.

Phil Mellor had been the talk of practice week after he unofficially slashed 15 seconds off the outright lap record on his Skoal Bandit Heron Suzuki. But if his average speed of 118.03mph worried Joey Dunlop any, the Irishman showed no signs of it come F1 race day when he emulated Mike Hailwood and Giacomo Agostini by becoming only the third man to win the same TT race five years running. But even though he won by over 50 seconds, Dunlop still had his share of problems as he admitted after the race. 'The exhaust came off,' he calmly announced. 'It was me own fault – I missed a gear and she blew the exhaust off.'

It proved to be Dunlop's only win in the eight-round F1 world championship that year and he was forced to concede the title he had held for five straight years to Italy's Virginio Ferrari. As the series eventually gave way to the World Superbike championship (which started in 1988), Dunlop would never regain his F1 title. Phil Mellor finished second in the race with Geoff Johnson taking third place after Roger Marshall suffered fuel starvation problems.

Mick Boddice won his fourth TT in the first leg of the Sidecars despite having no clutch for most of the race. But his passenger, Don Williams, must take the bravery award for hanging on despite having 47 pins in his leg from an earlier crash. Dennis and Julia Bingham scored yet another second place, seemingly destined to never win a TT. In the second leg, Ulsterman Lowry Burton became the oldest man to win a TT when he crossed the line first at the ripe old age of 49.

A young Borders rider named Steve Hislop stormed into the lead of the Junior race ahead of a quality field including Brian Reid, Graeme McGregor and Dubliner Eddie Laycock. After two laps, the 'Flying Haggis' had a lead of 51 seconds and looked set to take a debut TT win until his ignition packed up on the penultimate lap and forced him out of the race. His lead was inherited by Laycock who went on to take his first victory from Reid and McGregor.

For the F2 race, Hislop had a new ignition system, paid for by a fan who had overheard him say he couldn't afford one. Hizzy put it to good use. Again, it was Reid, McGregor and Laycock who provided the competition but even when Laycock set a new lap record during his pursuit of Hislop, he couldn't catch the runaway Scotsman who was talking his bike home on the last lap. 'It wasn't until I was heading over the Mountain for the last time that I started thinking "Yes, I can really do this." Then I became really distracted by the thought of winning and started talking to the bike saying "Come on, come on, please keep going, don't let me down this time girl" – just urging my little bike on.'

This time his old Yamaha TZ350 did make it home and Hizzy simply couldn't believe that he had finally won a TT. 'To explain what that win felt like is not really possible,' he said. 'My father had raced on that course, my brother had won a Manx GP on it and I had been trying to win there for five years. I had even been going to the Island since I was a kid and dreamed that one day I'd stand on the winner's rostrum. And this wasn't the Manx GP either, it was the TT proper and I simply couldn't have been more elated – and relieved.'

Trevor Nation had a 24-second lead in the Production B race (401-500cc two-strokes/601-750cc four-strokes) and was just three miles from victory when he ran out of fuel for the second year running. He managed to coax his spluttering Yamaha over the line but only after handing victory to his team-mate Geoff Johnson. Barry Woodland won the class D race (250cc two-strokes/400cc four-strokes), the only other Production race to be run in 1987.

The Senior was postponed from Friday to Saturday but was still run in atrocious weather conditions. Joey Dunlop won the race at an average speed of 99.85mph making it the slowest Senior since 1974. After his closest rival, Phil Mellor, slipped off at the Nook on lap three of the reduced four-lap race, Dunlop carefully nursed his Honda home to protest about the conditions. 'It was terrible,' he said. 'I never rode conditions like that before in my life. It never should have been run – it was desperate.'

Arai
GEMINI OIL
3

1988

NOBODY DOES IT BETTER

The 1988 Senior and Joey Dunlop heads for his second TT treble. He had already won the F1 and Junior races.

Steve Hislop started practice week by having his first taste of a Superbike on the Mountain course – an F1-spec Honda RC30 – and hated every minute of it. 'It was just too fast for me round the Island at that stage of my career,' he said. 'It felt so scary to ride and wanted to throw me off everywhere so in the end I just backed off and admitted defeat.'

Hislop was much happier on his production RC30 which was around 15mph slower and far less aggressive and flighty on acceleration. He used it to good effect in the opening event of the meeting, the Production Class B race, which he won by 12 seconds from fellow Scot, Brian Morrison.

Morrison turned the tables on Hislop by winning the Production C event and Barry Woodland took class D for the third year running, though in tragic circumstances. When Brian Warburton collided with him at Greeba Bridge, Woodland's brakes were badly affected yet he still managed to win by 16 seconds from Graeme McGregor. Warburton did not survive the collision – he was thrown from his bike and killed.

Mick Boddice had one ambition left to achieve at the TT and that was to win both Sidecar legs in the same week. He finally succeeded with the help of his long-time passenger Chas Birks, who had finally recovered from injuries sustained at the TT two years before. Boddice's first-leg win was made easier by a large fuel tank which negated the need for a fuel stop but he had a harder time of it in leg two when his clutch expired on the first lap.

Joey Dunlop no longer had the big time backing of Honda Britain or Rothmans Honda at the 1988 TT. The firm had scaled down its racing efforts and merely supplied Joey with a production RC30 and a race kit. Joey was not impressed but no-one could have guessed it from his performances that week. He sped off into an early lead in the F1 race and set a new absolute lap record at 118.54mph on his second circuit. Hislop, chasing hard on his standard production RC30, set a time just one second slower and had closed Joey's

Portrait of a master. Joey Dunlop was, quite simply, the greatest pure roads racer of all time.

Kings of the Mountain. Steve Hislop (left) watches winner Joey Dunlop break open the bubbly after the 1988 Senior. Geoff Johnson was third.

initial lead of 49 seconds down to just 20. But it was all in vain as his Honda's ignition switch failed on the fifth lap putting him out of the race. Geoff Johnson fought a tremendous battle with Nick Jefferies for second place until his Bimota failed him on the last lap. This allowed Roger Burnett to take third, despite the fact that he had ridden almost a full lap with a flat rear tyre.

The only drama for Dunlop in the Junior came in the pits when his filler cap fell into the bike's bellypan and caused some chaos. After the offending item had been reclaimed, Dunlop went on to win the race and set the first sub-20 minute lap on a 250cc machine. Second-placed finisher, Brian Reid, had trouble remembering to change gears with his left foot after breaking a toe on his right foot, while Eddie Laycock also rode through the pain barrier with a broken shoulder to clinch third spot.

The Production A race saw the closest ever finish in a TT with Dave Leach beating Geoff Johnson by just 0.8 seconds. Johnson had to console himself with a new lap record.

The Senior provided a classic battle between Joey Dunlop and his countryman Steve Cull who was riding Dunlop's old RS500 two-stroke Honda triple. It was still good enough, in Cull's hands, to set the fastest ever lap of the TT course – 119.08mph – as the two Irishmen slugged it out in the fastest TT to date. Perhaps Cull's pace was just too hot as his expansion chamber blew a hole in itself and dropped him off the pace. To add insult to mechanical injury, his hugely expensive Grand Prix-spec motorcycle then burst into flames on the super fast stretch between Creg-ny-Baa and Brandish while Cull watched helplessly from the side of the road.

Cull's demise promoted Steve Hislop to second place and he was ecstatic at being able to stand on the rostrum next to his TT hero, Dunlop. 'I was so pleased I just didn't know what to do with myself,' he said. 'There I was on the rostrum with the king of the roads himself – it was just incredible. I knew that when I got used to a full-on Superbike I could beat him so I couldn't wait for the following year's TT. But fate was to rob me of the chance to have a full on head-to-head with my hero as he was badly injured just months before the 1989 TT and wasn't able to ride.'

With that Senior win, Joey Dunlop became only the second man in history (the first being Mike Hailwood) to win three TTs in a week, two times over.

And this time around he achieved it without massive support from Honda. Dunlop had now amassed 13 TT victories, just one short of Hailwood and there was much talk about him trying to equal or beat Mike's all-time win tally. But when Dunlop was asked after the race if he planned to do so he replied: 'I don't know. That race took a lot out of me. I'm getting too old for this carry on.'

Roger Marshall finished fourth in what would prove to be his last TT. After coming so close on so many occasions, he never quite achieved the win he so dearly wanted. In his autobiography, *Roger and Out*, he reflected on his TT career: 'I think I was somewhat handicapped by always starting at number 11,' he said, 'because most of the real contenders start inside the first 10. If I had got mixed up in a dice on the road with Joey I know in my own mind I could have stayed with him. I could race against anyone in a man-to-man situation, but maybe I was not the best pacer. The main thing is I came out of the TT completely unscathed and with some great memories despite riding on what I still consider a dangerous course, because if your machine fails there, your life is in the lap of the gods.'

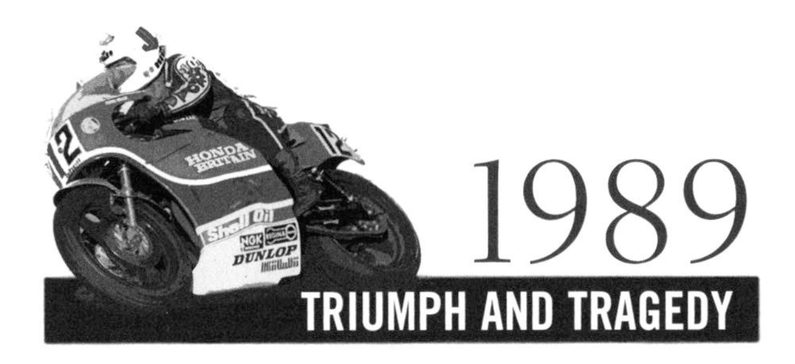

1989
TRIUMPH AND TRAGEDY

The two greatest TT riders of their era lay in hospital beds in Kent on Good Friday of 1989. Steve Hislop had crashed out of the Eurolantic Match races at Brands Hatch and had gravel in his eyes. In the same meeting, Joey Dunlop had sustained the worst injuries of his career. Dunlop had been clipped by Belgian rider Stephane Mertens and slammed hard into the tyre wall at the side of the track. He had broken his leg, shattered his wrist and broken several ribs. Hislop was gutted. 'I realised there was no way he was going to be fit in time to race at the TT. That was a real shame because I was looking forward to a head-to-head battle with us both in our prime.'

Hislop was soon fit and well again but Dunlop faced a long and painful journey back to full fitness. After leaving the hospital, he couldn't walk for six weeks. An 18-inch pin eventually sorted his leg out but it was his right wrist which gave him the most problems. 'I broke the joint in my wrist dozens of times,' Dunlop said. 'They had to piece it together and just wait. Then it started knitting together and it wasn't right so they had to re-break it and piece it together again.'

Hislop was left to carry Honda's hopes at the TT but no one could have expected him to triumph so completely. Three utterly dominant wins and a sensational new outright lap record of 121.34mph – the first ever lap over 120mph – left no one in any doubt that Hislop was the new man to beat. He had stunned the paddock with an unofficial lap of 121.99mph in practice and lined up as favourite for the first race of the week, the Supersport 600/400. In what was Honda's 30th year at the TT, Hizzy opened his account with a victory over Yamaha's Dave Leach by 28 seconds. Jamie Whitham was third ahead of Durex Suzuki team-mate Phil Mellor. Eddie Laycock on another Suzuki took his second TT win in the 400 class with victory over Graeme McGregor and Barry Woodland.

Expectations were high that Steve Hislop could become the first man in history to lap the TT course at 120mph in the Formula 1 race (his 121mph lap had been set in practice and therefore was not 'official'). He certainly had the machinery to do the job – the carburettors alone on his factory Honda RC30 were reckoned to be worth £20,000.

Hizzy set a scorching pace from the outset and broke the 120mph barrier from a standing start to take control of the race. On lap two, he raised his own outright record to 121.34mph. Yet while he looked fast, smooth and inch-perfect to most spectators, Hislop did admit to having the odd moment during the race. 'Coming into the village of Kirkmichael on one particular lap I reached for the brakes, squeezed hard on the lever, and was horrified to notice that nothing was happening – I'd forgotten to pump them and I was doing about 140mph and about to enter a high street lined with houses on both sides! There was nothing for it but to bounce up over the kerb and run onto the narrow pavement, desperately trying to haul the bike round and back onto the road before I smacked a house. I somehow managed to scrub off enough speed, which allowed me to get back on-line and back onto the road with a bump as I hopped off the kerb at about 120mph. It was a scary moment but everyone has them

The winner takes it all. Steve Hislop won three races in 1989 and set a new outright lap record. He is shown with the greatest prize in the sport – the Senior TT trophy.

from time to time at the TT and you've got to expect your fair share.'

Hislop won the race by almost two minutes from Brian Morrison on another Honda and Nick Jefferies on a Yamaha. His speed was such that his *race* average – which included a standing start and slowing down for two pit stops – was quicker than the old *lap* record. He also set the first sub-19-minute lap in TT history.

Hislop's pace inadvertently ended the TT career of future British Superbike star, John Reynolds. Riding in his first – and last – TT, Reynolds was stunned at how fast Hislop was prepared to ride on everyday public roads. Years later he recalled: 'I entered Barregarrow which is a very fast downhill section where the bike's suspension bottoms out and as far as I was concerned, I was going flat out until Stevie came past me like I was standing still. Sparks flew off his bike as the suspension bottomed out and he shot off into the distance towards Kirkmichael with the bike shaking its head all over the place. I thought there and then that if that's what you have to do to win a TT then it's not for me.'

The Sidecar race saw the first of many wins for Manxman Dave Molyneux. With another local, Colin Hardman, in the chair, 'Moly' took full advantage of Mick Boddice's early retirement to lead home Kenny Howles who had slowed up after being given inaccurate signals. Boddice won the second race and, in doing so, finally beat Jock Taylor's eight-year-old lap record.

The Ultra-Lightweight 125 race was reintroduced in 1989 after a 15 year lay-off. With Joey Dunlop out of the action, it fell to his younger brother Robert to uphold family honour and he did so with great success, taking his first TT win from two names that would soon feature prominently on the Isle of Man: Ian Lougher and Carl Fogarty. Dunlop beat Bill Ivy's 21-year-old lap record but, with a best lap of 103.02mph, he was only 3mph up on Ivy's speed, a clear indication of the Londoner's skill.

After finishing fourth in the F1 race and third in the 125s, Carl Fogarty won his first TT in the Production 750 event. Fogarty, Hislop and Dave Leach fought a terrific scrap on the roads together on the last lap, causing some spectators to think they had brought short circuit aggression to the roads and looked a trifle desperate. In his autobiography *Foggy*, Carl first seemed to admit to this then denied it in the same paragraph. 'Leach came back alongside me with the last few corners to go. I held him off through Signpost Corner and the three Governor's corners with some mad riding. People said I was short circuit scraping – throwing the bike on its side, braking as late as possible and running out onto the kerbs – but they were exaggerating as you simply cannot get away with that on the roads.'

Whatever the case, Fogarty won the race from Leach with Hislop in third place after what had been one of the most exciting last laps ever seen on the TT course.

Hislop was lucky to escape the Junior race with his life after a horrific accident at the ultra-fast Quarry Bends. After entering the series of bends slightly faster than he had done in practice, he was thrown from his 250 Honda at 140mph towards a stone wall. Fortunately, when he hit a kerb, it broke his speed and flipped him over so he slid harmlessly down the pavement instead of impacting with the wall. Hizzy had been leading the race by eight seconds before his accident and his exit from the race left Irishman Johnny Rea at the front of the field. Eddie Laycock had been detuned by witnessing what he thought was a fatal crash and it was only when Hizzy sat on a wall and gave him the thumbs up on the next lap that Laycock started charging again. He closed to within 2.8 seconds of Rea at the flag but effectively lost the race out of concern for his fallen comrade.

How lucky Hislop had been was clearly demonstrated in the following race, the Production 1300. Held just after the Junior, the Production race has gone down as one of the blackest moments in the TT's long history. Phil Mellor was one of the most popular riders in British racing and one of the favourites for the Production event. He was fighting for the lead when he crashed at Doran's Bend and sustained fatal head injuries. His team-mate, Jamie Whitham, rode through the wreckage of Mellor's crash and was seriously upset by what he saw. Just a few miles up the road, he too crashed at Quarry Bends but was uninjured. Steve Henshaw was not so fortunate. In trying to avoid Whitham's wreckage, he and Mike Seward touched and, while Seward suffered critical injuries – from which he later recovered – Henshaw lost his life in the crash.

Mick Grant was Mellor and Whitham's team manager in the Durex Suzuki squad and remembers 'Black Wednesday' like it was yesterday. 'I got a message that Mez had crashed and then, about ten minutes later, I got a message that James had crashed. You don't know how serious it is at that stage. As it happened, poor old Mez just made a riding mistake and unfortunately he paid for it with his life. I think he was just diving up the inside of somebody and lost it. In my opinion, James fell off because he'd seen Mez's accident and I think he lost concentration.'

As Grant sombrely admits, his job was made somewhat easier by the experienced TT organisers. 'There is a mechanism within the TT which is actually very good to cope with that sort of thing – unfortunately it's been very well rehearsed.'

While Dave Leach rode superbly to take the win by just 0.8 seconds from Geoff Johnson, his second TT victory has always been overshadowed by the loss of Mellor and Henshaw, two of the UK's best known riders. The fortnight had been one of the blackest ever with five riders in total losing their lives. Sidecar driver John Mulcahy, Sidecar passenger Marco Fattorelli, and Manx solo rider Phil Hogg had all been killed in practice.

For many riders and teams, Mellor and Henshaw's deaths were simply too much and many left the Island immediately, shocked and saddened. Brian Morrison, who had witnessed both fatal crashes flew straight home and Jamie Whitham, who had lost his team-mate and whose crash had inadvertently caused the death of Henshaw, never raced at the TT again.

Hislop decided to stay on for the Senior but faced a much-depleted grid. His attitude summed up the feelings of most other riders who stayed on to race. 'Naturally I was very sad but I had a job to do and I was prepared to do it even though my heart wasn't really in it.' Hizzy did his job in exemplary fashion and stuck in another couple of 120mph laps to win comfortably from Nick Jefferies and Graeme McGregor. In doing so, he became only the third man in TT history to win three races in a week but no one felt like celebrating, least of all Hislop. 'There was no celebration as there would have been any other year. It's ironic that my most successful TT to date had also been one of the most tragic for others. That was a TT I was glad to get home from – after all, five people never made the return trip.'

Out on his own.
Joey Dunlop heads for a 14th TT victory
to equal Mike Hailwood's all-time record.
1992 Ultra-Lightweight 125 race.

CHAPTER 8

1990-99

8
MICHELIN

1990

FOG ON THE MOUNTAIN

"Coming down the Mountain at the end of the last lap towards Creg-ny-Baa with the finish line in sight, the emotion of the moment became overwhelming. I began crying for the first time ever in a race. This was a race that I had seen my dad try and win so many times. It even meant more than the F1 win earlier in the week. This was the main race, before Formula 1 was even invented. To hold those massive trophies, which had been around since 1907, was an incredible feeling. The double TT victory still ranks as one of my biggest achievements.

Carl Fogarty was ecstatic after adding a Senior TT victory to his Formula 1 win earlier in the week. If the 1989 TT had been all about Steve Hislop, then the first year of the new decade belonged to Foggy. The two fastest TT riders of all time were team-mates in 1990 but that only added to the tension in the Honda garage as Hizzy explained. 'Knowing that I was the man he had to beat, Carl refused to speak to me all through TT fortnight, even though we were team-mates and based in the same garage. It was even more ridiculous because we'd been good friends since 1986 when we were both nobodies, but Carl has to do things like that to win. He has to hate his rivals in order to beat them.'

Foggy admitted the charge in his autobiography saying, 'I hardly spoke to him in the build-up to the races. I wanted to hate him because I was so determined to win. This was probably the first time that I had tried to psyche out an opponent.'

Yet the much-anticipated clash of the titans failed to materialise as Hislop had a week to forget, for various reasons, and Fogarty completely dominated the two big races with start-to-finish wins in both.

The deaths of Phil Mellor and Steve Henshaw the previous year had several repercussions on the 1990 TT. The 750 and 1300cc Production races were dropped from the programme on the grounds of safety and riders in all races were now started individually at ten-second intervals instead of in pairs. Sidecars were now restricted to Formula 2 specification, which was 350cc two-strokes or 600cc four-strokes and the number of races was cut from nine to seven.

Joey Dunlop was back at the TT following a year of recuperation but was still far from fully fit and didn't expect any miracles. 'This year I just want to try and finish. If I finish the races at all I'll be happy really.'

Right from the start of race week it was obvious the weather was going to play a big part in things. Rain and mist made tyre choice a lottery in the opening F1 event and when Hislop opted to change wheels just before setting off, he inadvertently cost himself any chance of a win. The new front wheel incorporated inferior brake discs and two trips up the slip roads at Ballacraine and Sulby Bridge put him out of

Carl Fogarty at Ginger Hall in 1990.
He took an F1/Senior double in what was his best year at the TT.

Dave Leach heads for victory in the 1990 Supersport 400 class.

contention. After pitting for another wheel change, he rejoined the race in 39th place but, on the final circuit, set a new absolute lap record at 122.63mph – just to prove a point.

With Hislop out of the running, Fogarty had things all his own way and collected the winner's £6,000 prize money, despite suffering pain from a torn arm muscle sustained in practice. 'I honestly wasn't even trying, ' he said of his first big bike win at the TT. 'I really felt in control. That's the way it goes here sometimes. You don't think you're going fast but you relax and get a good time.'

Nick Jefferies brought his Loctite Yamaha home in second place with Robert Dunlop scoring a superb third on the rotary-engined, British-built JPS Norton. Joey Dunlop had a steady ride round to eighth place.

Dave Leach slashed 14 seconds off the lap record from a standing start and went on to win the Supersport 400 race from Carl Fogarty. Run alongside the SS400 event, the 125cc TT was won by Robert Dunlop for the second year running. Brother Joey had been as high as third before retiring with mechanical problems.

If there was one TT that Steve Hislop was determined to win it was the Junior. He had led the race on several occasions before retiring or crashing but felt 1990 was going to be his year. A little-known Welshman called Ian Lougher thought different. Having never won a TT before, Lougher surprised everyone by battling with Hislop throughout. 'It was the first time I'd had a new bike for the TT and my confidence was up,' Lougher remembers. 'I'd been chatting with Hizzy earlier in the year and he reckoned the Junior lap times would be about 116mph. I was crapping myself because I thought I'd never be able to run at that pace. But I took about 18 seconds off the lap record in practice without trying too hard so by then I knew I could do it. I just thought it would be great to get on the rostrum with Hislop – to stand alongside him would have done me because he's the best TT rider I've ever seen. But to beat him . . .'

The two were never more than seconds apart and it was only a superhuman last lap from Lougher that ensured him of a famous win. He upped the lap record by more than 3mph from 114.04mph to 117.8mph on a lap which is still talked about to this day. 'As I was going down Bray Hill on the last lap I decided to try and put a really fast lap together; to concentrate on every single corner and get it spot-on. As it turned out, it was probably the best lap I've done in 24 years of racing the TT course.'

Hislop also gave it everything he knew on the final circuit. 'It's no exaggeration to say that the last lap of that race was without question the hardest I ever had, and ever would, ride a motorcycle round the Isle of Man,' he admitted. 'I had that thing sliding and decking out everywhere, I was brushing hedges and flying over jumps and just kept the throttle pinned to the stop. I rode the bloody wheels off that bike and thought nobody in the world could have put in a quicker lap but in the end it still wasn't enough.'

Hislop flashed over the line first and there was an agonising wait for Lougher who had started 1m 50s behind the Scotsman. As he took the chequered flag it was revealed that Lougher had won the race by just 1.8 seconds, the fourth closest finish in TT history.

With Sidecars now being restricted to Formula 2 specifications, there would be no more screaming 700cc two-stroke monsters capable of setting 108mph laps. Yet Dave Saville did manage a lap at 100.97mph on his 350 Yamaha and also managed to average over 100mph on his way to victory in both Sidecar legs. His ninth win put him equal with Siegfried Schauzu in the all-time winners' list.

The Supersport 600 race proved to be a race of attrition with fancied runners including Steve Hislop, Carl Fogarty, Dave Leach and Nick Jefferies dropping out early with technical problems. Their demise allowed Ulsterman Brian Reid to take his second TT

Together on the roads: but Steve Hislop's higher starting number means he has made up time on Carl Fogarty and he went on to win the 1991 F1 race.

win ahead of three of his countrymen, Johnny Rea, Steve Cull and Mark Farmer. All four were mounted on FZR600 Yamahas.

Carl Fogarty dominated a delayed Senior race which was run in dreadful mixed conditions – sunshine on one lap and pouring rain on another. Fogarty didn't seem to mind and after Steve Hislop, unhappy with the conditions, pulled out, he had it all his own way to such an extent that he was almost bored. 'When I got +50 and +80 signs,' he said, 'I did a few wheelies to keep myself interested and I waved to the crowds.'

Trevor Nation thrilled the patriotic crowds by finishing in second place on his British-built Norton ahead of the ever-popular Dave Leach. But there was no taking away from Fogarty's F1/Senior double. He had proved that whether it was wet, dry or anywhere in between, he could ride the TT course. In 1991, he would have to ride it faster than ever.

1991
GRUDGE MATCH

Steve Hislop: 'Both Foggy and I were terrified after the first lap of practice. The bikes were so much faster than anything we had ridden there before. I remember going down Sulby Straight for the first time and all I could see was a green blur. The bars were flapping from lock to lock so violently I had double vision and couldn't even see the black of the Tarmac in front.'

To spoil Yamaha's 30th anniversary at the TT, Honda shipped in two of the most exotic machines ever seen on the Isle of Man. The full factory RVFs

Steve Hislop kicks up a storm as he leaves Ramsey on the RVF in 1991.The exotic Honda was one of only two in existence. The other is behind him.

(assigned to Hislop and Fogarty for the F1 race then Hislop and Dunlop for the Senior) may have been two years old, but they were hand-built thoroughbred HRC racers and were the only two examples in existence. Mounted on equal machinery for the first time, Hislop and Fogarty's battle for dominance started from the first lap of practice with each rider setting a new unofficial lap record only to be bettered by the other. Even Fogarty was scared. 'I wasn't up for the race. I had scared myself too many times in the build-up and, at the kind of speeds we were forcing each other to ride at, someone was going to get hurt.'

After Hislop set a new unofficial lap record of 124.36mph, Honda boss, Koichi Oguma, sat his two riders down for a talking to. 'He was going mental at our antics,' Hislop recalled, 'and was terrified that we were going to crash and kill ourselves. He sat Foggy and I down at a table like naughty little schoolchildren. We got a real bollocking for going so fast; apparently we'd scared Oguma-san shitless when he watched us at the bottom of Bray Hill. He shouted: "You two not enemies. Must decide now which one will win big race." '

Naturally, neither rider had any intention of throwing the race and, as they left the meeting, both agreed that no quarter would be asked – or given.

Hislop later admitted that lining up on the Glencrutchery Road for the start of the 1991 F1 race was the most tense experience he ever had in racing. Perhaps fortunately – for safety's sake – the great head-to-head never truly materialised. Nine miles into the race, Hizzy had established a five-second lead and was never to relinquish it. Fogarty blamed fuel starvation problems for slowing him down but Hislop had no such worries. He was clocked at 192mph down the bumpy Sulby Straight and, by the second lap, had caught his team-mate on the roads. The pair then thrilled the crowds with an on-the-roads scrap until they were separated at the pit stops. Hislop went on to win the race at a record average of exactly 121mph. His fastest lap – 123.48mph – was also a new outright lap record.

Mick Boddice added to Honda's joy by taking the firm's first win in a Sidecar TT with victory in leg one then went one better by winning the second race too. What's more, it was the first time a 600cc four-stroke had won an F2 Sidecar race from the previously dominant 350cc Yamahas. Boddice's second win of the week put him on a par with Siggy Schauzu and Dave Saville as the most successful riders ever with nine wins each.

BARRULE PARK
LUXURY
DETACHED
Silkolene

With handlebars turned upside down to ease the pain from a broken collarbone, Robert Dunlop rides through the pain barrier to win the 1991 Junior.

Yamaha finally had something to smile about when Dave Leach had a winning ride in the Supersport 400 event. The Yorkshireman led throughout to take his second consecutive win in the class. Unsure of the wet conditions, Steve Hislop rode steadily to finish second with fellow Scotsman, Jim Moodie, taking his first TT podium in third.

The 125cc race was a family affair between the Dunlop brothers with Joey finally looking like a potential race winner for the first time since 1988. He held a 25-second lead over Robert by the second lap but a slow refuelling stop dropped him out of contention. A record last lap of 106.71mph by Robert was enough to assure him of victory but there was some resentment from Joey fans that his brother had not allowed him to equal Mike Hailwood's record of 14 TT wins. 'It won't help my popularity to have stopped Joey equalling the record,' Robert admitted, 'but we're a competitive family and I'd rather have beat him into second place than beat him for fifth spot.'

Robert Dunlop achieved a lifetime's ambition in winning the Junior race in what was proving to be his most successful TT to date – and he had only just been passed fit to ride after breaking his collarbone at Donington Park. Unperturbed by his injury, Dunlop simply turned his handlebars upside down to give him more leverage and ease the pain. The only concern the Irishman had after taking the chequered flag was how he was going to lift the heavy Junior TT trophy at the presentations with a broken collarbone.

Steve Hislop set the first 115mph lap on a Supersport 600 machine to win the race by 30 seconds from Steve Cull. Bob Jackson, whose last TT podium had been back in 1981, was third.

With Carl Fogarty off on World Superbike duties, Hislop was a clear favourite for the Senior race. While Honda had given Joey Dunlop use of the glorious factory RVF Foggy had raced in the F1 event, the Ulsterman had not had enough practice on the machine and could not match Hislop's pace, even though he set his first ever 120mph on his way to second place. 'It pulled the arms out of me on the first two laps,' he said of the Honda's awesome speed.

Although he was never pushed in the race, Hislop still set the fastest ever race average at 121.09mph and joined the exclusive company of Joey Dunlop and Mike Hailwood in becoming only the third man to achieve two TT trebles.

1992 MAKING HISTORY

'I was fighting the bike all the way but knew it was useless. There was an almighty bang on impact, total blackness and then I was just floating, higher and higher. The little white houses got smaller and smaller and I was thinking to myself, "This is definitely it – I'm on my way to Heaven!" The feeling wasn't bad at all, my mind was quite peaceful, except for the terrible noise which wouldn't stop. A girl's face floated into my vision and spoke to me. "Everything's fine, don't worry Phillip, you're okay now with us. You're in the helicopter and we're taking you to the hospital – you've only been out a few minutes." "Heaven will have to wait a bit longer for me then!" I thought – and that was the end of my TT for that year.'

Phillip McCallen's crash in the 1990 Senior hadn't put him off the TT. In fact, by 1992 the 14 times Irish champion was desperate to win the last big road race which had eluded him. After being the first man to win

Round the houses. Joey Dunlop is about to equal Mike Hailwood's all-time record of 14 TT wins. 1992 Ultra-Lightweight 125 race.

a Newcomer's race and a Manx GP proper in the same week in 1988, he had steadily worked his way up the TT leader board and now, as Honda Britain's main man for the TT, much was expected of him. He would not disappoint.

Honda's presence on the Island was significantly reduced for 1992. There were no exotic RVFs and star riders, Steve Hislop and Carl Fogarty, had left the team in order to pursue their short circuit ambitions. By the time the TT came around however, both riders were struggling in their new arenas and agreed to accept last-minute rides from unlikely sources. Against his better judgement, Hislop agreed to ride a leased Norton – a bike which he considered to be 'a bit of a joke'. There only remained the problem of the team finding £25,000 to finance the effort.

Fogarty accepted a Loctite Yamaha ride on an ageing OWO1 – ironically, the bike which Hislop would have been riding had he not quit the team earlier in the year.

Both machines were a far cry from the factory Hondas of the previous year but the sniggers in the paddock only strengthened Hislop's resolve. 'You could feel people were looking at the both of us sneering "Come on – let's see what you can do without your fancy factory bikes." It made me only more determined.'

From the drop of the flag in the opening F1 race, Carl Fogarty took control and built up a huge lead of 46 seconds before striking trouble on the penultimate lap. 'I changed down to second at the Bungalow and there was this horrible noise,' Fogarty explained. The 'horrible noise' turned out to be his Yamaha's gearbox destroying itself and putting Foggy out of the race. Hislop, in third place for the first five laps, had been having his own problems; his Norton was overheating

Oh brother!
Joey Dunlop is flanked by brother Robert (left) and Mick Lofthouse after winning the 1992 Ultra-lightweight race – a victory which put him level with Mike Hailwood on 14 TT wins.

Right: Carl Fogarty rode his Yamaha OW01 so hard in 1992 that it started 'falling apart.' His outright lap record of 123.61mph was not beaten for seven years.

and he spent precious time in the pits having the front mudguard removed to assist cooling. He was also suffering from lack of time on the bike – before TT practice started, he'd only managed eight laps of Oulton Park before the Norton blew up.

Fogarty's demise promoted Hislop up to second spot behind new race leader Phillip McCallen, who kept a consistent pace to take his first TT win.

After five years of trying, Geordie Telecom engineer Geoff Bell not only won a Sidecar TT, but did the double on his 600cc Yamaha. Bell's win in the first leg was helped when Mick Boddice and Dave Saville both suffered mechanical problems, but he led throughout the second race and set three consecutive 101mph laps to take a convincing victory.

The noise at the Villa Marina prize-giving ceremony was almost enough to bring the roof down when Joey Dunlop walked onstage with his young family to be awarded first prize in the 125cc race. Not only had he won his first TT since 1988, he had equalled Mike Hailwood's all-time record of 14 TT wins. Joey had fought a terrific scrap with his brother Robert to finally take victory by 8.4 seconds – partly thanks to Robert's cast-offs. 'We worked on the bike until 1.30 in the morning of the race,' he revealed, 'and found one of the engine mountings had broken. We couldn't get a replacement at that time of the day so we used one that Robert had thrown out.'

Joey had also starved himself to the point of illness in the two weeks leading up to the TT in order to

LAZER
4
DUNLOP
LOCTITE
MOTUL

In 1992, Steve Hislop (centre) won the Senior TT on a British bike for the first time since 1961 when Mike Hailwood also rode a Norton to victory. He is flanked by Carl Fogarty (right) and Robert Dunlop.

improve the power-to-weight ratio which is so crucial in 125 racing. He was so undernourished that he withdrew from the Senior race later in the week after suffering double vision.

In the Supersport 400 race, Brian Reid gave Yamaha its 100th win in its 31st year of TT competition. Reid continued his superb form in the Junior to take his fourth TT win in four different classes. Once again the Junior Jinx struck Steve Hislop as, in a near carbon-copy of the 1989 race, he was beaten in a last lap dash by just 3.2 seconds. 'I've never come down the Mountain that quick before,' Reid admitted after the race. 'I think I surprised Steve just how quick I got down.'

From having won no TTs at the beginning of the week, 14 times Irish champion, Phillip McCallen, bagged his second win in the Supersport 600 race. After guessing his suspension settings, the Irishman found his Honda CBR600 quite a handful. 'I had a few moments in the race because of it,' he said, 'but I felt under control. Mind you, I bet I didn't look under control!'

Motor Cycle News called the 1992 Senior TT 'The most exciting Senior since Hailwood and Agostini in 1967' and it was no exaggeration. It was not only the fastest race in TT history but also one of the closest, and it was fought out between the two fastest men of the era, Steve Hislop and Carl Fogarty. It would also result in an outright lap record which would stand for seven years.

As Hislop lined up on the machine his team boss described as 'a bike built in a shed in Lichfield', he was aware that the last time a Norton had won the Senior TT was in 1961 when Mike Hailwood rode one to victory. But Carl Fogarty wasn't in a sentimental mood and set a cracking pace to lead by the end of the first lap. Hislop chased hard on the viciously fast Norton but was struggling to control it. 'I was hitting bumps and getting lifted up out of my seat,' he said afterwards, 'and the wind at those speeds was really wrenching my neck and shoulders, threatening to blow me off the back of the bike.'

By the pit stops at the end of the second lap, Hislop was 2.8 seconds ahead but lost the lead by

Hail Hislop! 31 years after a British bike had last won the Senior TT, Steve Hislop regained the trophy for Norton.

taking on a fresh rear tyre while Fogarty only stopped for fuel. He had all the work to do again. At half race distance, Hislop had closed to within a second of his rival who was trying everything he knew to stay ahead. 'I was riding so hard that the bike was falling apart around me,' Fogarty said. 'None of the clocks were working, the front fork seal had gone, the rear brake was bent up, the rear shock was broken – the bike was an absolute mess.'

The lead continued to see-saw back and forth but, as the pair entered the final lap, Hislop held the advantage. Fogarty said: 'I was nine seconds behind at the start of the final lap which was a lot to make up. To make matters worse, the exhaust blew coming over the Mountain as I made that final push.'

Hislop knew his rival would pull out all the stops in a final bid for glory. 'There was no doubt in my mind that he'd try everything that he knew on that final circuit.'

Fogarty's final lap was astonishing: his speed of 123.61mph was faster than either rider had managed on infinitely superior factory machinery one year before. Yet it wasn't enough. After Fogarty flashed across the line there was an agonising three-minute wait before Hislop was due. 'On the last few miles I started talking to the bike,' Hislop admitted. 'I was urging it home, nursing it every inch and mile of the way.'

The commentator's countdown ensured everyone knew the result as Hislop flashed across the line – 4.4 seconds to the good. He had won the Senior TT on a British-built Norton: the impossible dream had come true. 'I'd never seen anything like it on my final circuit,' Hislop said. 'It must have been incredible for all those fans to see a British bike threatening to win the Senior TT after more than 30 years and it was very hard not to be distracted by them. Every vantage point was packed with fans hanging out onto the road, waving their programmes, cheering and taking photographs – it was a spectacular sight.'

After one of the greatest races of modern times, both Hislop and Fogarty announced they would not be returning to the TT.

Keeping it in the family. Nick Jefferies taking his only TT win – the 1993 F1. His father Allan, brother Tony, and nephew David, all raced on the Mountain course.

After nine years of trying and four second places, Nick Jefferies finally won a TT in 1993. The 41-year-old took control of the Formula 1 race on lap two and never looked back to record what would prove to be his one and only TT victory. 'I expected to get on the rostrum,' he said, 'but to win . . . it was a dream to win a TT – almost an impossible dream.'

Ulsterman Mark Farmer had set the early pace on his Ducati 888 and also set the fastest lap of the race at 120.58mph before striking mechanical trouble. Phillip McCallen was carrying injuries from a Mallory Park crash and struggled to control his Honda RC30 round the Mountain course. A lengthy pit stop then ruined any chance of a win and McCallen was forced to settle for second spot as veteran Steve Ward took third.

Manxman Dave Molyneux took his home-built outfit to a double win in the Sidecar races and denied both Dave Saville and Mick Boddice any chance of becoming the first man to score ten Sidecar TT race wins. Saville was second in the first leg – without a clutch – but retired in race two, while Boddice retired from both events. Molyneux set a new lap record of 104.27mph.

By the end of the 125cc race, Joey Dunlop had become the most successful rider in TT history with 15 wins compared to Mike Hailwood's 14. And the first person Dunlop paid tribute to after his incredible achievement was the late, great Hailwood himself. 'If he'd been here, I know he would have been the first man to congratulate me. He was that kind of bloke. I admired him.'

Joey's race had almost ended on the first lap when he struck clutch trouble, his lever coming right back to the bar with no effect. For the remainder of the lap, he rode single-handedly along the straights while adjusting the clutch with his left hand. Once he'd regained the use of his clutch, Dunlop's only major problem was with well-meaning fans who were going crazy round the course. 'The reception I got on the last lap was incredible,' he said. 'Way greater than last year when I equalled the record. But there were some fans *on* the track waving to me on the last lap which put me off a bit. Take Rhencullen. I always line up on one of the telegraph poles but I couldn't see the bottom of the pole for people waving. The crowd was going crazy – and I reckon every marshal on the TT course must have waved at me.'

Scotsman Jim Moodie took his first TT win in the Supersport 400 class. Shattering lap and race records on his FZR400 Yamaha, Moodie caught his closest challenger, fellow-Scot Iain Duffus, on the Mountain on the last lap and stuck with him to the flag. 'Jim was messing about, giving me the 'V' sign right across the Mountain,' Duffus said of his friend and countryman.

Two days later, Jim Moodie became the first man to do a Supersport double when he also won the 600 race. After leading from start to finish, the Scot, almost overcome with emotion said 'I can't believe it. Winning two TTs is the high point of my whole racing career.'

Having his first ride on a 250 since 1989, Moodie

Left: All-time greatest. By the end of this 1993 Ultra-Lightweight race, Joey Dunlop had won more TTs than any man in history.

Above: Steve Hislop returned to the TT in 1994 and blew everyone else into the dust.

enjoyed another good outing in the Junior, only losing out to eventual winner, Brian Reid, by 7.2 seconds. One of the pre-race favourites, Phillip McCallen, made an embarrassing error when he forgot to come in for fuel. The Irishman had been too dialled into a battle with Dave Milling to remember his stop. 'Dave was holding me up in the corners but I couldn't pass him on the straights because my bike was so slow,' McCallen says. 'I put my head down coming off the Mountain, really determined to get rid of him and get going. I was concentrating so hard that I forgot to come in for petrol. I just forgot. I got a real bollocking from Honda for that.'

McCallen made no such mistakes in the Senior, taking a start-to-finish win ahead of team-mate Nick Jefferies and privateer Steve Ward. Jefferies had caught a bug and slept for 15 hours the day before the race but crawled out of bed to record an impressive second. Ward's ride was equally heroic on a bike his wife had bought for him five years previously.

1994 BACK FOR MORE

The sensation of the 1994 TT was Steve Hislop's return, even if it was against his own better judgement. 'It's not that I wanted to race there,' he admitted, 'but Honda was very keen to promote the RC45 so it was written into my contract that I had to race at the TT.'

After just one lap on the new RC45, Hizzy was ready to pull out. 'If I had ever needed convincing that the TT was too dangerous, riding the RC45 round there was proof enough – it was absolutely lethal at the beginning of practice week. On my first lap I clipped a kerb at 150mph on Bray Hill then smacked my leg on a wall at Ginger Hall and ripped my leathers and my

Above: When the rear wheel of Robert Dunlop's Honda RC45 disintegrated, he was thrown into a stone wall and suffered a broken arm and leg as well as damage to his nervous system.

Right: Mark Farmer at Ballacraine in practice on the revolutionary Britten in 1994. He crashed and lost his life just a few miles farther down the road.

knee open. The bike had a mind of its own and just went wherever the hell it wanted. It was so out of control that, for the first time in my life, I considered withdrawing my entry and going home – and so, I think, did Joey Dunlop. He came into the garage on the first night of practice, threw the bike into his van and said "That thing's not going to kill me."'

As Hislop spent practice week trying to set up his bike, he was given another harsh reminder of how deadly the TT course can be when Mark Farmer, one of the UK's top riders, was killed at the Black Dub after crashing the revolutionary Britten V1000.

The Formula 1 race was to provide another shock when Robert Dunlop suffered a horrendous accident just after Ballaugh Bridge. As he landed from the famous jump and accelerated away, his rear wheel totally disintegrated and he was thrown into a stone wall at 130mph. Dunlop was rushed to intensive care with injuries to his nervous system as well as a broken arm and leg. As he lay fully conscious by the side of the road, Dunlop was not to know that he would never race a Superbike again and that his injuries would never fully heal. His Superbike career was over.

Dunlop's accident came in the second running of the F1 race after the first attempt had been called off. The race had been started in dry conditions on its traditional Saturday slot but riders encountered heavy rain, mist and fog during their first lap and most were on slick tyres. Many top riders, including Hislop and Dunlop, pulled in after one lap.

Nigel 'Cap' Davies was leading the race when it was finally red-flagged after two laps and, unsurprisingly, he was angered by the decision. 'I can't believe it,' he said. 'A wet race was my only chance of winning.'

The rerun was held in perfect conditions the following day and Hislop promptly did a disappearing act. With Phillip McCallen failing to find a rhythm in the early laps, the flying Scot built up an eventual lead of 1m 24.6s to draw level with Stanley Woods and Giacomo Agiostini on 10 TT wins. While Hislop had no real problems to report, Joey Dunlop had his hands full avoiding stray dogs and errant vans. 'I was just out of Barregarrow when I saw a van on the left-hand side of the road' said the Ulsterman, who just managed to swerve past the Highways Department worker who had 'forgotten' there was a race on. One lap later, the road was obstructed again, this time at the Highlander. 'A dog was running about on the track,' Dunlop said, 'but the marshals gave me a good warning just as they had for the truck.'

Despite his problems, Dunlop finished third behind team-mate McCallen whom he diced with on the roads for the last two laps.

In only his second TT, Cumbrian Rob Fisher and passenger Mick Wynn won both Sidecar races and set a new lap record just 2mph short of the outright record

Flying Scotsmen.
Ian Simpson leads Iain Duffus through Parliament Sqaure in the 1994 Supersport 600 race. Duffus took the win after Simmo swallowed his contact lens.

set five years previously before F2 restrictions came in. Wynn led every lap of both races to take home the maximum prize money, though still only a paltry £7,200. Mick Boddice, still chasing an elusive 10th win finished third in both legs while local ace Dave Molyneux secured two runner-up spots.

With Robert Dunlop lying in a hospital bed, Joey had no competition in the 125 class. The seemingly unstoppable Ballymoney publican flashed across the line 71 seconds ahead of fellow Ulsterman Dennis McCullough to take his TT win tally to 16. After dedicating the win to Robert, Joey said, 'I just wish Robert had been out there racing with me.'

Mark Farmer's death in practice left Jim Moodie agonising over his TT future. The two had been close friends as well as team-mates in the Loctite Yamaha team. Unable to sleep since the crash, Moodie eventually decided to do what he did best and went out and won the new Single-Cylinder race and dedicated the win to his late friend. Moodie finished the inaugural event – for thoroughbred single-cylinder racers – eight seconds ahead of Robert Holden after he had inadvertently sprayed the Kiwi with oil when his bike developed a leak. While Holden complained, Moodie responded: 'There was oil coming out of the bike and he was complaining that it was going over him. But it was actually going over my back tyre so I think I was getting the worst of it.'

Moodie was involved in an all-Scottish battle in the following Supersport 600 race. With his friends, Ian Simpson and Iain Duffus both gunning for their first TT wins, just one second split the three at Ramsey on lap one. Moodie posted the fastest lap of the race on the second circuit before crashing at the 130mph Black Dub – exactly where Mark Farmer had crashed in practice. As if to prove how random fate can be, he escaped an almost identical accident to that which killed his friend, with nothing more than a broken thumb. 'It was just a coincidence that I crashed at the same spot where Mark was killed,' Moodie says now. 'My bike wasn't handling well and I was desperate to try and break away from Ian Simpson and Iain Duffus and I just tried a wee bit too hard.'

A super-fast pit stop by Duffus allowed him to catch Simpson on the road and from that point on all he had to do was keep the Dalbeattie rider in sight to be sure of victory. Simpson, however, was struggling to keep Duffus in sight. 'I lost both my contact lenses and one of them got stuck to my lips and I got so annoyed with it I bit it and swallowed it. I couldn't see a thing so I just followed Iain Duffus for a lap and a half. It's a good job he never went into a hedge 'cos I'd have gone straight in behind him.'

Duffus towed Simpson home and was ecstatic with his victory. 'It's a dream come true,' he said. 'I can't believe this is happening.'

Phillip McCallen lost the Junior race for the second year in succession by running out of fuel. After he simply forgot to come into the pits in 1993, his team made sure he got 'Fuel' signals to remind him to stop this time around. He did stop, but pulled away again before his bike was fully fuelled up. While team boss Neil Tuxworth blamed his rider for pushing the fuel pump nozzle away too early, McCallen denies this. 'The mechanics just didn't put enough fuel in. It was just one of them things – we were all too keen to try and win.'

McCallen had been leading the race by 16 seconds from Joey Dunlop who had decided to settle for second place because of problems with his footrest. 'My right footpeg was hanging off so I had to rest my boot on the exhaust.' When McCallen ran out of fuel just five miles from home, Dunlop claimed an unexpected victory.

Jim Moodie won his second TT of the week in the Supersport 400 race. Riding with a broken thumb from his crash the previous day, the gritty Scot was still in turmoil over Mark Farmer's death but admitted: 'That was the best my head has been all week. I got my first lap sorted and won the race early on.'

Steve Hislop took his 11th and final TT win in the Senior race. The super Scot disappeared just as he had done in the F1 race at the beginning of the week and there was nothing that Phillip McCallen or Joey Dunlop could do about it. With no need to break the lap record, Hizzy eased up on the fifth lap but still won by 1m 15s. 'It was an easy run for me,' he admitted. 'I laughed to myself at Sulby Bridge on lap one when my first signal said plus six seconds. By the end of the race I was popping wheelies and waving to the crowd.'

Hislop's 11th win put him third in the all-time winners' list behind Dunlop and Mike Hailwood but he decided not to add to his tally. 'As I got older I became more aware of the risks,' he later admitted. 'The dangers of the TT just become more apparent and I started thinking about them more.'

Hislop went on to have a successful racing career on short circuits and won the British Superbike championship three times. He was the reigning champion in 2003 and on the verge of retiring from the sport when he lost his life in a helicopter crash near his home town of Hawick in the Scottish Borders. He is still regarded as one of the greatest TT riders of all time.

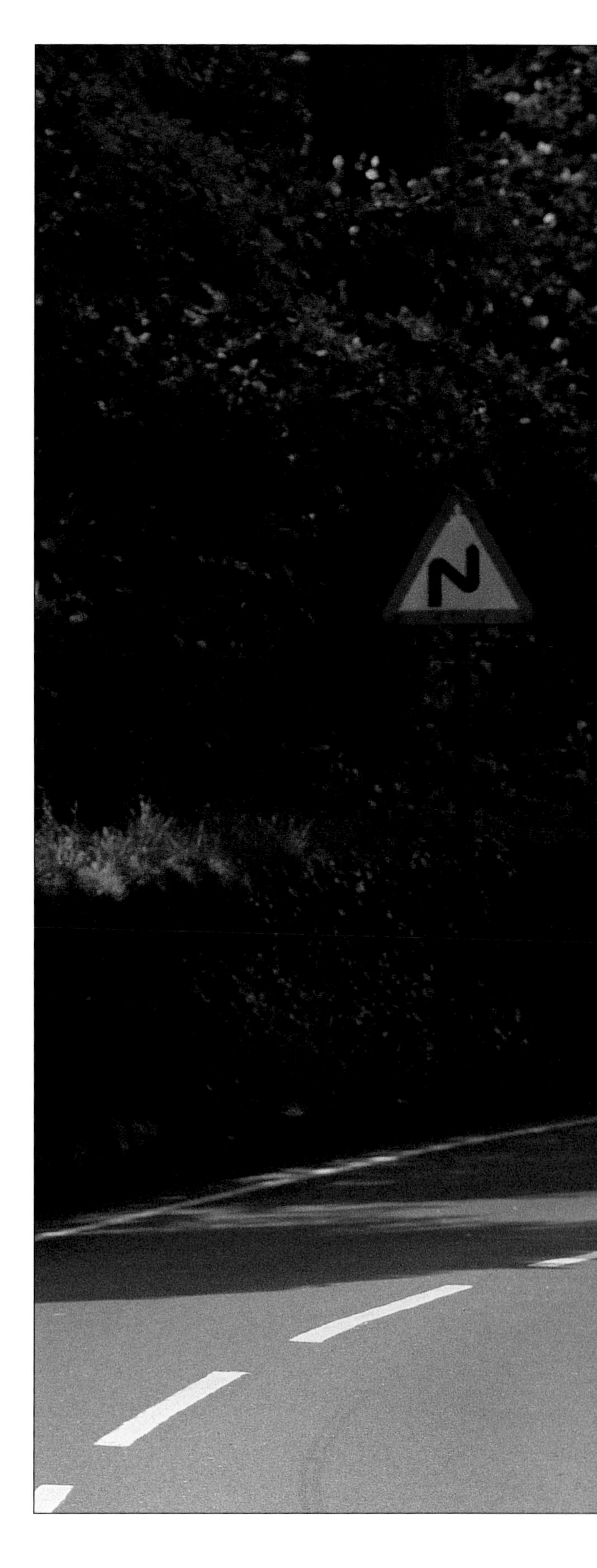

1995

OVER THE EDGE

"I didn't know what was wrong; I was in such a state of nervous tension it's difficult to describe. The only similar situation I can think of is if you can imagine you're the pilot of an aircraft. Now imagine it's got a terrible problem, you're hurtling towards the ground fighting the controls all the way, knowing any second now you're going to crash.

The Guv'nor. Joey Dunlop trickles into Governor's Bridge in 1995. He took his Honda RC45 to a long overdue victory in the Senior.

Phillip McCallen was racing round the TT course at 190mph with a loose rear wheel which threatened to fall off at any moment. It was no one's fault; the new wheel simply didn't fit his Honda RC45 as well as it should have done and the extra movement that caused had resulted in the wheel nut chewing right into the hub of the wheel. According to McCallen: 'The whole thing was only being held on by the remains of the nut, tight up against the fragile little sprung 'R' clip which is only designed to stop the nut coming off, not to hold a whole wheel on.

Sensing runaway leader McCallen was having problems, Joey Dunlop started closing the gap but, after having his own airbox problems to contend with, he lost out to McCallen by 18 seconds at the finish.

Privateer Simon Beck was thrilled with his third place finish on a Ducati 916 behind the two factory Hondas, yet one more mile and he would have been out of the race. 'The clutch exploded at the Nook,' he explained. 'I held it on the rev limiter all the way from Governor's and crossed the line in sixth gear doing about 30mph.' Beck was quick to thank his parents who had remortgaged their house to raise funds for his TT effort.

Rob Fisher pulled off another stunning double in the Sidecar events meaning he had won four races from six starts at the TT. He also set new lap and race records for the F2 class and predicted the less powerful machines would soon topple Mick Boddice's six-year-old outright lap record set on a 700cc two-stroke Yamaha. Fisher's best lap of 107.67mph was only eight seconds short of the fastest ever time.

With Joey Dunlop and Ian Lougher both retiring early on, the 125 race was thrown wide open. Mick

Robert Holden takes the equisite Ducati Supermono to victory in the Singles race.

Lofthouse held a six-second lead going into the last lap but was unaware of just how fast the largely unknown Mark Baldwin was chasing him. Lofthouse was already celebrating a TT victory in the paddock when Baldwin crossed the line two minutes later and the timekeepers announced he had won the race by six-tenths of a second. It was the third closest finish in TT history, and the closest ever in a staggered-start race. Lofthouse admitted he was 'gutted' on hearing the news as he'd eased up on the last lap thinking he was safe. Unemployed Baldwin also set a new lap record at 109.01mph and said, 'It's incredible – a dream come true. I thought a rostrum finish may be possible but I never thought I would take the lap record.' It would be Baldwin's one and only TT victory.

The Singles race, run alongside the 125s, saw another new winner in the shape of New Zealander Robert Holden. After six years of competing in the TT he finally took a victory on the exquisite little Ducati Supermono.

Joey Dunlop made up for his disappointment in the 125s with a perfect ride in the Lightweight 250 race, so-called because the Junior event (which had previously been for 250cc machines) was now for 600cc four-stroke bikes. His start-to-finish victory proved he could still cut it against much younger competition with young guns including James Courtney and Phillip McCallen left struggling in his wake.

With the Supersport 600 race being dropped from the programme, the Junior was now the only race for 600cc machines. Phillip McCallen started the race as hot favourite but when his CBR600 refused to pull top revs, he was forced to ride out of his skin in a bid to overtake race leader Iain Duffus. 'The bike wouldn't rev on the first lap because of dirt in the carbs,' he says. 'It got better with each lap and when it cleared on the fourth lap and revved out to 13,500rpm it felt like I had another cylinder. From that point on I rode that bike so hard – 200 per cent. I was drifting and sliding out of every single corner – doing two-wheeled slides right out to the kerbs. I had it flat on its side in fifth and sixth gear in places but I still felt I was in control – just because there was a kerb or a wall there, it didn't put me off. When you feel a bike that good, when the tyres are working and the suspension's working, there's just a super harmony between the rider and the machine and you can feel every single thing that's going on. You can take the bike to the edge without going over it. But mistakes can still happen and when I changed down for the Waterworks I hit neutral and couldn't get the bike stopped. I tried to bounce it off the kerb to try and stay on the course but it didn't happen and I crashed out.'

Iain Duffus en route to his second and last TT victory in the 1995 Junior.

McCallen's exit left Duffus with an unassailable lead and he took the win from Nick Jefferies by 25.5 seconds. Colin Gable took third place.

Even the most imaginative TT observers had run out of expletives by the time Joey Dunlop wrapped up the Senior TT. At 43 years of age, he once again showed younger challengers the way to ride a motorcycle and took his overall tally of wins to an unprecedented 19. It was Dunlop's first Senior victory since 1988 and it proved the doubters – who thought Joey's days on big bikes were over – wrong. His mechanic, Sammy Graham, put Dunlop's revival down to a new attitude. 'He stopped smoking, which helped a lot, and started training. It transformed him. He was tired after a TT, sure, but as sound as anyone else.'

Dunlop's task had been made somewhat easier when Phillip McCallen left the Island to race in a Thunderbike round at the Italian Grand Prix and therefore missed the Senior race, but he still managed to beat hard-charging Scot Iain Duffus on a Ducati by more than 30 seconds. Steve Ward, in his first ever factory ride took the Castrol Honda to third place and set the fastest lap of the week at 121.73mph. It would be his last TT. Steve Ward died after crashing in Sweden, just two months before TT96.

1996

FOUR IN A WEEK

An all-too familiar dark cloud hung over practice week in 1996 as the TT lost two of its best-known riders in separate incidents. Robert Holden was killed after crashing at Glen Helen and Mick Lofthouse lost his life near Milntown. Holden was top of the practice leader board on his Ducati 916 for both the F1 and Senior races while Lofthouse topped the 125 times and was second fastest in the 250s.

Yet no matter how great the tragedies at the TT, the racing always goes ahead and 1996 saw Phillip McCallen set a unique record of winning four TTs in a week. He remains the only man ever to have achieved this. With Joey Dunlop taking another two victories, Honda won every solo class it entered.

McCallen's winning streak began in the F1 race, though fuel starvation problems almost cost him the win. At times, his semi-factory Honda was pulling only 120mph instead of 180mph and to counter this, McCallen used the slipstream of Michael Rutter's Ducati to tow him along. He still won the race by over a minute from Nick Jefferies with Rutter in third.

Dave Molyneux went so fast in winning both Sidecar races that some of his rivals suspected he was using illegal avgas and an oversized engine. His new lap record of 111.02mph was way faster than anyone could have expected – the existing record being 107.67mph. Moly's speed was also much quicker than Mick Boddice's record from the old days of 700cc outfits and many thought that record would never be beaten. Molyneux was furious at the slurs on his reputation and offered to have his machine stripped and the fuel checked immediately after his second win of the week. Everything was found to be completely legal. 'They were even laying bets in the paddock that I would get found cheating,' said the Manxman. 'Even people I had real respect for were suggesting it. Now I know they are just a bunch of back-stabbers and, to be honest, it sickens me.'

In the year that he was awarded an MBE to add to his OBE – for his charity trips to Romania, Bosnia and

Unbeatable. Phillip McCallen took an unprecedented four wins in a week in 1996. He remains the only man to have done so.

Albania – Joey Dunlop scored his 20th TT win with an impressive ride in the Lightweight 250 race. The race had been shortened to two laps due to poor weather but visibility on the Mountain was so bad that many thought the race should never have been run at all. Dunlop had been neck and neck with Gavin Lee at Ramsey on the final lap but Joey used his superior course knowledge to eventually take the race win by four seconds. Lee who had led the previous day's 250 race before retiring, was hugely disappointed. 'I couldn't see a thing over the Mountain on lap two and I had to back off,' he said. 'I haven't got 20 years experience here like Joey.'

The Singles race was also shortened but it produced a close on-the-roads battle between Jim Moodie and David Morris. Moodie's bike misfired for most of the race and probably would not have lasted a full four laps but he managed to coax it round two circuits to beat Morris by ten seconds.

The Junior saw the TT debut of yet another member of the Jefferies family – David. Following in the footsteps of his grandfather Allan, his uncle Nick and his father Tony, David Jefferies finished in 16th place and loved every minute of his debut, saying, 'Racing on the roads is fun. It's like going down to the shops – only much faster.'

At the front of the race, Phillip McCallen dominated to take his second win of the week. Riding the same 600cc machine he'd been racing on short circuits all year, he had expected nothing less than a win. 'If I couldn't win this,' he said, 'I might as well have gone home.'

After the tragedies of 1989, Production racing made a return to the Isle of Man in 1996. By now it was agreed that the bikes handled much better than their predecessors and tyre technology had also improved vastly so, in theory at least, the machines should be much safer than before.

All time greats.
The legendary Geoff Duke presents new hero, Phillip McCallen with the Senior TT trophy in 1996.

Over half the entrants were mounted on Honda FireBlades, a bike which Phillip McCallen had helped to develop. And because of this, he felt he had to win the race. 'After being involved in the bike's development, I had no excuses not to win the TT. In fact, I felt obliged to win it for Honda, even though the bike was four years old by then.'

McCallen didn't disappoint his Honda bosses, winning the race by six seconds from fellow Blade rider, Iain Duffus. His success saw sales of the road bike double in the second half of the year, proving that the TT was still as important to road bike sales as it had been in its infancy. 'I told Mr Baba (Tadao Baba, creator of the FireBlade) that I'd win that race for him and it meant a lot to him,' says McCallen. 'He's a man who doesn't say much but he was very happy that day.'

With Phillip McCallen having already taken three wins, all eyes were on him in the Senior to see if he could become the first man in TT history to win four in a week. And the possibility of achieving that unique record even distracted McCallen himself during the race. 'I was going pretty steady until the fifth lap when I started to switch off and lose my concentration. I was thinking about getting my fourth TT win in a week and that's when I started making a few silly mistakes.'

Despite this, McCallen was never headed in the six-lap race and in a week totally dominated by Honda, Joey Dunlop and Nick Jefferies gave the Japanese firm a clean sweep of the Senior rostrum.

Even though McCallen had won more races in a week than any man in history, he still felt he could have done better. 'It should have been five wins that week but the Lightweight 250 didn't go to plan,' he says. 'The bike had a hole in the exhaust the size of your fist so it was losing power. The slower the bike got, the harder I rode it to compensate, and the harder I rode, the bigger the hole in the exhaust got as I scraped it round corners.'

A hero's return.
A sem-crippled Robert Dunlop returned to take third place in the 1997 125cc race three years after his near-fatal crash at Ballaugh.

1997
THE 11TH MILESTONE

Once again, practice week was marred by the death of a popular TT rider when Colin Gable was killed at Ballagarey and once again, his fellow riders did their best to push the dangers of the TT from their minds and carry on racing.

Phillip McCallen had a relatively easy win in the Formula 1 race after his two main rivals succumbed to problems. Michael Rutter was still in pain from three recently broken ribs and Joey Dunlop gave up the chase after a slow pit stop. Simon Beck had looked certain to take a podium position but ran out of fuel 400 yards from his second pit stop and had to push and paddle his bike into his pit. 'I ran alongside the bike in my helmet and leathers and got so hot I thought I was going to puke,' said Beck. An exhausted Beck refuelled and set off again but could only finish ninth after losing so much time.

After 30 years of trying, Roy Hanks finally won a TT with victory in Sidecar Race A. But there was even more for the Hanks family to celebrate when Roy's nephew, Tom Hanks, took the overall victory with a third in the first leg and second in race two. Rob Fisher bounced back from an engine blow up in race one to win the second race . Wendy Davis made history by becoming the first female Sidecar driver to compete in the TT. She finished in 41st and 42nd positions.

Phillip McCallen had still not won a 250cc race at the TT and by 1997, he was getting desperate. And when Joey Dunlop pulled out a healthy lead in the race, McCallen stepped over the edge. 'I got a sign that I was 20 seconds down and I just flipped,' he now admits. 'I rode like someone possessed – so hard it was unbelievable. I was a silly boy and tried to make all that time up in one section instead of over a full lap. Going through Rhencullen the bike was right on its side – I was just holding it flat out everywhere. I really shouldn't have been riding that hard but I was so mad with myself because I was more desperate than anything to win that 250 race. Coming into the first right-hander at Quarry Bends I'd usually knock it back a gear but I decided to hold it flat out in top then brake really hard and knock it down two gears for the following left. I held the throttle against the stop and tipped the bike in, flat on its side. Whether it was the camber change on the road or not, I don't know, but I just lost the front. Everything went dead quiet – so quiet that I actually heard the crowd gasp as I slid down the road. When I got up the pain was unbelievable – it was the first time I'd had a proper beating at 150mph. I had badly crushed my left hand and I had friction burns everywhere and gravel all through my legs. I got into a hot bath and my wife scrubbed the gravel out of my legs with a scrubbing brush. I had another race in two days so I just had to get better.'

With McCallen crashing out, Joey Dunlop took yet another victory in the class he had almost made his own. It was his fourth consecutive Lightweight win and his 22nd victory in all. Dunlop won the race by 47 seconds from Ian Lougher who in turn was just 1.4 seconds ahead of a new rising star at the TT – John McGuinness. Like most riders who race at the TT, McGuinness was fulfilling a lifelong ambition. 'I remember going to the TT with my folks when I was a kid,' he says, 'and we watched from Bray Hill and, like anyone who watches a race bike go down Bray Hill for the first time, I nearly jumped out of my skin. But at the same time, I decided there and then that I wanted to do that someday.'

McGuinness made his TT debut in 1996; a lack of funds preventing him mounting a challenge any earlier. 'I was brought up on a council estate and used to go club racing on Giros so the TT was completely out of my reach in my early days of racing. I even picked mussels in Morecambe Bay for a while to make ends meet. You need a good team and a good bike for the TT and I just didn't have the money.'

When he had outgrown his youthful enthusiasm, McGuinness began to have doubts about racing between stone walls and thought long and hard about whether it was the right thing to do. 'It took me a while to make up my mind about racing at the TT,' he admits. 'One day I'd decide that I wanted to do it then I'd think about the dangers and decide against it. Eventually, in 1996, I said to my team boss, Paul Bird, "Shall we do it then?" and that was that. We did.'

If he had needed any harsh reminders about just how dangerous the TT was, his debut year provided them. 'I shared a room with Mick Lofthouse during that first TT and he got killed in practice. You'd think

Double yellows.
Ian Simpson leads V&M Honda team-mate, Michael Rutter, over the yellow lines in Kirkmichael. Junior, 1997.

Jim Moodie on the Clarion Suzuki GSX-R750 in 1997. It wasn't a happy pairing but the Scot won a total of eight TTs on other machines.

that would put you off for life, but I suppose bike racers are just not right in the head so I carried on.'

After a nightmare three-year battle back to something like fitness, Robert Dunlop earned the hardest TT podium of his career in the 125cc race. His injuries were still such that he had been refused permission to race in the 1996 TT and even the North West 200 just a few weeks before the 1997 TT. Yet Dunlop claimed an incredible third place on a machine which was specially modified to account for the lack of mobility in his right arm and leg. The Ulsterman was jubilant at being back on the TT rostrum. 'I lost count of the number of times I questioned if I could run at the front again,' he said. 'I guess this is two fingers up to those who said I couldn't do it.'

Race winner, Ian Lougher, also had some harsh words for critics who claimed his last two TT wins had been flukes. The Welshman said: 'There were a lot of people who said my wins were down to other riders having bad luck and that I couldn't win purely on riding ability. Well, they can crawl back under their stones now! I think I've proved what I can do.'

The Singles class was under threat in 1997 with only 24 starters and 16 finishers making it a poor spectacle. But Dave Morris still had to ride his BMW hard to win the race from John Barton on a Ducati Supermono.

Phillip McCallen showed true grit by lining up for the Junior TT despite the fact that he couldn't use his crushed left hand – the hand which would normally operate the clutch. On the start line, a helper held the clutch lever while McCallen wrapped his hand around it and, after he'd let it out to get started, he never used it again. 'My arm was in such a state that, if I had let go of the handlebar, I wouldn't have been able to grab hold of it again, so I just had to hang onto that bar the whole way.' The Irishman rode a gutsy race to finish second but could do nothing with runaway winner Ian

Simpson who achieved a lifetime's ambition in winning his first TT.

Simpson had been around the TT paddock since he was a child and was there to witness his father Bill winning the 1976 Production race. Ever since then, 'Simmo' had dreamed of emulating his dad. 'Winning here is a dream come true,' said the 27-year-old Scot. 'This place has so many memories for me. I can remember coming here with my father all those years ago and being taken into the winner's enclosure to see him being presented with the laurels for his win. That has always stayed with me and ever since then I wanted to win here.'

Simpson set a blistering pace with new lap and race records but it was his time from Ramsey to Ramsey which created the biggest buzz when he unofficially clocked the first 120mph lap on a 600cc machine. His official time of 119.86mph was just shy of the landmark but it was more than enough to take the race from McCallen and Michael Rutter. Simpson became only the second son of a TT-winning father to take a race victory himself – the first was Stuart Graham who won the 1967 50cc race after his father Les had won the 1953 125cc event.

The Production TT ended in controversy over the fuel used by Honda-mounted winner, Phillip McCallen. After a close battle with Ducati's Ian Simpson, McCallen took his tenth TT win but then found himself at the centre of the fuel row. Ducati team boss Ben Atkins was unhappy that Honda had used special Elf race fuel rather than conventional pump fuel. He said, 'To use the special fuel was not racing with the spirit the proddie TT should be run in.' Ducati importer, Hoss Elm, even threatened to withdraw the Italian twins from the following year's TT after race officials threw the protest out. The fuel was legal however, and the result stood.

With his confidence regained, McCallen fought tooth and nail with Jim Moodie for top honours in the Senior race. Moodie was mounted on an NSR500 Honda V-twin Grand Prix and had a blistering ride which saw him lose out to McCallen by just eight seconds. 'The NSR was absolutely brilliant but we never had time to get the whole package set up just right,' Moodie says. 'And at that time, nobody in the world made tyres for a 500cc V-twin GP bike so I had to use Superbike tyres which were the wrong profile.'

It was McCallen's 11th TT win. It would also be his last.

1998

WALKING WOUNDED

Just days before the 1998 TT, two of the event's biggest stars were unsure if they would be given permission to compete.

After breaking his back in a crash at Thruxton in May, Phillip McCallen was told any further damage to his spine could leave him permanently paralysed. He was ruled out of the TT and was gutted at the news. 'It was Honda's 50th year and it was going to be a dream TT for me,' he says. 'I had a hand-built RVF coming – tailored exactly to my needs, right down to the last detail. Everything I wanted was on that bike. And a silly crash at Thruxton ended it all. I was thrown about 20 feet in the air and landed on my arse and drove my arse halfway up my back. Jesus, I was devastated at missing the TT. Gutted.'

McCallen was given the news just hours before travelling to the Isle of Man. And while he still made the trip, it was strictly as a spectator. 'The doctors told me there's absolutely no way my spine is stable enough for me to ride at the TT,' he said at the time. 'At the moment just one kick up my backside from a bucking bike could leave me unable to walk.'

Dunlop's injuries were no less gruesome; he had broken his left hand and collarbone and fractured his pelvis, as well as losing his wedding ring finger following a crash at the Tandragee 100 in May. Dunlop turned up at dawn for the first TT practice still unsure of whether he would be allowed to ride. Doctors passed him fit at the last minute but Joey decided to limit his outings to the smaller 125 and 250cc machines, the much heavier Superbikes proving too much of a handful – at least for now. 'I'll be back on a 750,' he said, 'because all I want to do is win another Formula 1 TT.' It may not have been on a 750, but Dunlop would get his wish.

Robert Dunlop was another of the walking wounded. He arrived on the Island on crutches after breaking his leg and a collarbone at the North West 200 just three weeks previously. With typical understatement, Dunlop explained that he didn't really need the broken

The Simpsons.
Bill Simpson won the 1976 Production Race. His son, Ian, is pictured here en route to an F1/Senior double in 1998.

leg anyway. 'It's not my gear-change foot – it just sits on the footrest and does nothing really.' He was given permission to ride at the beginning of practice week

Another faller at the NW200, Jim Moodie, was still suffering from a cracked bone in his wrist and was also doubtful about having enough strength to hang onto the larger machines. But the strangest injury of all had to belong to Honda's Iain Duffus who was ruled out of racing altogether – thanks to his son. 'There was about 10 minutes to go before the practice session and I was just getting my helmet on,' he explained. 'My wee boy decided to go for a walk on his own and I got into a bit of a panic looking for him. I saw him in the distance and just went to run to catch him and I heard my leg snap and I tumbled over and that was it – a broken leg.'

With Honda celebrating its 50th anniversary, it had expected to dominate the 1998 TT but with McCallen being ruled out and Dunlop not strong enough to ride a Superbike, it fell to young guns Ian Simpson and Michael Rutter to fly the Honda flag. They were given McCallen and Dunlop's full factory bikes and both rose to the challenge superbly. Rutter was leading the F1 race by six seconds on the last lap from Simpson when his contact lens fell out. Forced to slow his pace, Rutter was helpless to prevent a late charge from Simpson who clocked a 123.28mph lap on the last of four laps to win by 2.2 seconds. Simpson still remembers the huge difference between the works Honda machinery and his usual Honda mount. 'The full factory RC45 was incredible compared to the bike I usually rode – unbelievably better. The brakes were better, the clutch was better, the gearbox; it felt smaller to sit on, it was more comfortable. The throttle was lighter, the clutch was lighter, it was more stable – just everything you could imagine a bike doing, it did it better. It was a real sickener when I had to get back on my own bike after the TT 'cos then I realised what a heap of shit it really was!'

Bad weather forced the cancellation of Sidecar Race A and left crews rowing over what should become of the £32,000 prize fund for the race. The top riders wanted all the cash to be put into Race B but slower competitors felt the money should be split evenly amongst everyone. It was finally decided that all prize money would be carried over to Race B meaning Dave Molyneux picked up £10,000 – the richest purse in TT Sidecar history – for winning the three-lap dash.

Joey Dunlop put in one of the greatest performances of his career to win the Lightweight TT. Riding in great pain – the empty finger of his glove had been flapping maddeningly against the still-raw stump of his amputated ring finger – he employed brilliant tactics in the weather-hit event. The race was cut from four laps down to three just before the start and most riders planned to pit after one lap for fuel. Showing years of TT experience, Dunlop defied his Honda team and gambled on doing two straight laps, believing the weather would worsen and the race would be stopped after two laps. That was exactly what happened and Joey Dunlop won his 23rd TT in the most atrocious weather conditions and still in great pain.

There was more for the Dunlop family to celebrate after Robert made one of the greatest comebacks in TT history. Although conditions were wet at the start of the 125cc race, the injured Dunlop gambled on slick tyres and, when the course dried out, he went on to take his first Island victory since 1991. 'This is my best TT win ever,' said an emotional Dunlop. 'When I was lying in the road at the NW200 I didn't think I'd be riding here.' Dunlop had to mount the podium on crutches but the champagne never tasted sweeter.

The Singles TT was the only race Honda failed to win in its 50th anniversary year. After building an ultra-expensive XR650 special (rumoured to be worth more than its RC45 Superbikes), Honda's Jim Moodie had to settle for second best to BMW-mounted Dave Morris who did his bit to help BMW celebrate its own 75th anniversary.

Tony Rutter may have won seven TTs himself but when his son Michael flashed across the line to take his first victory Tony called it the happiest day of his life. Michael was no less pleased and beamed 'I can't believe I have finally won a TT. It's a dream come true.'

Ian Simpson had led the race at the start of the final lap but could do nothing to stop Rutter's late charge after a bungled fuel stop. 'I tried my best to catch him,' Simpson admitted, 'but it just wasn't good enough.'

Honda won its 100th TT since debuting in 1959 in the Production race thanks to a stunning ride by Jim Moodie. Despite never having ridden a FireBlade before, the Scot set the first ever 100mph lap by a production machine as he fended off Yamaha's R1 challenge. He was never headed in the race which was watched by Honda top brass including the FireBlade's designer, Tadao Baba. The race was marred by the death of Welshman Charles 'Ian' Hardisty who suffered fatal injuries after crashing at Kerrowmoar.

Waking up the neighbours. Michael Rutter's exhaust note reverberates off the houses in sleepy Kirkmichael village as he blasts to Junior victory in 1998.

Ian Simpson won the Senior race to add to his F1 victory earlier in the week then admitted he'd never ridden the Mountain as hard in his life. He was, he says, on the absolute limit. 'I don't think you're ever really scared while you're racing,' he reflects now, 'that comes more afterwards when you have time to think about it. But if you had to ride like that at the TT all the time it would catch you out eventually.'

Michael Rutter had been leading the race before suffering a puncture on the 160mph drop down Bray Hill on the third lap. He rode the following 37 miles with a flat rear tyre but still managed to hold onto 13th place. Bob Jackson opted to ride with a 32-litre fuel tank which meant he only needed to make one stop compared to everyone else's two. He was leading the race by over 30 seconds at the end of lap three but lost time in the pits and relinquished his lead. Simmo knew Jackson was reeling him in again as the pair headed for the Mountain for the final time and the Scotsman gave it everything to secure his name amongst the greats on the Senior TT trophy. He remains extremely proud of the achievement. 'When you think that some of the best riders who ever lived have their names on that trophy, and then you win it yourself and get your name engraved on it – it's quite an achievement really.'

1999

DAVID AND GOLIATH

Phillip McCallen leaps Ballaugh Bridge on the way to his last TT podium in the 1999 Production race. Injury and the death of a racing friend convinced him enough was enough.

David Jefferies changed the TT in more ways than he could have imagined when he beat the might of Honda on a private, production-based Yamaha R1 to lift the Formula 1 Trophy. Honda had won the F1 race every year since 1982 and, over the years, had shipped in some of the most exotic – and expensive – four-stroke motorcycles on the planet to guarantee victory. Cost was not an issue for the world's biggest motorcycle manufacturer. And it was no different in 1999 when Honda supplied Joey Dunlop and Jim Moodie with World Superbike-spec RC45s. *Motor Cycle News* estimated the cost of each bike to be around £500,000 and reckoned the team spent another £1 million on back-up.

In contrast, David Jefferies was mounted on a bike which started life as a bog standard £8,299 Yamaha R1 road bike. By the time it had been readied for racing by the V&M team, its total value was estimated at just £20,000. It seemed impudent to even think about challenging the might of Honda on such a budget but Jefferies and his V&M team were up for the challenge.

With depressing predictability, tragedy struck once again in practice week. After years of battling on privateer machinery, Simon Beck had fulfilled his life's dream by landing a factory Honda RC45 for the 1999 TT. He had just topped the practice leader board on the machine when he crashed at the 33rd Milestone and sustained fatal injuries.

Honda's F1 title defence got off to a bad start when Jim Moodie's RC45 expired just minutes into the race at Glen Lough. Moments later, the race was red-flagged for the first time since 1954 after Paul Orritt suffered the most horrendous tank-slapper ever seen on the flat-out plunge down Bray Hill. Finally losing control, Orritt crashed and slid up Ago's leap but escaped with relatively minor injuries.

The red flag spurred Moodie into action. 'I was down and out and then the race was red-flagged,' he says, 'so I ran the three-and-a-half mikes back to the paddock in my leathers, helmet in hand. But when I got back, there was no spare bike for me.'

Arai
9
micron
MICHELIN

In the four lap restart, Joey Dunlop quickly took the lead from Iain Duffus and David Jefferies and held it until the pit stops at the end of lap two. When Dunlop lost 20 seconds in the pits, he rode harder than ever to claw it back and set his fastest ever lap of the course at 123.06mph. But it wasn't enough: Jefferies responded with a lap at 123.36mph – just 3.1 seconds off Carl Fogarty's outright lap record. It was enough to give him his first TT win. 'I can't believe this,' he said, 'I never thought I'd win. I just didn't think I had the experience to do it. I can barely tell you how good it feels to take a win on a bike that costs about £20,000 in front of these massively expensive Hondas.'

Jefferies also admitted that, despite his awesome speed, he was dangerously short of knowing his way around in what was only his third TT (he sat out 1997 due to injury). He said 'It might sound daft but I don't really know my way around much of the course. I was all over the place at some of the corners and I don't think I got the line around the Veranda right more than once.'

Jefferies' win changed everyone's perception of the TT: if glorified street bikes could win, what was the point in building multi-million pound specials? Suddenly, even the most prestigious TT races were within the reach of modest teams. The TT had come full circle and returned to its 1907 roots.

Dave Molyneux won the first Sidecar race and was well on his way to doing another double when his engine blew on the last lap of leg two. A new lap record of 112.12mph was some consolation for the Manxman who had to sit back and watch Rob Fisher take the win.

John McGuinness took his first TT win in style in the Lightweight 250 race. Not only did he outclass Joey Dunlop, but he also beat the TT's longest standing lap record. McGuinness's speed of 118.29mph finally ousted Ian Lougher's 1990 record of 117.80mph. Dunlop had been put off after seeing his friend, James Courtney, crashing out of the race at 130mph, meaning Jason Griffiths was McGuinness's closest challenger. Yet even he was 37 seconds behind the Morecambe bricklayer who still remembers the race fondly. 'It was absolutely mega to take that first win. By 1999 I knew my way round and really felt I was ready to win one. I was leading the British championship at the time and my bike was the best thing on the track so I really had a good go at it on the first couple of laps and broke Lougher's lap record. It felt great to beat the likes of Joey Dunlop, Gary Dynes and Owen McNally because they were all great 250 riders. I had fulfilled one of my childhood dreams and my team boss, Paul Bird, was pretty speechless after that win. He never said a word, and if you can shut Birdie up you must have done alright!

Ian Lougher won the 125cc race for the third year in a row after the Dunlop brothers were dogged by problems. Robert could manage only fifth place due to lack of feeling in his so-often-injured hands, and Joey lost two minutes in the pits unblocking the fuel breather pipe on his Honda RS125.

John Barton and Steve Linsdell took full advantage of the very permissive rules in the Singles class and fitted additional under-seat fuel tanks for the race. The modifications meant neither rider would have to make a pit stop but their cunning plans came to nothing when mechanical problems ruled them both out of the race. Dave Morris took a third straight win on his BMW.

Just a quarter of a lap into the Junior race, Jim Moodie lost the use of his clutch but decided to carry on by simply banging the gears home. He recalls: 'It wasn't too bad because I'd raced with a broken left hand in 1998 and couldn't use the clutch then so I'd had some practice. The biggest problem was always going to be missing a gear. If I had missed a gear and hit a false neutral I'd have been fucked because I'd never have gotten it back into gear. I also got fuel sloshed in my eyes at the pit stop – and I wear contact lenses so it got between my eyes and the lenses. If I hadn't managed to work the lenses out I was finished. But I couldn't see too great after that – I certainly couldn't read my signal boards. So I just concentrated on catching Iain Duffus and used him as a bit of a gauge for the next two laps.'

Moodie overcame all his problems to take the win but Duffus had to settle for third after a flying last lap from David Jefferies hoisted him up to second place.

Duffus was then within two miles of victory in the Production race when his Yamaha R1 spluttered to a halt, out of fuel. The Scotsman was utterly distraught. 'No words can describe how bad this feels,' he said. 'To have a certain win taken away like that hurts so much.'

An extra second at the filler pump during his pit stop would have been enough to get him home but Duffus could only watch as David Jefferies inherited his lead and held it to the flag before admitting his own fuel warning light had been on for the last 17 miles of the race.

Phillip McCallen took his last ever podium on the Island in the Production race. Further injury and the shock of Simon Beck's death finally led to his decision to retire from racing. He describes the circumstances surrounding that last TT: 'I'd had a disagreement with Honda and was riding Yamahas that year. I'd spent a year recovering from my broken back and my dream was to go back to the TT and win on a Yamaha. But during a race at Donington just before the TT, I crashed and stretched all the muscles joining my right shoulder blade to my back. I rode at the NW200 and half way through the Superbike race I heard this almighty snap – it felt like someone had taken a hammer and smacked me right on the shoulder blade. What had happened was the muscles that hold the shoulder blade to my back had ripped. It was the greatest pain I'd ever felt in my life. I went to every physio, every doctor, every faith healer I could find and by the time I got to the TT I had full movement back in the arm but still no strength in it. I eventually realised that I had stretched the nerves in the shoulder and so I was losing feeling in my right hand. So I was effectually only using one arm to ride the bike and couldn't hold onto it properly. I wanted to cry – to die – because I was so gutted that I had the best bike out there but I couldn't give it my best shot. Had I been fit, there was no reason why I couldn't have won every race but as it was, the Production bike was the easiest to ride and that's the only one I got a result on.'

But the decision to retire had really been taken during practice. 'I saw Simon Beck's fatal crash and that hit me pretty hard because I knew him well. I felt sick inside' says McCallen. When I got back to the paddock I just thought "I don't need this." With the injuries I was carrying I couldn't ride properly and I felt I was letting people down so I just decided then and there to quit.'

Joey Dunlop didn't mince his words after he could only manage fifth place in the Senior TT. 'It's the end of the RC45 – it's time for something new. The bike has been outclassed by the R1 after five years at the top. We'll just have to wait and see what comes out next year.' It was the first year since 1991 that Dunlop had failed to win a TT race.

The R1s were even more dominant in the Senior than they had been in the F1 with David Jefferies winning again and team-mate Iain Duffus finishing second. Ian Lougher salvaged a little Honda pride by taking the last podium place on his NSR500V GP bike.

The first of many. John McGuinness took his first TT win on a 250 in the 1999 Junior.

Jim Moodie had set a scorching pace on his Honda RC45 in the early stages of the race, even catching radio commentators off guard as he approached commentary points much quicker than was expected. As Jim Moodie flashed across the line to begin lap two it was announced that he had broken Carl Fogarty's seven-year-old outright lap record by 7.4 seconds. Moodie's average speed of 124.45mph from a standing start seemed to indicate that he could easily crack the 125mph barrier on a flying lap but it was not to be: he was forced to pull out of the race with a shredded rear tyre. 'I think it was just a bad tyre' he says now 'but quite a lot of people stupidly thought I'd put a qualifying tyre on just to have a go at the lap record. Some time later a guy at a chat show handed me a fiver and said "That's for that lap record – I watched you do it and it was amazing." That's how much I got for breaking the lap record – five quid. Winning the race would have been worth about £15,000 and yet people thought I'd forego that to win a fiver?

The Scotsman's demise allowed Jefferies to take a relatively easy win as Duffus struggled with a broken steering damper. It was Jefferies's third win of the week and his treble left Honda wondering what it could come up with in 2000 to halt Yamaha's charge. The answer was something very special indeed: a rejuvenated Joey Dunlop.

Australia's Cameron Donald proved a fast learner at the TT, lapping at over 128mph in only his second visit to the Island.

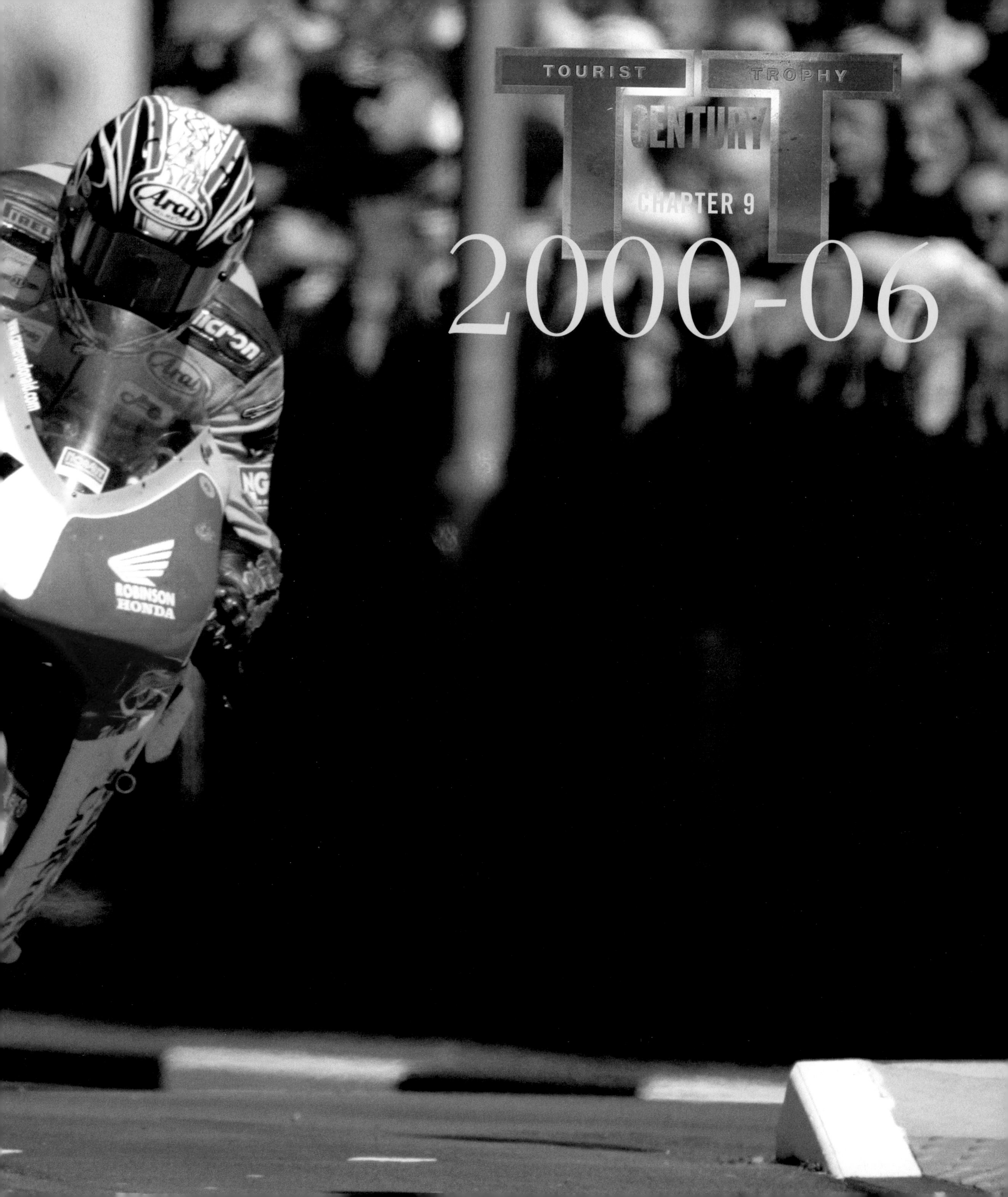

TOURIST TROPHY

TT CENTURY

CHAPTER 9

2000-06

Arai
3
Vimto
Demon
HONDA
DUNLOP
Vimto
Demon
NGK
DUNLOP
HONDA
elf
SCOTT

2000

THE LAST FAREWELL

Phillip McCallen probably summed it up best: 'I'm glad I'm not racing this year. How could I go home and say I've been beaten by a 48-year-old man when I'm supposed to be a good rider?'

With his hair now fully grey, Joey Dunlop turned in the performance of his life at TT 2000. On an unfamiliar bike, against far younger opposition, and 12 years after his last TT treble, he turned the clock back to score his third, and arguably finest, hat-trick of wins.

The fairy tale began more like a nightmare as Dunlop soon realised that the Honda FireBlade he was supposed to ride at the TT was not competitive. And when Honda then agreed to supply him with one of its new SP-1 V-twins – a type of bike Joey had never ridden before – things didn't get much better. He could finish only 5th in the Superbike race at the NW200 against the Yamaha R1s of David Jefferies and Michael Rutter, and declared that the SP-1 'Doesn't stand a chance against the R1s on the Island.'

Joey knew that he needed something special for the TT. With the help of Bob McMillan from Honda UK – who pleaded with his Japanese bosses for a better machine – Joey managed to secure the use of Aaron Slight's factory SP-1 World Superbike engine along with three Japanese engineers for the TT which many thought would be Joey's last. Yet still he had trouble. Throughout practice he suffered severe handling problems and it wasn't until the Dunlop tyre company shipped in some 1999-spec rubber that Joey finally thought he had a set-up capable of challenging for F1 honours.

It was still the longest of long shots. Dunlop was almost 50 years old and had suffered some horrendous injuries in more than 30 years of racing. His opposition consisted of young, aggressive riders who were all experienced in the cut-and-thrust world of international short circuit racing. Men like David Jefferies, Michael Rutter and John McGuinness should all, on paper at least, have had the beating of a man old enough to be their father.

But by the time Dunlop reached the bottom of Bray Hill on the opening lap it was obvious to all that he had his 'race face' on and meant business. Jefferies, Rutter and McGuinness chased hard but in the patchy conditions, Dunlop led the way and completed lap one with an advantage of 0.2 seconds over Rutter. But after Rutter suffered several massive slides on damp patches he lost his confidence and the race became a straight fight between Jefferies and Dunlop. On laps two and three, Dunlop held the advantage but, after posting the fastest lap of the race on lap four, Jefferies briefly snatched the lead only for Dunlop to regain it with a quicker pit stop. The duo were neck and neck in the early part of the fifth lap with both men clearly

Off the rails. The crowd went wild in 2000 when Joey Dunlop took his first F1 win since 1988. He was 48 years old.

Jason Griffiths sweeps through Keppel Gate on his way to second place in the 2000 Singles race. He was riding in honour of the late Dave Morris on a bike built by Morris's sons.

giving it everything they knew when suddenly the race was over: Jefferies's R1 had destroyed its clutch basket and he was forced to retire.

Although their hero still had more than a lap-and-a-half to go, Dunlop's fans – which meant practically everyone watching the race – sensed a fairy-tale victory was within reach. The reception he received all the way home was spectacular. Programmes waving, arms outstretched worshipping this God of Speed who continued to surpass himself and reach new levels of greatness. As he'd roared away from his last pit stop even rival teams had cheered him on. Like Hailwood's comeback in 1978, no one was immune to the emotions of witnessing one of the TT's greatest moments.

As he flashed across the finish line the crowds around the grandstand area rose as one to cheer home the most unlikely hero any sport had ever produced. The shy, humble folk hero of Ballymoney had achieved his last great ambition – to win back the Formula 1 crown which he had made his own in the 1980s when he had been a much younger man. Joey Dunlop was back where he belonged.

The tributes were universal. Four-times World Superbike champion Carl Fogarty said: 'To still be winning races at 48 on the hardest and most dangerous circuit in the world . . . well, he's got all my respect.' Steve Hislop added, 'What he's done is a great achievement. He seems to be more up for it now than ever.' And Phillip McCallen admitted that, 'When everything goes right for Joey, on his bike and in his mind, he's virtually unbeatable. There will never be another TT rider like him.'

Joey himself seemed relieved at the end of the race and admitted that 'The pressure was really on me because of having Slight's engine and because there were a lot of top men from Japan here. I'm just glad I could repay them for the faith they've shown.'

With Dave Molyneux opting to miss the TT to concentrate on the world championship, Rob Fisher won both Sidecar events on his Honda outfit. His task was made easier as his main rivals fell by the wayside in both races.

The Isle of Man had barely stopped celebrating Joey Dunlop's F1 triumph when the man from Ballymoney outdid himself yet again. With such a stunning win already in the bag, Dunlop could have been forgiven for taking it easy in his remaining races but he set such a pace in the Lightweight 250 event that his nearest rival, John McGuinness, destroyed his

Arai
Silkolene
52

engine trying to keep up. Using his unrivalled knowledge of the TT course, Dunlop consistently found the fastest lines round the damp roads to rack up win number 25. He finished 77 seconds ahead of New Zealander Bruce Anstey who was 'stoked' at taking his first TT podium ahead of Ian Lougher.

Geoff McMullan looked to have taken victory in the 400cc Lightweight race which was run alongside the 250cc main event – until his '400' was found to have a 600cc engine! McMullen claimed he was as surprised as everyone else to discover he had 200ccs more than his rivals. His exclusion meant New Zealander Brett Richmond was awarded the win.

The Singles race produced one of the most emotional victories ever witnessed at the TT. Dave Morris had won the event for three years in succession before losing his life in a crash at Croft in England in 1999. His sons, Neil and Lee, then went through the unimaginable grief of losing their mother Alison to a heart attack just one week later. Focusing their energies over the following nine months, the brothers vowed to continue their father's success at the TT. Using money left to them in their parents' wills, the brothers finished building the two machines Dave had been working on for TT 2000 and named them AMDMs – the initials of their parents. John McGuinness and Jason Griffiths were approached to ride the bikes and, after receiving special permission from their official teams, both agreed. The result was a real tear-jerker. McGuinness and Griffiths brought the bikes home in first and second places and as the sound of Dave Morris's engine roared across the line to victory, Neil and Lee wept openly as the whole paddock applauded their efforts. Of the brothers' awesome achievement, Neil Morris simply said, 'We've been through a lot but this was the best way to pay tribute to our parents and take a step into the future.'

Robert Dunlop started the 125cc race at number four, just ten seconds behind his brother Joey. If his plan had been to reel Joey in by having him in sight right from the start, it didn't work. After finishing in third place Robert admitted, 'There was nothing I could do to go any faster and I couldn't match him.'

In the late 1980s and early 1990s it had seemed that Joey Dunlop would never match the great Mike Hailwood's all-time record of 14 TT victories. Now, with victory over fellow Ulsterman, Dennis McCullough in the Ultra-Lightweight race, he had notched up an incredible 26 wins. No one knew it at the time, but it would prove to be the last victory for the TT's favourite son.

David Jefferies won the Junior after a fierce battle with rising star Adrian Archibald and old hand Ian Lougher. Archibald set a new lap record at 121.15mph on his way to second place while Jefferies set a new race record of 119.33mph.

Horrendous conditions meant the Production race was cut to two laps. After a five-hour delay, riders braved standing water and mist on the Mountain but many pulled in after just one lap claiming conditions were too dangerous. David Jefferies picked up his second win of the week but admitted after the race that 'They shouldn't really have run it. The conditions were bloody awful.' Third-placed finished, Michael Rutter, agreed. 'I'm just glad to have finished in one piece. It was *very* frightening.' Manxman Richard 'Milky' Quayle took a superb second spot in his first TT year, claiming he didn't mind the conditions.

A huge landmark was reached in the Senior when David Jefferies became the first man to lap the course at 125mph. On his way to securing another hat-trick, Jefferies clocked a lap at 125.69mph to lead team-mate Michael Rutter home by almost a minute. Joey Dunlop, riding in what would be his last ever TT race, held a joint lead with Jefferies in the early stages and recorded his fastest ever lap of his beloved course at 123.87mph but dropped to third place by the end of the race – and the end of a tiring week which saw him become the first man to achieve three TT hat-tricks.

After what was arguably his greatest ever TT, most people felt that Joey Dunlop had nothing left to prove and that he should retire from the sport while still on top. Honda's Bob McMillan even offered Dunlop money *not* to race at the TT again. Joey replied that since he had never raced for money, how could he entertain the idea of *not* racing for money? Racing motorcycles was all that Joey Dunlop knew and he had always panicked at the idea of retiring, claiming he simply 'wouldn't know how to do it.'

Just weeks after his victorious TT, Joey drove to Estonia to take part in an obscure race few people had even heard of. He won the Superbike class and was leading in the wet on the same 125cc Honda he had won the TT on when he crashed and struck a tree by the side of the course. He was killed instantly. More than 50,000 people attended the funeral of the greatest pure road racer, and one of the greatest racing characters of all time. The sport would never be the same again.

His greatest win?
Joey Dunlop's F1 victory in 2000 at the age of 48 must rank amongst his best.

And still they come.
Not everyone stayed away when the TT races were cancelled in 2001 due to the Foot and Mouth outbreak.

2001
THE TT THAT NEVER WAS

Few could imagine a TT without Joey Dunlop so it almost seemed right that the 2001 races were cancelled. With Foot and Mouth disease causing havoc on the UK mainland, the Manx authorities decided it posed too great a risk to have thousands of people standing in fields watching the TT and, quite possibly, spreading the disease. It was the first time since World War II that the races were cancelled.

2002
A RETURN TO RACING

If ever proof were needed that the TT Festival could not exist without the TT races then 2001 provided it. While a few thousand bikers still sailed to the Isle of Man during the fortnight, it was mostly because they had bookings they couldn't back out of. The fringe activities which have surrounded the TT since the late 1970s – fun fairs, beach racing, owners' gatherings, scrambles, live bands etc – play an important part in the meeting but they are only sideshows and, without the main event – the races themselves – the TT Festival would certainly die.

Fortunately for all concerned, the main event was back in 2002 and it was as thrilling as ever. David Jefferies picked up exactly where he left off with victory in the F1 race despite suffering a severe handicap on the last lap when his bike became stuck in third gear. 'I nearly lost control of all bodily functions when I went for the next gear up only to hear the limiter cut in and nothing happen,' said the burly Yorkshireman. 'I just left it alone and had to make do for the rest of the lap with only third gear.'

Smelling blood, John McGuinness hounded Jefferies over the Mountain on his Honda FireBlade on the last lap but Jefferies had built a big enough lead as a cushion and came home 36 seconds ahead of his rival and close friend. A new lap record of 126.68mph had helped Jefferies establish a one minute lead before his gear selector problem and it proved his saving grace at the end of the race.

McGuinness had his own problems, though they were of a more delicate nature. 'I got fuel splashed all over me bollocks and the pain was incredible,' he remembers. 'It was absolute agony all the way to Ballacraine and all I was thinking was "I need to stop, I need to stop to sort me bollocks – or at least make sure they were still there." It was so bad that I thought by the time I finished the race my knob would be gone. I made some 'adjustments' to the family jewels on one of the straights and eventually the pain disappeared and I was back in business. But it was pretty uncomfortable for a while, that's for sure.'

Big man, big trophy. David Jefferies has no problems lifting the Senior trophy in 2002.

Colin Hardman lived up to his name in the first Sidecar race. As passenger for Dave Molyneux, Hardman held on to grab fourth place despite having just broken his hand in a road bike accident on the morning of the race. Rob Fisher won the first leg using a Molyneux-tuned engine and joined Siggy Schauzu, Mick Boddice and Dave Saville on the all-time winners' list with his ninth victory – but not for long. By winning the second leg ahead of Molyneux, Fisher became the most successful Sidecar racer in TT history with 10 wins. His passenger, Rick Long became the first to win five in a row.

Ian Lougher outpaced all but two of the Supersport 400 machines on his 125 to pick up his fifth TT win. With the two classes being run concurrently, the Welshman's pace also saw him set a new lap record at 110.21mph. He explains just how hard the tiny machines can be ridden round the Island. 'I reckon we must have been holding the 125s on full throttle for about 85 per cent of the lap whereas you only have a Superbike at full throttle for around 13 per cent of the

Jim Moodie may look mellow in the sunshine but he was a ferocious competitor on the track.

Opposite: Number One – head down, flat out. The only way David Jefferies knew. Practice, 2003.

time. The most frustrating thing about 125s was trying to keep tucked in all the time – they really weren't comfortable. But they were probably faster than a Superbike through twisty sections like Glen Helen.'

Richard Quayle became the first Manxman to win a solo TT race for 35 years when he took the Lightweight 400 honours. The last local win had gone to Neil Kelly in the 1967 Production 500 race. Quayle was ecstatic. 'Other people want to be brain surgeons or climb Everest,' he said, 'but all I have ever wanted to do is win a TT race. It's so special to me as a Manxman.'

The lap time set by David Jefferies in the Production 1000 race made a mockery of the F1 class for which teams can spend unlimited amounts of cash in building a one-off Superbike. On a near-standard Suzuki GSX-R1000 on road-legal tyres, Jefferies lapped at 124.31mph – just 2.3mph slower than on his tuned F1 bike on slick tyres. Ian Lougher and Bruce Anstey rounded out the podium on similar machines proving that the GSX-R1000 was now *the* bike to have at the TT.

The Lightweight 250 race looked to be on its last legs as the class was in decline outside the Grand Prix world championship. But it still allowed Bruce Anstey to take his first TT win ahead of a poor field of 12 finishers from 18 starters. Racing journalist Ronnie Smith took a fine second.

Jim Moodie took his first TT win since 1999 with victory in the four-lap Junior. His task was made somewhat easier when arch rivals David Jefferies and John McGuinness went out on the first and second laps respectively, but a slipping clutch kept the Scotsman on his toes throughout the race. It was Moodie's eighth win, yet in the Production 600TT – using more standard versions of the tuned 600s raced in the Junior – he could manage no better than third and was amazed at the pace of his rivals. He said, 'I battled harder for that third than I did for the win in the Junior. I couldn't believe what I was seeing on the boards because I thought I was on the limit.'

Ahead of him, Ian Lougher did indeed set a blistering pace to take his second win of the week. He hustled a production GSX-R600 round the course at an average speed of 120.25mph to win from the identically-mounted Bruce Anstey. For Lougher, the relative lack of power meant the production bike was more fun to ride than tuned versions. He said, 'The bike was brilliant, and it was quite similar to riding the 125 because you just have to wring the neck of both of them all the way around this place.'

Thirty years after Giacomo Agostini last won the Senior TT he presented the magnificent trophy to David Jefferies as the Yorkshireman clocked up his third TT treble in three consecutive years. His victory took his overall win tally to nine, just one short of Agostini himself. The Italian was full of praise for Jefferies and the current crop of TT riders in general. He said: 'To see race speeds this high is wonderful and shows what respect should be shown for TT winners. Jefferies is a remarkable rider and will be one of the greatest.'

Jefferies's treble was made even more special by his setting a new outright lap record of 127.29mph in achieving it. He also became the first recipient of the Joey Dunlop Trophy, awarded to the rider with the best aggregate performance in the Formula 1 and Senior races. The trophy came with a bonus of £10,000 to cap Jefferies's amazing week. He said, 'It does feel pretty good, not only to win but to get close to the record of someone like Agostini who is a real hero of mine.'

Jefferies's TAS Suzuki team-mate Ian Lougher finished second despite being penalised for overshooting the stop box on the entry to pit lane, and John McGuinness took third on his FireBlade. While the top three enjoyed the luxury of top class machinery, Richard Quayle rode superbly to take fourth place on a standard Suzuki GSX-R100 which he had wheeled out of a local showroom only one week before.

As Jefferies celebrated his record-breaking victory in his usual jovial manner, no one could have imagined he would never see another chequered flag at the TT.

2003

DJ

John McGuinness: 'I came across what looked like a war zone. There's a wall on the right – which I'd never noticed before. I presumed he'd hit that because there were rocks all over the road. There was a telegraph pole down too. At first I couldn't make out whose bike it was because everything was such a mess. But I saw what looked like a brand new seat sitting in the road with the No.1 plate on it and then I knew it was DJ. Then I looked across and saw him motionless on the ground. It really shocked me and I had to walk away.'

The TT suffered one of the darkest periods in its long history during practice for the 2003 event. In Thursday's session, the event's biggest star, and one of the most popular riders in Britain, David Jefferies, was killed in a horrific 160mph crash. The outright lap record holder had been travelling flat-out in top gear through Crosby when he hit oil dropped by another machine. Against a backdrop of stone walls, houses and telegraph poles, Jefferies didn't stand a chance and was killed instantly. His close friend, John McGuinness, was the first rider on the scene and, while he managed to get his bike stopped in time, others were still approaching at speed. Among them was Jim Moodie who came perilously close to losing his life in the debris. Jefferies's crash had brought down a telegraph pole and its four cables lay perilously stretched across the track. As Moodie approached the cables, John McGuinness could only watch in horror. 'I honestly thought Jim was going to be decapitated,' he said. 'He must have been doing 50-60mph when the cable got caught around his neck. I turned away. How he's still alive is a miracle.'

'Everything happened in a split second,' Moodie said shortly afterwards, 'but I still had time to think "This is it." I saw four cables across the road – slightly below the level of my screen. The bike snapped three of them but one went over the screen and caught me across my neck. I got to the point where my right hand had lost grip, but just then the cable snapped. If the cable hadn't snapped, I was on the verge of blacking out.'

The last lap.
David Jefferies on his last complete lap of the TT circuit. Practice, 2003.

The day after Moodie had almost been beheaded and McGuinness lost the friend who was to be godfather to his son, both riders took the same corner at maximum speed as practice recommenced. As professional riders, it was the only thing to do as McGuinness explained. 'When I got there, I just went flat out through it. It was the only thing to do.'

Looking back, Moodie says, 'There's no way I wanted to race that week but I'm a professional rider and pulling out would have meant letting a lot of people down – my mechanics, my sponsors, Triumph . . . They would all have understood me pulling out under the circumstances but I'm professional and I had obligations to people, so I raced. Over the years you learn to deal with these things – it's not easy, but you learn to deal with them.'

McGuinness has also had time to think over the situation and has come to terms with it in his own way. 'I was the first man on the scene and it was the eeriest, weirdest feeling and just a horrific sight,' he says. 'But David was peaceful – he was gone. One second he was enjoying himself – the lap he did before that was the fastest of practice week. If there's anything positive you can take out of it it's that he was buzzing, he had his bike working right, he did a 125mph lap and was having a great time. Then, a split second later, for reasons that were out of David's hands, he was taken away.'

Despite the fact that the world of motorcycling was sent into deep shock by the news of Jefferies's death, his family insisted that the TT should go ahead as planned. David's father Tony, himself a three-times TT winner, said, 'It doesn't really change our attitude to the TT. We knew the risks and it's voluntary. But if there's anything that can be learned from this to make the place safer in future, let's do that.'

With everyone on the Isle of Man questioning whether they really wanted to be there, the riders lined up for the F1 race two days later. Jefferies's team-mate, Adrian Archibald, lined up on his TAS Suzuki with just one thought in his mind – to win his first TT and dedicate it to David. The TAS team had been ready to abandon the meeting out of respect for its fallen rider but the Jefferies family had insisted on business as usual. Team boss, Phillip Neil, said, 'The final decision to carry on was left to the Jefferies family. Tony Jefferies said DJ would have gone berserk if he had any idea the team was going to pull out.'

Carrying a 'DJ 1' sticker on his GSX-R1000 Suzuki, Adrian Archibald rode his heart out to claim his first ever TT win in honour of Jefferies. John McGuinness – who had seriously considered retiring from the sport – set the running in the early stages before suffering tyre and gearbox problems. He held on to finish third behind Ian Lougher and was disappointed that he couldn't win the race for his late friend. But Archibald did that for him and all three riders on the TT podium sombrely remembered their fallen comrade. There was no celebratory champagne – just intense sadness that the fastest man in the history of the TT could not have been there to push them harder.

Ian Bell finally took a TT win in Sidecar Race A after having twice led races before breaking down. Dave Molyneux won the second leg but complained that the race should never have been run in such poor weather conditions. He said, 'We wanted it stopped – it was crazy. The conditions were so dangerous you never knew what the outfit was going to do next.'

John McGuinness finally got the chance to dedicate a win to David Jefferies when he took victory in

Above left: Flying the flag. Bruce Anstey heading for victory on the British-built Triumph. Junior race, 2003.

Above: Anstey gave Triumph its first victory for 28 years.

the Lightweight 400 race from Ulstermen Richard Britton and Ryan Farquhar. Afterwards he revealed that he'd even asked his old pal for help during the race. He said, 'I'm not a believer or anything but when I went through Crosby I asked David to look after me.'

The 125 race produced the third new winner of the week when former British champion Chris Palmer scooped his first TT win ahead of Michael Wilcox and Ian Lougher. Robert Dunlop was fourth.

'I expected to be in tears but the emotion hasn't kicked in yet,' Shaun Harris said after winning the Production 1000 race. 'It's taken me a quarter of my life to win this one – as long as it took to lose my virginity!' The Kiwi beat his fellow countryman, Bruce Anstey, to take his second TT win, having won the 750cc Production class in 2000.

Anstey more than made up for being beaten in the Production race with an historic victory in the Junior. Riding a Daytona 600, he gave Triumph its first TT win for 28 years and set the first 120mph race average for a 600cc machine. The British firm had not had a presence at the TT since Dave Croxford and Alex George won the 10-lap Production race on a T150 Trident in 1975. Anstey's victory was also the first for a British machine since Steve Hislop's glorious Norton win in 1992. The Kiwi had only been signed as a third rider to back-up Jim Moodie and John McGuinness – who finished ninth and tenth respectively – but stole the show and established himself as a new star at the TT. The combined race times of Anstey, Moodie and McGuinness – who were both still trying to come to terms with David Jefferies' death – were also enough to earn Triumph the Manufacturer's award.

Triumph's greatest triumph was in beating the might of the Japanese factories, all of whom were represented in the keenly-contested race. Second place man Ian Lougher was on a Honda, Adrian Archibald rode a Suzuki to third and Ryan Farquhar had a good ride to fourth on a Kawasaki, while Jason Griffiths brought a Yamaha home in sixth spot.

Shaun Harris took his second win of the week in the shortened Production 600 race. With mist rolling in off the Irish Sea, the race was cut from four laps to two, leaving the Suzuki GSX-R600 rider a comfortable 16.21 seconds clear of Honda's Ian Lougher at the flag.

The Senior race produced an emotional end to TT 2003 for the TAS Suzuki team. Having never stood on the podium before his F1 win earlier in the week, Adrian Archibald took a perfect F1/Senior double for the small Irish team which had so tragically lost its star rider. Seldom can the highs and lows of the TT have been experienced so acutely by any one team. TAS boss Hector Neill was bursting with sadness, and pride, at the end of a roller-coaster fortnight. 'Mrs Jefferies had said "You can't pull out – David would go mad if you did that. You must stay and give Adrian the chance. Tell him to have a nice, safe week's racing and if he can win one, win it for our David." Well, we didn't win one, we won two – and the two main ones. It's recorded for evermore that TAS – a wee team from Ireland – won the Formula 1 and won the Senior.'

DJ would have been proud.

Former Manx GP winner Colin Breeze through Union Mills in practice, 2004. He lost his life in the F1 race the same year.

2004
PURE GENIUS

John McGuinness returned to the TT with a vengeance in 2004 and proved that he was the new man to beat round the Mountain course. After setting unofficial lap records in the F1 and Junior classes in practice, he picked up his first win of the week in what would be the last ever Formula 1 TT. The race was being axed to make way for a TT Superbike class with regulations more in line with British and World Superbikes.

On his way to winning his first 'big bike' TT, McGuinness set a new outright lap record of 127.68mph on his Yamaha R1. The race had been reduced to four laps in the name of safety, though few riders could understand why four laps should be any safer than six, and most wanted a return to the six-lap format – a wish which was granted the following year. McGuinness's record lap put him well clear of Adrian Archibald who in turn beat his new TAS Suzuki team-mate, Bruce Anstey.

At least part of McGuinness's success was down to Jim Moodie who, being unfit to race, took it upon himself to advise and manage McGuinness's 2004 TT campaign. The combination proved devastating as the fiery Scotsman seemed to have just the right knack of lighting the touchpaper under the normally placid McGuinness. 'Jim helped with my machine set-up and he'd helped me to train as well,' says McGuinness. 'He was one of my heroes and he's not an eight-times TT winner without reason – he knows what he's talking

about and he got where he is through a lot of hard work and dedication. When it came to work and preparation and aggression, Jim was way ahead of anyone else on the track. His advice was definitely worth a few seconds a lap.'

The F1 race was marred by the death of Colin Breeze following a crash at Quarry Bends. Winner of the 1999 Senior Manx GP, Breeze was also a well-known and popular racer of classic machinery. His death was the third since practice began: Frenchman Serge le Moal and Sidecar passenger, Paul Cowley, both sustained fatal injuries in separate incidents.

Former world champion, Klaus Klaffenbock, spiced up the Sidecar TT entry and achieved his ambition of setting a 100mph lap on his way to 19th place in the first leg. The race was won by Dave Molyneux with fellow Manxman, Daniel Sayle, in the chair. The second leg saw the same four men finish in the same positions (Molyneux, Nick Crowe, Steve Norbury and Roy Hanks) but Moly finally managed to beat his lap record set in 1999 with a speed of 113.17mph – just 0.3 seconds short of the first sub-20-minute lap by a Sidecar.

There were more than a few people, spectators and competitors alike, who were sad to see the flag drop on the 125cc race being, as it was, the last to be held at the TT. As world racing went almost exclusively four-stroke, entries had been falling for the 125 TT and the smell of two-stroke mixture would soon be but a memory on the Isle of Man – the 250 class had already been dropped in 2003. As a sign of mourning for the loss of the class, some competitors even rode with black armbands on their leathers.

The race also marked the last time one of the legendary Dunlop brothers would race in a TT. Robert's injuries meant he could only ride a 125 so, with the class's demise, he announced his retirement from TT racing with mixed emotions. 'I've lost a few

The result of Robert Dunlop's extensive injuries can clearly be seen in his awkward style as he wrestles his 125 through Union Mills.

Former motocrosser Martin Finnegan shows his all-action style as he leaves Ballaugh during the 2004 Junior.

friends here and I've got through two big ones so it's time to call it a day,' he said. 'I don't particularly like the Isle of Man. It's hard work, very unforgiving and very time-consuming. I've enjoyed it and still do but the dangers outweigh the benefits now.'

Dunlop came close to winning his last TT race but was eventually beaten into second spot by Chris Palmer who was close to tears after making a little bit of TT history in a class he loved. Ian Lougher had led the race before breaking down. He was amongst those who mourned the end of the two-stroke era at the TT. 'I was really sad to see the 125s and 250s go,' he says now. 'And I feel sorry for the Newcomers now because they were the perfect bikes to learn the course on. You had more time to look around a bit and learn the place. Now they have to start on 600s and they're really fast bikes. You also had to be more precise on the little bikes as there was less suspension movement so hitting the right line was crucial. Riding a 125 or 250 really taught you how to set a bike up properly too.'

Run concurrently with the 125s, the 400cc Lightweight race was also taking a curtain call before being scrapped from the programme. John McGuinness picked up his second win of the week on a little Honda he likened to 'a scooter' after riding a Superbike, but he could not better his team manager Jim Moodie's record lap set way back in 1994 – and Moodie didn't fail to remind him of the fact.

Bruce Anstey won the Production 1000 race on his Suzuki GSX-R1000 and set a new lap record at 125.10mph. After beating McGuinness by 12.8 seconds, he said, 'I took it steady on the first lap to see what the others were doing. But when I cracked the record on lap two I relaxed. Riding a GSX-R750, Maria Costello became the fastest woman in TT history with a lap at 114.74mph before retiring from the race on the second lap.

The tables were turned in the Junior with McGuinness this time getting the better of Anstey after another high speed battle. The Cumbrian set new lap and race records as he stormed to his third win of the week. Ryan Farquhar had been hot on the heels of McGuinness before his Kawasaki blew up halfway round the first lap, leaving the Irishman wondering what he had to do to see a chequered flag – he hadn't finished a race all week.

When Farquhar did finally make it to the end of a race, it was at the head of the field in the Production 600 event. Not only was it Farquhar's first TT victory,

Chris Palmer won the last ever Ultra-Lightweight 125 TT in 2004. The class was dropped as two-stroke machinery fell out of favour.

it was also the first time a Kawasaki had won on the Island for 20 years – Geoff Johnson had been the firm's last winner in 1984 when he took the Production C race. Incredibly, it was only the Japanese firm's sixth ever TT victory. John McGuinness had been leading the race until he lost his steering damper but Farquhar rode superbly in patchy conditions to become the first Irishman to win a race that week.

TAS Suzuki's Adrian Archibald then made it two Irish winners in a day with victory in the Senior after a troublesome week. Once again, McGuinness's luck deserted him when his clutch expired on the penultimate lap and ended his week's racing. But he wasn't the only one left as a spectator; his Yamaha team-mate, Jason Griffiths had already suffered similar problems and Ryan Farquhar and Ian Lougher were also forced out. Archibald took full advantage of his rivals' misfortunes and led Bruce Anstey home for a TAS Suzuki one-two. Finishing third, Gary Carswell became the first Manxman for 81 years to stand on the Senior podium. The last was Tommy Sheard who won the event in 1923.

PINE WOOD STUDIO
PINE WOOD STUDIO

2005
YOUNG GUNS

Toe-slider sparking off the road, Adrian Archibald rounds Ballacraine in the 2005 Superstock race. He led all the way until running out of fuel on the last lap.

The TT became a four-stroke-only event in 2005 and some argued that the race programme was too simple and the races too similar. It included the TT Superbike race, the Junior 600, Superstock, two 600cc Production races and the Senior, as well as the traditional two Sidecar races. For many, the bikes all looked, and sounded, far too much alike, and they bemoaned the loss of variety which had been provided by the combination of two-strokes, four-strokes, singles and multis. Those in favour welcomed the extra practice time this allowed as well as the reduction in expenditure which resulted from being able to enter more races with fewer bikes.

While the arguments continued, the racing got underway – eventually. After the weather had done its best to ruin practice week, it also caused the postponement of the first TT Superbike race meaning it fell to the Sidecars to launch TT 2005. Once again it was won by a Manxman but this time it wasn't Dave Molyneux, who was forced out with ignition failure. In his stead, Nick Crowe and Darren Hope took over the running and went on to score a maiden TT victory. Later in the week, Molyneux tore the record books apart. After setting a pace so fast that only two other crews received silver replicas, he won his 11th TT and set the first sub-20-minute lap by a Sidecar. His 116.04mph lap was 30 seconds inside his previous best but it took a toll on his self-built outfit – the rear wheel bearing collapsed at Governor's Bridge on the last lap and Moly could only trickle over the finish line at 30mph. After the race he admitted, 'Stuff's been breaking and cracking that we've never had problems with before. Maybe we've found the limit for this sort of technology.'

When the first TT Superbike race finally kicked off a day late, it was business as usual for John McGuinness. He led from start to finish to give Yamaha a victory exactly 40 years since its first TT success and in its 50th birthday year. Despite it being his seventh TT win, it was the first time McGuinness had won a six-lap event. Adrian Archibald finished second, some 36 seconds down, while Irishman, Martin Finnegan, scored his first TT podium with third place.

Finnegan's motocross background resulted in a spectacular style when he began road racing and, together with sixth-placed finisher, Guy Martin, the two young guns seemed to represent the future of the TT. Finnegan, 24, won the 250cc Newcomers Manx GP in 1999, just a year after his road race debut; while Guy Martin, 23, only tried his hand at the TT after being suspended from British championship racing for slamming a race boss's fingers in his laptop and telling him to 'stick his championship up his arse!' When he switched to the roads, he found his spiritual home and is still pleased that he took a stand against petty authority. 'If I hadn't fallen out with the fella in the British championship I'd probably never have done the TT and would still be working four jobs to pay £1,000 to go racing every weekend. It was definitely the right thing to do and if I had my time again I'd still do the same thing.'

In his TT debut in 2004, Martin lapped at an astonishing 122mph. While riders used to spend three years learning the TT course before truly getting up to speed, Martin believes the countless on-board camera laps of the course which are now widely available, speed up the learning process. 'I watched David Jefferies's on-board camera lap thousands of times. It's the only way to learn the course. Riding the course on a road bike is a waste of time – you're stuck up the arse of a car all the time and you don't learn bugger all. I did about 113mph on my first ever lap and that was all down to watching videos because as soon as I set off I knew where I was going.'

Martin also believes the days of riding at 80 per cent and still being able to win at the TT are over. He says 'I ride the TT now as hard as the bike will go. There's none of this riding at 80 per cent lark – it's as hard as she'll go. To win now, you've got to be using every inch of the Tarmac and you've got to be prepared to put your neck on the line. Absolutely.'

With most young riders opting to pursue careers in safer, and more lucrative, short circuit-based championships, the TT had looked likely to run out of new talent – a trend which would ultimately lead to its downfall. Riders like Finnegan and Martin are the future of pure road racing and their aggressive, spectacular style has already made them firm favourites with TT fans. And for Martin, riding at the TT is a much greater thrill than racing on a short circuit. 'There is no thrill for me in short circuit racing. I enjoy the British championship because it's so competitive and because I like riding motorbikes, but there's no buzz like the TT. Where else can you get so close to telegraph poles and walls and kerbs? You have to have risk to get the buzz and there's no real risk in BSB. If you come off you just slide into a gravel trap and nine times out of ten you walk away.'

TT veteran, Ian Lougher, welcomes new talent at the TT but has his reservations over safety. 'It's great for the TT having all these young fast guys coming through but maybe they're pushing a little too hard. I think at the TT you can push up to a point but then you need to step back that little bit. Some of these guys are pushing to that point and then pushing a bit more. I always keep a little in reserve at the TT – even when I'm really trying there's always a cushion. But these days I've probably had to up my game so I'm riding at about 96-97 per cent whereas before 95 per cent was enough to be competitive.'

John McGuinness was seriously spooked in the Superstock race which had replaced the Production 1000 event. Riding into Crosby – the scene of David Jefferies's fatal accident two years previously – he had a massive slide on his Yamaha R1. 'I lost the front, had me feet down and tore the sole of my boot off at 180mph. I thought "Fucking hell, that was a bit strange" because I hadn't done anything different. When you've done as many laps of the TT course as I've done you get to know absolutely *everywhere* that you can expect to get a slide so you're ready for them. It's when you get an entirely unexpected slide that it spooks you.'

McGuinness continued for half a lap but then decided to pull in at the Bungalow, clearly shaken from his experience. He's still not sure what went wrong. 'I've thought about that moment a lot,' he says, 'and the only thing I can suggest is that the 180bhp Superstock bikes are asking too much of treaded road tyres in places. I might have been distracted by the fact that David Jefferies was killed at that corner though – I really don't know. Every time I go past there I always have a little word with myself and it's the same at the spot where Mick Lofthouse was killed. I say a lot of strange things to myself. Every time before a race I pray to all the lads who have gone too.'

It was also at the Bungalow that the race was decided. Adrian Archibald had been leading through-

Over the mountain. Racing journalist Gus Scott was having the time of his life at TT2005 before tragedy struck.

out on his Suzuki GSX-R1000 but ran out of fuel exiting the Bungalow section, allowing his team-mate Bruce Anstey to take an unexpected win. Team boss, Hector Neill, openly admitted it was his own fault as he'd got his counting wrong while filling Archibald's tank. Fully expecting to be lynched by the Irish rider, Neill promised to retire from fuel-filling duties. Archibald's fastest lap, set on treaded road-legal tyres, had been just two seconds slower than McGuinness' best on a BSB-spec machine in the TT Superbike race.

Ian Lougher had a unique excuse for not winning the Superstock TT which he revealed after clinching the afternoon's Supersport Junior Race A. 'I had the shits basically, which is why I was off the pace early on in the Superstock race. In fact, I almost threw up going into Ramsey.' Lougher blamed a dodgy lasagne for his condition but it didn't slow him on the 600 Honda as he picked up his seventh TT victory ahead of John McGuinness and Jason Griffiths.

There were two Supersport Junior races in 2005 but the toll that eight laps in total (as well as a week of practice) took on the machines meant the exercise was never repeated. Of the fancied front runners, John McGuinness, Ian Lougher, Bruce Anstey, Adrian Archibald and Richard Britton were all forced out of the race when their over-stressed machines expired. In their absence, the ever-reliable Jason Griffiths scored yet another second place while Raymond Porter managed to limp home in third, despite running out of petrol a few miles from home.

As John McGuinness flashed across the finish line to take his first Senior TT win, he had no idea of the horrific news that awaited him. Just two years after David Jefferies's death, another of his closest friends had lost his life on the very circuit which was fast making McGuinness's name a legend. 'I saw a blue bike with a bit of pink on it by the side of the road but thought "Nah, it can't be Gus" so I carried on. After the race I was whisked to the podium and was being interviewed and stuff and I felt on top of the world after winning three races – it was amazing. It was my first Senior win and I'd always wanted to lift that big trophy so it was brilliant. Then I went into the press room and was told about Gus and then my win seemed totally insignificant.'

Ian 'Gus' Scott was a hugely popular motorcycle journalist and racer and had been enjoying a steady TT debut, increasing his lap times in a methodical manner and not trying to set the world alight at his first attempt. Like all competitors, he knew the dangers of the TT – but what he didn't expect was a marshal to walk straight into his path in the flat-out blind kink exiting Kirkmichael village. Neither Scott, nor the marshal, stood a chance. His death was mercifully quick but, it has to be said, completely avoidable. The TT is dangerous enough without the added hazard of people who are supposed to be watching out for riders, crossing the track in front of them. The future of the meeting was again called into doubt as rows broke out about the standard of marshalling on the 37.73-mile course.

Guy Martin at the Bungalow. The British championship's loss was the TT's gain.

Gus Scott was thrilled to be taking part in 'the biggest race in the world' and would not have wanted the TT to be banned but it was clear that lessons would have to be learned from his tragic death so that the dangers faced by TT riders are reduced, not increased, by the presence of marshals. Ryan Farquhar best summed up the feelings of fellow riders when he angrily commented on the marshalling following the fatal accident. He fumed: 'The flags should have been at Douglas Road Corner (on the entry to Kirkmichael village), not when you're right on the incident. It's a fucking disgrace.'

Following Scott's death, more efforts were made to recruit and properly train marshals, and it can only be hoped that standards will continue to improve so that such a needless tragedy is never repeated. John McGuinness, devastated as he was by his friend's death, was still determined to carry on racing on the world's most dangerous course, yet he's still unsure how he manages to continue in the face of such frequent tragedy. 'I don't know how we do it really – how we somehow manage to switch off to all the deaths. We're kind of brought up that way as Brits – the old stiff upper lip thing. I remember a foreign rider got killed and his mate went straight home and said he'd never come back and you can't really blame him for that, but here I am – ready for more. I can't explain it.'

The Senior race, as always, continued, and Ian Lougher, by far the most experienced TT rider still racing, had another consistent finish in second place. Behind him was the New Order: Guy Martin and Martin Finnegan. The youngsters fought a titanic battle for the last podium spot with Guy Martin just getting the verdict at the flag by two seconds to take his first TT podium. 'I didn't know it was Finnegan,' says Martin. 'But I knew it was tight because I got a board on the Mountain saying plus zero so I thought I best get me finger out. All week I'd been desperate to get on the podium. I think I was the only rider to finish all five races in the top five but I hadn't got on the podium so to finally get up there was brilliant. There's nothing to beat it.'

In only his second TT, Martin lapped at an incredible 126.48mph while Finnegan posted the fastest ever lap by an Irishman and third fastest of all time at 127.01mph. The future of the TT looked in good hands.

John McGuinness: 'Ten years ago there was a gentleman's agreement to take it steady then race for the last lap or so. These days, especially this year with the level of riding far better than I've ever known it, you have to go for it from the start.'

On the eve of its 100th anniversary, it seemed the TT had already moved on in preparation for its second century. Competition had intensified, speeds had risen dramatically, lap records were shattered, more young riders had come to the fore to challenge the old guard, the organisation had improved, and more top teams were being lured back to the last great road race. It seemed the future of the world's oldest motorcycle race was secure.

Even the weather played a part in making TT 2006 one of the best in modern times. For the first time since 1957, every session of practice week was held in dry weather. And the top speeds achieved by the top men shocked even seasoned TT veterans. The onboard telemetry on Bruce Anstey's Suzuki GSX-R1000 showed he was travelling at 206mph down Sulby Straight; houses, walls, trees, a pub and a shop on either side of him. It was simply mind-blowing. 'You can't really see much at 206mph,' he admitted. 'I just keep it pinned.'

Hot on the heels of Guy Martin and Martin Finnegan, were new rising stars including Ian Hutchinson and Cameron Donald. Hutchinson, a top British championship racer and former Manx GP winner, had set practice week alight by setting the third fastest time at over 120mph – on his 600cc Kawasaki, against the full factory Superbikes! And by the end of the meeting, Cameron Donald would lap at over 128mph in only his second visit to the Island.

As always, however, the triumphs were matched with tragedies. Japanese rider Jun Maeda, died several days after crashing in practice, and reminded everyone that riding motorcycles at over 200mph between stone walls is a hideously dangerous game.

All-time Sidecar great, Dave Molyneux, also crossed the fine line between control and disaster when he flipped his outfit at Rhencullen during practice. The 11 times winner found a perfect line through the tricky section for what he claimed was the first time, but the extra speed he gained meant the front of his machine lifted, the wind got under it and flipped it over at around 140mph. After rider and passenger were thrown clear, the outfit burst into flames and was completely burnt out. Molyneux, who suffered a dislocated shoulder as well as friction burns and cuts, immediately announced his retirement but retracted the statement several days later. He may have been ruled out of TT 2006, but like so many other competitors, he couldn't resist the lure of racing round the Isle of Man and being bitten certainly didn't turn him shy.

Racing got under way with a record-breaking Superbike race in which John McGuinness, now Honda-mounted, broke the outright lap record from a standing start with an average speed of 127.83mph. With the TAS Suzukis of Bruce Anstey and Adrian Archibald and the AIM Yamaha of Guy Martin all breaking down, and with Ryan Farquhar ruled out of the TT with a broken arm, it was down to the latest TT hot shot, Ian Hutchinson, and old stager, Ian Lougher, to hound McGuinness. Lougher's experience eventually told and he took second place, 39 seconds behind McGuinness to record his 25th podium since his debut in 1984. 'Hutch' was delighted to fly the flag for the next generation of TT racers in third place.

In the absence of Dave Molyneux, Nick Crowe did the double for the first time and became only the second driver to post a sub-20-minute lap. Perhaps even more overjoyed than Crowe was 58-year-old stalwart, Roy Hanks, who took third place in what was his 40th TT. As chairman of the TT Supporters' Club, Hanks has been a lifelong fan of the event and no one more deserved a podium place. Reflecting on the continuing costs of pursuing his dream Hanks said, 'We've had no carpets or wallpaper for the past 10 years but it's worth it for moments like this.'

Bruce Anstey won his fifth TT with victory in the Superstock event after a close-fought battle with Ian Hutchinson. The pair were never more than a few seconds apart but the experienced Kiwi eventually managed to cross the line with eight seconds to spare over the relative newcomer. Jason Griffiths, who only races once a year at the TT, took yet another third place but seemed destined never to win a TT.

Jason Griffiths is one of the best riders to never have won a TT. Here the Welshman aviates his Yamaha at the top of Bray Hill.

Aussie sensation Cameron Donald is just one of the new young riders who will help guarantee the TT's future. He finished second in the 2006 Senior in what was only his second year of racing on the Island.

John McGuinness considered his Supersport 600 Junior win his finest ever performance at the TT. After another race-long battle with Ian Hutchinson, he took his second – and most satisfying – win of the week. 'People had written me off on the 600 saying I was a bit of a fat boy but that just lit my fire more. Everyone who doubts my ability just winds me up all the more so they're actually doing me a favour because I'll try even harder to prove them wrong. The bike wasn't that good in practice either but we changed a few bits on it and won the race. That was probably the best I've ever ridden round the TT course.'

Unfortunately, Hutchinson was later excluded from the results after a technical infringement. The cam lobe lift on his exhaust camshaft was found to measure 7.25mm when the accepted tolerance was 7mm. Even though officials admitted it would have offered no advantage, all Hutch's efforts had been in vain. Hutchinson's exclusion promoted Bruce Anstey to second and Jason Griffiths to third.

McGuinness had set a new lap record of 123.97mph in the Junior but, impressive as that was, it was completely overshadowed by his performance in the Senior. In winning the race, he took his 11th TT victory which put him third-equal with Steve Hislop and Phillip McCallen in the all-time winners' list. Only Joey Dunlop and Mike Hailwood have more wins to their credit. It was also Honda's 130th TT win and, to cap the statistics nicely, McGuinness became the first man to lap at 129mph when he set a new outright lap record at 129.45mph – a speed even he couldn't believe. 'I sat in the pit box at the end of that lap,' he said, 'and I could hear the Manx Radio commentator shouting I'd done 129mph. I was like "Fuck me! Did I really do that?" I thought 128.5mph was just about possible. It took me half a lap for it to sink in. I was riding along thinking "If I can do that, why do I need to ever come back?" then I got a plus seven on my board and Cameron Donald does 128mph and I'm thinking "What the hell is going on?" So, just like in the Supersport race, I had to push hard all the way.'

Cameron Donald's performance was incredible. In only his second visit to the TT, the Australian was pushing the acknowledged master of the toughest course on earth. His ambition had been a top-four finish and to do a 125mph lap. Instead, he finished second in the biggest race of the week and posted a lap at 128mph. In that one race, Donald marked himself out as one of the TT's top stars and his Australian passport also helped loan the event an international flavour it had been missing for some years.

New Zealanders were one of the few exceptions to this omission, and Bruce Anstey also raised some eyebrows when he followed McGuinness's lead and posted a 129mph lap on his final circuit to become the second fastest man in TT history. He finished third in what was the fastest race ever seen around the Mountain circuit. And with that race, the TT course became the fastest circuit in the world: McGuinness's new lap record eclipsed Anstey's previous record of 129.03mph set at the Ulster Grand Prix at Dundrod. There seems little doubt that the Centennial TT in 2007 will see the first ever 130mph lap of the Mountain circuit. The only question is, in a new era of such intense competition – who will set it?

Charlie Collier and Rem Fowler, who had ridden their hearts out in 1907 to set average lap times of just over 40mph would never have believed such speeds were possible. So much has changed in the century since those two pioneers became the first winners of an Isle of Man Tourist Trophy race; the motorcycles have gone from making 2 horsepower to over 200bhp and top speeds have risen from 55mph to 205mph. Riding gear has changed from flat caps and tweed jackets to one-piece leathers and full-face crash helmets, medical back-up has moved on from boy scouts to emergency helicopters, and the paddock has changed from being a field full of beer crates to a multi-million pound gathering of articulated trucks and hospitality units. Yet there is one constant in all this change – the TT riders themselves. While they may differ from the rest of us in their biological make-up, there is no difference at all between current stars like John McGuinness and Guy Martin and the pioneers of the TT like Collier and Fowler. It was the same brand of courage which allowed Rem Fowler to ride though a wall of flame in 1907, not knowing if he would come out the other side alive, as it took for McGuinness to set an outright lap record of almost 130mph on the course which had already claimed the lives of two of his best friends.

The times may have changed, but the heroism and courage of *every* man and woman who has tackled the Isle of Man Tourist Trophy races over the last hundred years has remained the same. It will be a sad day for mankind if we ever deny those kind of heroes the challenge that makes them feel truly alive.

Into the light.
New TT hero Guy Martin breaks out of the shadows in 2006. He set a 122mph lap in his first year at the TT.

The sky's the limit.
John McGuinness, 2006. The man everybody had to beat.

Jim Moodie on the Clarion Suzuki GSX-R750 in 1997. It wasn't a happy pairing but the Scot won a total of eight TTs on other machines.

CHAPTER 10

RESULTS 1907-2006

DUN
SHELL
CONVENIENCES

ISLE OF MAN TOURIST TROPHY RACE RESULTS 1907-2006

** Indicates new lap record*

1907

Single-cylinder

Only eight finishers

	(10 laps/158 miles)	St John's course
1.	C. Collier	Matchless
	4h 08m 0.82s/38.2mph	
2.	J. Marshall	Triumph
3.	F. Hulbert	Triumph
4.	R. Brice	Brown
5.	M. Geiger	NSU
6.	J. Smyth	Rex
7.	R. Ayton	Coventry
8.	F. Applebee	Rex
	Fastest lap: H. Collier, 23m 05s/41.81mph	

Twin-cylinder

Only three finishers

	(10 laps/158 miles)	St John's course
1.	R. Fowler	Norton
	4h 21m 52.8s/36.2mph	
2.	W. Wells	Vindec
3.	W. Heaton	Rex
	Fastest lap: R. Fowler, 22m 06s/42.91mph	

1908

Single-cylinder

	(10 laps/158 miles)	St John's course
1.	J. Marshall	Triumph
	3h 54m 50s/40.49mph	
2.	C. Collier	Matchless
3.	R. Arbuthnot	Triumph
4.	W. Newsome	Triumph
5.	W. McMinnies	Triumph
6.	C. Franklin	Chater-Lea
7.	H. Lister-Cooper	Triumph
8.	O. Godfrey	Triumph
9.	R. Brice	Brown
10.	G. Gibson	Triumph
	Fastest lap: J. Marshall. 22m 20s/42.48mph*	

Twin-cylinder

	(10 laps/158 miles)	St John's course
1.	H. Reed	DOT
	4h 05m 58s/38.5mph	
2.	W. Bashall	BAT
3.	R. Clark	FN
4.	W. Wells	Vindec
5.	J. Lang	NSU
6.	N. Drury	Matchless
7.	A. Moorhouse	Rex
8.	J. Dixon	Vindec
9.	H. Colver	Matchless
10.	S. Perryman	Norton
	Fastest lap: W. Bashall, 22m 27s/42.45mph	

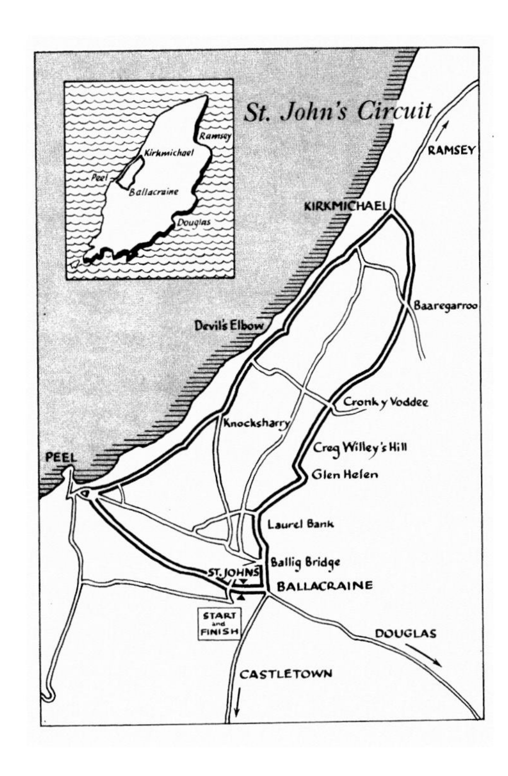

1909

500cc Single/750cc Twin-cylinder

	(10 laps/158 miles)	St John's course
1.	H. Collier	Matchless
	3h 13m 37s/49.01mph	
2.	G. Evans	Indian
3.	W. Newsome	Triumph
4.	O. Godfrey	Rex
5.	C. Franklin	Triumph
6.	F. Applebee	Rex
7.	J. Munro	BAT
8.	B. Jones	Premier
9.	A. Moorhouse	Rex
10.	H. Colver	Matchless
	Fastest lap: H. Collier, 18m 05s/52.27mph*	

1910

500cc Single/670cc Twin-cylinder

	(10 laps/158 miles)	St John's course
1.	C. Collier	Matchless
	3h 7m 24s/50.63mph	
2.	H. Collier	Matchless
3.	W. Creyton	Triumph
4.	J. Adamson	Triumph
5.	J. Scriven	Rex
6.	J. Marshall	Triumph
7.	H. Lister-Cooper	Triumph
8.	W. Newsome	Triumph
9.	F. Phillip	Scott
10.	H. Colver	Matchless
	Fastest lap: H. Bowen, 17m 51s/53.15mph*	

1911

Junior

	(4 laps/151 miles)	Four-Inch course
1.	P. Evans	Humber
	3h 37m 07s/41.45mph	
2.	H. Collier	Matchless
3.	H. Cox	Forward
4.	D. Brown	Humber
5.	H. Greaves	Enfield
6.	K. Gassert	NSU
7.	W. Douglas	Douglas
8.	A. Fenn	Humber
9.	F. Johnson	Humber
10.	J. Haslam	Zenith
	Fastest lap: P. Evans, 53m 24s/42.00mph	

Senior

	(5 laps/187.5 miles)	Four-Inch course
1.	O. Godfrey	Indian
	3h 56m 10s/47.63mph	
2.	C. Franklin	Indian
3.	A. Moorhouse	Indian
4.	H. Collier	Matchless
5.	H. Mason	Matchless
6.	J. Carvill	Triumph
7.	W. Bashall	BAT
8.	Q. Smith	Triumph
9.	H. Lister-Cooper	Triumph
10.	J. Bashall	BAT
	Fastest lap: F. Philipp, 44m 52s/50.11mph	

1912

Junior

(4 laps/151 miles)		Four-Inch course
1.	W.H. Bashall	Douglas
	3h 46m 59s/39.65mph	
2.	E. Kickham	Douglas
3.	H. Cox	Forward
4.	J. Stewart	Douglas
5.	P. Owen	Forward
6.	R. Ellis	NUT
7.	H. Petty	Singer
8.	J. Haslam	Douglas
9.	E. Pratt	OK
10.	H. Newman	OK
Fastest lap: E Kickham, 53m 53s/41.76mph		

Senior

(5 laps/187.5 miles)		Four-Inch course
1.	F. Applebee	Scott
	3h 51m 03s/48.69mph	
2.	J. Haswell	Triumph
3.	H. Collier	Matchless
4.	C. Collier	Matchless
5.	J. Hoffmann	Triumph
6.	J. Adamson	Triumph
7.	A. Kirk	Triumph
8.	J. Alexander	Indian
9.	C. Martin	Triumph
10.	A. Alexander	Indian
Fastest lap: F. Applebee, 45m 31s/49.44mph		

1913

Junior

(6 laps/225 miles)		Four-Inch course
1.	H. Mason	NUT
	5h 08m 34s/43.73mph	
2.	W. Newsome	Douglas
3.	H. Newman	Ivy-Precision
4.	D. O'Donavan	NSU
5.	F. Ball	Douglas
6.	S. Wright	Humber
7.	R. Bell	NSU
8.	R. Ellis	NUT
9.=	J. Haslam	Douglas
9.=	W. Heaton	AJS
Fastest lap: H. Mason, 49m 32s/45.42mph*		

Senior

(7 laps/262.5 miles)		Four-Inch course
1.	T. Wood	Scott
	5h 26m 18s/48.28mph	
2.	A. Abbott	Rudge
3.	A. Alexander	Indian
4.	C. Franklin	Indian
5.	J. Cocker	Singer
6.	T. Sheard	Rudge
7.	E. Moxey	Zenith
8.	S. Gerrett	Regal Green
9.	V. Busby	Ariel
10.	N. Brown	Indian
Fastest lap: T. Wood, 43m 10s/52.12mph*		

1914

Junior

(5 laps/187.5 miles)		Four-Inch course
1.	E. Williams	AJS
	4h 06m 50s/45.58mph	
2.	C. Williams	AJS
3.	F. Walker	Enfield
4.	W. Jones	AJS
5.	F. Barker	Zenith
6.	B. Haddock	AJS
7.	E. Elwell	Douglas
8.	E. Keyte	Enfield
9.	D. Bolton	Douglas
10.	T. Knowles	Humber
Fastest lap: E. Williams, 47m 18s/47.57mph*		

Senior

(6 laps/225 miles)		Four-Inch course
1.	C. Pullin	Rudge
	4h 32m 48s/49.49mph	
2.=	H. Davies	Sunbeam
2.=	O. Godfrey	Indian
4.	H. Colver	Matchless
5.	G. Boyton	Triumph
6.	J. Emerson	ABC
7.	H. Mason	NUT
8.	C. Franklin	Indian
9.	Q. Smith	Triumph
10.	J. Sirett	Motosacoche
Fastest lap: T. Wood, 42m 16s/53.50mph*		

1920

Junior

(5 laps/188.65 miles)		Mountain course
1.	C. Williams	AJS
	4h 37m 57s/40.74mph	
2.	J. Watson-Bourne	Blackburne
3.	J. Holroyd	Blackburne
4.	R. Clark	Levis
5.	E. Longdon	DOT
6.	N. Loughton	Douglas
7.	G. Khun	Levis
8.	H. Prescott	AJS
9.	F. Applebee	Levis
10.	S. Haden	New Comet
Fastest lap: E. Williams, 44m 06s/51.36mph		

Senior

(6 laps/226.38 miles)		Mountain course
1.	T. de la Hay	Sunbeam
	4h 22m 23s/51.79mph	
2.	D. Brown	Norton
3.	R. Brown	Sunbeam
4.	N. Slacter Junior	Norton
5.	H. Harveyson	Indian
6.	A. Alexander	Indian
7.	J. Shaw	Norton
8.	N. Brown	Norton
9.	F. Townshend	Sunbeam
10.	F. North	Norton
Fastest lap: G. Dance, 40m 43s/55.62mph*		

1921

Junior

(5 laps/188.65 miles)		Mountain course
1.	E. Williams	AJS
	3h 37m 23s/52.1mph	
2.	H. Davies	AJS
3.	T. Sheard	AJS
4.	G. Kelly	AJS
5.	J. Whalley	Massey-Arran
6.	O. Wade	AJS
7.	W. Howarth	DOT
8.	H. Harris	AJS
9.	R. Carey	Blackburne
10.	D. Prentice	New Imperial
Fastest lap: H. Davies, 41m 04s/55.15mph*		

Senior

(6 laps/226.38 miles)		Mountain course
1.	H. Davies	AJS
	4h 09m 22s/54.49mph	
2.	F. Dixon	Indian
3.	H. le Vack	Indian
4.	A. Bennett	Sunbeam
5.	J. Watson-Bourne	Triumph
6.	J. Mitchell	Norton
7.	F. Edmond	Triumph
8.	G. Danve	Sunbeam
9.	T. Sheard	Sunbeam
10.	F. Townshend	Triumph
Fastest lap: F. Edmond, 40m 08s/56.40mph*		

1922

Lightweight 250

(5 laps/188.65 miles)		Mountain course
1.	G. Davison	Levis
	3h 46m 56.8s/49.89mph	
2.	D. Young	Rex-Acme
3.	S. Jones	Velocette
4.	L. Padley	Sheffield-Henderson
5.	D. Prentice	New Imperial
6.	F. North	OK
7.	N. Hall	OK
8.	C. Hopwood	Levis
9.	L. Nicholson	Coulson
10.	R. Loughton	Francis Barnett
Fastest lap: W. Handley, 44m 24s/51.00mph*		

Junior

(5 laps/188.65 miles)		Mountain course
1.	T. Sheard	AJS
	3h 26m 48.2s/54.75mph	
2.	G. Grinton	AJS
3.	J. Thomas	Sheffield-Henderson
4.	R. Lucas	Coulson
5.	S. Woods	Cotton
6.	J. Haslam	Douglas
7.	P. Newman	Ivy
8.	G. Shepherd	Edmund
9.	J. Bance	Blackburne
10.	T. Jones	Ivy
Fastest lap: H. le Vack, 40m 07s/56.46mph*		

Senior

(6 laps/226.5 miles)	Mountain course
1. A. Bennett	Sunbeam
3h 53m 00.2s/58.31mph	
2. W. Brandish	Triumph
3. H. Langman	Scott
4. C. Wood	Scott
5. G. Walker	Norton
6. T. de la Hay	Sunbeam
7. A. Alexander	Douglas
8. V. Olsson	Sunbeam
9. G. Clapham	Scott
10. J. Adamson	Indian
Fastest lap: A. Bennett, 37m 46s/59.99mph*	

1923

Junior

(6 laps/226.38 miles)	Mountain course
1. S. Woods	Cotton
4h 03m 47s/55.74mph	
2. H. Harris	AJS
3. A. Alexander	Douglas
4. J. Watson-Bourne	Matador
5. V. Anstice	Douglas
6. F. Longman	AJS
7. F. Morgan	Cotton
8. G. Tottey	New Imperial
9. C. Pullin	Douglas
10. G. Strange	OK
Fastest lap: J. Simpson, 38m 00s/59.59mph*	

Lightweight 250

(6 laps/226.38 miles)	Mountain course
1. J. Porter	New Gerrard
4h 21m 37s/51.93mph	
2. H. le Vack	New Imperial
3. D. Hall	Rex-Acme
4. R. Gray	Rex-Acme
5. N. Black	Cedos
6. L. Horton	New Imperial
7. P. Pike	Levis
8. W. Handley	OK
9. P. Walker	Excelsior
10. G. Davison	Levis
Fastest lap: W. Handley, 41m 58s/53.95mph*	

Sidecar

(3 laps/113 miles)	Mountain course
1. F. Dixon	Douglas
2h 07m 48s/53.15mph	
2. G. Walker	Norton
3. G. Tucker	Norton
4. D. Davidson	Douglas
5. H. Reed	DOT
6. F. Hatton	Douglas
7. H. Langman	Scott
8. A. Taylor	OEC-Blackburne
9. R. Wetherall	Wetherall
10. F. Longman	Scott
Fastest lap: H. Langman, 41m 24s/54.69mph	

Senior

(6 laps/226.38 miles)	Mountain course
1. T. Sheard	Douglas
4h 04m 33s/55.55mph	
2. G. Black	Norton
3. F. Dixon	Indian
4. G. Walker	Norton
5. T. Simister	Norton
6. J. Emerson	Douglas
7. J. Shaw	Norton
8. T. Allchin	Douglas
9. T. de la Hay	Sunbeam
10. A. Bennett	Douglas
Fastest lap: J. Whalley, 37m 54s/59.74mph	

1924

Junior

(6 laps/226.38 miles)	Mountain course
1. K. Twemlow	New Imperial
4h 41m 21s/55.67mph	
2. S. Ollerhead	DOT
3. H. Scott	AJS
4. C. Ashby	Montgomery
5. H. Willis	Montgomery
6. J. Emerson	DOT
7. F. Simpson	Excelsior
8. L. Nicholson	OEC-Blackburne
9. F. Marston	AJS
10. J. Shaw	Zenith
Fastest lap: J. Simpson, 35m 05s/64.54mph	

Ultra-Lightweight 175cc

Massed start

(3 laps/113.19 miles)	Mountain course
1. J. Porter	New Gerrard
2h 12m 40.4s/51.2mph	
2. F. Morgan	Cotton
3. C. Stead	Cotton
4. G. Davison	Levis
5. H. Brockbank	Cotton
6. T. Meeten	Francis Barnett
7. B. Smith	Wee MacGregor
8. J. Oates	Powell
9. A. Bennett	Diamond
10. D. Young	Wee MacGregor
Fastest lap: J. Porter, 43m 02s/52.61mph	

Sidecar

Only five finishers

(4 laps/150.92 miles)	Mountain course
1. G. Tucker	Norton
2h 56m 34.2s/51.31mph	
2. H. Reed	DOT
3. A. Tinkler	Matador
4. J. Taylor	New Scale
5. G. Grinton	Norton
Fastest lap: F. Dixon, 43m 32s/53.23mph	

Lightweight 250

(6 laps/226.38 miles)	Mountain course
1. E. Twemlow	New Imperial
4h 05m 03s/55.44mph	
2. H. Brockbank	Cotton
3. J. Cooke	DOT
4. L. Cridland	JES
5. P. Pike	Levis
6. H. Harris	New Imperial
7. F. Simpson	Excelsior
8. C. Gleare	OK-Blackburne
9. C. Johnston	Cotton
10. G. Povey	Velocette
Fastest lap: E. Twemlow, 38m 51s/58.28mph*	

Senior

(6 laps/226.38 miles)	Mountain course
1. A. Bennett	Norton
3h 40m 24.6s/61.64mph	
2. H. Langman	Scott
3. F. Dixon	Douglas
4. C. Young	Triumph
5. H. Hassall	Norton
6. C. Hough	AJS
7. A. Alexander	Douglas
8. F. Longman	AJS
9. J. Stuart	Norton
10. H. Loader	Norton
Fastest lap: F. Dixon, 35m 31s/63.75mph*	

1925

Junior

(6 laps/226.38 miles)	Mountain course
1. W. Handley	Rex-Acme
3h 28m 56.4s/65.02mph	
2. H. Davies	HRD
3. J. Simpson	AJS
4. C. Hough	AJS
5. H. Harris	HRD
6. L. Horton	New Imperial
7. C. Young	Royal Enfield
8. C. Dodson	Sunbeam
9. F. Testall	Sunbeam
10. R. Mundey	New Hudson
Fastest lap: W. Handley, 34m 23s/65.89mph*	

Ultra-Lightweight 175cc

Only six finishers

(4 laps/150.92 miles)	Mountain course
1. W. Handley	Rex-Acme
2h 49m 27.0s/53.45mph	
2. C. Johnston	Cotton
3. J. Porter	New Gerrard
4. J. Morgan	Cotton
5. C. Barrow	Excelsior
6. C. Dodson	DOT
Fastest lap: W. Handley, 41m 52s/54.12mph*	

Senior

(6 laps/226.38 miles)	Mountain course
1. H. Davies	HRD
3h 25m 25.8s/66.13mph	
2. F. Longman	AJS
3. A. Bennett	Norton
4. T. Bulluss	Panther
5. H. Langman	Scott
6. L. Randles	Sunbeam
7. C. Waterhouse	Sunbeam
8. A. Varzi	Sunbeam
9. H. Willis	Montgomery
10. F. Tetstall	Sunbeam
Fastest lap: J. Simpson, 32m 50s/68.97mph*	

1926

Junior

(7 laps/264.11 miles)		Mountain course
1.	A. Bennett	Velocette
	3h 57m 37s/66.70mph	
2.	J. Simpson	AJS
3.	W. Handley	Rex-Acme
4.	F. Dixon	Douglas
5.	G. Kuhn	Velocette
6.	J. Burney	Royal Enfield
7.	C. Hough	AJS
8.	F. Longman	AJS
9.	G. Povey	Velocette
10.	J. Amott	Montgomery
Fastest lap: A. Bennett, 32m 56s/68.75mph*		

Lightweight 250

Only seven finishers

(7 laps/264.11 miles)		Mountain course
1.	C. Johnston	Cotton
	4h 23m 16s/60.24mph	
2.	F. Morgan	Cotton
3.	W. Colgan	Cotton
4.	W. Bicknell	Royal Enfield
5.	E. Archibald	OK
6.	S. Gleave	Diamond
7.	G. Shepherd	New Imperial
Fastest lap: P. Ghersi (disqualified), 35m 49s/63.12mph*		

Senior

(7 laps/264.11 miles)		Mountain course
1.	S. Woods	Norton
	3h 54m 39.8s/67.54mph	
2.	W. Handley	Rex-Acme
3.	F. Longman	AJS
4.	J. Craig	Norton
5.	C. Wood	HRD
6.	G. Rowley	AJS
7.	A. Varzi	Sunbeam
8.	S. Jackson	HRD
9.	K. Twemlow	HRD
10.	G. Walker	Sunbeam
Fastest lap: J. Simpson, 32m 09s/70.43mph*		

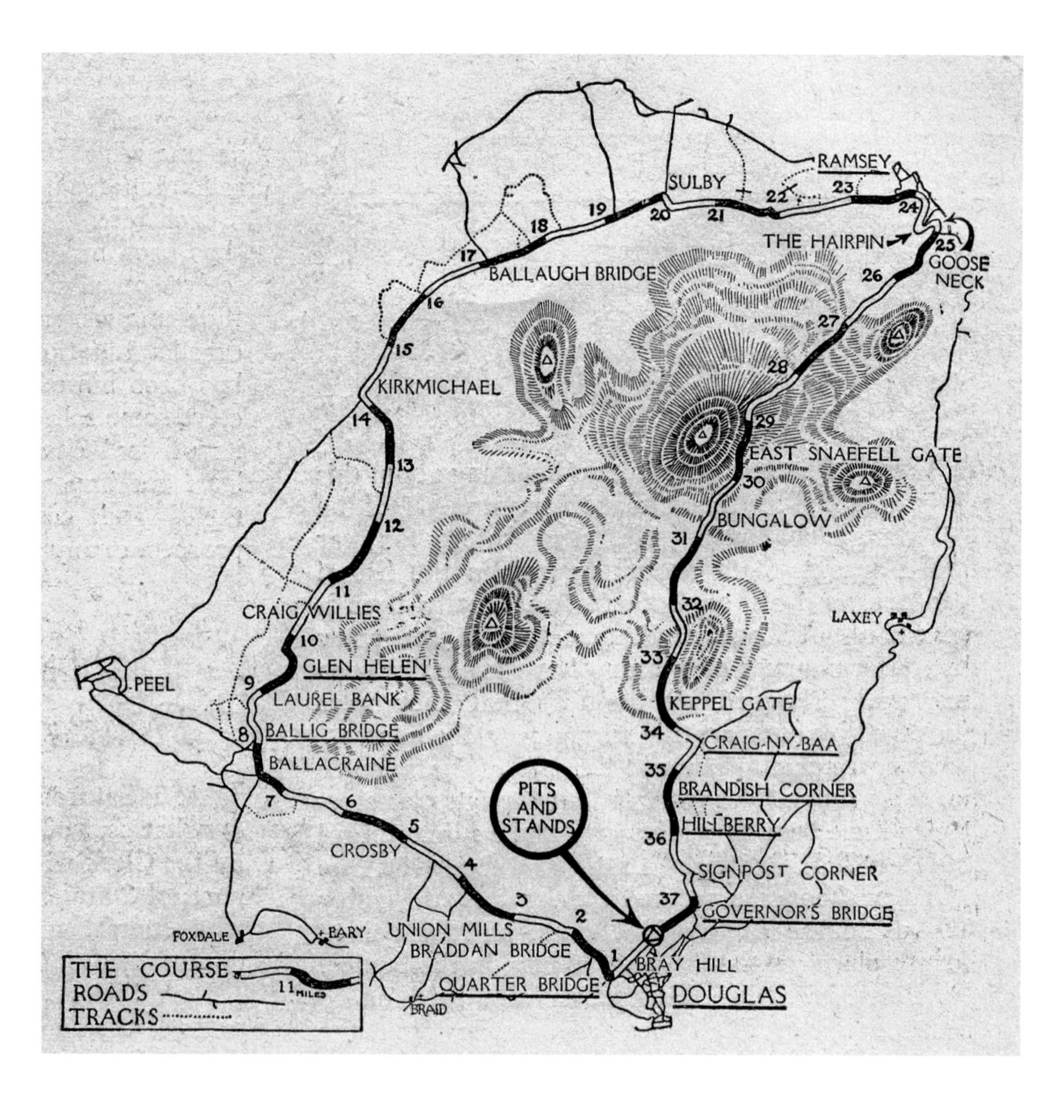

1927

Junior

(7 laps/264.11 miles)		Mountain course
1.	F. Dixon	HRD
	3h 55m 54s/67.19mph	
2.	H. Willis	Velocette
3.	J. Simpson	AJS
4.	G. Reynard	Royal Enfield
5.	C. Johnston	Cotton
6.	E. Twemlow	Excelsior
7.	C. Barrow	Royal Enfield
8.	L. Cohen	AJS
9.	W. Pearce	DOT
10.	G. Himming	Zenith
Fastest lap: W. Handley, 32m 44s/69.18mph*		

Lightweight 250

(7 laps/264.11 miles)		Mountain circuit
1.	W. Handley	Rex-Acme
	4h 10m 22s/63.30mph	
2.	L. Archangeli	Moto Guzzi
3.	C. Ashby	OK-Supreme
4.	S. Crabtree	Crabtree
5.	A. Varzi	Moto Guzzi
6.	F. Hall	New Imperial
7.	C. Barrow	Royal Enfield
8.	S. Gleave	DOT
9.	G. Davison	Rex-Acme
10.	L. Higson	Montgomery
Fastest lap: A. Bennett, 35m 08s/64.45mph*		

Senior

(7 laps/264.11 miles)		Mountain course
1.	A. Bennett	Norton
	3h 51m 42s/68.41mph	
2.	J. Guthrie	New Hudson
3.	T. Simister	Triumph
4.	J. Shaw	Norton
5.	G. Walker	Sunbeam
6.	F. Dixon	HRD
7.	O. Langton	New Hudson
8.	C. Dodson	Sunbeam
9.	G. Rowley	AJS
10.	W. Braidwood	P&M
Fastest lap: S. Woods, 31m 54s/70.90mph*		

1928

Junior

(7 laps/264.11 miles)		Mountain course
1.	A. Bennett	Velocette
	3h 50m 52s/68.65mph	
2.	H. Willis	Velocette
3.	K. Twemlow	DOT
4.	S. Crabtree	Excelsior
5.	F. Hicks	Velocette
6.	G. Reynard	Royal Enfield
7.	C. Ashby	Raleigh
8.	S. Jackson	Montgomery
9.	B. Hieatt	Cotton
10.	C. Tattersall	DOT
Fastest lap: A. Bennett, 32m 13s/70.28mph*		

Lightweight 250

(7 laps/264.11 miles)		Mountain course
1.	F. Longman	OK-Supreme
	4h 11m 59s/62.87mph	
2.	C. Barrow	Royal Enfield
3.	E. Twemlow	DOT
4.	G. Himing	OK-Supreme
5.	C. Ashby	OK-Supreme
6.	V. Anstice	OK-Supreme

7. S. Jones	New Imperial
8. J. Porter	New Gerrard
9. S. Gleave	New Imperial
10. J. Burney	Royal Enfield
Fastest lap: F. Longman, 35m 08s/64.65mph	

Senior

(7 laps/264.11 miles)	Mountain course
1. C. Dodson	Sunbeam
4h 11m 40s/62.98mph	
2. G. Rowley	AJS
3. T. Hatch	Scott
4. H. Tyrell-Smith	Rudge
5. S. Woods	Norton
6. E. Mellors	Norton
7. F. Franconi	Sunbeam
8. J. Duncan	Raleigh
9. A. Warwick	P&M
10. A. Quinn	Triumph
Fastest lap: J. Simpson, 33m 20s/67.98mph	

1929

Junior

(7 laps/264.11 miles)	Mountain course
1. F. Hicks	Velocette
3h 47m 23s/69.71mph	
2. W. Handley	AJS
3. A. Bennett	Velocette
4. C. Dodson	Sunbeam
5. T. Simister	Velocette
6. D. Hall	Velocette
7. S. Crabtree	Velocette
8. W. Burrows	DOT
9. K. Twemlow	DOT
10. J. Shaw	Velocette
Fastest lap: F. Hicks, 31m 05s/70.95mph*	

Lightweight 250

(7 laps/264.11 miles)	Mountain course
1. S. Crabtree	Excelsior
4h 08m 10s/63.87mph	
2. K. Twemlow	DOT
3. F. Longman	OK-Supreme
4. J. Sarkis	OK-Supreme
5. C. Johnston	Cotton
6. S. Jackson	Montgomery
7. E. Twemlow	DOT
8. J. Whalley	Cotton
9. J. Shaw	OK-Supreme
10. H. Lester	SOS
Fastest lap: P. Ghersi, 35m 49s/66.63mph	

Senior

(7 laps/264.11 miles)	Mountain course
1. C. Dodson	Sunbeam
3h 39m 59s/72.05mph	
2. A. Bennett	Sunbeam
3. H. Tyrell-Smith	Rudge
4. P. Hunt	Norton
5. G. Nott	Velocette
6. F. Hicks	Velocette
7. A. Simcock	Sunbeam
8. C. Johnston	Cotton
9. E. Twemlow	DOT
10. S. Jackson	Montgomery
Fastest lap: C. Dodson, 30m 47s/73.55mph*	

1930

Junior

(7 laps/264.11 miles)	Mountain course
1. H.G. Tyrell-Smith	Rudge
3h 43m 00s/71.08mph	
2. G.E. Nott	Rudge
3. G.W. Walker	Rudge
4. D. Hall	Velocette
5. C. Williams	Raleigh
6. S. Woods	Norton
7. A. Mitchell	Velocette
8. G. Himing	AJS
9. P. Hunt	Norton
10. L. Davenport	AJS
Fastest lap: G. Nott, 31m 21s/72.02mph*	

Lighweight 250

(7 laps/264.11 miles)	Mountain course
1. J. Guthrie	AJS
4h 04m 56.0s/64.71mph	
2. C. Johnston	OK-Supreme
3. C. Barrow	OK-Supreme
4. S. Gleave	SGS
5. J. Lind	AJS
6. E. Mellors	New Imperial
7. E. Twemlow	Cotton
8. C. Tattersall	SGS
9. C. Needham	Rex-Acme
10. V. Anstice	Excelsior
Fastest lap: W. Handley, 33m 52s/68.86mph*	

Senior

(7 laps/264.11 miles)	Mountain course
1. W. Handley	Rudge
3h 33m 30s/74.24mph	
2. G. Walker	Rudge
3. J. Simpson	Norton
4. C. Dodson	Sunbeam
5. T. Bullus	Sunbeam
6. H. Tyrell-Smith	Rudge
7. G. Nott	Rudge
8. V. Brittain	Sunbeam
9. J. Lind	AJS
10. J. Duncan	Raleigh
Fastest lap: W. Handley, 29m 41s/76.28mph*	

1931

Junior

(7 laps/264.11 miles)	Mountain course
1. P. Hunt	Norton
3h 34m 21s/73.94mph	
2. J. Guthrie	Norton
3. G. Nott	Rudge
4. S. Woods	Norton
5. G. Walker	Rudge
6. C. Dodson	Excelsior
7. A. Mitchell	Velocette
8. J. Simpson	Norton
9. G. Rowley	AJS
10. E. Mellors	New Imperial
Fastest lap: P. Hunt, 30m 05s/75.27mph*	

Lightweight 250

(7 laps/264.11 miles)	Mountain course
1. G. Walker	Rudge
3h 49m 47s/68.98mph	
2. H. Tyrell-Smith	Rudge
3. E. Mellors	New Imperial
4. G. Nott	Rudge
5. F. Longman	OK-Supreme
6. P. Ghersi	New Imperial
7. S. Williams	New Imperial
8. C. Johnston	Moto Guzzi
9. C. Needham	OK-Supreme
10. C. Taylor	OK-Supreme
Fastest lap: G. Nott, 31m 34s/71.73mph*	

Senior

(7 laps/264.11 miles)	Mountain course
1. P. Hunt	Norton
3h 23m 28s/77.90mph	
2. J. Guthrie	Norton
3. S. Woods	Norton
4. G. Nott	Rudge
5. G. Walker	Rudge
6. E. Mellors	NSU
7. A. Tyler	Raleigh
8. E. Simcock	OK-Supreme
9. J. Lind	Velocette
10. S. Gleave	SGS
Fastest lap: J. Simpson, 28m 01s/80.82mph*	

1932

Junior

(7 laps/264.11 miles)	Mountain course
1. S. Woods	Norton
3h 25m 25s/77.16mph	
2. W. Handley	Rudge
3. H. Tyrell-Smith	Rudge
4. C. Dodson	Excelsior
5. G. Walker	Rudge
6. L. Archer	Velocette
7= L. Davenport	New Imperial
7= A. Bennett	Velocette
9. S. Gleave	New Imperial
10. C. Williams	Velocette
Fastest lap: S. Woods, 28m 48s/78.62mph*	

Lightweight 250

Only eight finishers

(7 laps/264.11 miles)	Mountain course
1. L. Davenport	New Imperial
3h 41m 53s/70.48mph	
2. G. Walker	Rudge
3. W. Handley	Rudge
4. T. Spann	New Imperial
5. C. Tattersall	CTS
6. J. Fairweather	Cotton
7. J. Lind	OK-Supreme
8. H. Warburton	Excelsior
Fastest lap: W. Handley, 30m 34s/74.08mph*	

Senior

(7 laps/264.11 miles)		Mountain course
1.	S. Woods	Norton
	3h 19m 40s/79.38mph	
2.	J. Guthrie	Norton
3.	J. Simpson	Norton
4.	G. Nott	Rudge
5.	C. Dodson	Excelsior
6.	G. Walker	Rudge
7.	J. Duncan	Cotton
8.	H. Tyrell-Smith	Rudge
9.	E. Simcock	Sunbeam
10.	G. Emery	Sunbeam
Fastest lap: J. Simpson, 27m 47s/81.50mph*		

1933

Junior

(7 laps/264.11 miles)		Mountain course
1.	S. Woods	Norton
	3h 23m 00s/78.08mph	
2.	P. Hunt	Norton
3.	J. Guthrie	Norton
4.	A. Mitchell	Velocette
5.	H. Tyrell-Smith	Velocette
6.	G. Emery	Velocette
7.	W. Handley	Velocette
8.	H. Newman	Velocette
9.	D. Hall	Velocette
10.	E. Thomas	Velocette
Fastest lap: S. Woods, 28m 35s/79.22mph*		

Lightweight 250

(7 laps/264.11 miles)		Mountain course
1.	S. Gleave	Excelsior
	3h 41m 23s/71.59mph	
2.	C. Dodson	New Imperial
3.	C. Manders	Rudge
4.	L. Davenport	New Imperial
5.	S. Crabtree	Excelsior
6.	P. Ghersi	Moto Guzzi
7.	E. Mellors	New Imperial
8.	L. Martin	Rudge
9.	C. Taylor	OK-Supreme
10.	J. Fairweather	Cotton
Fastest lap: S. Gleave, 31m 11s/72.62mph*		

Senior

(7 laps/264.11 miles)		Mountain course
1.	S. Woods	Norton
	3h 15m 35s/81.04mph	
2.	J. Simpson	Norton
3.	P. Hunt	Norton
4.	J. Guthrie	Norton
5.	G. Nott	Rudge
6.	A. Mitchell	Velocette
7.	J. Duncan	Cotton
8.	S. Wood	Jawa
9.	H. Tyrell-Smith	Rudge
10.	J. Williams	Norton
Fastest lap: S. Woods, 27m 22s/82.74mph*		

1934

Junior

(7 laps/264.11 miles)		Mountain course
1.	J. Guthrie	Norton
	3h 20m 14s/79.16mph	
2.	J. Simpson	Norton
3.	G. Nott	Husqvarna
4.	H. Newman	Velocette
5.	A. Mitchell	Velocette
6.	L. Archer	Velocette
7.	W. Rusk	Velocette
8.	F. Aranda	Velocette
9.	V. Brittain	Velocette
10.	H. Lamacraft	Velocette
Fastest lap: J. Guthrie, 28m 16s/80.11mph*		

Lightweight 250

Only eight finishers

(7 laps/264.11 miles)		Mountain course
1.	J. Simpson	Rudge
	3h 43m 50s/70.81mph	
2.	G. Nott	Rudge
3.	G. Walker	Rudge
4.	S. Woods	Moto Guzzi
5.	C. Manders	New Imperial
6.	S. Gleave	Excelsior
7.	C. Tattersall	CTS
8.	T. Martin	Cotton
Fastest lap: J. Simpson, 30m 45s/73.64mph		

Senior

(7 laps/264.11 miles)		Mountain course
1.	J. Guthrie	Norton
	3h 23m 10s/78.01mph	
2.	J. Simpson	Norton
3.	W. Rusk	Velocette
4.	L. Archer	Velocette
5.	V. Brittain	Norton
6.	G. Walker	Rudge
7.	H. Tyrell-Smith	AJS
8.	H. Newman	Velocette
9.	H. Daniell	AJS
10.	A. Mitchell	AJS
Fastest lap: S. Woods, 28m 08s/80.49mph		

1935

Junior

(7 laps/264.11 miles)		Mountain course
1.	J. Guthrie	Norton
	3h 20m 16s/79.14mph	
2.	W. Rusk	Norton
3.	J. White	Norton
4.	D. Pirie	Velocette
5.	G. Nott	Velocette
6.	E. Thomas	Velocette
7.	J. Duncan	Norton
8.	H. Daniell	AJS
9.	L. Archer	Velocette
10.	H. Tyrell-Smith	AJS
Fastest lap: W. Rusk, 28m 19s/79.96mph		

Lightweight 250

(7 laps/264.11 miles)		Mountain course
1.	S. Woods	Moto Guzzi
	3h 41m 29s/71.56mph	
2.	H. Tyrell-Smith	Rudge
3.	G. Nott	Rudge
4.	S. Wood	New Imperial
5.	J. Williams	Rudge
6.	C. Manders	Excelsior
7.	A. Geiss	DKW
8.	G. Burnley	Moto Guzzi
9.	L. Hill	Rudge
10.	S. Smith	Excelsior
Fastest lap: S. Woods, 30m 31s/74.19mph*		

Senior

(7 laps/264.11 miles)		Mountain course
1.	S. Woods	Moto Guzzi
	3h 07m 10s/84.68mph	
2.	J. Guthrie	Norton
3.	W. Rusk	Norton
4.	J. Duncan	Norton
5.	O. Steinbach	NSU
6.	E. Mellors	NSU
7.	C. Williams	Vincent
8.	C. Barrow	Royal Enfield
9.	N. Christmas	Vincent
10.	H. Lamacraft	Vincent
Fastest lap: S. Woods, 26m 10s/86.53mph*		

1936

Junior

(7 laps/264.11 miles)		Mountain course
1.	F. Frith	Norton
	3h 17m 46s/80.14mph	
2.	J. White	Norton
3.	E. Mellors	Velocette
4.	E. Thomas	Velocette
5.	J. Guthrie	Norton
6.	O. Steinbach	NSU
7.	H. Fleischmann	NSU
8.	D. Hall	Norton
9.	H. Daniell	AJS
10.	G. Rowley	AJS

Fastest lap: F. Frith, 27m 38s/81.94mph*

Lightweight 250

(7 laps/264.11 miles)		Mountain course
1.	R. Foster	New Imperial
	3h 33m 22s/74.28mph	
2.	H. Tyrell-Smith	Excelsior
3.	A. Geiss	DKW
4.	D. Fairweather	Cotton
5.	C. Manders	Excelsior
6.	W. Cornfield	Excelsior
7.	H. Hartley	Rudge
8.	S. Sorenson	Excelsior
9.	H. Lamacraft	Excelsior
10.	J. Galway	Excelsior

Fastest lap: S. Woods, 29m 43s/76.20mph*

Senior

(7 laps 264.11 miles)		Mountain course
1.	J. Guthrie	Norton
	3h 04m 43s/85.80mph	
2.	S. Woods	Velocette
3.	F. Frith	Norton
4.	J. White	Norton
5.	N. Pope	Norton
6.	C. Goldberg	Velocette
7.	W. Tiffen	Velocette
8.	J. West	Vincent
9.	J. Galway	Norton
10.	J. Beevers	Norton

Fastest lap: S. Woods, 26m 02s/86.98mph*

1937

Junior

(7 laps/264.11 miles)		Mountain circuit
1.	J. Guthrie	Norton
	3h 07m 42s/84.43mph	
2.	F. Frith	Norton
3.	J. White	Norton
4.	S. Woods	Velocette
5.	H. Daniell	Norton
6.	E. Thomas	Velocette
7.	H. Tyrell-Smith	Excelsior
8.	G. Rowley	AJS
9.	J. Galway	Norton
10.	J. Williams	Norton

Fastest lap: F. Frith/J. Guthrie, 26m 35s/85.18mph*

Lightweight 250

Only nine finishers

(7 laps/264.11 miles)		Mountain course
1.	O. Tenni	Moto Guzzi
	3h 32m 06s/74.72mph	
2.	S. Wood	Excelsior
3.	E. Thomas	DKW
4.	L. Archer	New Imperial
5.	S. Wunsche	DKW
6.	C. Tattersall	CTS
7.	C. Moore	New Imperial
8.	S. Smith	Excelsior
9.	L. Martin	Cotton

Fastest lap: O. Tenni, 29m 08s/77.72mph*

Senior

(7 laps/264.11 miles)		Mountain course
1.	F. Frith	Norton
	2h 59m 41s/88.21mph	
2.	S. Woods	Velocette
3.	J. White	Norton
4.	E. Mellors	Velocette
5.	H. Daniell	Norton
6.	J. West	BMW
7.	J. Galway	Norton
8.	L. Archer	Velocette
9.	N. Pope	Norton
10.	J. Williams	Norton

Fastest lap: F. Frith, 25m 05s/90.27mph*

1938

Junior

(7 laps/264.11 miles)		Mountain course
1.	S. Woods	Velocette
	3h 8m 30s/84.08mph	
2.	E. Mellors	Velocette
3.	F. Frith	Norton
4.	J. White	Norton
5.	H. Daniell	Norton
6.	M. Whitworth	Velocette
7.	N. Croft	Norton
8.	J. Williams	Norton
9.	R. Loyer	Velocette
10.	W. Craine	Norton

Fastest lap: S. Woods, 26m 33s/85.30mph*

Lightweight 250

(7 laps/264.11 miles)		Mountain course
1.	E. Kluge	DKW
	3h 21m 56s/78.48mph	
2.	S. Wood	Excelsior
3.	H. Tyrell-Smith	Excelsior
4.	M. Cann	Excelsior
5.	C. Manders	Excelsior
6.	J. Forbes	Excelsior
7.	L. Martin	Excelsior
8.	G. Paterson	New Imperial
9.	J. Galway	Excelsior
10.	S. Miller	OK-Supreme

Fastest lap: E. Kluge, 28m 11s/80.35mph*

Senior 500

(7 laps/264.11 miles)		Mountain course
1.	H. Daniell	Norton
	2h 57m 50.6s/89.11mph	
2.	S. Woods	Velocette
3.	F. Frith	Norton
4.	J. White	Norton
5.	J. West	BMW
6.	E. Mellors	Velocette
7.	L. Archer	Velocette
8.	J. Galway	Norton
9.	J. Weddell	Norton
10.	J. Boardman	Norton

Fastest lap: H. Daniell, 24m 52.6s/91.00mph*

1939

Junior

(7 laps/264.11 miles)		Mountain course
1.	S. Woods	Velocette
	3h 10m 30s/83.10mph	
2.	H. Daniell	Norton
3.	H. Fleischmann	DKW
4.	E. Mellors	Velocette
5.	M. Whitworth	Velocette
6.	S. Wunsche	DKW
7.	M. Cann	Norton
8.	S. Wood	Velocette
9.	J. Little	Velocette
10.	F. Mussett	Velocette

Fastest lap: H. Daniell, 26m 38s/85.05mph

Lightweight 250

(7 laps/264.11 miles)		Mountain course
1.	E. Mellors	Benelli
	3h 33m 26s/74.26mph	
2.	E. Kluge	DKW
3.	H. Tyrell-Smith	Excelsior
4.	L. Martin	Excelsior
5.	S. Wunsche	DKW
6.	C. Manders	Excelsior
7.	H. Hartley	Rudge
8.	E. Thomas	DKW
9.	S. Wood	Rudge
10.	C. Tattersall	CTS

Fastest lap: S. Woods, 28m 58s/78.16mph

Senior

(7 laps/264.11 miles)		Mountain course
1.	G. Meier	BMW
	2h 57m 19s/89.28mph	
2.	J. West	BMW
3.	F. Frith	Norton
4.	S. Woods	Velocette
5.	J. White	Norton
6.	L. Archer	Velocette
7.	E. Mellors	Velocette
8.	S. Wood	Norton
9.	M. Cann	Moto Guzzi
10.	J. Galway	Norton

Fastest lap: G. Meier, 24m 57s/90.75mph

1947

Junior

(7 laps/264.11 miles)		Mountain course
1.	R. Foster	Velocette
	3h 17m 20s/80.31mph	
2.	D. Whitworth	Velocette
3.	J. Weddell	Velocette
4.	P. Goodman	Velocette
5.	L. Martin	Norton
6.	F. Hudson	Norton
7.	G. Newman	Velocette
8.	T. Wood	Velocette
9.	E. Oliver	Norton
10.	G. Murdoch	Norton
Fastest lap: D. Whitworth, 27m 45s/81.61mph		

Lightweight 250

(7 laps/264.11 miles)		Mountain course
1.	M. Barrington	Moto Guzzi
	3h 36m 26.6s/73.22mph	
2.	M. Cann	Moto Guzzi
3.	B. Drinkwater	Excelsior
4.	L. Archer	New Imperial
5.	W. Pike	Rudge
6.	G. Paterson	New Imperial
7.	S. Sorenson	Excelsior
8.	C. Johnston	CTS
9.	L. Martin	Excelsior
10.	J. Brett	Excelsior
Fastest lap: M. Cann, 30m 17s/74.75mph		

Senior

(7 laps/264.11 miles)		Mountain course
1.	H. Daniell	Norton
	3h 11m 22.2s/82.81mph	
2.	A. Bell	Norton
3.	P. Goodman	Velocette
4.	E. Frend	Norton
5.	G. Newman	Norton
6.	E. Evans	Norton
7.	N. Christmas	Norton
8.	J. Beevers	Norton
9.	L. Graham	AJS
10.	L. Dear	Norton
Fastest lap: A. Bell/P. Goodman, 26m 56s/84.07mph		

Clubman's Lightweight

(3 laps/113.19 miles)		Mountain course
1.	W. McVeigh	Triumph
	1h 45m 42s/64.27mph	
2.	B. Keys	AJS
3.	L. Archer	Velocette
Fastest lap: B. Keys, 34m 56s/64.77mph		

Clubman's Junior

(4 laps/150.92 miles)		Mountain course
1.	D. Parkinson	Norton
	2h 08m 01s/70.74mph	
2.	R. Pratt	Norton
3.	W. Sleightholme	AJS
Fastest lap: D. Parkinson, 31m 03s/72.92mph		

Clubman's Senior

(4 laps/150.92 miles)		Mountain course
1.	E. Briggs	Norton
	1h 55m 08s/78.67mph	
2.	A. Jefferies	Triumph
3.	G. Parsons	Ariel
Fastest lap: E. Briggs, 28m 18s/80.02mph		

1948

Junior

(7 laps/264.11 miles)		Mountain course
1.	F. Frith	Velocette
	3h 14m 33.6s/81.45mph	
2.	R. Foster	Velocette
3.	A. Bell	Norton
4.	J. Lockett	Norton
5.	M. Cann	AJS
6.	E. Briggs	Norton
7.	L. Graham	AJS
8.	E. Oliver	Velocette
9.	S. Miller	Norton
10.	G. Paterson	AJS
Fastest lap: F. Frith, 27m 28s/82.45mph		

Lightweight 250

Only six finishers

(7 laps/264.11 miles)		Mountain course
1.	M. Cann	Moto Guzzi
	3h 30m 49s/75.l18mph	
2.	R. Pike	Rudge
3.	D. Beasley	Excelsior
4.	B. Drinkwater	Moto Guzzi
5.	R. Petty	New Imperial
6.	J. McCredie	Excelsior
Fastest lap: M. Cann, 29m 31s/76.72mph		Massed start

Senior

(7 laps/264.11 miles)		Mountain course
1.	A. Bell	Norton
	3h 06m 31s/84.97mph	
2.	W. Doran	Norton
3.	J. Weddell	Norton
4.	G. Murdoch	AJS
5.	N. Pope	Norton
6.	C. Petch	Norton
7.	H. Pinnington	Norton
8.	J. Brett	Norton
9.	O. Tenni	Moto Guzzi
10.	E. Oliver	Velocette
Fastest lap: O. Tenni, 25m 43s/88.06mph		

Clubman's Lightweight

(3 laps/113.19 miles)		Mountain course
1.	M. Lockwood	Excelsior
	1h 44m 37.6s/64.93mph	
2.	W. Dehany	Excelsior
3.	R. Carvill	Triumph
Fastest lap: M. Lockwood, 34m 06s/66.40mph		

Clubman's Junior

(4 laps/150.92 miles)		Mountain course
1.	R. Hazlehurst	Velocette
	2h 08m 47.2s/70.33mph	
2.	G. Robinson	AJS
3.	M. Sunderland	Norton
Fastest lap: R. Pratt, 30m 42s/73.76mph		

Clubman's Senior

(4 laps/150.92 miles)		Mountain course
1.	J. Daniels	Vincent
	1h 52m 29.6s/80.51mph	
2.	F. Heath	Vincent
3.	G. Stevens	Norton
Fastest lap: G. Brown, 27m 24s/82.65mph		

1949

Junior

(7 laps/264.11 miles)		Mountain course
1.	F. Frith	Velocette
	3h 10m 26s/83.15mph	
2.	E. Lyons	Velocette
3.	A. Bell	Norton
5.	H. Armstrong	AJS
6.	R. Foster	Norton
7.	J. Lockett	Norton
8.	E. Frend	AJS
9.	E. Briggs	Velocette
10.	T. McEwan	Velocette
Fastest lap: F. Frith, 26m 53s/84.23mph		

Lightweight 250

(7 laps/264.11 miles)		Mountain course
1.	M. Barrington	Moto Guzzi
	3h 23m 13.2s/77.99mph	
2.	T. Wood	Moto Guzzi
3.	R. Pike	Rudge
4.	R. Mead	Norton
5.	S. Sorenson	Excelsior
6.	E. Thomas	Moto Guzzi
7.	W. Pike	Rudge
8.	L. Bayliss	Elbee Special
9.	R. Edwards	CTS
10.	R. Petty	New Imperial

Fastest lap: R. Dale/T. Wood, 28m 09s/80.44mph*

Senior

(7 laps/264.11 miles)		Mountain course
1.	H. Daniell	Norton
	3h 02m 18.6s/86.93mph	
2.	J. Lockett	Norton
3.	E. Lyons	Velocette
4.	A. Bell	Norton
5.	S. Jensen	Triumph
6.	C. Stevens	Triumph
7.	H. Armstrong	AJS
8.	W. Doran	AJS
9.	H. Hinton	Norton
10.	L. Graham	AJS

Fastest lap: R. Foster, 25m 14s/89.75mph

Clubman's Lightweight

(2 laps/75.46 miles)		Mountain course
1.	C. Taft	Excelsior
	1h 06m 30.2s/68.10mph	
2.	D. Ritchie	Velocette
3.	B. Hargreaves	Velocette

Fastest lap: C. Taft, 32m 57.2s/68.70mph

Clubman's Junior

(3 laps/113.19 miles)		Mountain course
1.	H. Clark	BSA
	1h 30m 21.6s/75.18mph	
2.	J. Simister	Norton
3.	A. Taylor	Norton

Fastest lap: H. Clark, 29m 52s/75.81mph

Clubman's Senior

(3 laps/113.19 miles)		Mountain course
1.	G. Duke	Norton
	1h 21m 53s/82.97mph	
2.	A. Jefferies	Triumph
3.	L. Starr	Triumph

Fastest lap: G. Duke, 27m 03s/83.70mph*

Clubman's 1000cc

(3 laps/113.19 miles)		Mountain course
1.	D. Lashmar	Vincent
	1h 29m 01.8s/76.30mph	
2.	J. Wright	Vincent
3.	P. Wilson	Vincent

Fastest lap: C. Horn, 26m 28s/85.55mph

1950

Junior

(7 laps/264.11 miles)		Mountain course
1.	A. Bell	Norton
	3h 03m 35s/86.32mph	
2.	G. Duke	Norton
3.	H. Daniell	Norton
4.	L. Graham	AJS
5.	E. Frend	AJS
6.	J. Lockett	Norton
7.	R. Dale	AJS
8.	W. McCandless	Norton
9.	K. Bills	Velocette
10.	H. Hinton	Norton

Fastest lap: A. Bell, 25m 56s/87.31mph*

Lightweight 250

(7 laps/264.11 miles)		Mountain course
1.	D. Ambrosini	Benelli
	3h 22m 58s/78.08mph	
2.	M. Cann	Moto Guzzi
3.	R. Mead	Velocette
4.	R. Pike	Rudge
5.	L. Bayliss	Elbee Special
6.	R. Watts	Moto Guzzi
7.	S. Sorenson	Excelsior
8.	E. Cope	AJS
9.	R. Edwards	CTS
10.	W. Webb	Excelsior

Fastest lap: D. Ambrosini, 27m 59s/80.90mph

Senior

(7 laps/264.11 miles)		Mountain course
1.	G. Duke	Norton
	2h 51m 45.6s/92.37mph	
2.	A. Bell	Norton
3.	J. Lockett	Norton
4.	L. Graham	AJS
5.	H. Daniell	Norton
6.	R. Armstrong	Velocette
7.	R. Dale	Norton
8.	W. McCandless	Norton
9.	J. Brett	Norton
10.	H. Hinton	Norton

Fastest lap: G. Duke, 24m 16s/93.33mph*

Clubman's Lightweight

(4 laps/150.92 miles)		Mountain course
1.	F. Fletcher	Excelsior
	1h 41m 34.3s/66.89mph	
2.	A. Wellstead	Triumph
3.	J. Dulson	Velocette

Fastest lap: F. Fletcher, 33m 33.4s/67.50mph

Clubman's Junior

(4 laps/150.92 miles)		Mountain course
1.	B. Jackson	BSA
	2h 01m 58.2s/74.25mph	
2.	I. McGuffie	BSA
3.	A. Brown	Norton

Fastest lap: B. Jackson, 29m 45s/76.12mph

Clubman's Senior

(4 laps/150.92 miles)		Mountain course
1.	P. Carter	Norton
	1h 59m 50.4s/75.60mph	
2.	A. Hill	Triumph
3.	K. Dixon	Norton

Fastest lap: I. Wicksteed, 28m 29s/79.51mph

Clubman's 1000cc

(4 laps/150.92 miles)		Mountain course
1.	A. Phillip	Vincent HRD
	1h 55m 18s/78.85mph	
2.	J. Alexander	Vincent HRD
3.	F. Young	Vincent HRD

Fastest lap: A. Phillip, 27m 57s/81.01mph

1951

Junior

(7 laps/264.11 miles)		Mountain course
1.	G. Duke	Norton
	2h 56m 17.6s/89.90mph	
2.	J. Lockett	Norton
3.	J. Brett	Norton
4.	M. Featherstone	AJS
5.	W. Lomas	Velocette
6.	A. Foster	Velocette
7.	W. McCandless	Norton
8.	R. Coleman	AJS
9.	R. Amm	Norton
10.	L. Graham	Velocette

Fastest lap: G. Duke, 24m 47s/91.38mph*

Lightweight 250

(4 laps/150.92 miles)		Mountain course
1.	T. Wood	Moto Guzzi
	1h 51m 15.8s/81.39mph	
2.	D. Ambrosini	Benelli
3.	E. Lorenzetti	Moto Guzzi
4.	W. Hutt	Moto Guzzi
5.	A. Wheeler	Velocette
6.	F. Purslow	Norton
7.	S. Sorenson	Excelsior
8.	E. Cope	AJS
9.	A. Jones	Excelsior
10.	H. Hartley	Rudge

Fastest lap: F. Anderson, 27m 03s/83.70mph*

Lightweight 125

(2 laps/75.46 miles)		Mountain course
1.	W. McCandless	Mondial
	1h 0m 30s/74.85mph	
2.	C. Ubbiali	Mondial
3.	G. Leoni	Mondial
4.	N. Pagani	Mondial
5.	J. Bulto	Montesa
6.	J. Loblet	Montesa
7.	E. Hardy	DOT
8.	H. Grindley	DMW
9.	L. Caldecutt	BSA
10.	R. Holton	Pankhurst Special

Fastest lap: W. McCandless, 30m 03s/75.34mph

Senior

	(7 laps/264.11 miles)	Mountain course
1.	G. Duke	Norton
	2h 48m 56.8s/93.83mph	
2.	W. Doran	AJS
3.	W. McCandless	Norton
4.	T. McEwan	Norton
5.	M. Barrington	Norton
6.	A. Parry	Norton
7.	E. Briggs	Norton
8.	A. Moule	Norton
9.	L. Perry	Norton
10.	L. Dear	Norton
	Fastest lap: G. Duke, 23m 47s/95.22mph*	

Clubman's Junior

	(4 laps/150.92 miles)	Mountain course
1.	B. Purslow	BSA
	2h 0m 10s/75.36mph	
2.	G. Read	Norton
3.	G. Draper	Norton
	Fastest lap: K. James, 29m 35s/76.55mph	

Clubman's Senior

	(4 laps/150.92 miles)	Mountain course
1.	K. Arder	Norton
	1h 53m 37.6s/79.70mph	
2.	I. Wickstead	Triumph
3.	G. Draper	Triumph
	Fastest lap: I. Wickstead, 27m 56s/81.06mph	

1952

Junior

	(7 laps/264.11 miles)	Mountain course
1.	G. Duke	Norton
	2h 55m 30.6s/90.29mph	
2.	H. Armstrong	Norton
3.	R. Coleman	AJS
4.	W. Lomas	AJS
5.	S. Lawton	AJS
6.	G. Brown	AJS
7.	W. McCandless	Norton
8.	E. Ring	AJS
9.	C. Sandford	Velocette
10.	P. Carter	Norton
	Fastest lap: G. Duke, 24m 53s/91mph*	

Lightweight 250

	(4 laps/150.92 miles)	Mountain course
1.	F. Anderson	Moto Guzzi
	1h 48m 08.6s/83.82mph	
2.	E. Lorenzetti	Moto Guzzi
3.	S. Lawton	Moto Guzzi
4.	L. Graham	Velocette
5.	M. Cann	Moto Guzzi
6.	B. Ruffo	Moto Guzzi
7.	R. Mead	Velocette
8.	R. Petty	Norton
9.	A. Wheeler	Moto Guzzi
10.	C. Salt	Rudge
	Fastest lap: B. Ruffo, 26m 42s/84.82mph*	

Lightweight 125

	(3 laps/113.19 miles)	Mountain course
1.	C. Sandford	MV Agusta
	1h 29m 54.8s/75.54mph	
2.	C. Ubbiali	Mondial
3.	A. Parry	Mondial
4.	W. McCandless	Mondial
5.	A. Copeta	MV Agusta
6.	F. Burman	EMC Puch
7.	H. Williams	BSA
8.	H. Grindley	DMW Royal Enfield
9.	M. Mavrogordato	EMC Puch
10.	E. Hardy	DOT
	Fastest lap: C. Sandford, 29m 46s/76.07mph*	

Senior

	(7 laps/264.11 miles)	Mountain course
1.	H. Armstrong	Norton
	2h 50m 28.4s/92.97mph	
2.	L. Graham	MV Agusta
3.	R. Amm	Norton
4.	R. Coleman	AJS
5.	W. Lomas	AJS
6.	W. McCandless	Norton
7.	G. Brown	Norton
8.	K. Mudford	Norton
9.	A. Moule	Norton
10.	P. Carter	Norton
	Fastest lap: G. Duke, 23m 52s/94.88mph	

Clubman's Junior

	(4 laps/150.92 miles)	Mountain course
1.	E. Houseley	BSA
	1h 54m 45.2s/78.92mph	
2.	R. McIntyre	BSA
3.	K. James	Norton
	Fastest lap: R. McIntyre, 28m 16.4s/80.09mph	

Clubman's Senior

	(4 laps/150.92 miles)	Mountain course
1.	B. Hargreaves	Triumph
	1h 49m 50s/82.45mph	
2.	K. James	Norton
3.	J. Clark	Norton
	Fastest lap: B. Hargreaves, 27m 16s/83.05mph	

1953

Junior

	(7 laps/264.11 miles)	Mountain course
1.	R. Amm	Norton
	2h 55m 14.6s/90.52mph	
2.	K. Kavanagh	Norton
3.	F. Anderson	Moto Guzzi
4.	J. Brett	Norton
5.	W. Doran	AJS
6.	D. Farrant	AJS
7.	K. Mudford	AJS
8.	G. Murphy	AJS
9.	P. Carter	AJS
10.	H. Clark	AJS
	Fastest lap: R. Amm, 24m 40s/91.82mph*	

Lightweight 250

	(4 laps/150.92 miles)	Mountain course
1.	F. Anderson	Moto Guzzi
	1h 46m 53s/84.73mph	
2.	W. Haas	NSU
3.	S. Wunsche	DKW
4.	A. Wheeler	Moto Guzzi
5.	S. Willis	Velocette
6.	T. Wood	Moto Guzzi
7.	R. Petty	Norton
8.	A. Jones	Excelsior
9.	W. Webster	Velocette
10.	R. Geeson	REG
	Fastest lap: F. Anderson, 26m 29s/85.52mph*	

Lightweight 125

	(3 laps/113.19 miles)	Mountain course
1.	L. Graham	MV Agusta
	1h 27m 19s/77.79mph	
2.	W. Haas	NSU
3.	C. Sandford	MV Agusta
4.	A. Copeta	MV Agusta
5.	A. Jones	MV Agusta
6.	W. Webster	MV Agusta
7.	A. Fenn	Mondial
8.	W. Webb	MV Agusta
9.	J. Thompson	MV Agusta
10.	F. Purslow	MV Agusta
	Fastest lap: L. Graham, 28m 57s/78.21mph*	

Senior

	(7 laps/264.11 miles)	Mountain course
1.	R. Amm	Norton
	2h 48m 51.8s/93.85mph	
2.	J. Brett	Norton
3.	H. Armstrong	Gilera
4.	R. Coleman	AJS
5.	W. Doran	AJS
6.	P. Davey	Norton
7.	E. Frend	Norton
8.	R. Sherry	AJS
9.	H. Pearce	Matchless
10.	J. Grace	Norton
	Fastest lap: R. Amm, 23m 15s/97.41mph*	

Clubman's Junior

	(4 laps/150.92 miles)	Mountain course
1.	D. Powell	BSA
	1h 52m 57.8s/80.17mph	
2.	O. Greenwood	BSA
3.	J. Bottomley	Norton
	Fastest lap: D. Powell, 27m 58s/80.96mph*	

Clubman's Senior

	(3 laps/113.19 miles)	Mountain course
1.	R. Keeler	Norton
	1h 20m 43.4s/84.14mph	
2.	E. Crookes	Norton
3.	W. Holmes	Norton
	Fastest lap: R. Keeler, 26m 48s/84.50mph*	

Clubman's 1000cc

(4 laps/150.92 miles)		Mountain course
1.	G. Douglas	Vincent
	1h 51m 04s/81.54mph	
2.	G. Clark	Vincent
3.	P. Peters	Vincent
Fastest lap: G. Douglas, 27m 21s/82.80mph		

1954

Junior

(5 laps/188.65 miles)		Mountain course
1.	R. Coleman	AJS
	2h 03m 41.8s/91.51mph	
2.	D. Farrant	AJS
3.	R. Keeler	Norton
4.	L. Simpson	AJS
5.	P. Davey	Norton
6.	J. Clark	AJS
7.	W. Lomas	MV Agusta
8.	G. Murphy	AJS
9.	E. Houseley	AJS
10.	A. Wheeler	AJS
Fastest lap: R. Amm, 23m 65s/94.61mph*		

Lightweight 250

(3 laps/113.19 miles)		Mountain course
1.	W. Haas	NSU
	1h 14m 44.4s/90.88mph	
2.	R. Hollaus	NSU
3.	H. Armstrong	NSU
4.	H. Muller	NSU
5.	F. Anderson	Moto Guzzi
6.	H. Baltisberger	NSU
7.	A. Wheeler	Moto Guzzi
8.	E. Houseley	Velocette
9.	R. Petty	Norton
10.	J. Horne	Rudge
Fastest lap: W. Haas, 24m 49.9s/91.22mph*		

Lightweight 125

Only nine finishers

(10 laps/107.9 miles)		Clypse course
1.	R. Hollaus	NSU
	1h 33m 03.4s/69.57mph	
2.	C. Ubbiali	MV Agusta
3.	C. Sandford	MV Agusta
4.	H. Baltisberger	NSU
5.	I. Loyd	MV Agusta
6.	B. Purslow	MV Agusta
7.	J. Grace	Montesa
8.	M. Webster	MV Agusta
9.	J. Thompson	MV Agusta
Fastest lap: R. Hollaus, 9m 03.4s/71.53mph		

Sidecar

(10 laps/107.9 miles)		Clypse course
1.	E. Oliver/L. Nutt	Norton
	1h 34m 0.2s/68.87mph	
2.	F. Hillebrand/M. Grunwald	BMW
3.	W. Noll/F. Cron	BMW
4.	W. Schneider/H. Strauss	BMW
5.	J. Drion/I. Stoll-Laforge	Norton
6.	W. Boddice/W. Storr	Norton
7.	J. Beeton/C. Billingham	Norton
8.	E. Walker/D. Roberts	Norton
9.	F. Taylor/R. Taylor	Norton
10.	L. Taylor/P. Glover	Norton
Fastest lap: E. Oliver/L. Nutt, 9m 09s/70.85mph		

Senior

(4 laps/150.92 miles)		Mountain course
1.	R. Amm	Norton
	1h 42m 46.8s/88.12mph	
2.	G. Duke	Gilera
3.	J. Brett	Norton
4.	H. Armstrong	Gilera
5.	R. Allison	Norton
6.	G. Laing	Norton
7.	R. Dale	MV Agusta
8.	R. Keeler	Norton
9.	J. Ahearn	Norton
10.	M. Quincey	Norton
Fastest lap: R. Amm, 25m 12.8s/89.82mph		

Clubman's Junior

(4 laps/150.92 miles)		Mountain course
1.	P. Palmer	BSA
	1h 50m 39.4s/81.83mph	
2.	D. Wright	BSA
3.	J. Davie	BSA
Fastest lap: D. Wright, 27m 15.8s/83.05mph*		

Clubman's Senior

(4 laps/150.92 miles)		Mountain course
1.	A. King	BSA
	1h 45m 36s/85.76mph	
2.	J. Denton	BSA
3.	E. Haldane	BSA
Fastest lap: A. King, 26m 01s/87.02mph*		

1955

Junior

(7 laps/264.11 miles)		Mountain course
1.	W. Lomas	Moto Guzzi
	2h 51m 38.2s/92.33mph	
2.	R. McIntyre	Norton
3.	C. Sandford	Moto Guzzi
4.	J. Surtees	Norton
5.	M. Quincey	Norton
6.	J. Hartle	Norton
7.	D. Ennett	AJS
8.	D. Agostini	Moto Guzzi
9.	G. Murphy	AJS
10.	J. Ahearn	Norton
Fastest lap: W. Lomas, 24m 03.2s/94.13mph*		

Lightweight 250

Only eight finishers

(9 laps/97.11 miles)		Clypse course
1.	W. Lomas	MV Agusta
	1h 21m 38.2s/71.37mph	
2.	C. Sandford	Moto Guzzi
3.	H. Muller	NSU
4.	A. Wheeler	Moto Guzzi
5.	D. Chadwick	RD Special
6.	W. Webster	Velocette
7.	P. Carter	Norton
8.	W. Maddrick	Moto Guzzi
Fastest lap: W. Lomas, 8m 52s/73.13mph		

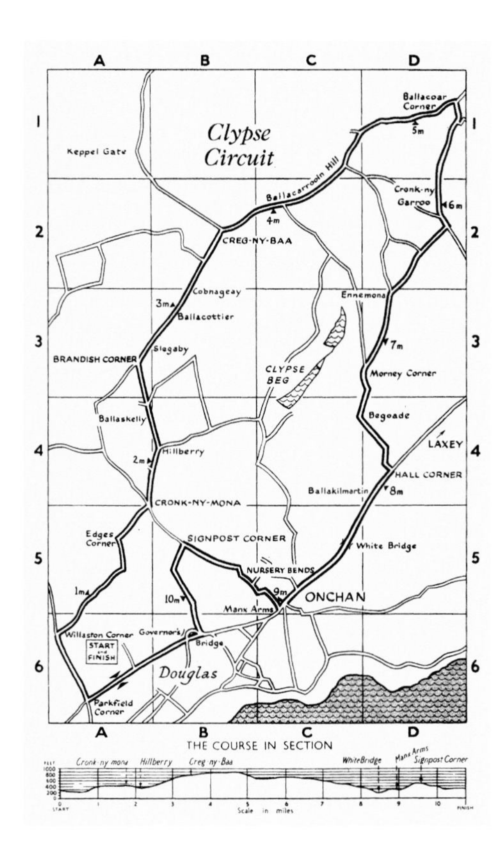

Lightweight 125

Only eight finishers

(9 laps/97.11 miles)		Clypse course
1.	C. Ubbiali	MV Agusta
	1h 23m 38.2s/69.67mph	
2.	L. Taveri	MV Agusta
3.	G. Lattanzi	Mondial
4.	W. Lomas	MV Agusta
5.	W. Webster	MV Agusta
6.	R. Porter	MV Agusta
7.	F. Burman	EMC Puch
8.	L. Hartfield	LCH
Fastest lap: C. Ubbiali, 9m 02.2s/71.65mph*		

Sidecar

(9 laps/97.11 miles)		Clypse course
1.	W. Schneider/H. Strauss	BMW
	1h 23m 14s/70.01mph	
2.	W. Boddice/W. Storr	Norton
3.	P. Harris/R. Campbell	Matchless
4.	J. Beeton/C. Billingham	Norton
5.	F. Taylor/R. Taylor	Norton
6.	E. Walker/D. Roberts	Norton
7.	F. Hanks/E. Dorman	Matchless
8.	D. Yorke/R. Eden	Norton
9.	A. Skein/F. Westaway	Norton
10.	F. Muhlemann/K. Tuscher	BSA
Fastest lap: W. Noll, 9m 00.00s/71.93mph*		

Senior

(7 laps/264.11 miles)		Mountain course
1.	G. Duke 2h 41m 49.8s/97.93mph	Gilera
2.	H. Armstrong	Gilera
3.	K. Kavanagh	Moto Guzzi
4.	J. Brett	Norton
5.	R. McIntyre	Norton
6.	D. Ennett	Matchless
7.	W. Lomas	Moto Guzzi
8.	E. Jones	Norton
9.	D. Powell	Matchless
10.	P. Davey	Norton
Fastest lap: G. Duke, 22m 39s/99.97mph*		

Clubman's Junior

(9 laps/97.11 miles)		Clypse course
1.	J. Buchan 1h 25m 24s/68.23mph	BSA
2.	D. Joubert	BSA
3.	P. Ferbrache	BSA
Fastest lap: D. Joubert, 9m 18s/69.78mph		

Clubman's Senior

(9 laps/97.11 miles)		Clypse course
1.	W. Dow 1h 22m 23s/70.73mph	BSA
2.	I Atkinson	Triumph
3.	R. Kelly	Triumph
Fastest lap: J. Drysdale, 31m 13.2s/72.53mph		

1956

Junior

(7 laps/264.11 miles)		Mountain course
1.	K. Kavanagh 2h 57m 29.4s/89.29mph	Moto Guzzi
2.	D. Ennett	AJS
3.	J. Hartle	Norton
4.	C. Sandford	DKW
5.	E. Grant	Norton
6.	A. Trow	Norton
7.	D. Powell	AJS
8.	F. Perris	AJS
9.	D. Agostini	Moto Guzzi
10.	T. Shepherd	Norton
Fastest lap: K. Kavanagh, 24m 18.8s/93.15mph		

Lightweight 250

(9 laps/97.11 miles)		Clypse course
1.	C. Ubbiali 1h 26m 54s/67.05mph	MV Agusta
2.	R. Colombo	MV Agusta
3.	H. Baltisberger	NSU
4.	H. Kassner	NSU
5.	F. Bartos	CZ
6.	A. Wheeler	Moto Guzzi
7.	P. Carter	RDS
8.	A. Jones	Norton
9.	E. Cope	Norton
10.	N. Webb	Moto Guzzi
Fastest lap: H. Baltisberger, 9m 21.6s/69.35mph		

Lightweight 125

Only nine finishers

(9 laps/97.11 miles)		Clypse course
1.	C. Ubbiali 1h 24m 16.8s/69.13mph	MV Agusta
2.	M. Cama	Montesa
3.	F. Gonzalez	Montesa
4.	E. Sirera	Montesa
5.	D. Chadwick	LEF
6.	V. Parus	CZ
7.	D. Allen	Mondial
8.	D. Edlin	MV Agusta
9.	E. Cope	MV Agusta
Fastest lap: C. Ubbiali, 9m 09.8s/70.75mph		

Sidecar

(9 laps/97.11 miles)		Clypse course
1.	F. Hillebrand/M. Grunwald 1h 23m 12.2s/70.03mph	BMW
2.	P. Harris/R. Campbell	Norton
3.	W. Boddice/W. Storr	Norton
4.	R. Mitchell/E. Bliss	Norton
5.	J. Beeton/L. Nutt	Norton
6.	E. Walker/D. Roberts	Norton
7.	F. Hanks/E. Dorman	Matchless
8.	A. Young/A. Partridge	Norton
9.	J. Beevers/W. Munday	Norton
10.	L. Taylor/F. Glover	Norton
Fastest lap: W. Noll, 9m 01.6s/71.74mph		

Senior

(7 laps/264.11 miles)		Mountain course
1.	J. Surtees 2h 44m 05.8s/96.57mph	MV Agusta
2.	J. Hartle	Norton
3.	J. Brett	Norton
4.	W. Zeller	BMW
5.	W. Lomas	Moto Guzzi
6.	D. Ennett	Matchless
7.	A. Trow	Norton
8.	G. Dunlop	Matchless
9.	G. Salt	Norton
10.	D. Chapman	Norton
Fastest lap: J. Surtees, 23m 09.4s/97.79mph		

Clubman's Junior

(3 laps/113.19 miles)		Mountain course
1.	B. Codd 1h 22m 48.4s/82.02mph	BSA
2.	J. Eckart	BSA
3.	A. Shepherd	Norton
Fastest lap: B. Codd, 27m 30.4s/82.33mph		

Clubman's Senior

(3 laps/113.19 miles)		Mountain course
1.	B. Codd 1h 18m 40.6s/86.33mph	BSA
2.	R. Jerrard	BSA
3.	A. Jenkins	BSA
Fastest lap: B. Codd, 26m 10.4s/86.52mph		

1957

Junior

(7 laps/264.11 miles)		Mountain course
1.	R. McIntyre 2h 46m 50.2s/94.99mph	Gilera
2.	K. Campbell	Moto Guzzi
3.	R. Brown	Gilera
4.	J. Surtees	MV Agusta
5.	E. Hinton	Norton
6.	G. Murphy	AJS
7.	G. Tanner	Moto Guzzi
8.	J. Clarke	Moto Guzzi
9.	N. McCutcheon	AJS
10.	A. Trow	Norton
Fastest lap: R. McIntyre, 23m 14.2s/97.42mph*		

Lightweight 250

(10 laps/107.9 miles)		Clypse course
1.	C. Sandford 1h 25m 25.4s/75.80mph	Mondial
2.	L. Taveri	MV Agusta
3.	R. Colombo	MV Agusta
4.	F. Bartos	Jawa
5.	S. Miller	Mondial
6.	D. Chadwick	MV Agusta
7.	J. Kostir	CZ
8.	A.Wheeler	Moto Guzzi
9.	F. Camathias	NSU
10.	M. O'Rourke	MV Agusta
Fastest lap: T. Provini, 8m 18.0s/78.00mph*		

Lightweight 125

(10 laps/107.9 miles)		Clypse course
1.	T. Provini 1h 27m 51.0s/73.69mph	Mondial
2.	C. Ubbiali	MV Agusta
3.	L. Tavern	MV Agusta
4.	S. Miller	Mondial
5.	C. Sandford	Mondial
6.	R. Colombo	MV Agusta
7.	F. Bartos	CZ
8.	M. O'Rourke	MV Agusta
9.	D. Edlin	MV Agusta
10.	D. Allen	Mondial
Fastest lap: T. Provini, 8m 41.8s/74.44mph*		

Sidecar

(10 laps/107.9 miles)		Clypse course
1.	F. Hillebrand/M. Grunwald 1h 30m 03.4s/71.89mph	BMW
2.	W. Schneider/H. Strauss	BMW
3.	F. Camathias/J. Galliker	BMW
4.	J. Beeton/C. Billingham	Norton
5.	C. Freeman/J. Chisnall	Norton
6.	P. Woollett/G. Loft	Norton
7.	E. Young/D. Young	Triumph
8.	V. Rowlands/D. Alcock	Norton
9.	D. Yorke/G. Tyler	Norton
10.	G. Humby/G. Deakin	Norton
Fastest lap: F. Hillebrand/M. Grunwald, 8m 55.4s/72.55mph*		

Senior

(8 laps/301.84 miles)	Mountain course
1. R. McIntyre	Gilera
3h 02m 57.0s/98.99mph	
2. J. Surtees	MV Agusta
3. R. Brown	Gilera
4. R. Dale	Moto Guzzi
5. K. Campbell	Moto Guzzi
6. A. Trow	Norton
7. A. King	Norton
8. G. Murphy	Matchless
9. J. Buchan	Norton
10. R. Barker	Norton
Fastest lap: R. McIntyre, 22m 23.2s/101.12mph*	

1958

Junior

(7 laps/264.11 miles)	Mountain course
1. J. Surtees	MV Agusta
2h 48m 38.4s/93.97mph	
2. D. Chadwick	Norton
3. G. Tanner	Norton
4. T. Shepherd	Norton
5. G. Catlin	Norton
6. A. King	Norton
7. K. Campbell	Norton
8. R. Anderson	Norton
9. D. Minter	Norton
10. J. Buchan	Norton
Fastest lap: J. Surtees, 23m 43.4s/95.42mph	

Lightweight 250

(10 laps/107.9 miles)	Clypse course
1. T. Provini	MV Agusta
1h 24m 12.0s/76.89mph	
2. C. Ubbiali	MV Agusta
3. M. Hailwood	NSU
4. R. Brown	NSU
5. D. Falk	Adler
6. S. Miller	CZ
7. E. Hinton	NSU
8. T. Robb	NSU
9. F. Purslow	NSU
10. D. Andrews	NSU
Fastest lap: T. Provini, 8m 06.2s/79.90mph*	

Lightweight 125

(10 laps/107.9 miles)	Clypse course
1. C. Ubbiali	MV Agusta
1h 28m 51.2s/72.86mph	
2. R. Ferri	Ducati
3. D. Chadwick	Ducati
4. S. Miller	Ducati
5. E. Degner	MZ
6. H. Fugner	MZ
7. M. Hailwood	Paton
8. F. Purslow	Ducati
9. A. Wheeler	Mondial
10. D. Allen	Mondial
Fastest lap: C. Ubbiali, 8m 44.0s/74.13mph	

Sidecar

(10 laps/107.9 miles)	Clypse course
1. W. Schneider/H. Strauss	BMW
1h 28m 40.0s/73.01mph	
2. F. Camathias/H. Cecco	BMW
3. J. Beeton/E. Bulgin	Norton
4. A. Ritter/E. Baulth	BMW
5. E. Walker/D. Roberts	Norton
6. P. Woollett/ G. Loft	Norton
7. G. de Orfe/D. Flynn	Norton
8. B. Green/R. Eden	Norton
9. E. Young/A. Young	Triumph
10. E. Oliver/P. Wise	Norton
Fastest lap: W. Schneider/H. Strauss, 8m 44.4s/74.07mph*	

Senior

(7 laps/264.11 miles)	Mountain course
1. J. Surtees	MV Agusta
2h 40m 39.8s/98.63mph	
2. R. Anderson	Norton
3. R. Brown	Norton
4. D. Minter	Norton
5. D. Chadwick	Norton
6. J. Anderson	Norton
7. G. Catlin	Norton
8. E. Haldane	Norton
9. P. Pawson	Norton
10. R. Dale	BMW
Fastest lap: J. Surtees, 22m 30.4s/100.58mph	

1959

Formula 1, 500cc

(3 laps/113.19 miles)	Mountain course
1. R. McIntyre	Norton
1h 09m 28.4s/97.77mph	
2. R. Brown	Norton
3. T. Shepherd	Norton
4. K. Kavanagh	Norton
5. J. Buchan	Norton
6. D. Chapman	Norton
7. D. Powell	Matchless
8. R. Ingram	Norton
9. B. Daniels	Norton
10. R. Miles	Norton
Fastest lap: R. McIntyre, 23m 01.0s/98.35mph	

Formula 1, 350cc

(3 laps/113.19miles)	Mountain course
1. A. King	AJS
1h 11m 45.4s/94.66mph	
2. R. Anderson	Norton
3. M. Hailwood	Norton
4. D. Chadwick	Norton
5. T. Phillis	Norton
6. W. Mizen	AJS
7. J. Redman	Norton
8. W. Smith	AJS
9. V. Cottle	Norton
10. W. Roberton	AJS
Fastest lap: A. King, 23m 45.6s/95.27mph	

Junior

(7 laps/264.11 miles)	Mountain course
1. J. Surtees	MV Agusta
2h 46m 08.0s/95.38mph	
2. J. Hartle	MV Agusta
3. A. King	Norton
4. G. Duke	Norton
5. R. Anderson	Norton
6. D. Chadwick	Norton
7. R. Brown	Norton
8. D. Minter	Norton
9. T. Shepherd	Norton
10. G. Catlin	AJS
Fastest lap: J. Surtees, 23m 19.2s/97.08mph	

Lightweight 250

(10 laps/107.9 miles)	Clypse course
1. T. Provini	MV Agusta
1h 23m 18.8s/77.77mph	
2. C. Ubbiali	MV Agusta
3. D. Chadwick	MV Agusta
4. T. Robb	GMS
5. H. Kassner	NSU
6. R. Thalhammer	NSU
7. A. Wheeler	NSU
8. J. Autengruber	NSU
9. F. Purslow	NSU
10. S. Lohmann	Adler
Fastest lap: T. Provini, 8m 04.2s/80.22mph*	

Lightweight 125

(10 laps/107.9 miles)	Clypse course
1. T. Provini	MV Agusta
1h 27m 25.2s/74.06mph	
2. L. Taveri	MZ
3. M. Hailwood	Ducati
4. H. Fugner	MZ
5. C. Ubbiali	MV Agusta
6. N. Taniguchi	Honda
7. G. Suzuki	Honda
8. T. Tanaka	Honda
9. T. Robb	Ducati
10. F. Purslow	Ducati
Fastest lap: L. Taveri, 8m 38.0s/74.99mph*	

Sidecar

(10 laps/107.9 miles)	Clypse course
1. W. Schneider/H. Strauss	BMW
1h 29m 03.8s/72.69mph	
2. F. Camathias/H. Cecco	BMW
3. F. Scheidegger/H. Burklhardt	BMW
4. H. Fath/A. Wholgemuth	BMW
5. E. Strub/M. Woollett	BMW
6. O. Greenwood/T. Fairbrother	Triumph
7. L. Neussner/ A. Partridge	BMW
8. C. Freeman/B. Nelson	Norton
9. R. Cheney/J. Gibbins	Norton
10. R. Yorke/M. Merrick	Norton
Fastest lap: W. Schneider/H. Strauss, 8m 49.8s/73.32mph	

Senior

(7 laps/264.11 miles) Mountain course

Pos	Rider	Machine
1.	J. Surtees	MV Agusta
	3h 00m 13.4s/87.94mph	
2.	A. King	Norton
3.	R. Brown	Norton
4.	D. Powell	Matchless
5.	R. McIntyre	Norton
6.	E. Driver	Norton
7.	A. Shepherd	Matchless
8.	G. Catlin	Matchless
9.	R. Bensen	Norton
10.	P. Pawson	Norton

Fastest lap: J. Surtees, 22m 22.4s/101.18mph*

1960

Note: From 1960 all races were held on the 37.73-mile Mountain Course

Lightweight 125 (3 laps/113.19 miles)

Pos	Rider	Machine
1.	C. Ubbiali	MV Agusta
	1h 19m 21.2s/85.60mph	
2.	G. Hocking	MV Agusta
3.	L. Taveri	MV Agusta
4.	L. Hempleman	MZ
5.	R. Anderson	MZ
6.	N. Taniguchi	Honda
7.	G. Suzuki	Honda
8.	S. Shimazaki	Honda
9.	T. Tanaka	Honda
10.	T. Phillis	Honda

Fastest lap: C. Ubbiali, 26m 17.6s/86.10mph*

Sidecar (3 laps/113.19 miles)

Pos	Rider	Machine
1.	H. Faith/A. Wohlgemuth	BMW
	1h 20m 45.8s/84.10mph	
2.	P. Harris/R. Campbell	BMW
3.	C. Freeman/B. Nelson	Norton
4.	L. Wells/T. Cook	Norton
5.	F. Camathias/R. Foll	BMW
6.	A. Ritter/E. Horner	BMW
7.	J. Beevers/J. Chisnall	BMW
8.	P. Millard/G. Spence	Norton
9.	B. Green/D. Flynn	Norton
10.	W. Yorke/G. Mason	Norton

Fastest lap: H. Fatih/A. Wohlgemuth, 26m 23.4s/85.79mph

Lightweight 250 (5 laps/188.65 miles)

Pos	Rider	Machine
1.	G. Hocking	MV Agusta
	2h 00m 53.0s/93.64mph	
2.	C. Ubbiali	MV Agusta
3.	T. Provini	Morini
4.	R. Brown	Honda
5.	M. Kitano	Honda
6.	M. Taniguchi	Honda
7.	M. O'Rourke	Ariel
8.	L. Taveri	MV Agusta
9.	O. Perfetti	Bianchi
10.	A. Dugdale	NSU

Fastest lap: C. Ubbiali, 23m 42.8s/95.47mph*

Junior (6 laps/226.38 miles)

Pos	Rider	Machine
1.	J. Hartle	MV Agusta
	2h 20m 28.8s/96.70mph	
2.	J. Surtees	MV Agusta
3.	R. McIntyre	AJS
4.	D. Minter	Norton
5.	R. Rensen	Norton
6.	R. Anderson	Norton
7.	A. Shepherd	AJS
8.	J. Lewis	Norton
9.	B. Setchell	Norton
10.	G. Catlin	AJS

Fastest lap: J. Surtees, 22m 49.4s/99.20mph*

Senior (6 laps/226.38 miles)

Pos	Rider	Machine
1.	J. Surtees	MV Agusta
	2h 12m 35.2s/102.44mph	
2.	J. Hartle	MV Agusta
3.	M. Hailwood	Norton
4.	T. Phillis	Norton
5.	R. Dale	Norton
6.	R. Brown	Norton
7.	A. Godfrey	Norton
8.	R. Anderson	Norton
9.	E. Driver	Norton
10.	R. Renson	Norton

Fastest lap: J. Surtees, 21m 45.0s/104.08mph*

1961

Lightweight 125 (3 laps/113.19 miles)

Pos	Rider	Machine
1.	M. Hailwood	Honda
	1h 16m 58.6s/88.23mph	
2.	L. Taveri	Honda
3.	T. Phillis	Honda
4.	J. Redman	Honda
5.	S. Shimazaki	Honda
6.	R. Rensen	Bultaco
7.	T. Godfrey	EMC
8.	N. Taniguchi	Honda
9.	D. Shorey	Bultaco
10.	J. Grace	Bultaco

Fastest lap: L. Taveri, 23m 35.6s/88.45mph*

Sidecar (3 laps/113.19 miles)

Pos	Rider	Machine
1.	M. Deubel/E. Horner	BMW
	1h 17m 29.8s/87.65mph	
2.	F. Scheidegger/H. Burkhadt	BMW
3.	P. Harris/R. Campbell	BMW
4.	A. Rohsiepe/L. Bottcher	BMW
5.	C. Freeman/B. Nelson	Norton
6.	C. Seeley/W. Rawlings	Matchless
7.	A. Parry/L. Carter	Norton
8.	E. Pickup/J. Biggs	BMW
9.	O. Greenwood/T. Fairbrother	Triumph
10.	H. Scholes/R. Lindsay	BMW

Fastest lap: M. Deubel/E. Horner, 25m 44.0s/87.97mph*

Lightweight 250 (5 laps/188.65 miles)

Pos	Rider	Machine
1.	M. Hailwood	Honda
	1h 55m 03.6s/98.38mph	
2.	T. Phillis	Honda
3.	J. Redman	Honda
4.	K. Tagahashi	Honda
5.	N. Taniguchi	Honda
6.	F. Ito	Yamaha
7.	A. Wheeler	Moto Guzzi
8.	D. Shorey	NSU
9.	P. Chatterton	NSU
10.	H. Anderson	Suzuki

Fastest lap: R. McIntyre, 22m 44.0s/99.58mph*

Junior (6 laps/226.38 miles)

Pos	Rider	Machine
1.	P. Read	Norton
	2h 22m 50.0s/95.10mph	
2.	G. Hocking	MV Agusta
3.	R. Rensen	Norton
4.	D. Minter	Norton
5.	F. Stastny	Jawa
6.	R. Ingram	Norton
7.	H. Anderson	AJS
8.	E. Boyce	AJS
9.	F. Stevens	Norton
10.	E. Driver	Norton

Fastest lap: G. Hocking, 22m 41.0s/99.80mph*

Senior (6 laps/226.38 miles)

Pos	Rider	Machine
1.	M. Hailwood	Norton
	2h 15m 02.0s/100.60mph	
2.	R. McIntyre	Norton
3.	T. Phillis	Norton
4.	A. King	Norton
5.	R. Langston	Matchless
6.	T. Godfrey	Norton
7.	R. Ingram	Norton
8.	P. Pawson	Matchless
9.	E. Boyce	Norton
10.	F. Stevens	Norton

Fastest lap: G. Hocking, 22m 03.6s/102.62mph

1962

Sidecar (3 laps/113.19 miles)

Pos	Rider	Machine
1.	C. Vincent/J. Bliss	BSA
	1h 21m 16.4s/83.57mph	
2.	O. Kolle/K. Hess	BMW
3.	C. Seeley/W. Rawlings	Matchless
4.	C. Lambert/A. Herzig	BMW
5.	H. Luthringshauser/H. Knopp	BMW
6.	G. Auerbacher/J. Zach	BMW
7.	A. Birch/P. Birch	Matchless
8.	D. Brindley/J. Waugh	BSA
9.	B. Green/D. Fynn	Norton
10.	J. Melhuish/I. McDonald	Norton

Fastest lap: M. Duebel/E. Horner, 24m 57.6s/90.70mph*

Lightweight 250 (6 laps/226.38 miles)

Pos	Rider	Machine
1.	D. Minter	Honda
	2h 20m 30.0s/96.68mph	
2.	J. Redman	Honda
3.	T. Phillis	Honda
4.	A. Wheeler	Moto Guzzi
5.	A. Pagani	Aermacchi
6.	S. Shorey	Bultaco
7.	F. Hardy	REG

Fastest lap: R. McIntyre, 22m 51.2s/99.06mph

Only seven finishers

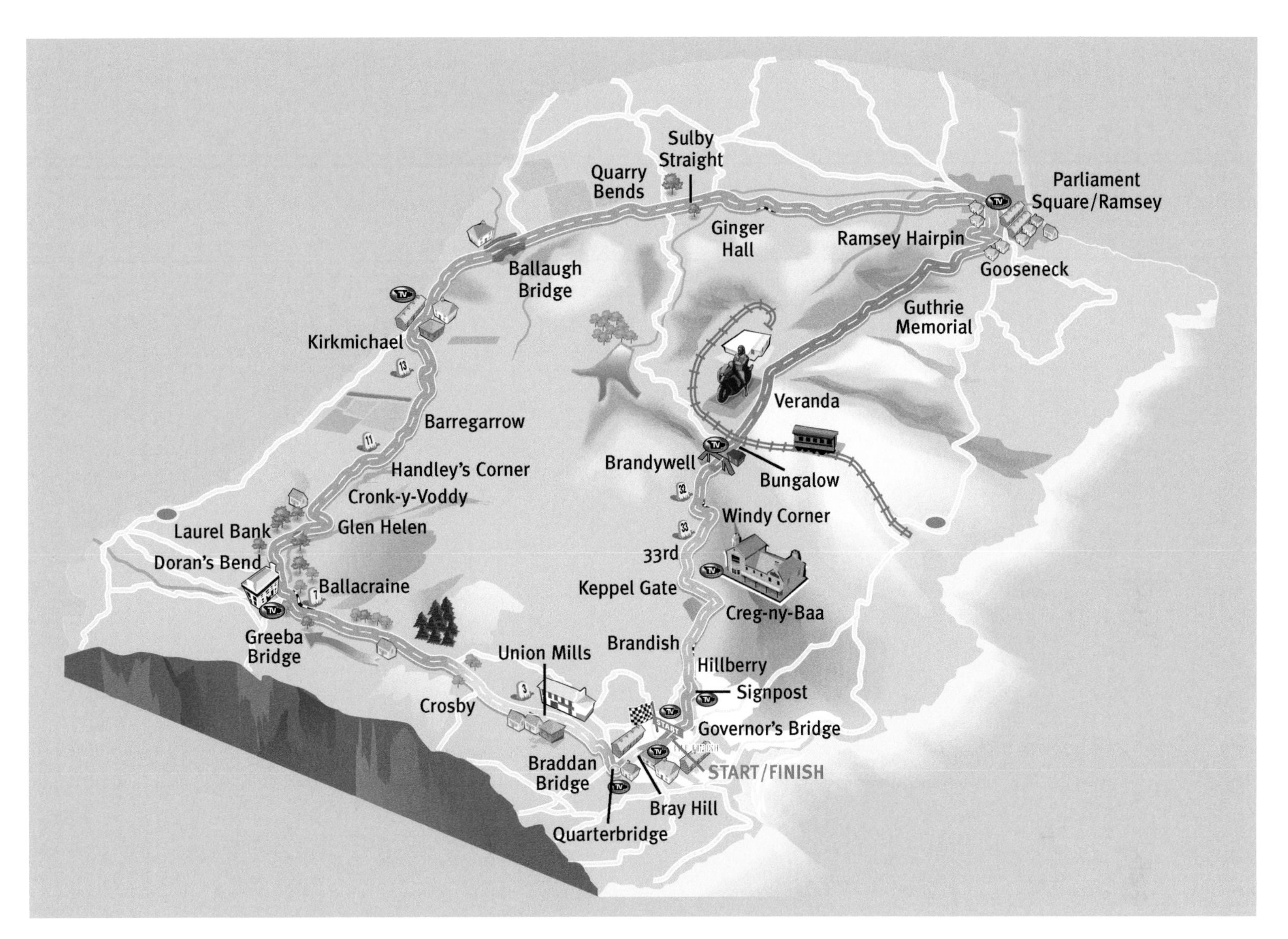

Lightweight 125 (3 laps/113.19 miles)

1.	L. Taveri 1h 15m 34.2s/89.88mph	Honda
2.	T. Robb	Honda
3.	T. Phillis	Honda
4.	D. Minter	Honda
5.	J. Redman	Honda
6.	R. Avery	EMC
7.	S. Malina	CZ
8.	E. Degner	Suzuki
9.	F. Stevens	Bultaco
10.	M. O'Rourke	Bultaco

Fastest lap: L. Taveri, 25m 07.0s/90.13mph*

Junior (6 laps/226.38 miles)

1.	M. Hailwood 2h 16m 24.2s/99.59mph	MV Agusta
2.	G. Hocking	MV Agusta
3.	F. Stastny	Jawa
4.	R. Ingram	Norton
5.	M. Duff	AJS
6.	H. Anderson	AJS
7.	P. Read	Norton
8.	F. Stevens	Norton
9.	E. Boyce	AJS
10.	D. Woodman	AJS

Fastest lap: M. Hailwood, 22m 17.2s/101.58mph

50cc (2 laps/75.46 miles)

1.	E. Degner 1h 00m 16.4s/75.12mph	Suzuki
2.	L. Taveri	Honda
3.	T. Robb	Honda
4.	H.G. Anscheidt	Kreidler
5.	M. Itoh	Suzuki
6.	M. Ichino	Suzuki
7.	J. Huberts	Kreidler
8.	S. Suzuki	Suzuki
9.	D. Minter	Honda
10.	S. Shimazaki	Honda

Fastest lap: E. Degner, 29m 58.6s/75.52mph

Senior (6 laps/226.38 miles)

1.	G. Hocking 2h 11m 13.4s/103.51mph	MV Agusta
2.	E. Boyce	Norton
3.	F. Stevens	Norton
4.	B. Schneider	Norton
5.	R. Ingram	Norton
6.	B. Setchell	Norton
7.	T. Thorp	Norton
8.	C. Conn	Norton
9.	D. Powell	Matchless
10.	D. Woodman	Matchless

Fastest lap: G. Hocking, 21m 24.4s/105.75mph*

1963

Sidecar (3 laps/113.19 miles)

1.	F. Camathias/ A. Herzig 1h 16m 51.0s/88.38mph	BMW
2.	F. Scheidegger/J. Robinson	BMW
3.	A. Birch/P. Birch	BMW
4.	O. Kolle/K. Hess	BMW
5.	G. Auerbacher/B. Heim	BMW
6.	C. Seeley/W. Rawlings	Matchless
7.	O. Greenwood/T. Fairbrother	Matchless
8.	M. Deubel/B. Dungworth	BMW
9.	T. Jackson/J. Harthill	BMW
10.	E. Sanders/H. Estwick	BMW

Fastest lap: F. Camathias/A. Herzig, 25m 19.0s/89.42mph

Lightweight 250 (6 laps/226.38 miles)

Pos	Rider	Machine
1.	J. Redman	Honda
	2h 23m 13.2s/94.85mph	
2.	F. Ito	Yamaha
3.	W. Smith	Honda
4.	H. Hasegawa	Yamaha
5.	T. Robb	Honda
6.	J. Kidson	Moto Guzzi
7.	J. Isherwood	NSU
8.	A. Harris	Greeves
9.	D. Shorey	Bultaco
10.	D. Gallagher	Velocette

Fastest lap: J. Redman, 23m 17.0s/97.23mph

Lightweight 125 (3 laps/113.19 miles)

Pos	Rider	Machine
1.	H. Anderson	Suzuki
	1h 16m 05.0s/89.27mph	
2.	F. Perris	Suzuki
3.	E. Degner	Suzuki
4.	L. Taveri	Honda
5.	B. Schneider	Suzuki
6.	J. Redman	Honda
7.	T. Robb	Honda
8.	K. Takahashi	Honda
9.	R. Bryans	Honda
10.	R. Dickinson	Honda

Fastest lap: H. Anderson, 24m 47.4s/91.32mph*

Junior (6 laps/226.38 miles)

Pos	Rider	Machine
1.	J. Redman	Honda
	2h 23m 08.2s/94.91mph	
2.	J. Hartle	Gilera
3.	F. Stastny	Jawa
4.	W. Mizen	AJS
5.	J. Ahearn	Norton
6.	M. Duff	AJS
7.	M. Low	AJS
8.	D. Woodman	AJS
9.	E. Driver	AJS
10.	E. Boyce	Norton

Fastest lap: J. Redman, 22m 20.8s/101.30mph

50cc (3 laps/113.19 miles)

Pos	Rider	Machine
1.	M. Itoh	Suzuki
	1h 26m 10.6s/78.81mph	
2.	H. Anderson	Suzuki
3.	H.G. Anscheidt	Kreidler
4.	I. Morishita	Suziki
5.	M. Ichino	Suzuki
6.	I. Plumridge	Honda
7.	W. Ivy	Sheene Spl
8.	M. Simmonds	Tohatsu

Fastest lap: E. Degner, 28m 37.2s/79.10mph*

Only eight finishers

Senior (6 laps/226.38 miles)

Pos	Rider	Machine
1.	M. Hailwood	MV Agusta
	2h 09m 48.4s/104.64mph	
2.	J. Hartle	Gilera
3.	P. Read	Gilera
4.	M. Duff	Matchless
5.	J. Dunphy	Norton
6.	F. Stevens	Norton
7.	E. Driver	Matchless
8.	W. Smith	Matchless
9.	J. Ahearn	Norton
10.	E. Boyce	Norton

Fastest lap: M. Hailwood, 21m 16.4s/106.41mph*

1964

Sidecar (3 laps/113.19 miles)

Pos	Rider	Machine
1.	M. Deubel/E. Horner	BMW
	1h 16m 13.0s/89.12mph	
2.	C. Seeley/W. Rawlings	FCSB
3.	G. Auerbacher/B. Heim	BMW
4.	A. Butcher/W. Kalauch	BMW
5.	T. Vinicombe/G. Golder	Triumph
6.	T. Jackson/J. Harthill	BMW
7.	D. Ajax/M. Caley	Norton
8.	A. Birch/P. Cropper	BMW
9.	D. Yorke/G. Mason	Norton
10.	H. Wohlfahrt/W. Zielaff	BMW

Fastest lap: M. Deubel/E. Horner, 25m 15.4s/89.63mph

Lightweight 250 (6 laps/226.38 miles)

Pos	Rider	Machine
1.	J. Redman	Honda
	2h 19m 23.6s/97.45mph	
2.	A. Shepherd	MZ
3.	A. Pagani	Paton
4.	S. Malina	CZ
5.	R. Boughey	Yamaha
6.	C. Hunt	Aermacchi
7.	T. Robb	Yamaha
8.	R. Everett	Greeves
9.	A. Willmott	Norton
10.	P. Walsh	Ariel

Fastest lap: P. Read, 22m 46.2s/99.42mph

Lightweight 125 (3 laps/113.19 miles)

Pos	Rider	Machine
1.	L. Taveri	Honda
	1h 13m 43.0s/92.14mph	
2.	J. Redman	Honda
3.	R. Bryans	Honda
4.	S. Malina	CZ
5.	W. Scheimann	Honda
6.	B. Beale	Honda
7.	W. Smith	Honda
8.	R. Dickinson	Honda
9.	D. Simmonds	Tohatsu
10.	R. Foll	Honda

Fastest lap: L. Taveri, 24m 12.2s/93.53mph

Junior (6 laps/226.38 miles)

Pos	Rider	Machine
1.	J. Redman	Honda
	2h 17m 55.4s/98.50mph	
2.	P. Read	AJS
3.	M. Duff	AJS
4.	D. Minter	Norton
5.	D. Woodman	AJS
6.	J. Dunphy	AJS
7.	P. Darvill	AJS
8.	W. Mizen	AJS
9.	E. Driver	AJS
10.	C. Conn	AJS

Fastest lap: J. Redman, 22m 28.0s/100.76mph

50cc (3 laps/113.19 miles)

Pos	Rider	Machine
1.	H. Anderson	Suzuki
	1h 24m 13.4s/80.64mph	
2.	R. Bryans	Honda
3.	I. Morishita	Suzuki
4.	H.G. Anscheidt	Kreidler
5.	M. Itoh	Suzuki
6.	N. Taniguchi	Honda
7.	L. Taveri	Kreidler
8.	T. Provini	Kreidler
9.	D. Simmonds	Tohatsu
10.	I. Plumridge	Honda

Fastest lap: H. Anderson, 27m 54.2s/81.13mph*

Senior (6 laps/226.38 miles)

Pos	Rider	Machine
1.	M. Hailwood	MV Agusta
	2h 14m 33.8s/100.95mph	
2.	D. Minter	Norton
3.	F. Stevens	Matchless
4.	D. Woodman	Matchless
5.	G. Jenkins	Norton
6.	W. McCosh	Matchless
7.	B. Setchell	Norton
8.	C. Ward	Norton
9.	J. Cooper	Norton
10.	D. Lee	Matchless

Fastest lap: M. Hailwood, 22m 05.0s/102.51mph

1965

Sidecar (3 laps/113.19 miles)

Pos	Rider	Machine
1.	M. Deubel/E. Horner	BMW
	1h 14m 59.8s/90.57mph	
2.	F. Scheidegger/J. Robinson	BMW
3.	G. Auerbacher/P. Rykers	BMW
4.	H. Luthringshauser/H. Hahn	BMW
5.	C. Vincent/T. Harrison	BSA
6.	C. Freeman/B. Nelson	Norton
7.	T. Vinicombe/J. Flaxman	BSA
8.	N. Huntingford/R. Lindsay	Matchless
9.	B. Thompson/R. Bradley	BMW
10.	A. Butscher/W. Kalauch	BMW

Fastest lap: M. Deubel/E.Horner, 24m 39.6s/91.80mph*

Lightweight 250 (6 laps/226.38 miles)

Pos	Rider	Machine
1.	J. Redman	Honda
	2h 19m 45.8s/97.19mph	
2.	M. Duff	Yamaha
3.	F. Perris	Suzuki
4.	T. Provini	Benelli
5.	F. Stastny	Jawa
6.	D. Williams	Mondial
7.	G. Milani	Aermacchi
8.	B. Setchell	Aermacchi
9.	D. Minter	Cotton
10.	J. Findlay	BMW

Fastest lap: J. Redman, 22m 37.0s/100.09mph*

Lightweight 125 (3 laps/113.19 miles)

Pos	Rider	Machine
1.	P. Read	Yamaha
	1h 12m 02.6s/94.28mph	
2.	L. Taveri	Honda
3.	M. Duff	Yamaha
4.	D. Woodman	MZ

5.	H. Anderson	Susuki
6.	R. Bryans	Honda
7.	W. Ivy	Yahama
8.	E. Degner	Suzuki
9.	K. Cass	Bultaco
10.	I. Burne	Bultaco

Fastest lap: H. Anderson, 23m 34.6s/96.02mph*

Junior (6 laps/226.38 miles)

1.	J. Redman 2h 14m 52.2s/100.72mph	Honda
2.	P. Read	Yahama
3.	G. Agostini	MV Agusta
4.	B. Beale	Honda
5.	G. Jenkins	Norton
6.	G. Milani	Aermacchi
7.	C. Conn	Norton
8.	B. Setchell	Aermacchi
9.	J. Dunphy	Norton
10.	W. Smith	AJS

Fastest lap: M. Hailwood, 22m 00.6s/102.85mph*

50cc (3 laps/113.19 miles)

1.	L. Taveri 1h 25m 15.6s/79.66mph	Honda
2.	H. Anderson	Suzuki
3.	E. Degner	Suzuki
4.	C. Mates	Honda
5.	I. Plumridge	Derbi
6.	E. Griffiths	Honda
7.	J. Pink	Honda
8.	B. Kettle	Honda
9.	G. Ashton	Honda
10.	K. Burgess	Itom

Fastest lap: L. Taveri, 28m 00.4s/80.83mph

Senior (6 laps/226.38 miles)

1.	M. Hailwood 2h 28m 09.0s/91.69mph	MV Agusta
2.	J. Dunphy	Norton
3.	M. Duff	Matchless
4.	I. Burne	Norton
5.	S. Griffiths	Matchless
6.	W. McCosh	Matchless
7.	A. Dugdale	Norton
8.	G. Marsovsky	Matchless
9.	J. Ahearn	Norton
10.	J. Findlay	Matchless

Fastest lap: M. Hailwood, 23m 48.2s/95.11mph

1966

Sidecar (3 laps/113.19 miles)

1.	F. Scheidegger/J. Robinson 1h 14m 50.0s/90.76mph	BMW
2.	M. Deubel/E. Horner	BMW
3.	G. Auerbacher/W. Kalauch	BMW
4.	K. Enders/R. Engelhardt	BMW
5.	C. Seeley/W. Rawlings	BMW
6.	B. Dungworth/N. Caddow	BMW
7.	S. Schauzu/H. Schneider	BMW
8.	A. Butscher/A. Neumann	BMW
9.	T. Vinicombe/J. Flaxman	BMW
10.	B. Thompson/G. Wood	BMW

Fastest lap: M. Deubel/E. Horner, 24m 42.4s/91.63mph

Lightweight 250 (6 laps/226.38 miles)

1.	M. Hailwood 2h 13m 26.0s/101.79mph	Honda
2.	S. Graham	Honda
3.	P. Inchley	Villiers
4.	F. Stastny	Jawa-CZ
5.	J. Findlay	Bultaco
6.	W. Smith	Bultaco
7.	T. Grotefeld	Padgett
8.	T. Butcher	Aermacchi
9.	G. Plenderleith	Honda
10.	B. Richards	Bultaco

Fastest lap: M. Hailwood, 21m 42.2s/104.29mph*

Lightweight 125 (3 laps/113.19 miles)

1.	W. Ivy 1h 09m 32.8s/97.66mph	Yamaha
2.	P. Read	Yamaha
3.	H. Anderson	Suzuki
4.	M. Duff	Yamaha
5.	F. Perris	Suzuki
6.	M. Hailwood	Honda
7.	R. Bryans	Honda
8.	L. Taveri	Honda
9.	J. Curry	Honda
10.	K. Cass	Bultaco

Fastest lap: W. Ivy, 22m 58.2s/98.55mph*

Junior (6 laps/226.38 miles)

1.	G. Agostini 2h 14m 40.4s/100.87mph	MV Agusta
2.	P. Williams	AJS
3.	C. Conn	Norton
4.	J. Hearn	Norton
5.	F. Brocek	Jawa-CZ
6.	J. Blanchard	AJS
7.	G. Jenkins	Norton
8.	D. Simmonds	Honda
9.	F. Stastny	Jawa-CZ
10.	W. Smith	AJS

Fastest lap: G. Agostini, 21m 57.6s/103.09mph*

50cc (3 laps/113.19 miles)

1.	R. Bryans 1h 19m 17.2s/85.66mph	Honda
2.	L. Taveri	Honda
3.	H. Anderson	Suzuki
4.	E. Degner	Suzuki
5.	B. Gleed	Honda
6.	D. Simmonds	Honda
7.	E. Griffiths	Honda
8.	J. Pink	Honda
9.	M. Allen	Honda
10.	B. Kettle	Honda

Fastest lap: R. Bryans, 26m 10.2s/86.49mph*

Senior (6 laps/226.38 miles)

1.	M. Hailwood 2h 11m 44.8s/103.11mph	Honda
2.	G. Agostini	MV Agusta
3.	C. Conn	Norton
4.	J. Blanchard	Matchless
5.	R. Chandler	Matchless
6.	F. Stastny	Jawa-CZ
7.	P. Williams	Matchless
8.	J. Findlay	Matchless
9.	W. McCosh	Matchless
10.	M. Stanton	Norton

Fastest lap: M. Hailwood, 21m 08.6s/107.07mph*

1967

Production 750 (3 laps/113.19 miles)

1.	J. Hartle 1h 09m 56.8s/97.10mph	Triumph
2.	P. Smart	Norton
3.	A. Smith	BSA
4.	L. Weil	Triumph
5.	P. Butler	Triumph
6.	A. Godfrey	Norton
7.	G. Bailey	Triumph
8.	M. Rice	BSA
9.	A. McGurk	Triumph
10.	J. Strijbs	Triumph

Fastest lap: J. Hartle, 23m 07.8s/97.87mph

Production 500 (3 laps/113.19 miles)

1.	N. Kelly 1h 15m 33.8s/89.89mph	Velocette
2.	K. Heckles	Velocette
3.	D. Nixon	Triumph
4.	G. Penny	Honda
5.	N. Hanks	BSA
6.	A. Peck	Triumph
7.	A. Dunnel	Honda
8.	R. Baylie	Triumph
9.	D. Doyle	Norton
10.	R. Biscardine	Velocette

Fastest lap: N. Kelly, 24m 52.6s/91.01mph

Production 250 (3 laps/113.19 miles)

1.	W. Smith 1h 16m 38.2s/88.63mph	Bultaco
2.	T. Robb	Bultaco
3.	B. Smith	Suzuki
4.	F. Whiteway	Suzuki
5.	K. Carruthers	Suzuki
6.	K. Cass	Bultaco
7.	D. Simmonds	Kawasaki
8.	C. Vincent	Suzuki
9.	E. Crooks	Suzuki
10.	C. Thompsett	Ducati

Fastest lap: W. Smith, 25m 19.4s/89.41mph

Sidecar (3 laps/113.19 miles)

1.	S. Schauzu/H. Schneider 1h 14m 40.6s/90.96mph	BMW
2.	K. Enders/R. Engelhardt	BMW
3.	C. Seeley/R. Lindsey	BMW
4.	P. Harris/J. Thornton	BMW
5.	B. Dungworth/N. Caddow	BMW
6.	T. Vinicombe/J. Flaxman	BSA
7.	H. Wohlfahrt/H. Vester	BMW
8=	A. Butscher/A. Neumann	BMW
8=	M. Boddice/D. Loach	BSA
10.	J. Attenberger/J. Schillinger	BMW

Fastest lap: G. Auerbacher/E. Dein, 24m 41.2s/91.70mph

Lightweight 250 (6 laps/226.38 miles)

1.	M. Hailwood 2h 11m 47.6s/103.07mph	Honda
2.	P. Read	Yamaha
3.	R. Bryans	Honda
4.	D. Simmonds	Kawasaki
5.	W. Smith	Kawasaki
6.	M. Chatterton	Yamaha
7.	G. Marsovsky	Bultaco
8.	T. Holdsworth	Greeves
9.	R. Farmer	Yamaha
10.	T. Robb	Bultaco

Fastest lap: M. Hailwood, 21m 39.8s/104.50mph*

Lightweight 125 (3 laps/113.19 miles)

1.	P. Read 1h 09m 40.8s/97.48mph	Yamaha
2.	S. Graham	Suzuki
3.	A. Motohashi	Yamaha
4.	D. Simmonds	Kawasaki
5.	K. Carruthers	Honda
6.	J. Curry	Honda
7.	T. Robb	Bultaco
8.	P. Inchley	TSR
9.	B. Gustafsson	Honda
10.	M. Carney	Bultaco

Fastest lap: P. Read, 23m 00.8s/98.36mph

Junior (6 laps/226.38 miles)

1.	M. Hailwood 2h 09m 45.6s/104.68mph	Honda
2.	G. Agostini	MV Agusta
3.	D. Woodman	MZ
4.	A. Pagani	Aermacchi
5.	C. Conn	Aermacchi
6.	G. Milani	Aermacchi
7.	J. Hartle	Aermacchi
8.	S. Spencer	Norton
9.	J. Cooper	Norton
10.	K. Carruthers	Aermacchi

Fastest lap: M. Hailwood, 21m 00.8s/107.73mph*

50cc (3 laps/113.19 miles)

1.	S. Graham 1h 21m 56.8s/82.89mph	Suzuki
2.	H.G. Anscheidt	Suzuki
3.	T. Robb	Suzuki
4.	C. Walpole	Honda
5.	E. Griffiths	Honda
6.	S. Lawley	Honda
7.	T. Fearns	Honda
8.	B. Gleed	Honda
9.	T. Burgess	Yamaha
10.	J. Lawley	Honda

Fastest lap: S. Graham, 26m 34.4s/85.19mph

Senior (6 laps/226.38 miles)

1.	M. Hailwood 2h 08m 36.2s/105.62mph	Honda
2.	P. Williams	Matchless
3.	S. Spencer	Norton
4.	J. Cooper	Norton
5.	F. Stevens	Paton
6.	J. Hartle	Matchless
7.	T. Dickie	Matchless
8.	W. McCosh	Matchless
9.	R. Chandler	Matchless
10.	D. Lee	Matchless

Fastest lap: M. Hailwood, 20m 48.8s/108.77mph*

1968

Sidecar, 500cc (3 laps/113.19 miles)

1.	S. Schauzu/H. Schneider 1h 14m 34.2s/91.09mph	BMW
2.	J. Attenberger/J. Schillinger	BMW
3.	H. Luthringshauser/G. Hughes	BMW
4.	H. Fath/W. Kalauch	BMW
5.	J. Brandon/C. Holland	BMW
6.	M. Toombs/T. Tombs	BMW
7.	W. Copson/F. Higginbottom	BMW
8.	K. Enders/R. Engelhardt	BMW
9.	J. Philpott/R. Turrington	Norton
10.	D. Hawes/J. Mann	Seeley

Fastest lap: K. Enders/R. Engelhardt, 24m 00.0s/94.32mph*

Sidecar, 750cc (3 laps/113.19 miles)

1.	T. Vinicombe/J.Flaxman 1h 19m 07.4s/85.85mph	BSA
2.	N. Hanks/R. Arnold	BSA
3.	P. Brown/D. Bean	BSA
4.	M. Horspole/G. Horspole	Triumph
5.	J. Crick/D. Senior	Triumph
6.	K. Graham/G. Sewell	Triumph
7.	E. Leece/J. Molyneux	LMS
8.	D. Plummer/M. Brett	Triumph
9.	T. Windle/R. Honchcliffe	Triumph
10.	D. Saville/E. Fletcher	Sabre

Fastest lap: C. Vincent/K. Scott, 25m 25s/89.11mph

Lightweight 250 (6 laps/226.38 miles)

1.	W. Ivy 2h 16m 24.8s/99.58mph	Yamaha
2.	R. Pasolini	Benelli
3.	H. Rosner	MZ
4.	M. Uphill	Suzuki
5.	R. Gould	Yamaha
6.	W. Smith	Yamaha
7.	S. Herrero	Ossa
8.	J. Cooper	Yamaha
9.	A. McGurk	Yamaha
10.	D. Chatterton	Yamaha

Fastest lap: W. Ivy, 21m 27.4s/105.51mph*

50cc (3 laps/113.19 miles)

1.	B. Smith 1h 33m 10.4s/72.90mph	Derbi
2.	C. Walpole	Honda
3.	E. Griffiths	Honda
4.	D. Lock	Honda
5.	J. Pink	Honda
6.	R. Udall	Honda
7.	J. Lawley	Honda
8.	R. Stopford	Heldun
9.	N. Mayo	Heldun
10.	F. Redfern	Honda

Fastest lap: B. Smith, 21m 46s/73.44mph

Production, 750cc (3 laps/113.19 miles)

1.	R. Pickrell 1h 09m 13.2s/98.13mph	Dunstall Dominator
2.	B. Nelson	Norton
3.	A. Smith	BSA
4.	G. Bailey	Triumph
5.	M. Uphill	Triumph
6.	T. Godfrey	Norton

Fastest lap: R. Pickrell, 22m 46.6s/99.39mph*
Only six finishers

Production, 500cc (3 laps/113.19 miles)

1.	R. Knight 1h 15m 23.6s/90.09mph	Triumph
2.	J. Blanchard	Velocette
3.	D. Nixon	Triumph
4.	T. Kelly	Velocette
5.	G. Robinson	Honda
6.	G. Barnacle	Triumph
7.	H. Evans	BSA
8.	C. Mortimer	Ducati
9.	T. Walker	Triumph

Fastest lap: R. Knight, 24m 52.2s/91.03mph*
Only nine finishers

Production, 250cc (3 laps/113.19 miles)

1.	T. Burgess 1h 17m 53.4s/87.21mph	Ossa
2.	G. Leigh	Bultaco
3.	B. Smith	Suzuki
4.	B. Richards	Bultaco
5.	G. Keith	Suzuki
6.	T. Robb	Suzuki
7.	K. Carruthers	Suzuki
8.	A. Rogers	Ducati
9.	A. Cooper	Suzuki
10.	E. Johnson	Suzuki

Fastest lap: T. Burgess, 25m 45.4s/87.89mph

Junior (6 laps/226.38 miles)

1.	G. Agostini 2h 09m 38.6s/104.78mph	MV Agusta
2.	R. Pasolini	Benelli
3.	W. Smith	Honda
4.	D. Woodman	Aermacchi
5.	J. Cooper	Seeley
6.	J. Findlay	Aermacchi
7.	J. Curry	Aermacchi
8.	A. Barnett	Metisse
9.	B. Steenson	Aermacchi
10.	M. Uphill	Suzuki

Fastest lap: G. Agostini, 21m 12.2s/106.77mph

Lightweight 125 (3 laps/113.19 miles)

1.	P. Read 1h 08m 31.4s/99.12mph	Yamaha
2.	W. Ivy	Yamaha
3.	K. Carruthers	Honda
4.	T. Robb	Bultaco
5.	G. Keith	Brown Spl
6.	S. Murray	Honda
7.	J. Kiddie	Honda
8.	R. Dickinson	Honda
9.	G. Pienderleith	Honda
10.	J. Shacklady	Bultaco

Fastest lap: W. Ivy, 22m 34s/100.32mph*

Senior (6 laps/226.38 miles)

1.	G. Agostini	MV Agusta
	2h 13m 39.4s/11.63mph	
2.	B. Ball	Seeley
3.	B. Randle	Norton
4.	W. Smith	Matchless
5.	B. Lund	Matchless
6.	K. Carruthers	Norton
7.	B. Nelson	Paton
8.	R. Butcher	Matchless
9.	D. Woodman	Seeley
10.	K. Turner	Matchless

Fastest lap: G. Agostini, 21m 34.8s/104.91mph

1969

Sidecar, 750cc (3 laps/113.19 miles)

1.	S. Schauzu/H. Schneider	BMW
	1h 15m36.8s/89.83mph	
2.	P. Brown/M. Casey	BSA
3.	W. Currie/F. Kay	LWC
4.	M. Boddice/C. Pollington	BSA
5.	D. Plummer/M. Brett	Triumph
6.	M. Horspole/G. Horspole	Triumph
7.	G. Fox/M. Sanderson	Triumph
8.	W. Cooper/D. Argent	WEC
9.	R. Kewley/D. Tucker	BSA
10.	D. Keen/M. Wotherspoon	Triumph

Fastest lap: S. Schauzu/H. Schneider, 24m 35.4s/92.06mph*

Sidecar, 500cc (3 laps/113.19 miles)

1.	K. Enders/R. Engelhardt	BMW
	1h 13m 27.0s/92.48mph	
2.	S. Schauzu.H. Scheider	BMW
3.	H. Fath/W. Kalauch	URS
4.	A. Butsher/J. Huber	BMW
5.	F. Linnarz/P. Kuchnmund	BMW
6.	R. Hawes/J. Mann	Seeley
7.	N. Hanks/R. Arnold	BSA
8.	B. Copson/D. Rowe	BMW
9.	D. Keen/M. Wotherspoon	Triumph
10.	T. Harris/B. Harris	Triumph

Fastest lap: K. Enders/R. Engelhardt, 24m 27.8s/92.54mph*

Lightweight 250 (6 laps/226.38 miles)

1.	K. Carruthers	Benelli
	2h 21m 35.2s/95.95mph	
2.	F. Perris	Suzuki
3.	S. Herrero	Ossa
4.	M. Chatterton	Yamaha
5.	F. Whiteway	Suzuki
6.	D. Chatterton	Yamaha
7.	S. Woods	Yamaha
8.	F. Stastny	Jawa
9.	I. Richards	Yamaha
10.	G. Keith	Yamaha

Fastest lap: K. Carruthers, 22m 51s/99.01mph

Production, 750cc (3 laps/113.19 miles)

1.	M. Uphill	Triumph
	1h 07m 55.4s/99.99mph	
2.	P. Smart	Norton
3.	D. Pendlebury	Triumph
4.	M. Andrew	Norton
5.	S. Jolly	Triumph
6.	A. Jefferies	Triumph
7.	M. Carney	Triumph
8.	P. Mahoney	BSA
9.	P. Butler	Triumph
10.	L. Phelps	Triumph

Fastest lap: M. Uphill, 22m 33.2s/100.37mph*

Production, 500cc (3 laps/113.19 miles)

1.	W. Penny	Honda
	1h 17m 01.6s/88.18mph	
2.	R. Knight	Triumph
3.	R. Baylie	Triumph
4.	A. Cooper	Suzuki
5.	H. Evans	BSA
6.	M. Chatterton	Triumph
7.	B. Warburton	Triumph
8.	A. Allen	Triumph

Fastest lap: T. Dunnell, 24m 55.2s/90.84mph

Only eight finishers

Production, 250cc (3 laps/113.19 miles)

1.	A. Rogers	Ducati
	1h 21m 03.8s/83.79mph	
2.	F. Whiteway	Suzuki
3.	C. Mortimer	Ducati
4.	G. Leigh	Bultaco
5.	G. Thompsett	Ducati
6.	W. Benson	Suzuki
7.	T. Holdsworth	Suzuki
8.	T. Loughridge	Suzuki
9.	C. Mates	Yamaha
10.	J. Williams	Honda

Fastest lap: C. Mortimer, 26m 35.6s/85.13mph

Junior (6 laps/226.38 miles)

1.	G. Agostini	MV Agusta
	2h 13m 25.4s/101.81mph	
2.	B. Steenson	Aermacchi
3.	J. Findlay	Aermacchi
4.	T. Dickie	Seeley
5.	T. Grotefeld	Yamaha
6.	S. Griffiths	AJS
7.	J. Findlay	Norton
8.	W. Guthrie	Yamaha
9.	M. Hatherill	Aermacchi
10.	R. Graham	Aermacchi

Fastest lap: G. Agostini, 21m 46.0s/104.00mph

Lightweight 125 (3 laps/113.19 miles)

1.	D. Simmonds	Kawasaki
	1h 14m 34.6s/91.08mph	
2.	K. Carruthers	Aermacchi
3.	R. Dickinson	Honda
4.	S. Murray	Honda
5.	J. Kiddie	Honda
6.	C. Ward	Bultaco
7.	J. Shacklady	Bultaco
8.	C. Garner	Bultaco
9.	J. Pasquier	Bultaco
10.	T. Loughridge	Bultaco

Fastest lap: D. Simmond, 24m 29s/92.46mph

Senior (6 laps/226.38 miles)

1.	G. Agostini	MV Agusta
	2h 09m 40.2s/107.75mph	
2.	A. Barnett	Metisse
3.	T. Dickie	Seeley
4.	D. Woodman	Seeley
5.	J. Findlay	Norton
6.	R. Chandler	Seeley
7.	S. Jolly	Seeley
8.	S. Griffiths	Matchless
9.	P. Darvill	Norton
10.	S. Spencer	Metisse

Fastest lap: G. Agostini, 21m 18.4s/106.25mph

1970

Production, 750cc		(5 laps/188.65 miles)
1.	M. Uphill	Triumph
	1h 55m 51.0s/97.71mph	
2.	P. Williams	Norton
3.	R. Pickrell	Norton
4.	T. Dickie	Triumph
5.	B. Heath	BSA
6.	H.O. Butenuth	BMW
7.	S. Spencer	Norton
8.	T. Robb	Honda
9.	J. Cooper	Honda
10.	P. Mahoney	Norton
Fastest lap: P. Williams, 22m 38.4s/99.99mph		

Production, 500cc		(5 laps/188.65 miles)
1.	F. Whiteway	Suzuki
	2h 05m 52s/89.94mph	
2.	G. Pantall	Suzuki
3.	R. Knight	Triumph
4.	R. Baylie	Triumph
5.	G. Penny	Triumph
6.	J. Wade	Suzuki
7.	B. Finch	Velocette
Fastest lap: F. Whiteway, 24m 57s/90.75mph		
Only seven finishers		

Production, 250cc		(5 laps/188.65 miles)
1.	C. Mortimer	Ducati
	2h 13m 23.4s/84.87mph	
2.	J. Williams	Honda
3.	S. Woods	Suzuki
4.	G. Hunter	Ducati
5.	R. Boughey	Honda
6.	R. Ashcroft	Honda
7.	T. Loughridge	Suzuki
8.	C. Luton	Ducati
Fastest lap: C. Mortimer, 26m 25.6s/86.71mph		
Only eight finishers		

Sidecar, 750cc		(3 laps/113.19 miles)
1.	S. Schauzu/H. Schneider	BMW
	1h 15m 18.0s/90.20mph*	
2.	P. Brown/M. Casey	BSA
3.	E. Leece/J. Molyneux	LMS
4.	W. Cooper/D. Argent	WEC
5.	M. Horspole/E. McPherson	Triumph
6.	A. Sansum/A. Macfazdean	Triumph
7.	M. Hobson/G. Atkinson	BSA
8.	A. Swindells/D. Bayer	Norton
9.	R. Woodhouse/D. Woodhouse	Honda
10.	P. Krukowski/A. Lewis	BSA
Fastest lap: K. Enders/W. Kalauch, 24m 30.6s/92.37mph*		

Lightweight 250		(6 laps/226.38 miles)
1.	K. Carruthers	Yamaha
	2h 21m 19.2s/96.13mph	
2.	R. Gould	Yamaha
3.	G. Bartusch	MZ
4.	C. Mortimer	Yamaha
5.	P. Berwick	Suzuki
6.	A. George	Yamaha
7.	I. Richards	Yamaha
8.	B. Jansson	Yamaha
9.	T. Smith	Yamaha
10.	W. Smith	Yamaha
Fastest lap: K. Carruthers, 23m 05.4s/98.04mph		

Sidecar, 500cc		(3 laps/113.19 miles)
1.	K. Enders/W. Kalauch	BMW
	1h 13m 05.6s/92.93mph	
2.	S. Schauzu/H. Schneider	BMW
3.	H. Luthringshauser/H. Cusnik	BMW
4.	J. Castella/A. Castella	BMW
5.	H. Owesle/J. Kremer	Munch URS
6.	G. Auerbacher/H. Hahn	BMW
7.	A. Butscher/K. Lauterbach	BMW
8.	C. Freeman/E. Fletcher	Norton
9.	L. Currie/F. Kay	GSM
10.	M. Horspole/E. McPherson	Triumph
Fastest lap: K. Enders/W. Kalauch, 24m 08.2s/93.79mph*		

Junior		(6 laps/226.38 miles)
1.	G. Agostini	MV Agusta
	2h 13m 28.6s/101.77mph	
2.	A. Barnett	Aermacchi
3.	P. Smart	Yamaha
4.	M. Uphill	Yamaha
5.	T. Rutter	Yamaha
6.	P. Berwick	Aermacchi
7.	R. Pickrell	Aermacchi
8.	R. Duffy	Aermacchi
9.	T. Robb	Yamaha
10.	J. Findlay	Norton
Fastest lap: G. Agostini, 21m 39s/104.56mph		

Lightweight 125		(3 laps/113.19 miles)
1.	D. Braun	Suzuki
	1h 16m 05.0s/89.27mph	
2.	B. Jansson	Maico
3.	G. Bartusch	MZ
4.	S. Murray	Honda
5.	F. Launchbury	Bultaco
6.	J. Curry	Honda
7.	T. Robb	Maico
8.	J. Kiddie	Honda
9.	B. Dickinson	Honda
10.	K. Armstrong	Honda
Fastest lap: D. Simmonds, 24m 54.2s/90.90mph		

Senior		(6 laps/226.38 miles)
1.	G. Agostini	MV Agusta
	2h 13m 47.6s/101.52mph	
2.	P. Williams	Matchless
3.	W. Smith	Kawasaki
4.	J. Findlay	Seeley
5.	J. Williams	Matchless
6.	A. Jefferies	Matchless
7.	S. Griffiths	Matchless
8.	B. Adams	Norton
9.	V. Duckett	Matchless
10.	S. Spencer	Norton
Fastest lap: G. Agostini, 21m 30s/105.29mph		

1971

Formula 750		(3 laps/113.19 miles)
1.	A. Jefferies	Triumph
	1h 06m 02.0s/102.85	
2.	R. Pickrell	BSA
3.	P. Williams	Norton
4.	B. Clark	Yamaha
5.	D. Robinson	Yamaha
6.	D. Nixon	Triumph
7.	W. Smith	Kawasaki
8.	T. Dickie	BMW
9.	P. Darvill	Honda
10.	C. Dobson	Norton
Fastest lap: A. Jefferies, 21m 56.0s/103.21mph		

Sidecar TT, 750cc		(3 laps/113.19 miles)
1.	G. Auerbacher/H. Hahn	BMW
	1h 18m 12.0s/86.86mph	
2.	A. Sansum/D. Jose	Triumph
3.	R. Williamson/J. McPherson	Weslake
4.	R. Woodhouse/D. Woodhouse	Honda
5.	D. Wood/D. Coomber	Norton

6.	D. Plummer/M. Brett	Triumph
7.	L. Currie/K. Scott	Weslake
8.	M. Potter/P. Burleigh	BSA
9.	R. Hawes/J. Mann	Seeley
10.	A. Methersill/M. Mitchinson	AMS

Fastest lap: S. Schauzu/W. Kalauch, 24m 13.6s/93.44mph*

Junior (5 laps/188.65 miles)

1.	A. Jefferies 2h 05m 48.6s/89.91mph	Yamsel
2.	G. Pantall	Yamaha
3.	W. Smith	Honda
4.	J. Williams	AJS
5.	M. Chatterton	Yamaha
6.	G. Mateer	Aermacchi
7.	M. Grant	Yamaha
8.	B. Guthrie	Yamaha
9.	G. Bartusch	MZ
10.	P. Berwick	Suzuki

Fastest lap: P. Read, 22m 33.2s/100.37mph

Sidecar, 500cc (3 laps/113.19 miles)

1.	S. Schauzu/W. Kalauch 1h 18m 47.8s/86.21mph	BMW
2.	G. Auerbacher/H. Hahn	BMW
3.	A. Butcher/J. Huber	BMW
4.	J. Gawley/G. Alcock	BMW
5.	R. Wegener/A. Heinrichs	BMW
6.	C. Vincent/M. Casey	BSA
7.	R. Hawes/P. Mann	Seeley
8.	R. Williamson/J. McPherson	Triumph
9.	J. Mines/G. Davis	Matchless
10.	P. Brown/F. Holden	BSA

Fastest lap: G. Auerbacher/W. Kalauch, 25m 56.2s/87.27mph

Lightweight 250 (4 laps/150.92 miles)

1.	P. Read 1h 32m 23.6s/98.02mph	Yamaha
2.	B. Randle	Yamaha
3.	A. Barnett	Yamaha
4.	R. Gould	Yamaha
5.	B. Henderson	Yamaha
6.	G. Marsovsky	Yamaha
7.	P. Berwick	Yamaha
8.	I. Richards	Yamaha
9.	B. Jansson	Yamaha
10.	G. Pantall	Yamaha

Fastest lap: P. Read, 22m 37.2s/100.08mph

Production, 750cc (4 laps/150.92 miles)

1.	R. Pickrell 1h 30m 30.2s/100.07mph	Triumph
2.	A. Jefferies	Triumph
3.	B. Heath	BSA
4.	H.O. Butenuth	BMW
5.	D. Nixon	Triumph
6.	B. Clark	Norton
7.	T. Dickie	BMW
8.	K. Heckles	Norton
9.	T. Anderson	BMW

Fastest lap: P. Williams, 22m 24.0s/101.06mph*
Only nine finishers

Production, 500cc (4 laps/150.92 miles)

1.	J. Williams 1h 39m 28.8s/91.04mph	Honda
2.	G. Penny	Honda
3.	A. Cooper	Suzuki
4.	G. Bailey	Suzuki
5.	T. Loughridge	Suzuki
6.	M. Ashwood	Suzuki
7.	D. Shimmin	Suzuki
8.	P. Jones	Suzuki
9.	B. Milne	Kawasaki

Fastest lap: J. Williams, 24m 45.4s/91.45mph*
Only nine finishers

Production, 250cc (4 laps/150.92 miles)

1.	W. Smith 1h 47m 43.6s/84.14mph	Honda
2.	C. Williams	Yamaha
3.	T. Tobb	Honda
4.	P. Berwick	Suzuki
5.	G. Daniels	Suzuki
6.	L. Porter	Suzuki
7.	R. Simmons	Suzuki
8.	J. Evans	Montesa
9.	B. Barker	Honda

Fastest lap: C. Williams, 26m 44.8s/84.64mph
Only nine finishers

Lightweight 125 (3 laps/113.19 miles)

1.	C. Mortimer 1h 20m 54.0s/83.96mph	Yamaha
2.	B. Jansson	Maico
3.	J. Kiddie	Honda
4.	P. Courtney	Yamaha
5.	R. Watts	Honda
6.	C. Ward	Maico
7.	F. Smart	Honda
8.	L. Porter	Honda
9.	B. Rae	Maico
10.	J. Pearson	Bultaco

Fastest lap: C. Mortimer, 26m 00.2s/87.05mph

Senior (6 laps/226.38 miles)

1.	G. Agostini 2h 12m 24.4s/102.59mph	MV Agusta
2.	P. Williams	Matchless
3.	F. Perris	Suzuki
4.	S. Griffiths	Matchless
5.	G. Pantall	Kawasaki
6.	R. Sutcliffe	Matchless
7.	K. Turner	Suzuki
8.	C. Sanby	Seeley
9.	T. Dickie	Matchless
10.	H.O. Butenuth	BMW

Fastest lap: G. Agostini, 21m 35.4s/104.86mph

1972

Production, 750cc (4 laps/150.92 miles)

1.	R. Pickrell 1h 30m 34.0s/100.00mph	Triumph
2.	P. Williams	Norton
3.	D. Nixon	Triumph
4.	H. Dahne	BMW
5.	M. Ashwood	Norton
6.	A. Copland	Triumph
7.	W. Baxter	Norton
8.	D. Lunn	Honda
9.	T. Waterer	Norton
10.	R. Baylie	Honda

Fastest lap: R. Pickrell, 22m 16.8s/101.61mph*

Production, 500cc (4 laps/150.92 miles)

1.	S. Woods 1h 38m 13.8s/92.20mph	Suzuki
2.	R. Bowler	Triumph
3.	B. Smith	Honda
4.	R. Knight	Triumph
5.	H. Evans	Kawasaki
6.	G. Penny	Honda
7.	B. Milne	Kawasaki
8.	T. Loughridge	Suzuki
9.	R. Boughey	Honda
10.	R. Ashcroft	Honda

Fastest lap: S. Woods, 24m 11.0s/93.61mph*

Production, 250cc (4 laps/150.92 miles)

1.	J. Williams 1h 46m 08.8s/85.32mph	Honda
2.	C.Williams	Yamaha
3.	E. Roberts	Suzuki
4.	D. Arnold	Ducati
5.	N. Tuxworth	Suzuki
6.	J. Evans	Yamaha
7.	V. Soussan	Suzuki
8.	J. Kiddie	Honda
9.	C. Garner	Honda
10.	L. Notman	Yamaha

Fastest lap: J. Williams, 26m 24.4s/85.73mph

Sidecar, 750cc (3 laps/113.19 miles)

1.	S. Schauzu/W. Kalauch 1h 14m 40.0s/90.97mph	BMW
2.	A. Sansum/C. Emmins	Triumph
3.	J. Barker/A. Macfazdean	BSA
4.	J. Brandon/C. Holland	Honda
5.	R. Wegener/A. Heinrichs	BMW
6.	R. Hanks/J. Mann	BSA
7.	M. Horspole/G. Horspole	Triumph
8.	R. Woodhouse/D. Woodhouse	Honda
9.	R. Williamson/D. Smith	Triumph
10.	T. Ireson/N. Smith	Triumph

Fastest lap: S. Schauzu/W. Kalauch, 24m 47.2s/91.33mph*

Junior (5 laps/188.65 miles)

1.	G. Agostini 1h 50m 56.8s/102.03mph	MV Agusta
2.	T. Rutter	Yamaha
3.	M. Grant	Yamaha
4.	J. Findlay	Yamaha
5.	D. Chatterton	Yamaha
6.	S. Griffiths	Yamaha
7.	M. Chatterton	Yamaha
8.	L. Szabo	Yamaha
9.	B. Rae	Yamaha
10.	B. Lee	Yamaha

Fastest lap: G. Agostini, 21m 54.4s/103.34mph

Sidecar, 500cc (3 laps/113.19 miles)

1.	S. Schauzu/W. Kalauch 1h 13m57.2s/91.85mph	BMW
2.	H. Luthringshauser/J. Cusnik	BMW
3.	G. Boret/N. Boret	Konig
4.	W. Klenk/N. Scheerer	BMW
5.	B. Dungworth/R. Turrington	BMW
6.	R. Hanks/J. Mann	BSA
7.	R. Woodhouse/D. Woodhouse	BSA
8.	R. Dutton/T. Wright	BMW
9.	G. O'Dell/W. Boldison	BSA
10.	J. Barker/A. Macfazdean	BSA

Fastest lap: H. Luthringshauser/J. Cusnik, 24m 28s/92.53mph

Lightweight 250 (4 laps/150.92 miles)

1.	P. Read 1h 30 51.2s/99.68mph	Yamaha
2.	R. Gould	Yamaha
3.	J. Williams	Yamaha
4.	C. Williams	Yamaha
5.	W. Pfirter	Yamaha
6.	B. Henderson	Yamaha
7.	D. Chatterton	Yamaha
8.	D. Robinson	Yamaha
9.	B. Randle	Yamaha
10.	B. Rae	Yamaha

Fastest lap: P. Read, 22m 30.0s/100.61mph

Formula 750 (5 laps/188.65 miles)

1.	R. Pickrell 1h 48m 36.0s/104.23mph	Triumph
2.	T. Jefferies	Triumph
3.	J. Findlay	Suzuki
4.	D. Nixon	Triumph
5.	C. Williams	Yamaha
6.	B. Steele	Norton
7.	J. Williams	Honda
8.	R. Nicholls	Suzuki
9.	D. Trollope	Triumph
10.	C. Brown	Suzuki

Fastest lap: R. Pickrell, 21m 25.2s/105.68mph*

Lightweight 125 (3 laps/113.19 miles)

1.	C. Mortimer 1h 17m 38.2s/87.49mph	Yamaha
2.	C. Williams	Yamaha
3.	B. Rae	Maico
4.	L. Porter	Honda
5.	R. Hackett	Honda
6.	R. Watts	Honda
7.	F. Launchbury	Maico
8.	L. Notman	Yamaha
9.	A. Morris	Yamaha
10.	M. Evans	Yamaha

Fastest lap: C. Mortimer, 24m 59.6s/90.58mph

Senior (6 laps/226.38 miles)

1.	G. Agostini 2h 10m 34.4s/104.02mph	MV Agusta
2.	A. Pagani	MV Agusta
3.	M. Grant	Kawasaki
4.	K. Cowley	Seeley
5.	D. Chatterton	Yamaha
6.	C. Williams	Yamaha
7.	S. Griffiths	Matchless
8.=	C. Brown	Suzuki
8.=	P. Cott	Seeley
10.	C. Sanby	Suzuki

Fastest lap: G. Agostini, 21m 28.8s/105.39mph

1973

Production, 750cc (4 laps/150.92 miles)

1.	A. Jefferies 1h 34m 41.6s/95.62mph	Triumph
2.	J. Williams	Triumph
3.	D. Nixon	Triumph
4.	H. Dahne	BMW
5.	E. Pitt	Triumph
6.	D. Pendlebury	Triumph
7.	H.O. Butenuth	BMW
8.	H. Evans	Honda
9.	R. Corbett	Triumph
10.	K. Huggett	Triumph

Fastest lap: P. Williams, 21m 31.2s/100.52mph

Production, 500cc (4 laps/150.92 miles)

1.	W. Smith 1h 42m 47.0s/88.10mph	Honda
2.	S. Woods	Suzuki
3.	K. Martin	Kawasaki
4.	C. Brown	BSA
5.	R. Bowler	Triumph
6.	B. Milne	Kawasaki
7.	R. Knight	Triumph
8.	N. Rollason	BSA
9.	J. Wilkinson	Suzuki
10.	G. Benson	Suzuki

Fastest lap: S. Woods, 23m 58.2s/94.44mph*

Production, 250cc (4 laps/150.92 miles)

1.	C. Williams 1h 50m 45.0s/81.76mph	Yamaha
2.	E. Roberts	Yamaha
3.	T. Robb	Yamaha
4.	R. Hunter	Suzuki
5.	P. Courtney	Kawasaki
6.	P. Carpenter	Honda
7.	J. Curry	Honda
8.	J. Kiddie	Honda
9.	L. Porter	Suzuki
10.	J. Kidson	Honda

Fastest lap: E. Roberts, 26m 58.8s/84.06mph

Sidecar, 750cc (3 laps/113.19 miles)

1.	K. Enders/R. Engelhardt 1h 13m 00.1s/93.01mph	BMW
2.	S. Schauzu/W. Kalauch	BMW
3.	J. Brandon/C. Holland	Honda
4.	M. Boddice/K. Williams	Kawasaki
5.	W. Crook/K. Arthur	BSA
6.	R. Williamson/J. McPherson	BMW
7.	R. Hawes/E. Kiff	Weslake
8.	R. Wegner/D. Jacobson	BMW
9.	M. Vanneste/S. Vanneste	BMW
10.	M. Potter/B. Coverdale	BMW

Fastest lap: K. Enders/R. Engelhardt, 23m 22.2s/96.86mph*

Junior (5 laps/188.65 miles)

1.	T. Rutter 1h 50m 58.5s/101.99mph	Yamaha
2.	K. Huggett	Yamaha
3.	J. Williams	Yamaha
4.	B. Randle	Yamaha
5.	P. Carpenter	Yamaha
6.	D. Chatterton	Yamaha
7.	A. George	Yamaha
8.	H. Kassner	Yamaha
9.	T. Dickie	Yamaha
10.	P. Cott	Yamaha

Fastest lap: T. Rutter, 21m 43.2s/104.22mph

Sidecar, 500cc (3 laps/113.19 miles)

1.	K. Enders/ R. Engelhardt 1h 11m 32.4s/94.93mph	BMW
2.	S. Schauzu/W. Kalauch	BMW
3.	R. Steinhausen/K. Scheurer	Konig
4.	M. Vanneste/S. Vanneste	BMW
5.	R. Williamson/J. McPherson	BMW
6.	R. Dutton/T. Wright	BMW
7.	G. O'Dell/N. Boldison	BSA
8.	R. Hawes/E. Kiff	Weslake
9.	R. Woodhouse/D. Woodhouse	Honda
10.	M. Candy/E. Fletcher	BSA

Fastest lap: K. Enders/R. Engelhardt, 23m 46.4s/95.22mph*

Lightweight 250 (4 laps/150.92 miles)

1.	C. Williams 1h 30m 30.0s/100.05mph	Yamaha
2.	J. Williams	Yamaha
3.	B. Rae	Yamaha
4.	D. Chatterton	Yamaha
5.	A. George	Yamaha
6.	T. Rutter	Yamaha
7.	P. Carpenter	Yamaha
8.	H. Kassner	Yamaha
9.	T. Herron	Yamaha
10.	B. Randle	Yamaha

Fastest lap: C. Williams, 22m 08.4s/102.24mph

Formula 750 (5 laps/188.65 miles)

1.	P. Williams 1h 47m 19.2s/105.47mph	Norton
2.	M. Grant	Norton
3.	T. Jefferies	Triumph
4.	C. Williams	Yamaha
5.	S. Woods	Suzuki
6.	K. Huggett	Yamaha
7.	G. Barry	Seeley
8.	P. Cott	Yamaha
9.	H. Dahne	BMW
10.	G. Bailey	Triumph

Fastest lap: P. Williams, 21m 06.2s/107.27mph*

Lightweight 125 (3 laps/113.19 miles)

1.	T. Robb 1h 16m 23.6s/88.90mph	Yamaha
2.	J. Kostwinder	Yamaha
3.	N. Tuxworth	Yamaha
4.	I. Hodgkinson	Yamaha
5.	A. Jones	Maico
6.	L. Porter	Yamaha
7.	C. Horton	Yamaha
8.	R. Stevens	Maico

9.	B. Ware	Yamaha
10.	J. Kiddie	Honda

Fastest lap: T. Robb, 25m 22.0s/89.24mph

Senior (6 laps/226.38 miles)

1.	J. Findlay 2h 13m 45.2s/101.55mph	Suzuki
2.	P. Williams	Matchless
3.	C. Sanby	Suzuki
4.	A. George	Yamaha
5.	R. Nicholls	Suzuki
6.	D. Hughes	Matchless
7.	D. Robinson	Suzuki
8.	J. Taylor	Suzuki
9.	S. Griffiths	Matchless
10.	G. Bailey	Kawasaki

Fastest lap: M. Grant, 21m 40.8s/104.41mph

1974

Junior (5 laps/188.65 miles)

1.	T. Rutter 1h 48m 22.2s/104.44mph	Yamaha
2.	M. Grant	Yamaha
3.	P. Cott	Yamaha
4.	T. Herron	Yamaha
5.	B. Nelson	Yamaha
6.	B. Guthrie	Yamaha
7.	A. Rogers	Yamaha
8.	R. Nicholls	Yamaha
9.	P. Gurner	Yamaha
10.	N. Clegg	Yamaha

Fastest lap: C. Mortimer, 21m 16.6s/106.39mph*

Sidecar, 750cc (3 laps/113.19 miles)

1.	S. Schauzu/W. Kalauch 1h 10m 18.4s/96.59mph	BMW
2.	H. Luthringshauser/H. Hahn	BMW
3.	M. Horspole/G. Horspole	Weslake
4.	J. Barker/C. Emmins	BSA
5.	B. Crook/S. Collins	BSA
6.	R.Bell/G. Russell	Konig
7.	B. Moran/K. Moran	Norton
8.	D. Bexley/D. Tyler	Honda
9.	W. Schilling/H. Matthews	BMW
10.	M. Wortley/R. Crellin	Triumph

Fastest lap: R. Steinhausen/K. Scheurer, 23m 03.4s/98.18mph*

Production, 1000cc (4 laps/150.92 miles)

1.	M. Grant 1h 30m 48.0s/99.72mph	Triumph
2.	H.-O. Butenuth	BMW
3.	H. Dahne	BMW
4.	G. Barry	Norton
5.	C. Williams	Honda
6.	A. Walsh	Triumph
7.	R. Corbett	Triumph
8.	G. Bentham	Norton
9.	M. Russell	BSA
10.	G. Dixon	Triumph

Fastest lap: M. Grant, 22m 28.2s/100.74mph

Production, 500cc (4 laps/150.92 miles)

1.	K. Martin 1h 36m 28.6s/93.85mph	Kawasaki
2.	A. Rogers	Triumph
3.	P. Gurner	BSA
4.	N. Tuxworth	Honda
5.	R. Sutcliffe	Suzuki
6.	T. Loughridge	Suzuki
7.	C. Revett	Honda
8.	A. Jackson	Suzuki
9.	T. McGurk	Honda
10.	P. Crew	Honda

Fastest lap: K. Martin, 23m 46.6s/95.21mph*

Production, 250cc (4 laps/150.92 miles)

1.	M. Sharpe 1h 44m 09.2s/86.94mph	Yamaha
2.	E. Roberts	Yamaha
3.	B. Rae	Suzuki
4.	G. Benson	Yamaha
5.	J. Kiddie	Honda
6.	B. Robertson	Suzuki
7.	R. Nicholls	Ducati
8.	B. Murray	Benelli
9.	K. Heckles	Honda
10.	T. Christian	Yamaha

Fastest lap: E. Roberts, 25m 35.0s/88.48mph

Sidecar, 500cc (3 laps/113.19 miles)

1.	H. Luthringshauser/H. Hahn 1h 13m 36.2s/92.27mph	BMW
2.	G. O'Dell/B. Boldison	Konig
3.	D. Hawes/E. Kiff	Weslake
4.	M. Hobson/J. Armstrong	Yamaha
5.	T. Ireson/G. Hunt	Konig
6.	B. Crook/S. Collins	BSA
7.	M. Aldrick/M. Skeels	Honda
8.	R. Perry/A. Craig	BSA
9.	S. Schauzu/W. Kalauch	BMW
10.	R. Aldous/P. Lucock	Triumph

Fastest lap: J. Gawley/K. Birch, 24m 14.8s/93.36mph

Lightweight 250 (4 laps/150.92 miles)

1.	C. Williams 1h 36m 09.8s/94.16mph	Yamaha
2.	M. Grant	Yamaha
3.	C. Mortimer	Yamaha
4.	T. Herron	Yamaha
5.	T. Rutter	Yamaha
6.	P. McKinley	Yamaha
7.	I. Richards	Yamaha
8.	G. Mateer	Yamaha
9.	B. Warburton	Yamaha
10.	B. Randle	Yamaha

Fastest lap: M. Grant, 23m 08s/97.85mph

Senior (5 laps/188.65 miles)

1.	P. Carpenter 1h 56m 41.6s/96.99mph	Yamaha
2.	C. Williams	Yamaha
3.	T. Rutter	Yamaha
4.	B. Guthrie	Yamaha
5.	P. Cott	Yamaha
6.	H. Kassner	Yamaha
7.	B. Nelson	Yamaha
8.	P. McKinley	Yamaha
9.	S. Griffiths	Matchless
10.	G. Barry	Matchless

Fastest lap: C. Williams, 22m 12.6s/101.92mph

Lightweight 125 (3 laps/113.19 miles)

1.	C. Horton 1h 16m 47s/88.44mph	Yamaha
2.	I. Hodgkinson	Yamaha
3.	T. Herron	Yamaha
4.	K. Daniels	Yamaha
5.	F. Launchbury	Maico
6.	J. Kostwinder	Yamaha
7.	B. Kirkwood	Yamaha
8.	A. Jones	BSA
9.	R. Gooch	Yamaha
10.	B. Dickinson	Yamaha

Fastest lap: A. Hockley/C. Horton, 25m 29.8s/88.78mph

Formula 750 (6 laps/226.38 miles)

1.	C. Mortimer 2h 15m 07.2s/100.52mph	Yamaha
2.	C. Williams	Yamaha
3.	T. Rutter	Yamaha
4.	P. Tait	Triumph
5.	B. Guthrie	Yamaha
6.	A. Hockley	Yamaha
7.	A. George	Yamaha
8.	N. Clegg	Yamaha
9.	D. Lunn	Ducati
10.	D. Chatterton	Yamaha

Fastest lap: C. Williams, 21m 14s/106.61mph

1975

Production (10 laps/377.37 miles)

1.	D. Croxford/A. George 3h 47m 17.2s/99.60mph	Triumph
2.	C. Mortimer/B. Guthrie	Yamaha
3.	S. Griffiths/D. Williams	Triumph
4.	S. Jones/W. Simpson	Triumph
5.	A. North/M. Patrick	Yamaha
6.	S. Ward/G. Waring	Yamaha
7.	M. Sharp/A. Alexander	BMW
8.	C. Williams/E. Roberts	Honda
9.	R. Hunter/M. Scutt	Suzuki
10.	R. Stevens/P. Casey	Yamaha

Fastest lap: A. George/D. Croxford, 22m 01.0s/102.82mph

Junior (5 laps/188.65 miles)

1.	C. Williams 1h 48m 26.4s/104.38mph	Yamaha
2.	C. Mortimer	Yamaha
3.	T. Herron	Yamaha
4.	S. Tonkin	Yamaha
5.	D. Chatterton	Yamaha
6.	B. Guthrie	Yamaha
7.	G. Mateer	Yamaha
8.	G. Barry	Yamsel
9.	N. Clegg	Yamaha
10.	M. Sharpe	Yamaha

Fastest lap: A. George, 21m 17.8s/106.29mph

Sidecar, 500cc (3 laps/113.19 miles)

1.	R. Steinhausen/J. Huber 1h 10m 47.0s/95.94mph	Konig
2.	M. Hobson/G. Russell	Yamaha
3.	D. Greasley/C. Holland	Yamaha
4.	H. Schilling/F. Knights	BMW
5.	D. Plummer/C. Birks	Konig
6.	G. Pape/F. Kallenberg	Konig
7.	A. Campbell/J. Pearson	Yamaha
8.	R. Williamson/J. McPherson	Magnum
9.	R. Dutton/T. Wright	Yamaha
10.	T. Jansson/P. Sales	Konig

Fastest lap: M. Hobson/G. Russell, 23m 24.4s/96.71mph*

Senior (6 laps/226.38 miles)

1.	M. Grant 2h 15m 27.6s/100.27mph	Kawasaki
2.	J. Williams	Yamaha
3.	C. Mortimer	Yamaha
4.	B. Guthrie	Yamaha
5.	S. Tonkin	Yamaha
6.	G. Barry	Yamsel
7.	C. Williams	Yamaha
8.	T. Rutter	Yamaha
9.	H. Kassner	Yamaha
10.	L. Kennedy	Yamaha

Fastest lap: M. Grant, 21m 59.6s/102.93mph

Sidecar, 1000cc (3 laps/113.19 miles)

1.	S. Schauzu/W. Kalauch 1h 09m 37.0s/97.55mph	BMW
2.	D. Greasley/C. Holland	Yamaha
3.	G. Boret/N. Boret	Konig
4.	G. Milton/D. Smith	Magnum
5.	K. Graham/D. Tower	Suzuki
6.	D. Lawrence/J. Brromham	Limpet
7.	R. Williamson/J. Mc Pherson	Magnum
8.	R. Dutton/T. Wright	Yamaha
9.	J. Trustham/J. Cowley	BMW
10.	N. Rollason/P. Shiner	BSA

Fastest lap: S. Schauzu/W. Kalauch, 22m 47.6s/99.31mph*

Lightweight 250 (4 laps/150.92 miles)

1.	C. Mortimer 1h 28m 57.8s/101.78mph	Yamaha
2.	D. Chatterton	Yamaha
3.	J. Williams	Yamaha
4.	T. Rutter	Yamaha
5.	A. George	Yamaha
6.	B. Henderson	Yamaha
7.	N. Tuxworth	Yamaha
8.	H. Kassner	Yamaha
9.	E. Roberts	Yamaha
10.	C. Horton	Yamaha

Fastest lap: D. Chatterton, 21m 51.8s/103.54mph

Classic (6 laps/226.38 miles)

1.	J. Williams 2h 08m 56.8s/105.33mph	Yamaha
2.	P. Tait	Yamaha
3.	C. Sanby	Suzuki
4.	N. Tuxforth	Yamaha
5.	D. Chatterton	Yamaha
6.	B. Henderson	Yamaha
7.	J. Weedon	Yamaha
8.	P. Grove	Yamaha
9.	H. Dahne	BMW
10.	B. Rae	Yamaha

Fastest lap: M. Grant, 20m 36.8s/109.82mph*

1976

Junior (5 laps/188.65 miles)

1.	C. Mortimer 1h 46m 00.2s/106.78mph	Yamaha
2.	T. Rutter	Yamaha
3.	B. Guthrie	Yamaha
4.	M. Sharpe	Yamaha
5.	J. Weedon	Yamaha
6.	D. Chatterton	Yamaha
7.	N. Tuxworth	Yamaha
8.	J. Findlay	Yamaha
9.	T. Katayama	Yamaha
10.	S. McClements	Yamaha

Fastest lap: T. Rutter, 20m 49.6s/108.69mph*

Sidecar, 500cc (3 laps/113.19 miles)

1.	R. Steinhausen/J. Huber 1h 10m 26.0s/96.42mph	Konig
2.	D. Greasley/C. Holland	Yamaha
3.	M. Hobson/M. Burns	Yamaha
4.	S. Schauzu/W. Kalauch	Aro
5.	J. Gawley/K. Birch	Yamaha
6.	G. Milton/J. Brushwood	Magnum
7.	H. Schilling/R. Gundel	Aro
8.	A. Campbell/R. Campbell	Yamaha
9.	W. Ohrmann/B.Grube	Yamaha
10.	T. Wakefield/C. Newbold	Magnum

Fastest lap: S. Schauzu/W. Kalauch, 23m 13.0s/97.50mph*

Production (10 laps/377.37 miles)

1.	B. Simpson/C. Mortimer 4h 05m 09.8s/87.0mph	Yamaha
2.	T. Rutter/D. Hughes	Suzuki
3.	F. Rutter/M. Poxon	Honda
4.	J. Kidson/B. Hendeson	Honda
5.	H. Dahne/H.-O. Butenuth	BMW
6.	K. Martin/J. Riley	Yamaha
7.	N. Rollason/L. Trotter	Suzuki
8.	D. Randall/J. Lavender	Yamaha
9.	D. Hunter/M. Kirwan	Suzuki
10.	K. Trubshaw/J. Higham	Honda

Fastest lap: S. Tonkin/R. Nicholls, 21m 57.0s/103.13mph

Senior (6 laps/226.38 miles)

1.	T. Herron 2h 09m 10.0s/105.15mph	Yamaha
2.	I. Richards	Yamaha
3.	B. Guthrie	Yamaha
4.	T. Katayama	Yamaha
5.	R. Nicholls	Yamaha
6.	J. Ekerold	Yamaha
7.	J. Williams	Yamaha
8.	G. Pantall	Yamaha
9.	J. Weedon	Yamaha
10.	W. Smith	Yamaha

Fastest lap: J. Williams, 20m 09.8s/112.27mph*

Sidecar, 1000cc (3 laps/113.19 miles)

1.	M. Hobson/M. Burns 1h 09m 27.8s/97.77mph	Yamaha
2.	S. Schauzu/W. Kalauch	BMW
3.	D. Greasley/C. Holland	Yamaha
4.	R. Steinhausen/J. Huber	Konig
5.	O. Haller/E. Haselbeck	BMW
6.	A. Campbell/R. Campbell	Yamaha

7.	B. Hodgkins/J. Parkins	Yamaha
8.	G. Fox/H. Sanderson	Yamaha
9.	G. Pape/F. Kellenberg	Konig
10.	N. Rollason/M. Coomber	BSA

Fastest lap: M. Hobson/M. Burns, 22m 38.8s/99.96mph*

Lightweight 250 (4 laps/150.92 miles)

1.	T. Herron 1h 27m 26.8s/103.55mph	Yamaha
2.	T. Katayama	Yamaha
3.	C. Mortimer	Yamaha
4.	T. Rutter	Yamaha
5.	E. Roberts	Yamaha
6.	A. George	Yamaha
7.	J. Weedon	Yamaha
8.	I. Richards	Yamaha
9.	D. Casement	Yamaha
10.	N. Tuxworth	Yamaha

Fastest lap: T. Herron, 21m 27.8s/105.47mph*

Classic (6 laps/226.38 miles)

1.	J. Williams 2h 05m 33.0s/108.18mph	Suzuki
2.	A. George	Yamaha
3.	T. Rutter	Yamaha
4.	C. Williams	Yamaha
5.	T. Herron	Yamaha
6.	E. Roberts	Yamaha
7.	I. Richards	Yamaha
8.	W. Smith	Yamaha
9.	G. Pantall	Yamaha
10.	G. Mateer	Yamaha

Fastest lap: J. Williams, 20m 32.4s/110.21mph*

1977

Junior (3 laps/113.19 miles)

1.	C. Williams 1h 08m 10.0s/99.62mph	Yamaha
2.	I. Richards	Yamaha
3.	T. Herron	Yamaha
4.	A. George	Yamaha
5.	S. Woods	Yamaha
6.	E. Roberts	Yamaha
7.	M. Grant	Kawasaki
8.	C. Horton	Yamaha
9.	J. Lindsay	Yamsel
10.	J. Dunlop	Yamsel

Fastest lap: I. Richards, 22m 18.8s/101.45mph

Formula 1 (4 laps/150.92 miles)

1.	P. Read 1h 33m 19.6s/97.02mph	Honda
2.	R. Nicholls	Ducati
3.	I. Richards	Honda
4.	S. Woods	Honda
5.	M. Lucas	BSA
6.	M. Hunt	Laverda
7.	R. Corbett	Triumph
8.	I. Tomkinson	BSA
9.	J. Kirkby	Laverda
10.	J. Wilkinson	Suzuki

Fastest lap: P. Read, 22m 15.0s/101.74mph

Senior (5 laps/188.65 miles)

1.	P. Read 1h 45m 48.4s/106.97mph	Suzuki
2.	T. Herron	Yamaha
3.	E. Roberts	Suzuki
4.	J. Dunlop	Yamsel
5.	P. Hennen	Suzuki
6.	J. Lindsay	Yamsel
7.	C. Mortimer	Yamaha
8.	W. Smith	Yamaha
9.	B. Guthrie	Yamaha
10.	J. Scott	Yamaha

Fastest lap: P. Read, 20m 34.6s/110.01mph*

Sidecar 1st leg (3 laps/113.19 miles)

1.	G. O'Dell/K. Arthur 1h 30m 31.2s/100.03mph	Yamaha
2.	D. Greasley/M. Skeels	Yamaha
3.	R. Steinhausen/W. Kalauch	Konig
4.	G. Milton/J. Brushwood	Magnum
5.	M. Boddice/C. Birks	Yamaha
6.	B. Hodgkins/J. Parkins	Yamaha
7.	G. Oates/J. Molyneux	Kawasaki
8.	M. Aldrick/P. Beasley	Yamaha
9.	B. Mee/A. Widdowson	Kawasaki
10.	B. Hall/P. Mionion	Kawasaki

Fastest lap: G. O'Dell/K. Arthur, 22m 01.2s/102.80mph

Classic (6 laps/226.38 miles)

1.	M. Grant 2h 02m 37.4s/110.76mph	Kawasaki
2.	C. Williams	Yamaha
3.	E. Roberts	Yamaha
4.	C. Mortimer	Yamaha
5.	W. Smith	Yamaha
6.	S. Woods	Suzuki
7.	J. Dunlop	Yamaha
8.	S. Tonkin	Yamaha
9.	S. Parrish	Yamaha
10.	A. George	Yamaha

Fastest lap: M. Grant, 20m 04.4s/112.77mph*

Sidecar 2nd leg (3 laps/113.19 miles)

1.	M. Hobson/S.Collins 1h 30m 47.0s99.74mph	Yamaha
2.	R. Biland/K. Williams	Yamaha
3.	R. Steinhausen/W. Kalauch	Konig
4.	D. Greasley/M. Skeels	Yamaha
5.	M. Boddice/C. Birks	Yamaha
6.	G. Hilditch/V. Biggs	Yamaha
7.	S. Sinnott/J. Williamson	Yamaha
8.	B. Hall/P. Minion	Kawasaki
9.	R. Spooner/D. Smith	Konig
10.	R. Philpott/M. Buxton	Laverda

Fastest lap: M. Hobson/S. Collins, 22m 15.0s/101.74mph

Formula 2 (4 laps/150.92 miles)

1.	A. Jackson 1h 31m 08.0s/99.36mph	Honda
2.	N. Tuxworth	Honda
3.	D. Casement	Honda
4.	J. Crick	Honda
5.	D. McMillan	Triumph
6.	T. McKane	Honda
7.	A. Copland	Benelli
8.	R. Arian	Honda

Fastest lap: A. Jackson, 22m 22.8s/101.15mph

Only eight finishers

Formula 3 (4 laps/150.92 miles)

1.	J. Kidson 1h 37m 04.4s/93.28mph	Honda
2.	D. Loan	Suzuki
3.	B. Peters	Suzuki
4.	A. Walsh	Honda
5.	G. Bentman	Honda
6.	F. Launchbury	Maico
7.	M. Kirwan	Honda
8.	N. Watts	Honda
9.	R. Stevens	Yamaha
10.	J. Riley	Yamaha

Fastest lap: J. Kidson, 23m 52.6s/94.81mph

Jubilee TT (4 laps/150.92 miles)

1.	J. Dunlop 1h 23m 10.6s/108.86mph	Yamaha
2.	G. Fogarty	Suzuki
3.	S. Tonkin	Yamaha
4.	W. Smith	Suzuki
5.	D. Huxley	Yamaha
6.	J. Findlay	Yamaha
7.	D. Chatterton	Suzuki
8.	D. Casement	Yamaha
9.	N. Tuxworth	Yamaha
10.	J. Scott	Yamaha

Fastest lap: J. Dunlop, 20m 24.4s/110.93mph

1978

Formula 1 (6 laps/226.38 miles)

1.	M. Hailwood 2h 05m 10.2s/108.51mph	Ducati
2.	J. Williams	Honda
3.	I. Richards	Kawasaki
4.	H. Dahne	Honda
5.	A. George	Triumph
6.	C. Mortimer	Suzuki
7.	M. Lucas	BSA
8.	K. Wrettom	Kawasaki
9.	D. Casement	Honda
10.	I. Tomkinsson	Triumph

Fastest lap: M. Hailwood, 20m 27.8s/110.62mph*

Senior (6 laps/226.38 miles)

1.	T. Herron 2h 01m 33.4s/111.74mph	Suzuki
2.	B. Guthrie	Suzuki
3.	C. Mortimer	Yamaha
4.	G. Fogarty	Suzuki
5.	A. George	Suzuki
6.	W. Smith	Suzuki
7.	D. Ireland	Suzuki
8.	G. Waring	Yamaha
9.	J. Woodley	Suzuki
10.	B. Ingham	Yamaha

Fastest lap: P. Hennen, 19m 53.2s/113.83mph

Sidecar 1st leg (3 laps/113.19 miles)

1.	D. Greasley/G. Russell	Yamaha
	1h 06m 44.6s/101.75mph	
2.	J. Taylor/K. Arthur	Yamaha
3.	G. Milton/J. Brushwood	Magnum
4.	G. Hilditch/V. Biggs	Yamaha
5.	M. White/P. Spendlove	Yamaha
6.	T. Wakefield/E. Kiff	Magnum
7.	A. May/M. Gray	Yamaha
8.	D. Jones/B. Ayres	Yamaha
9.	P. Coney/B. Leigh	Yamaha
10.	J. Brandon/P. Wynne	Yamaha

Fastest lap: R. Biland/K. Williams, 21m 48.4s/103.81mph*

Junior (5 laps/188.65 miles)

1.	C. Mortimer	Yamaha
	1h 52m 23.8s/100.70mph	
2.	C. Williams	Yamaha
3.	T. Herron	Yamaha
4.	G. Waring	Yamaha
5.	J. Lindsay	Yamaha
6.	B. Ingham	Yamaha
7.	D. Chatterton	Yamaha
8.	J. Weedon	Yamaha
9.	T. Katayama	Yamaha
10.	I. Richards	Yamaha

Fastest lap: C. Mortimer, 22m 10.8s/102.06mph

Sidecar 2nd leg (3 laps/113.19 miles)

1.	R. Steinhausen/W. Kalauch	Yamaha
	1h 12m 30.0s/93.67mph	
2.	M. Boddice/C. Birks	Yamaha
3.	J. Taylor/K. Arthur	Yamaha
4.	A. Steele/A. Barrow	Yamaha
5.	T. Ireson/M. Allsworth	Yamaha
6.	A. May/M. Gray	Yamaha
7.	M. White/P. Spendlove	Yamaha
8.	G. Milton/J. Brushwood	Magnum
9.	M. Joyce/A. Collins	Suzuki
10.	B. Hall/P. Minion	Kawasaki

Fastest lap: R. Steinhausen/W. Kalauch, 23m 32.8s/96.14mph

Formula 2 (4 laps/150.92 miles)

1.	A. Jackson	Honda
	1h 31m 08.6s/99.35mph	
2.	I. Mason	Honda
3.	N. Tuxworth	Honda
4.	R. Haslam	Honda
5.	J. Dunlop	Benelli
6.	P. Davies	Laverda
7.	J. Kirkby	Honda
8.	T. Williamson	Honda
9.	D. Casement	Honda
10.	D. Kerby	Honda

Fastest lap: A. Jackson, 21m 56.0s/103.21mph*

Formula 3 (4 laps/150.92 miles)

1.	W. Smith	Honda
	1h 35m 50.8s/94.47mph	
2.	D. Mortimer	Yamaha
3.	J. Stephens	Honda
4.	M. Poxon	Honda
5.	A. Cathcart	Harley-Davidson
6.	F. Launchbury	Maico
7.	K. Inwood	Yamaha
8.	J. Middleton	Honda
9.	D. Trollope	Yamaha
10.	B. Barker	Honda

Fastest lap: W. Smith, 23m 32.6s/96.13mph*

Classic (6 laps/226.38 miles)

1.	M. Grant	Kawasaki
	2h 00m 50.2s/112.40mph	
2.	J. Williams	Suzuki
3.	A. George	Yamaha
4.	P. Read	Honda
5.	B. Simpson	Yamaha
6.	D. Ireland	Suzuki
7.	M. Lucas	Yamaha
8.	J. Sayle	Yamaha
9.	S. Tonkin	Yamaha
10.	W. Smith	Yamaha

Fastest lap: M. Grant, 19m 48s/114.33mph*

1979

Formula 1 (6 laps/226.38 miles)

1.	A. George	Honda
	2h 02m 50.6s/110.57mph	
2.	C. Williams	Honda
3.	R. Haslam	Honda
4.	G. Crosby	Kawasaki
5.	M. Hailwood	Ducati
6.	R. Bowler	Honda
7.	G. Fogarty	Ducati
8.	H. Dahne	Honda
9.	A. Moyce	Kawasaki
10.	R. Corbett	Kawasaki

Fastest lap: A. George, 20m 02.6s/112.94mph*

Sidecar 1st leg (3 laps/113.19 miles)

1.	T. Ireson/C. Pollington	Yamaha
	1h 06m 29.4s/102.14mph	
2.	D. Greasley/J. Parkins	Yamaha
3.	M. Boddice/C. Birks	Yamaha
4.	B. Hargreaves/N. Burgess	Yamaha
5.	D. Saville/H. Sanderson	Yamaha
6.	N. Rollason/D. Homer	Barton Phoenix
7.	M. White/P. Spendlove	Yamaha
8.	P. Campbell/D. Goodwin	Yamaha
9.	R. Biland/K. Waltisperg	Yamaha
10.	A. Steele/A. Barrow	Yamaha

Fastest lap: M. Boddice/C. Birks, 21m 55.4s/103.26mph*

Senior (6 laps/226.38 miles)

1.	M. Hailwood	Suzuki
	2h 01m 32.4s/111.75mph	
2.	T. Rutter	Suzuki
3.	D. Ireland	Suzuki
4.	S. Ward	Suzuki
5.	S. Tonkin	Yamaha
6.	C. Mortimer	Yamaha
7.	I. Richards	Yamaha
8.	K. Blake	Yamaha
9.	B. Murray	Yamaha
10.	B. Ingham	Yamaha

Fastest lap: M. Hailwood, 19m 51.2s/114.02mph*

Junior (6 laps/226.38 miles)

1.	C. Williams	Yamaha
	2h 09m 11.8s/105.12mph	
2.	G. McGregor	Yamaha
3.	I. Richards	Yamaha
4.	C. Mortimer	Yamaha
5.	J. Sayle	Yamaha
6.	S. Tonkin	Yamaha
7.	B. Ingham	Yamaha
8.	B. Simpson	Yamaha
9.	E. Roberts	Yamaha
10.	K. Harrison	Yamaha

Fastest lap: C. Williams, 21m 11.4s/106.83mph*

Sidecar 2nd leg (3 laps/113.19 miles)

1.	T. Ireson/C. Pollington	Yamaha
	1h 07m 22.6s/100.79mph	
2.	N. Rollason/D. Homer	Barton Phoenix
3.	D. Saville/H. Sanderson	Yamaha
4.	M. White/P. Spendlove	Yamaha
5.	G. Milton/J. Brushwood	Magnum
6.	B. Hargreaves/N. Burgess	Yamaha
7.	P. Campell/D. Goodwin	Yamaha
8.	R. Biland/K. Waltisperg	Yamaha
9.	M. Joyce/A. Collins	Suzuki
10.	D. Hawes/B. Boldison	Yamaha

Fastest lap: R. Steinhausen/K. Arthur, 22m 09.4s/102.17mph

Formula 2 (4 laps/150.92 miles)

1.	A. Jackson	Honda
	1h 29m 09.8s/101.55mph	
2.	R. Bowler	Honda
3.	S. Tonkin	Honda
4.	I. Richards	Honda
5.	S. Ward	Benelli
6.	M. Hunt	Laverda
7.	P. Odlin	Honda
8.	R. Knight	Honda
9.	P. Davies	Laverda
10.	D. Goodfellow	Honda

Fastest lap: A. Jackson, 21m 53.6s/103.40mph*

Formula 3 (4 laps/150.92 miles)

1.	B. Smith	Yamaha
	1h 32m 33.8s/97.82mph	
2.	R. Hunter	Honda
3.	M. Wheeler	Aermacchi
4.	T. Rutter	Honda
5.	T. Robb	Suzuki
6.	N. Tuxworth	Honda
7.	W. Smith	Honda
8.	J. Hammond	Aermacchi
9.	A. Cathcart	Aermacchi
10.	H. Grasse	Yamaha

Fastest lap: B. Smith, 22m 46.8s/99.37mph*

Classic (6 laps/226.38 miles)

1.	A. George	Honda
	2h 00m 07.0s/113.08mph	
2.	M. Hailwood	Suzuki
3.	C. Williams	Yamaha
4.	J. Sayle	Yamaha
5.	G. McGregor	Yamaha
6.	J. Dunlop	Yamaha
7.	C. Mortimer	Yamaha

8.	K. Blake	Yamaha
9.	S. Moynihan	Yamaha
10.	D. Huxley	Yamaha

Fastest lap: A. George, 19m 49.6s/114.18mph*

1980

Formula 1 (6 laps/226.38 miles)

1.	M. Grant 2h 08m 59.8s/105.29mph*	Honda
2.	G. Crosby	Suzuki
3.	S. McClements	Honda
4.	A. Jackson	Kawasaki
5.	M. Hunt	Kawasaki
6.	K. Buckley	Honda
7.	J. Jones	Suzuki
8.	S. Woods	Honda
9.	J. Wells	Kawasaki
10.	A. Copeland	Honda

Fastest lap: S. McClements, 21m 10.8s/106.88mph*

Sidecar 1st leg (3 laps/113.19 miles)

1.	T. Ireson/C. Pollington 1h09m 12.2s/98.13mph	Yamaha
2.	J. Taylor/B. Johansson	Yamaha
3.	D. Greasley/J. Parkins	Yamaha
4.	M. Boddice/C. Birks	Yamaha
5.	N. Rollason/D. Homer	Barton Phoenix
6.	F. Wrathall/D. Fort	Yamaha
7.	W. Coates/E. Coates	Yamaha
8.	M. White/P. Spendlove	Yamaha
9.	M. Burcombe/D. Rumble Jnr	Yamaha
10.	F. Illingworth/R. Crowther	Yamaha

Fastest lap: J. Taylor/B. Johansson, 22m 20.0s/100.61mph

Sidecar 2nd leg (3 laps/113.19 miles)

1.	J. Taylor/B. Johansson 1h 05m 34.8s/103.19mph	Yamaha
2.	T. Ireson/C. Pollington	Yamaha
3.	N. Rollason/D. Homer	Barton Phoenix
4.	M. Boddice/C. Birks	Yamaha
5.	L. Burton/M. Murphy	Yamaha
6.	W. Coates/E. Coates	Yamaha
7.	S. Sinnott/N. Walker	Yamaha
8.	D. Hallam/J. Havercroft	Yamaha
9.	D. Bingham/J. Bingham	Yamaha
10.	D. Keen/A. Symons	Yamaha

Fastest lap: J. Taylor/B. Johansson, 21m 20.4s/106.08mph

Senior (6 laps/226.38 miles)

1.	G. Crosby 2h 03m 52.2s/109.65mph	Suzuki
2.	S. Cull	Suzuki
3.	S. Ward	Suzuki
4.	S. Woods	Suzuki
5.	T. Rutter	Yamaha
6.	S. Tonkin	Yamaha
7.	D. Randall	Suzuki
8.	C. Mortimer	Suzuki
9.	J. Dunlop	Yamaha
10.	D. Robinson	Yamaha

Fastest lap: S. Woods, 20m 19.6s/111.37mph

Formula 2 (4 laps/150.92 miles)

1.	C. Williams 1h 34m 04.0s/96.24mph	Yamaha
2.	C. Guy	Honda
3.	M. Lucas	Honda
4.	P. Odin	Honda
5.	P. Davies	Laverda
6.	H.-O. Butenuth	Honda
7.	G. Fogarty	Laverda
8.	R. Corbett	Kawasaki
9.	L. Backstrom	Laverda
10.	D. Dean	Yamaha

Fastest lap: C. Williams, 23m 03.6s/98.17mph

Formula 3 (4 laps/150.92 miles)

1.	B. Smith 1h 38m 26.4s/91.98mph	Yamaha
2.	C. Griffiths	Aermacchi
3.	R. Haslam	Honda
4.	R. Hunter	Suzuki
5.	D. Casement	Yamaha
6.	M. Wheeler	Aermacchi
7.	R. Jones	Yamaha
8.	D. Arnold	Aermacchi
9.	J. Stephens	Honda
10.	M. Poxon	Honda

Fastest lap: B. Smith, 23m 37.4s/95.82mph

Junior (4 laps/150.92 miles)

1.	C. Williams 1h 28m 34.8s/102.22mph	Yamaha
2.	D. Robinson	Yamaha
3.	S. Tonkin	Cotton
4.	K. Blake	Yamaha
5.	I. Richards	Yamaha
6.	B. Murray	Yamaha
7.	L. Backstrom	Yamaha
8.	J. Sayle	Yamaha
9.	D. Chatterton	Yamaha
10.	R. Swallow	Yamaha

Fastest lap: D. Robinson, 21m 39.4s/104.53mph*

Classic (6 laps/226.38 miles)

1.	J. Dunlop 2h 00m 29.8s/112.72mph	Yamaha
2.	M. Grant	Honda
3.	R. Haslam	Honda
4.	C. Mortimer	Suzuki
5.	S. Cull	Suzuki
6.	S. Mclements	Honda
7.	D. Ireland	Suzuki
8.	D. Robinson	Yamaha
9.	C. Guy	Honda
10.	K. Harrison	Yamaha

Fastest lap: J. Dunlop, 19m 38.8s/115.22mph*

1981

Formula 1 (6 laps/226.38 miles)

1.	G. Crosby 2h 01m 28.8s/111.81mph	Suzuki
2.	R. Haslam	Honda
3.	J. Dunlop	Honda
4.	J. Newbold	Suzuki
5.	S. McClements	Suzuki
6.	A. George	Honda
7.	A. Jackson	Suzuki
8.	S. Woods	Honda
9.	C. Mortimer	Kawasaki
10.	F. Rutter	Honda

Fastest lap: G. Crosby, 19m 54.6s/113.70mph*

Sidecar 1st leg (3 laps/113.19 miles)

1.	J. Taylor/B. Johansson 1h 03m 27.4s/107.02mph	Yamaha
2.	M. Boddice/C. Birks	Yamaha
3.	D. Bayley/R. Bryson	Yamaha
4.	D. Keen/G. Leitch	Yamaha
5.	R. Hanks/V. Biggs	Yamaha
6.	N. Rollason/D. Williams	Barton Phoenix
7.	F. Illingworth/G. Miller	Yamaha
8.	D. Plummer/R. Tomlinson	Kawasaki
9.	K. Galtress/N. Shelton	Yamaha
10.	E. Cornes/R. Holmes	Yamaha

Fastest lap: J. Taylor/B. Johansson, 20m 56.2s/108.12mph*

Sidecar 2nd leg (3 laps/113.19 miles)

1.	J. Taylor/B. Johansson 1h 04m 57.2s/104.55mph	Yamaha
2.	D. Greasley/S. Atkinson	Yamaha
3.	R. Hanks/V. Biggs	Yamaha
4.	N. Rollason/D. Williams	Barton Phoenix
5.	D. Bayley/R. Bryson	Yamaha
6.	D. Hallam/J. Havercroft	Yamaha
7.	S. Abbott/S. Smith	Yamaha
8.	F. Wrathall/P. Spendlove	Yamaha
9.	D. Keen/G. Leitch	Yamaha
10.	G. Davies/E. Davies	Yamaha

Fastest lap: J. Taylor/B. Johansson, 21m 03.0s/107.54mph

Senior (6 laps/226.38 miles)

1.	M Grant 2h 07m 58.2s/106.14mph	Suzuki
2.	D. Robinson	Yamaha
3.	J. Newbold	Suzuki
4.	A. George	Suzuki
5.	B. Guthrie	Suzuki
6.	C. Law	Yamaha
7.	B. Jackson	Suzuki
8.	G. Johnson	Yamaha
9.	D. Ireland	Suzuki
10.	P. Mellor	Suzuki

Fastest lap: M. Grant, 20m 0.4s/112.68mph

Junior (6 laps/226.38 miles)

1.	S. Tonkin 2h 07m 53.0s/106.21mph	Armstrong
2.	B. Jackson	Yamaha
3.	C. Williams	Yamaha
4.	J. Sayle	Armstrong
5.	D. Robinson	Rotax
6.	B. Simpson	Yamaha
7.	P. Wild	Yamaha
8.	R. Swallow	Yamaha
9.	D. Huxley	Yamaha
10.	K. Harrison	Yamaha

Fastest lap: G. McGregor, 20m 43.6s/109.22mph*

Formula 2 (4 laps/150.92 miles)

1.	T. Rutter	Ducati
	1h 28m 51.4s/101.91mph	
2.	P. Odlin	Honda
3.	C. Williams	Yamaha
4.	B. Jackson	Yamaha
5.	G. Johnson	Yamaha
6.	D. Mason	Honda
7.	H.-O. Butenuth	Ducati
8.	G. Bentman	Honda
9.	M. Keen	Honda
10.	P. Davies	Laverda

Fastest lap: T. Rutter, 21m 52.2s/103.51mph*

Formula 3 (4 laps/150.92 miles)

1.	B. Smith	Yamaha
	1h 30m 51.4s/99.66mph	
2.	D. Raybon	Yamaha
3.	D. Casement	Yamaha
4.	R. Hunter	Yamaha
5.	D. Arnold	Aermacchi
6.	J. Miller	Aermacchi
7.	M. Wheeler	Aermacchi
8.	J. Stephens	Honda
9.	D. Gallagher	Aermacchi
10.=	D. Mortimer	Yamaha
10.=	P. Barrett	Aermacchi

Fastest lap: B. Smith, 22m 20.6s/101.31mph*

Classic (6 laps/226.38 miles)

1.	G. Crosby	Suzuki
	1h 59m 34.8s/113.58mph	
2.	M. Grant	Suzuki
3.	A. George	Honda
4.	J. Newbold	Suzuki
5.	A. Jackson	Suzuki
6.	B. Murray	Yamaha
7.	S. Ward	Yamaha
8.	B. Simpson	Yamaha
9.	I. Richards	Kawasaki
10.	W. Smith	Suzuki

Fastest lap: J. Dunlop, 19m 37.0s/115.40mph*

1982

Formula 1 (6 laps/226.38 miles)

1.	R. Haslam	Honda
	1h 59m 50.6s/113.33mph	
2.	J. Dunlop	Honda
3.	D. Hiscock	Suzuki
4.	G. Johnson	Kawasaki
5.	B. Murray	Kawasaki
6.	D. Shimmin	Suzuki
7.	A. Jackson	Suzuki
8.	A. Moyce	Kawasaki
9.	W. Smith	Honda
10.	F. Rutter	Honda

Fastest lap: M. Grant, 19m 41.8s/114.93mph*

Sidecar 1st leg (3 laps/113.19 miles)

1.	T. Ireson/D. Williams	Yamaha
	1h 03m 53.4s/106.29mph	
2.	D. Greasley/S. Atkinson	Yamaha
3.	R. Hanks/V. Biggs	Yamaha
4.	D. Keen/G. Leitch	Yamaha
5.	D. Plummer/R. Tomlinson	Yamaha
6.	N. Rollason/C. Blair	Barton Phoenix
7.	B. Offen/I. Watson	Yamaha
8.	K. Plaschke/W. Jager	Busch
9.	D. Saville/D. Hall	Yamaha
10.	D. Davies/E. Davies	Yamaha

Fastest lap: M. Boddice/C. Birks, 21m 03.2s/107.52mph

Senior, 350cc (6 laps/226.38 miles)

1.	T. Rutter	Yamaha
	2h 05m 09.0s/108.53mph	
2.	P. Mellor	Yamaha
3.	G. Cannell	Yamaha
4.	E. Roberts	Yamaha
5.	B. Heath	Yamaha
6.	T. Nation	Yamaha
7.	J. Weedon	Yamaha
8.	S. Cull	Yamaha
9.	N. Tuxworth	Yamaha
10.	G. Padgett	Yamaha

Fastest lap: G. McGregor, 20m 12.4s/112.03mph*

Senior, 500cc (6 laps/226.38 miles)

1.	N. Brown	Suzuki
	2h 02m 22.8s/110.98mph	
2.	J. Ekerold	Suzuki
3.	D. Ireland	Suzuki
4.	P. Read	Suzuki
5.	B. Woodland	Suzuki
6.	C. Law	Yamaha
7.	S. McClements	Suzuki
8.	S. Henshaw	Suzuki
9.	B. Reid	Suzuki
10.	S. Parrish	Yamaha

Fastest lap: C. Williams, 19m 40.2s/115.08mph*

Sidecar 2nd leg (3 laps/113.19 miles)

1.	J. Taylor/B. Johansson	Yamaha
	1h 4m 00.6s/106.09mph	
2.	D. Bingham/J. Bingham	Yamaha
3.	S. Abbott/S. Smith	Yamaha
4.	D. Bayley/R. Bryson	Yamaha
5.	R. Hanks/V. Biggs	Yamaha
6.	D. Saville/D. Hall	Yamaha
7.	D. Plummer/R.Tomlinson	Yamaha
8.	E. Bregazzi/J. Creer	Yamaha
9.	K. Cousins/P. Hookman	Yamaha
10.	N. Edwards/B. Marris	Yamaha

Fastest lap: J. Taylor/B. Johansson, 20m 54.2s/108.29mph*

Junior (6 laps/226.38 miles)

1.	C. Law	Waddon
	2h 08m 57.6s/105.32mph	
2.	N. Brown	Yamaha
3.	P. Wild	Yamaha
4.	B. Reid	Yamaha
5.	D. Huxley	Yamaha
6.	P. Cranston	Yamaha
7.	R. Vine	Yamaha
8.	D. Ashton	Yamaha
9.	E. Roberts	Yamaha
10.	R. Swallow	Yamaha

Fastest lap: C. Williams, 20m 57.6s/108.00mph

Formula 2 (4 laps/150.92 miles)

1.	T. Rutter	Ducati
	1h 23m 48.2s/108.05mph	
2.	S. Moynihan	Yamaha
3.	P. Odlin	Yamaha
4.	M. Wheeler	Laverda
5.	G. Fogarty	Ducati
6.	B. Hill	Honda
7.	J. Stephens	Honda
8.	H.-O. Butenuth	Ducati
9.	G. Johnson	Yamaha
10.	H. Lees	Ducati

Fastest lap: T. Rutter, 20m 43.0s/109.27mph*

Formula 3 (4 laps/150.92 miles)

1.	G. Padgett	Yamaha
	1h 34m 09.2s/96.17mph	
2.	R. Hunter	Yamaha
3.	P. Barrett	Aermacchi
4.	D. Mason	Honda
5.	D. Linton	Aermacchi
6.	R. Claude	Yamaha
7.	J. Hammond	Aermacchi
8.	D. Smith	Yamaha

9.	J. Kiddie	Yamaha
10.	R. Niven	Aermacchi

Fastest lap: G. Padgett, 23m 15.0s/97.36mph

Classic (6 laps/226.38 miles)

1.	D. Ireland 2h 04m 21.8s/109.21mph	Suzuki
2.	J. Ekerold	Suzuki
3.	T. Rutter	Yamaha
4.	K. Klein	Suzuki
5.	B. Woodland	Suzuki
6.	G. Johnson	Suzuki
7.	G. Linder	Yamaha
8.	R. Vine	Yamaha
9.	D. Hiscock	Suzuki
10.	D. East	Suzuki

Fastest lap: C. Williams, 19m 57s/113.47mph

1983

Formula 1 (6 laps/226.38 miles)

1.	J. Dunlop 1h 59m 06.4s/114.03mph	Honda
2.	M. Grant	Suzuki
3.	R. McElnea	Suzuki
4.	R. Marshall	Honda
5.	T. Nation	Suzuki
6.	S. McClements	Suzuki
7.	J. Wells	Kawasaki
8.	D. Hiscock	Suzuki
9.	M. Hunt	Kawasaki
10.	A. Jackson	Suzuki

Fastest lap: J. Dunlop, 19m 33.6s/115.73mph*

Sidecar 1st leg (3 laps/113.19 miles)

1.	D. Greasley/S. Atkinson 1h 05m 08.6s/104.25mph	Yamaha
2.	D. Bingham/J. Bingham	Yamaha
3.	K. Cousins/P. Hookham	Yamaha
4.	N. Edwards/B. Marris	Yamaha
5.	D. Plummer/R. Tomlinson	Yamaha
6.	L. Burton/P. Cushnahan	Yamaha
7.	D. Keen/C. Hardman	Yamaha
8.	S. Sinnott/N. Burgess	Yamaha
9.	D. Bayley/B. Nixon	Yamaha
10.	B. Hargreaves/J. Hennigan	Yamaha

Fastest lap: D. Greasley/S. Atkinson, 21m 33.4s/105.01mph

Junior (6 laps/226.38 miles)

1.	C. Law 2h 05m 39.6s/108.09mph	EMC
2.	G. McGregor	Yamaha
3.	N. Brown	Yamaha
4.	E. Roberts	Rotax
5.	S. Cull	Armstrong
6.	B. Jackson	Armstrong
7.	J. Ekerold	Bimota
8.	A. Cooper	Yamaha
9.	M. Booys	Rotax
10.	D. Dean	Yamaha

Fastest lap: C. Law, 20m 34.4s/110.03mph*

Sidecar 2nd leg (3 laps/113.19 miles)

1.	M. Boddice/C. Birks 1h 04m 36.6s/105.11mph	Yamaha
2.	N. Edwards/B. Marris	Yamaha
3.	R. Hanks/D. Williams	Yamaha
4.	N. Rollason/C. Bairnson	Barton Phoenix
5.	D. Lawrence/G. Leitch	Yamaha
6.	K. Cousins/P. Hookham	Yamaha
7.	B. Brindley/C. Jones	Yamaha
8.	D. Holmes/S. Bagnall	Yamaha
9.	J. Phillips/M.Hollis	Yamaha
10.	B. Hargreaves/J. Hennigan	Suzuki

Fastest lap: M. Boddice/C. Birks, 21m 19s/106.19mph

Formula 2 (4 laps/150.92 miles)

1.	T. Rutter 1h 23m 41.2s/108.20mph	Ducati
2.	G. McGregor	Ducati
3.	P. Mellor	Yamaha
4.	S. Tonkin	Ducati
5.	M. Wheeler	Laverda
6.	P. Wild	Yamaha
7.	S. Henshaw	Yamaha
8.	A. Walsh	Honda
9.	S. Cull	Ducati
10.	D. Arnold	Ducati

Fastest lap: T. Rutter, 20m 41s/109.44mph*

Junior (6 laps/226.38 miles)

1.	P. Mellor 2h 06m 25.2s/107.44mph	Yamaha
2.	T. Nation	Yamaha
3.	C. Mortimer	Yamaha
4.	S. McClements	Yamaha
5.	S. Tonkin	Yamaha
6.	R. Vine	Yamaha
7.	N. Tuxworth	Wicks
8.	D. Dean	Yamaha
9.	B. Heath	Yamaha
10.	G. Young	Yamaha

Fastest lap: C. Law, 20m 38s/109.71mph

Senior Classic (6 laps/226.38 miles)

1.	R. McElnea 1h 58m 18.2s/114.81mph	Suzuki
2.	C. Law	Suzuki
3.	J. Dunlop	Honda
4.	C. Williams	Honda
5.	M. Grant	Suzuki
6.	B. Murray	Kawasaki
7.	G. McGregor	Yamaha
8.	T. Nation	Suzuki
9.	K. Harrison	Yamaha
10=	S. Williams	Yamaha
10=	P. Mellor	Yamaha

Fastest lap: N. Brown, 19m 29s/116.19mph*

1984

Formula 1 (6 laps/226.38 miles)

1.	J. Dunlop 2h 01m 37.0s/111.68mph	Honda
2.	R. Marshall	Honda
3.	T. Rutter	Ducati
4.	A. McGladdery	Kawasaki
5.	T. Nation	Ducati
6.	A. Moyce	Ducati
7.	J. Heselwood	Suzuki
8.	A. Jackson	Suzuki
9.	A. Frame	BSA
10.	D. Shimmin	Suzuki

Fastest lap: J. Dunlop, 19m 32.0s/115.89mph*

Sidecar 1st leg (3 laps/113.19 miles)

1.	M. Boddice/C. Birks 1h 05m 19.0s/103.97mph	Yamaha
2.	D. Bingham/J. Bingham	Yamaha
3.	S. Abbott/S. Smith	Yamaha
4.	D. Plummer/B. Marris	Yamaha
5.	L. Burton/P.Cushnahan	Yamaha
6.	D. Hallam/B. Dunn	Yamaha
7.	D. Bayley/B. Nixon	Yamaha
8.	A. Oates/E. Oates	Yamaha
9.	J. Barker/N. Cutmore	Yamaha
10.	E. Bregazzi/J. Creer	Yamaha

Fastest lap: M. Boddice/C. Birks, 21m 04.0s/107.45mph

Historic TT, 500cc (3 laps/113.19 miles)

1.	D. Roper 1h 10m 39.6s/96.11mph	Matchless
2.	I. Lougher	Matchless
3.	G. Johnson	Norton
4.	R. Knight	Triumph
5.	K. Inwood	Norton
6.	N. Jefferies	Norton
7.	J. Hurlstone	Norton
8.	J. Raybold	Norton
9.	J. Findlay	Norton
10.	A. Dugdale	Matchless

Fastest lap: D. Roper, 23m 17.2s/97.21mph

Historic TT, 350cc (3 laps/113.19 miles)

1.	S. Cull 1h 12m 02.6s/94.26mph	Aermacchi
2.	J. Millar	Aermacchi
3.	P. Barrett	Aermacchi
4.	A. Cathcart	Aermacchi
5.	J. Stephens	Norton
6.	R. Roebury	Honda
7.	S. McDiarmid	Suzuki
8.	R. Fitzsimmons	Suzuki
9.	J. Curry	Honda
10.	J. Kiddie	Honda

Fastest lap: J. Millar, 23m 45.4s/95.28mph

Senior (6 laps/226.38 miles)

1.	R. McElnea 1h 57m 26.2s/115.66mph	Suzuki
2.	R. Marshall	Honda
3.	T. Nation	Suzuki
4.	B. Reid	Suzuki
5.	M. Johns	Suzuki
6.	M. Grant	Suzuki
7.	S. Cull	Suzuki
8.	S. Parrish	Yamaha
9.	N. Jefferies	Suzuki
10.	T. Rutter	Yamaha

Fastest lap: J. Dunlop, 19m 06.4s/118.47mph*

Sidecar 2nd leg (3 laps/113.19 miles)

1.	S. Abbott/S. Smith	Yamaha
	1h 04m 30.0s/105.29mph	
2.	L. Burton/P. Cushnahan	Yamaha
3.	D. Hallam/B. Dunn	Yamaha
4.	A. Oates/E. Oates	Yamaha
5.	M. Burcombe/S. Parker	Yamaha
6.	D. Keen/C. Hardman	Yamaha
7.	J. Barker/N. Cutmore	Yamaha
8.	J. Phillips/M. Hollis	Yamaha
9.	D. Bayley/B. Nixon	Yamaha
10.	M. Murphy/C. Jordan	Yamaha

Fastest lap: M. Boddice/C. Birks, 21m 04.0s/107.45mph

Junior (6 laps/226.38 miles)

1.	G. McGregor	EMC
	2h 03m 57.6s/109.57mph	
2.	C. Williams	Yamaha
3.	B. Reid	EMC
4.	S. Williams	Yamaha
5.	G. Padgett	Yamaha
6.	P. Tinker	Armstrong
7.	K. Shepherd	Armstrong
8.	G. McDonnell	EMC
9.	P. Nicholls	Yamaha
10.	R. Vine	Maxton

Fastest lap: G. McGregor, 20m 23.0s/111.06mph*

Formula 2 (4 laps/150.92 miles)

1.	G. McGregor	Yamaha
	1h 23m 14.6s/108.78mph	
2.	T. Rutter	Ducati
3.	T. Nation	Ducati
4.	P. Mellor	Yamaha
5.	G. Padgett	Yamaha
6.	M. Booys	Yamaha
7.	M. Wheeler	Ducati
8.	D. Griffith	Yamaha
9.	S. Cull	Yamaha
10.	M. Barr	Yamaha

Fastest lap: G. McGregor, 20m 34.6s/110.01mph*

Classic (6 laps/226.38 miles)

1.	R. McElnea	Suzuki
	1h 56m 58.2s/116.12mph	
2.	J. Dunlop	Honda
3.	M. Grant	Suzuki
4.	K. Klein	Suzuki
5.	M. Johns	Suzuki
6.	B. Woodland	Suzuki
7.	N. Jefferies	Suzuki
8.	M. Salle	Suzuki
9.	T. Rutter	Yamaha
10.	J. Rea	Suzuki

Fastest lap: R. McElnea, 19m 19.6s/117.13mph*

Production Class C (3 laps/113.19 miles)

1.	G. Johnson	Kawasaki
	1h 04m 30.4s/105.28mph	
2.	H. Selby	Kawasaki
3.	P. Linden	Honda
4.	S. Parrish	Yamaha
5.	J. Gow	Kawasaki
6.	M. Grant	Suzuki
7.	B. Jackson	Honda
8.	N. Jefferies	BMW
9.	J. Wells	Kawasaki
10.	K. Dieplod	Honda

Fastest lap: G. Johnson, 21m 19.8s/106.13mph*

Production Class B (3 laps/113.19 miles)

1.	T. Nation	Honda
	1h 06m 25.2s/102.24mph	
2.	H. Dahne	Honda
3.	D. Dean	Honda
4.	H. Kerner	Honda
5.	K. Dobson	Honda
6.	M. Salle	Honda
7.	F. Rutter	Honda
8.	M. Lucas	Honda
9.	R. Vine	Yamaha
10.	P. Iddon	Suzuki

Fastest lap: T. Nation, 21m 59.0s/102.97mph*

Production Class A (3 laps/113.19 miles)

1.	P. Mellor	Yamaha
	1h 13m 21.4s/92.58mph	
2.	C. Fargher	Suzuki
3.	M. Oxley	Suzuki
4.	G. Padgett	Yamaha
5.	C. Williams	Yamaha
6.	J. Weedon	Suzuki
7.	I. Lougher	Suzuki
8.	R. Sutcliffe	Suzuki
9.	S. Collister	Yamaha
10.	M. McGarrity	Honda

Fastest lap: P. Mellor, 24m 04.8s/94.01mph*

1985

Formula 1 (6 laps/226.38 miles)

1.	J. Dunlop	Honda
	1h 59m 12.0s/113.95mph	
2.	T. Rutter	Suzuki
3.	S. McClements	Yamaha
4.	P. Rubatto	Honda
5.	D. Dean	Suzuki
6.	M. Salle	Suzuki
7.	R. Vine	Yamaha
8.	H. Dahne	Yamaha
9.	E. Roberts	Suzuki
10.	W. Simpson	Kawasaki

Fastest lap: J. Dunlop, 19m 26.6s/116.42mph*

Formula 2 (6 laps/226.38 miles)

1.	T. Rutter	Ducati
	2h 06m 00.6s/107.79mph	
2.	J. Weedon	Yamaha
3.	G. PAdgett	Yamaha
4.	C. Law	Yamaha
5.	S. Cull	Cagiva
6.	J. Brindley	Yamaha
7.	W. Hoffman	Yamaha
8.	B. McCormack	Kawasaki
9.	M. Hunt	Kawasaki
10.	N. Jefferies	Yamaha

Fastest lap: B. Reid, 20m 29.6s/110.46mph*

Sidecar Race A (3 laps/113.19 miles)

1.	D. Hallam/J. Gibbard	Yamaha
	1h 05m 01.2s104.45mph	
2.	M. Boddice/C. Birks	Yamaha
3.	N. Rollason/D. Williams	Barton Phoenix
4.	D. Plummer/B. Marris	Yamaha
5.	W. Newman/E. Yarker	Yamaha
6.	N. Murphy/J. Cush	Yamaha
7.	D. Keen/C. Hardman	Yamaha
8.	S. Sinnott/T. Dwyer	Yamaha
9.	C. McCombe/P. Brady	Yamaha
10.	A. May/M. Gray	Yamaha

Fastest lap: M. Boddice/C. Birks, 21m 08.2s/107.10mph

Junior (6 laps/226.38 miles)

1.	J. Dunlop	Honda
	2h 03m 35.0s/109.91mph	
2.	S. Cull	Honda
3.	E. Roberts	Kimoco
4.	G. Cannell	Yamaha
5.	G. McDonnell	EMC
6.	J. Rea	EMC
7.	M. McGarrity	Honda
8.	K. Mitchell	Harris
9.	P. Nicholls	Yamaha
10.	P. Tinker	Armstrong

Fastest lap: B. Reid, 20m 11.8s/112.08mph*

Sidecar Race B (3 laps/113.19 miles)

1.	M. Boddice/C. Birks	Yamaha
	1h 04m 31.0s/105.27mph	
2.	L. Burton/A. Langton	Yamaha
3.	D. Bingham/J. Bingham	Yamaha
4.	A. Oates/E. Oates	Yamaha
5.	D. Hallam/J. Gibbard	Yamaha
6.	D. Plummer/B. Marris	Yamaha
7.	W. Newman/E. Yarker	Yamaha
8.	L. Schwartz/L. Gustavsson	Yamaha
9.	T. Baker/P. Harper	Yamaha
10.	S. Pullan/P. Stirk	Yamaha

Fastest lap: M. Boddice/C. Birks, 21m 05s/107.37mph

Production Class A (3 laps/113.19 miles)

1.	M. Oxley	Honda
	1h 11m 36.4s/94.84mph	
2.	G. Cannell	Yamaha
3.	G. Padgett	Honda
4.	M. McGarrity	Honda
5.	P. Nicholls	Honda
6.	R. Dunlop	Honda
7.	P. Bateson	Honda
8.	G. Brennan	Honda
9.	S. Collister	Kawasaki
10.	C. Fargher	Suzuki

Fastest lap: M. Oxley, 23m 29s/96.40mph*

Production Class B (3 laps/113.19 miles)

1.	M. Grant	Suzuki
	1h 05m 04.6s/104.36mph	
2.	K. Wilson	Suzuki
3.	T. Rutter	Suzuki
4.	G. Williams	Suzuki
5.	H. Dahne	Yamaha
6.	S. Parrish	Yamaha
7.	D. Dean	Suzuki

8.	R. Vine	Yamaha
9.	K. Hughes	Suzuki
10.	S. Hislop	Yamaha

Fastest lap: G. Williams, 21m 22.2s/105.93mph*

Production Class C (3 laps/113.19 miles)

1.	G. Johnson 1h 04m 36.2s/105.12mph	Honda
2.	B. Simpson	Kawasaki
3.	H. Selby	Kawasaki
4.	D. Ireland	Kawasaki
5.	P. Linden	Honda
6.	D. Leach	Kawasaki
7.	N. Jefferies	BMW
8.	I. Duffus	Kawasaki
9.	B. Morrison	Kawasaki
10.	M. Hunt	Kawasaki

Fastest lap: B. Simpson, 21m 23.4s/105.83mph

Senior (6 laps/226.38 miles)

1.	J. Dunlop 1h 59m 28.2s/113.69mph	Honda
2.	R. Marshall	Honda
3.	M. Johns	Suzuki
4.	S. McClements	Suzuki
5.	B. Woodland	Suzuki
6.	S. Cull	Suzuki
7.	A. McGladdery	Suzuki
8.	R. Burnett	Honda
9.	P. Linden	Honda
10.	B. Heath	Yamaha

Fastest lap: R. Marshall, 19m 30.2s/116.07mph

1986

Formula 1 (4 laps/150.92 miles)

1.	J. Dunlop 1h 20m 09.4s/112.96mph	Honda
2.	G. Johnson	Honda
3.	A. McGladdery	Suzuki
4.	J. Weedon	Suzuki
5.	P. Mellor	Suzuki
6.	T. Nation	Suzuki
7.	G. McGregor	Suzuki
8.	G. Padgett	Suzuki
9.	G. Williams	Suzuki
10.	K. Klein	Suzuki

Fastest lap: J. Dunlop, 19m 51.6s/113.98mph

Sidecar Race A (3 laps/113.19 miles)

1.	L. Burton/P. Cushnahan 1h 04m 58.2s/104.53mph	Yamaha
2.	W. Newman/E. Yarker	Yamaha
3.	M. Burcombe/S. Parker	Yamaha
4.	D. Hallam/J. Gibbard	Yamaha
5.	G. Rushbrook/G. Leitch	Yamaha
6.	E. Cornes.G. Wellington	Yamaha
7.	L. Schwartz/L. Gustavsson	Yamaha
8.	S. Pullan/A. Smith	Yamaha
9.	D. Bayley/B. Nixon	Yamaha
10.	R. Bellas/G. Knight	Suzuki

Fastest lap: L. Burton/P.Cushnahan, 21m 22.6s/105.90mph

Formula 2 (4 laps/150.92 miles)

1.	B. Reid 1h 22m 31.4s/109.72mph	Yamaha
2.	J. Weedon	Yamaha
3.	N. Tuxworth	Yamaha
4.	R. Swann	Kawasaki
5.	E. Laycock	Yamaha
6.	S. Hislop	Yamaha
7.	C. Faulkner	Yamaha
8.	B. Heath	Yamaha
9.	D. Barry	Yamaha
10.	S. Williams	Yamaha

Fastest lap: B. Reid, 20m 15.4s/111.75mph*

Production Class B (3 laps/113.19 miles)

1.	P. Mellor 1h 02m 10.2s/109.23mph	Suzuki
2.	H. Dahne	Suzuki
3.	K. Wilson	Suzuki
4.	T. Nation	Suzuki
5.	D. Leach	Honda
6.	A. McGladdery	Suzuki
7.	D. Dean	Suzuki
8.=	G. Johnson	Honda
8.=	K. Hughes	Honda
10.	N. Jefferies	Suzuki

Fastest lap: P. Mellor, 20m 27.0s/111.69mph*

Production Class D (3 laps/113.19 miles)

1.	B. Woodland 1h 08m 0202s/99.82mph	Suzuki
2.	G. Cannell	Yamaha
3.	M. Oxley	Yamaha
4.	P. Bateson	Honda
5.=	G. Williams	Suzuki
5.=	C. Fargher	Suzuki
7.	G. Padgett	Yamaha
8.	K. Mawdsley	Honda
9.	S. Williams	Yamaha
10.	J. Whitham	Suzuki

Fastest lap: M. Oxley, 22m 27.2s/100.82mph*

Junior (6 laps/226.38 miles)

1.	S. Cull 2h 03m 54.0s/109.623mph	Honda
2.	P. Mellor	EMC
3.	G. Cannell	Honda
4.	D. Leach	Yamaha
5.	J. Weedon	Armstrong
6.	G. Padgett	Yamaha
7.	C. Fargher	Yamaha
8.	K. Shepherd	Spondon
9.	S. Hislop	Cotton
10.	K. de Cruz	EMC

Fastest lap: P. Mellor, 20m 19.0s/111.42mph

Sidecar Race B (3 laps/113.19 miles)

1.	N. Rollason/D. Williams 1h 05m 25.2s/103.81mph	Phoenix
2.	D. Plummer/B. Marris	Yamaha
3.	W. Newman/E. Yarker	Yamaha
4.	M. Burcombe/S. Parker	Yamaha
5.	D. Bingham/J. Bingham	Yamaha
6.	S. Pullan/A. Smith	Yamaha
7.	K. Howles/S. Pointer	Yamaha
8.	D. Keen/C. Hardman	Yamaha
9.	H. Lunemann/M. Cain	Yamaha
10.	R. Bellas/G. Knight	Suzuki

Fastest lap: D. Hallam/J. Gibbard, 21m 27.8s/105.47mph

Production Class A (3 laps/113.19 miles)

1.	T. Nation 1h 00m 38.4s/111.99mph	Suzuki
2.	K. Wilson	Suzuki
3.	B. Morrison	Suzuki
4.	N. Jefferies	Suzuki
5.	B. Woodland	Suzuki
6.	H. Dahne	Suzuki
7.	I. Duffus	Suzuki
8.	A. Batson	Suzuki
9.	D. Leach	Kawasaki
10.	S. Henshaw	Suzuki

Fastest lap: T. Nation, 19m 59.2s/113.26mph*

Production Class C (3 laps/113.19 miles)

1.	G. Padgett 1h 05m 56.6s/102.98mph	Suzuki
2.	M. Wheeler	Kawasaki
3.	S. Linsdell	Yamaha
4.	J. Dunlop	Honda
5.	P. Nicholls	Honda
6.	R. Burnett	Honda
7.	B. Jackson	Honda
8.	S. Boyes	Honda
9.	R. Price	Kawasaki
10.	A. Jackson	Honda

Fastest lap: G. Padgett, 21m 40.6s/104.43mph*

Senior (6 laps/226.38 miles)

1.	R. Burnett 1h 59m 09.8s/113.98mph	Honda
2.	G. Johnson	Honda
3.	B. Woodalnd	Suzuki
4.	J. Dunlop	Honda
5.	P. Mellor	Suzuki
6.	R. Marshall	Honda
7.	D. Leach	Yamaha
8.	K. Wilson	Suzuki
9.	S. McClements	Suzuki
10.	G. McGregor	Suzuki

Fastest lap: T. Nation, 19m 25.4s/116.55mph

1987

Formula 1 (6 laps/226.38 miles)

1.	J. Dunlop 1h 58m 04.4s/115.03mph	Honda
2.	P. Mellor	Suzuki
3.	G. Johnson	Yamaha
4.	R. Marshall	Suzuki
5.	T. Nation	Yamaha
6.	N. Jefferies	Honda
7.	P. Rubatto	Yamaha
8.	D.Leach	Suzuki
9.	G. Williams	Suzuki
10.	S. Linsdell	Yamaha

Fastest lap: J. Dunlop, 19m 15.4s/117.55mph*

Sidecar Race A (3 laps/113.19 miles)

1.	M. Boddice/D. Williams	Yamaha
	1h 04m 49.6s/104.76mph	
2.	D.Bingham/J.Bingham	Yamaha
3.	G.Rushbrook/G. Leitch	Yamaha
4.	W. Newman/E. Yarker	Yamaha
5.	K. Howles/S. Pointer	Yamaha
6.	M. Murphy/A. Langton	Yamaha
7.	D. Greasley/S. Atkinson	Yamaha
8.	E. Cornes/G. Wellington	Yamaha
9.	N. Smith/P. Gravel	Yamaha
10.	D. Molyneux/P. Kneale	Yamaha

Fastest lap: M. Boddice/D. Williams, 21m 24.6s/105.73mph

Junior (6 laps/226.38 miles)

1.	E. Laycock	EMC
	2h 05m 09.2s/108.52mph	
2.	B. Reid	EMC
3.	G. McGregor	Yamaha
4.	C. Fogarty	Honda
5.	J. Rea	Yamaha
6.	B. Heath	Yamaha
7.	D. Chatterton	Yamaha
8.	J. Dunlop	Honda
9.	M. Johns	Yamaha
10.	R. Coates	Yamaha

Fastest lap: S. Hislop, 20m 18.0s/111.51mph

Sidecar Race B (3 laps/113.19 miles)

1.	L. Burton/P. Cushnahan	Yamaha
	1h 04m 21.0s/105.53mph	
2.	K. Howles/S. Pointer	Yamaha
3.	W. Newman/E. Yarker	Yamaha
4.	L. Schwartz/L. Gustavsson	Yamaha
5.	N. Rollason/D. Huntingdon	Phoenix
6.	N. Smith/P. Gravel	Yamaha
7.	A. Oates/E. Oates	Yamaha
8.	E. Cornes/G. Wellington	Yamaha
9.	G. Rushbrook/G. Leitch	Yamaha
10.	D. Brown/W. Nelson	Yamaha

Fastest lap: L. Burton/P. Cushnahan, 21m 22.2s/105.93mph

Formula 2 (6 laps/226.38 miles)

1.	S. Hislop	Yamaha
	2h 03m 01.4s/110.40mph	
2.	E. Laycock	Yamaha
3.	B. Heath	Yamaha
4.	J. Rea	Yamaha
5.	R. Dunlop	Yamaha
6.	D. Chatterton	Yamaha
7.	M. Seward	Honda
8.	D. Dean	Honda
9.	K. Hughes	Honda
10.	I. Lougher	Yamaha

Fastest lap: E. Laycock, 20m 08.8s/112.36mph*

Production Class B (3 laps/113.19 miles)

1.	G. Johnson	Yamaha
	1h 01m 45.0s/109.98mph	
2.	B. Morrison	Suzuki
3.	T. Nation	Yamaha
4.	K. Wilson	Suzuki
5.	G. McGregor	Yamaha
6.	N. Jefferies	Honda
7.	T. Haynes	Kawasaki
8.	G. Williams	Suzuki
9.	S. Ward	Suzuki
10.	I. Dufus	Yamaha

Fastest lap: T. Nation, 20m 16.6s/111.64mph*

Production Class D (3 laps/113.19 miles)

1.	B. Woodland	Yamaha
	1h 05m 56.8s/102.98mph	
2.	M. Wheeler	Yamaha
3.	M. Oxley	Yamaha
4.	G. Cannell	Yamaha
5.	S. Hislop	Yamaha
6.	R. Dunlop	Honda
7.	P. Nicholls	Honda
8.	C. Fargher	Suzuki
9.	C. Fogarty	Honda
10.	P. Bateson	Honda

Fastest lap: B. Woodland, 21m 54.0s/103.36mph*

Senior TT (4 laps/150.92 miles)

1.	J. Dunlop	Honda
	1h 30m 41.2s/99.85mph	
2.	G. Johnson	Yamaha
3.	R. Marshall	Suzuki
4.	A. McGladdery	Suzuki
5.	N. Jefferies	Honda
6.	T. Nation	Yamaha
7.	D. Griffith	Yamaha
8.	B. Morrison	Suzuki
9.	G. McGregor	Suzuki
10.	E. Laycock	Yamaha

Fastest lap: J. Dunlop, 21m 21.22s/108.08mph

1988

Production Class C (4 laps/150.92 miles)

1.	B. Morrison	Honda
	1h 23m 30.8s/108.42mph	
2.	R. Hurst	Kawasaki
3.	S. Hislop	Honda
4.	D. Leach	Honda
5.	S. Ward	Honda
6.	A. Batson	Honda
7.	K. Mawdsley	Honda
8.	R. Swann	Kawasaki
9.	M. Seward	Honda
10.	N. Jefferies	Honda

Fastest lap: S. Hislop, 20m 36.6s/109.83mph*

Production Class D (4 laps/150.92 miles)

1.	B. Woodland	Yamaha
	1h 28m 35.2s/102.21mph	
2.	G. McGregor	Suzuki
3.	B. Reid	Yamaha
4.	M. Oxley	Yamaha
5.	E. Laycock	Yamaha
6.	I. Duffus	Yamaha
7.	C. Bevan	Yamaha
8.	S. Cull	Suzuki
9.	N. Tuxworth	Yamaha
10.	C. Faulkner	Yamaha

Fastest lap: B. Woodland, 21m 48.6s/103.79mph*

Production Class B (4 laps/150.92 miles)

1.	S. Hislop	Honda
	1h 20m 38.2s/112.39mph	
2.	B. Morrison	Honda
3.	G. Johnson	Yamaha
4.	J. Whitham	Suzuki
5.	J. Dunlop	Honda
6.	N. Jefferies	Honda
7.	K. Wilson	Suzuki
8.	D. Leach	Yamaha
9.	A. Batson	Suzuki
10.	S. Ward	Suzuki

Fastest lap: G. Johnson, 20m 02.2s/112.98mph*

Sidecar Race A (3 laps/113.19 miles)

1.	M. Boddice/C. Birks	Yamaha
	1h 03m 54.4s/106.27mph	
2.	K. Howles/S. Pointer	Yamaha
3.	L. Burton/P. Cushnahan	Yamaha
4.	D. Plummer/B. Marris	Yamaha
5.	D. Hallam/S. Parker	Yamaha
6.	D. Molyneux/A. Langton	Yamaha
7.	M. Burcombe/C. Hardman	Yamaha
8.	D. Brown/W. Nelson	Yamaha
9.	A. Oates/J. Gibbard	Yamaha
10.	E. Cornes/G. Wellington	Yamaha

Fastest lap: M. Boddice/C. Birks, 21m 07.6s/107.15mph

Formula 1 (6 laps/226.38 miles)

1.	J. Dunlop	Honda
	1h 56m 50.2s/116.25mph	
2.	N. Jefferies	Honda
3.	R. Burnett	Honda
4.	C. Fogarty	Honda
5.	P. Iddon	Yamaha
6.	M. Farmer	Suzuki
7.	B. Morrison	Honda
8.	S. Ward	Suzuki
9.	D. Leach	Yamaha
10.	B. Reid	Kawasaki

Fastest lap: J. Dunlop, 19m 05.8s/118.54mph*

Junior (4 laps/150.92 miles)

1.	J. Dunlop	Honda
	1h 20m 56.6s/111.87mph	
2.	B. Reid	EMC
3.	E. Laycock	EMC
4.	B. Morrison	Honda
5.	J. Rea	Yamaha
6.	S. Cull	Honda
7.	B. Heath	Yamaha
8.	M. Seward	Honda
9.	S. Williams	Yamaha
10.	I. Young	Honda

Fastest lap: S. Hislop, 19m 57.6s/113.41mph*

Sidecar Race B (3 laps/113.19 miles)

1.	M. Boddice/C. Birks	Yamaha
	1h 03m 47.4s/106.46mph	
2.	L. Burton/P. Cushnahan	Yamaha
3.	K. Howles/S. Pointer	Yamaha
4.	D. Hallam/S. Parker	Yamaha
5.	M. Burcombe/C. Hardman	Yamaha
6.	D. Plummer/B. Marris	Yamaha
7.	M. Murphy/J. Cusnahan	Yamaha
8.	A. Oates/J. Gibbard	Yamaha

9.	E. Cornes/G. Wellington	Yamaha
10.	S. Pullan/T. Darby	Yamaha

Fastest lap: L. Burton/P. Cushnahan, 21m 01.6s/107.66mph

Production Class A (4 laps/150.92 miles)

1.	D. Leach 1h 19m 12.2s/114.32mph	Yamaha
2.	G. Johnson	Yamaha
3.	K. Wilson	Suzuki
4.	P. Mellor	Suzuki
5.	R. Haynes	Kawasaki
6.	N. Jefferies	Honda
7.	R. Hurst	Kawasaki
8.	M. Seward	Yamaha
9.	H. Selby	Suzuki
10.	R. Marshall	Suzuki

Fastest lap: G. Johnson, 19m 25.4s/116.55mph*

Senior (6 laps/226.38 miles)

1.	J. Dunlop 1h 55m 42.6s/117.38mph	Honda
2.	S. Hislop	Honda
3.	G. Johnson	Yamaha
4.	R. Marshall	Suzuki
5.	R. Burnett	Honda
6.	B. Morrison	Honda
7.	C. Fogarty	Honda
8.	E. Laycock	Honda
9.	S. Ward	Suzuki
10.	S. McClements	Honda

Fastest lap: S. Cull, 19m 00.6s/119.08mph*

1989

Supersport 600 (4 laps/150.92 miles)

1.	S. Hislop 1h 20m 25.8s/112.58mph	Honda
2.	D. Leach	Yamaha
3.	J. Whitham	Suzuki
4.	P. Mellor	Suzuki
5.	B. Morrison	Honda
6.	N. Jefferies	Yamaha
7.	I. Young	Honda
8.	H. Selby	Yamaha
9.	A. Batson	Yamaha
10.	J. Rea	Honda

Fastest lap: D. Leach, 19m 55.6s/113.60mph*

Supersport 400 (4 laps/150.92 miles)

1.	E. Laycock 1h 26m 01.0s/105.27mph	Suzuki
2.	G. McGregor	Suzuki
3.	B. Woodland	Yamaha
4.	N. Tuxworth	Yamaha
5.	M. Oxley	Yamaha
6.	M. Langton	Suzuki
7.	D. Glass	Suzuki
8.	N. Crawford	Kawasaki
9.	J. Reynolds	Kawasaki
10.	I. McMillan	Suzuki

Fastest lap: E. Laycock, 21m 10.6s/106.90mph

Formula 1 (6 laps/226.38 miles)

1.	S. Hislop 1h 53m 47.4s/119.36mph	Honda
2.	B. Morrison	Honda
3.	N. Jefferies	Yamaha
4.	C. Fogarty	Honda
5.	G. McGregor	Honda
6.	J. Whitham	Suzuki
7.	R. Dunlop	Honda
8.	A. McGladdery	Honda
9.	S. McClements	Honda
10.	C. Gable	Honda

Fastest lap: S. Hislop, 18m 39.4s/121.34mph*

Sidecar Race A (3 laps/113.19 miles)

1.	D. Molyneux/C. Hardman 1h 04m 57.0s/104.56mph	Yamaha
2.	K. Howles/S. Pointer	Yamaha
3.	N. Smith/D. Wood	Yamaha
4.	D. Brown/W. Nelson	Yamaha
5.	L. Schwartz/L. Gustavsson	Yamaha
6.	D. Plummer/A. Darby	Yamaha
7.	V. Jefford/P. Hill	Yamaha
8.	A. Oates/E. Oates	Yamaha
9.	G. Bell/J. Tailford	Yamaha
10.	D. Low/J. Low	Yamaha

Fastest lap: K. Howles/S. Pointer, 21m 25.6s/105.65mph

Ultra-Lightweight 125 (2 laps/75.46 miles)

1.	R. Dunlop 44m 08.0s/102.58mph	Honda
2.	I. Lougher	Honda
3.	C. Fogarty	Honda
4.	I. Newton	Honda
5.	M. McGarrity	Honda
6.	R. Swallow	Honda
7.	P. McCallen	Honda
8.	D. Nobbs	Honda
9.	S. Ward	Morbidelli
10.	D. Shields	Honda

Fastest lap: R. Dunlop, 21m 54.4s/103.02mph*

Production 750 (4 laps/150.92 miles)

1.	C. Fogarty 1h 18m 57.6s/114.68mph	Honda
2.	D. Leach	Yamaha
3.	S. Hislop	Honda
4.	N. Jefferies	Yamaha
5.	B. Morrison	Honda
6.	I. Young	Honda
7.	B. Jackson	Honda
8.	K. Harrison	Yamaha
9.	P. Mellor	Suzuki
10.	M. Farmer	Kawasaki

Fastest lap: D. Leach, 19m 21.8s/116.91mph*

Sidecar Race B (3 laps/113.19 miles)

1.	M. Boddice/C. Birks 1h 03m 22.0s/107.19mph	Yamaha
2.	D. Brown/W. Nelson	Yamaha
3.	D. Molyneux/C. Hardman	Yamaha
4.	G. Rushbrook/G. Leitch	Yamaha
5.	D. Hallam/J. Gibbard	Yamaha
6.	G. Bell/J. Tailford	Yamaha
7.	L. Schwartz/L. Gustavsson	Yamaha
8.	E. Cornes/G. Wellington	Yamaha
9.	D. Rumble Jnr/G. Keep	Yamaha
10.	A. Oates/E. Oates	Yamaha

Fastest lap: M. Boddice/C. Birks, 20m 54.0s/108.31mph*

Junior (4 laps/150.92 miles)

1.	J. Rea 1h 20m 45.8s/112.12mph	Yamaha
2.	E. Laycock	Yamaha
3.	S. Hazlett	EMC
4.	C. Fogarty	Honda
5.	I. Young	Yamaha
6.	B. Woodland	Yamaha
7.	D. Chatterton	Yamaha
8.	R. Coates	Yamaha
9.	R. Swallow	Honda
10.	R. Boland	Yamaha

Fastest lap: E. Laycock, 19m 51.0s/114.04mph*

Production 1300 (4 laps/150.92 miles)

1.	D. Leach 1h 18m 19.4s/115.61mph	Yamaha
2.	N. Jefferies	Yamaha
3.	A. Batson	Yamaha
4.	H. Selby	Yamaha
5.	C. Gable	Yamaha
6.	K. Harrison	Yamaha
7.	S. Hazlett	Yamaha
8.	A. McGladdery	Yamaha
9.	I. Duffus	Suzuki
10.	S. Ward	Kawasaki

Fastest lap: N. Jefferies, 19m 18.2s/117.27mph*

Senior (6 laps/226.38 miles)

1.	S. Hislop 1h 54m 52.6s/118.23mph	Honda
2.	N. Jefferies	Yamaha
3.	G.McGregor	Honda
4.	R. Dunlop	Honda
5.	E. Laycock	Honda
6.	A. McGladdery	Honda
7.	S. McCLements	Honda
8.	I. Young	Honda
9.	C. Gable	Yamaha
10.	K. Harrison	Yamaha

Fastest lap: S. Hislop, 18m 45.4s/120.69mph*

1990

Formula 1 (6 laps/226.38 miles)

1.	C. Fogarty 1h 54m 45.6s/118.35mph	Honda
2.	N. Jefferies	Yamaha
3.	R. Dunlop	Norton
4.	B. Morrison	Honda
5.	D. Leach	Yamaha
6.	T. Nation	Norton
7.	G. McGregor	Honda
8.	J. Dunlop	Honda
9.	S. Hislop	Honda
10.	B. Jackson	Honda

Fastest lap: S. Hislop, 18m 27.6s/122.63mph*

Supersport 400 (3 laps/113.19 miles)

1.	D. Leach	Yamaha
	1h 03m 02.2s/107.73mph	
2.	C. Fogarty	Honda
3.	S. Ward	Kawasaki
4.	N. Jefferies	Yamaha
5.	B. Reid	Yamaha
6.	S. Hislop	Honda
7.	S. Cull	Kawasaki
8.	B. Woodland	Yamaha
9.	J. Moodie	Honda
10.	J. Rea	Suzuki

Fastest lap: D. Leach, 20m 41.6s/109.39mph*

Ultra-Lightweight 125 (3 laps/113.19 miles)

1.	R. Dunlop	Honda
	1h 05m 40.2s/103.41mph	
2.	I. Newton	Honda
3.	M. Toping	Honda
4.	A. Caughey	Honda
5.	A. Jackson	Honda
6.	A. McCauley	Honda
7.	F. Duffy	Honda
8.	J. Barton	EMC
9.	R. Mortimer	Honda
10.	M. Chatterton	Honda

Fastest lap: R. Dunlop, 21m 44.8s/104.09mph*

Junior (4 laps/150.92 miles)

1.	I. Lougher	Yamaha
	1h 18m 37.6s/115.16mph	
2.	S. Hislop	Honda
3.	E. Laycock	Yamaha
4.	C. Fogarty	Honda
5.	J. Rea	Yamaha
6.	P. McCallen	Honda
7.	S. Williams	Yamaha
8.	S. Hazlett	EMC
9.	B. Heath	Honda
10.	D. Leach	Yamaha

Fastest lap: I. Lougher, 19m 13s/117.8mph*

Sidecar Race A (3 laps/113.19 miles)

1.	D. Saville/N. Roache	Yamaha
	1h 07m 25.6s/100.72mph	
2.	M. Boddice/D. Wells	Honda
3.	N. Smith/S. Mace	Yamaha
4.	K. Howles/S. Pointer	Yamaha
5.	A. Oates/S. Pitts	Kawasaki
6.	E. Wright/A. Hetherington	Yamaha
7.	D. Plummer/G. Keep	Kawasaki
8.	P. Krukowski/C. McGahan	Yamaha
9.	D. Rumble/D. Jewell	Yamaha
10.	R. Crossley/K. Ellison	Yamaha

Fastest lap: D. Saville/N. Roache, 22m 25.2s/100.97mph*

Sidecar Race B (2 laps/75.46 miles)

1.	D. Saville/N. Roache	Yamaha
	45m 11.8s/100.17mph	
2.	G. Bell/J. Cochrane	Yamaha
3.	P. Krukowski/C. McGahan	Yamaha
4.	A. Oates/S. Pitts	Kawasaki
5.	R. Hanks/T. Hanks	Yamaha
6.	E. Wright/A. Hetherington	Yamaha
7.	D. Plummer/G. Keep	Kawasaki
8.	D. Hawes/E. Kiff	Kawasaki
9.	D. Founds/P. Yarwood	Yamaha
10.	B. Gray/P. Basile	Yamaha

Fastest lap: D. Saville/N. Roache, 22m 30.8s/100.55mph

Supersport 600 (4 laps/150.92 miles)

1.	B. Reid	Yamaha
	1h 20m 51.6s/111.98mph	
2.	J. Rea	Yamaha
3.	S. Cull	Yamaha
4.	M. Farmer	Yamaha
5.	B. Jackson	Yamaha
6.	J. Moodie	Honda
7.	H. Selby	Yamaha
8.	B. Morrison	Yamaha
9.	S. Ward	Kawasaki
10.	B. Woodland	Yamaha

Fastest lap: D. Leach, 19m 49.2s/114.21mph*

Senior (6 laps/226.38 miles)

1.	C. Fogarty	Honda
	2h 02m 25.2s/110.95mph	
2.	T. Nation	Norton
3.	D. Leach	Yamaha
4.	S. Ward	Honda
5.	B. Morrison	Honda
6.	S. Williams	Yamaha
7.	E. Laycock	Honda
8.	S. Hazlett	Honda
9.	B. Jackson	Honda
10.	N. Barton	Honda

Fastest lap: D. Leach, 19m 26.2s/116.47mph

1991

Formula 1 (6 laps/226.38 miles)

1.	S. Hislop	Honda
	1h 52m 15.0s/121.00mph	
2.	C. Fogarty	Honda
3.	B. Morrison	Yamaha
4.	P. McCallen	Honda
5.	S. Ward	Honda
6.	B. Jackson	Honda
7.	N. Jefferies	Honda
8.	S. Linsdell	Yamaha
9.	G. Williams	Kawasaki
10.	I. Duffus	Honda

Fastest lap: S. Hislop, 18m 20s/123.48mph*

Sidecar Race A (3 laps/113.19 miles)

1.	M. Boddice/D. Wells	Honda
	1h 08m 25.2s/99.26mph	
2.	N. Smith/S. Mace	Yamaha
3.	A. Oates/S. Pitts	Kawasaki
4.	E. Wright/A. Hetherington	Yamaha
5.	R. Hanks/T. Hanks	Yamaha
6.	G.Bell/K. Cornbill	Yamaha
7.	V. Biggs/J. Biggs	Yamaha
8.	J. Holden/I. Watson	Kawasaki
9.	D. Holden/B. Threlfall	Yamaha
10.	B. Grey/P. Basile	Yamaha

Fastest lap: M. Boddice/D. Wells, 22m 40.2s/99.85mph

Supersport 400 (4 laps/150.92 miles)

1.	D. Leach	Yamaha
	1h 25m 50.0s/105.49mph	
2.	S. Hislop	Honda
3.	J. Moodie	Yamaha
4.	B. Morrison	Yamaha
5.	S. Linsdell	Yamaha
6.	S. Ives	Yamaha
7.	H. Selby	Yamaha
8.	N. Jefferies	Honda
9.	I. Lougher	Yamaha
10.	D. Goodley	Kawasaki

Fastest lap: D. Leach, 20m 41.6s/109.39mph

Ultra-Lightweight 125 (4 laps/150.92 miles)

1.	R. Dunlop	Honda
	1h 27m 19.8s/103.68mph	
2.	J. Dunlop	Honda
3.	B. Heath	Honda
4.	P. McCallen	Honda
5.	B. Jackson	Honda
6.	S. Ward	Honda
7.	M. Topping	Honda
8.	N. Clegg	Honda
9.	D. Young	Honda
10.	N. Wood	Honda

Fastest lap: R. Dunlop, 21m 12.8s/106.71mph*

Sidecar Race B (3 laps/113.19 miles)

1.	M. Boddice/D. Wells	Honda
	1h 08m 24.8s/99.27mph	
2.	G. Bell/K. Cornbill	Yamaha
3.	D. Molyneux/K. Ellison	Kawasaki
4.	K. Howles/A. Langton	Yamaha
5.	J. Holden/I. Watson	Yamaha
6.	A. Oates. S. Pitts	Kawasaki
7.	R. Crossley/C. Jenkins	Suzuki
8.	D. Holden/B. Threlfall	Yamaha
9.	H. Lunemann/G. Morscher	Kawasaki
10.	D. Hawes/N. Cutmore	Kawasaki

Fastest lap: M. Boddice/D. Wells, 22m 36.2s/100.15mph

Junior (4 laps/150.92 miles)

1.	R. Dunlop	Yamaha
	1h 18m 48.8s/114.89mph	
2.	P. McCallen	Honda
3.	S. Hazlett	Yamaha
4.	I. Newton	Yamaha
5.	J. Dunlop	Honda
6.	D. Leach	Yamaha
7.	B. Heath	Honda
8.	S. Johnson	Yamaha
9.	M. Birkinshaw	Yamaha
10.	J. Rea	Yamaha

Fastest lap: P. McCallen, 19m 23.4s/116.75mph*

Supersport 600 (4 laps/150.92 miles)

1.	S. Hislop	Honda
	1h 19m 14.2s/114.28mph	
2.	S. Cull	Yamaha
3.	B. Jackson	Honda
4.	S. Ives	Yamaha
5.	P. McCallen	Honda
6.	J. Dunlop	Honda
7.	B. Morrison	Yamaha
8.	J. Rea	Yamaha

9.	S. Allen	Yamaha
10.	M. Farmer	Yamaha

Fastest lap: S. Hislop, 19m 34s/115.69mph*

Senior (6 laps/226.38 miles)

1.	S. Hislop 1h 52m 10.1s/121.09mph	Honda
2.	J. Dunlop	Honda
3.	P. McCallen	Honda
4.	B. Morrison	Yamaha
5.	N. Jefferies	Honda
6.	B. Jackson	Honda
7.	G. Williams	Kawasaki
8.	I. Morris	Honda
9.	G. Radcliffe	Honda
10.	K. Harrison	Honda

Fastest lap: S. Hislop, 18m 21.8s/123.27mph*

1992

Formula 1 (6 laps/226.38 miles)

1.	P. McCallen 1h 53m 22.4s/119.80mph	Honda
2.	S. Hislop	Norton
3.	J. Dunlop	Honda
4.	N. Jefferies	Honda
5.	M. Farmer	Yamaha
6.	S. Ward	Honda
7.	B. Jackson	Honda
8.	T. Nation	Ducati
9.	I. Duffus	Kawasaki
10.	J. Griffiths	Honda

Fastest lap: S. Hislop, 18m 21.6s/123.3mph

Sidecar Race A (3 laps/113.19 miles)

1.	G. Bell/K. Cornbill 1h 06m 54.4s/101.50mph	Honda
2.	E. Wright/P. Hill	Honda
3.	M. Boddice/D. Wells	Honda
4.=	R. Hanks/T. Hanks	Yamaha
4.=	N. Smith/T Salone	Yamaha
6.	D. Molyneux/K. Ellison	Kawasaki
7.	R. Crossley/K. Waller	Yamaha
8.	D. Hawes/E. Kiff	Kawasaki
9.	G. Porteous/J. Spencer	Kawasaki
10.	P. Nuttall/R. Burns	Honda

Fastest lap: G. Bell/K. Cornbill, 22m 04.6s/102.54mph*

Supersport 400 (4 laps/150.92 miles)

1.	B. Reid 1h 21m 56.6s/110.50mph	Yamaha
2.	P. McCallen	Honda
3.	S. Linsdell	Yamaha
4.	N. Jefferies	Honda
5.	I. Duffus	Yamaha
6.	M. Farmer	Yamaha
7.	D. Morris	Yamaha
8.	R. Hayes	Yamaha
9.	M. Langton	Yamaha
10.	C. Petty	Yamaha

Fastest lap: B. Reid, 20m 09.8s/112.27mph*

Ultra-Lightweight 125 (4 laps/150.92 miles)

1.	J. Dunlop 1h 25m 01.6s/106.49mph	Honda
2.	R. Dunlop	Honda
3.	M. Lofthouse	Honda
4.	S. Rea	Honda
5.	S. Johnson	Honda
6.	D. McCullough	Honda
7.	I. Lougher	Honda
8.	M. Westmorland	Honda
9.	N. Clegg	Honda
10.	A. Caughey	Honda

Fastest lap: J. Dunlop, 20m 49.6s/108.69mph*

Sidecar Race B (3 laps/113.19 miles)

1.	G. Bell/K. Cornbill 1h 06m 55.0s/101.49mph	Yamaha
2.	M. Boddice/D. Wells	Honda
3.	D. Molyneux/K. Ellison	Kawasaki
4.	N. Smith/T. Salone	Yamaha
5.	P. Krukowski/C. McGahan	Yamaha
6.	D. Saville/N. Roache	Yamaha
7.	V. Biggs/J. Biggs	Yamaha
8.	R. Crossley/K. Walter	Yamaha
9.	G. Porteous/J. Spencer	Kawasaki
10.	D. Dawes/E. Kiff	Kawasaki

Fastest lap: G. Bell/K. Cornbill, 22m 16.0s/101.66mph

Junior (4 laps/150.92 miles)

1.	B. Reid 1h 18m 38.8s/115.13mph	Yamaha
2.	S. Hislop	Yamaha
3.	R. Dunlop	Yamaha
4.	S. Johnson	Yamaha
5.	I. Lougher	Yamaha
6.	B. Jackson	Yamaha
7.	B. Heath	Honda
8.	S. Williams	Yamaha
9.	J. Griffiths	Yamaha
10.	L. Pullan	Yamaha

Fastest lap: S. Hislop, 19m 15.8s/117.51mph

Supersport 600 (4 laps/150.92 miles)

1.	P. McCallen 1h 18m 42.8s/115.04mph	Honda
2.	S. Hislop	Honda
3.	S. Ward	Honda
4.	N. Jefferies	Honda
5.	B. Jackson	Honda
6.	J. Rea	Yamaha
7.	R. Holden	Yamaha
8.	D. Young	Honda
9.	J. Dunlop	Honda
10.	I. Duffus	Honda

Fastest lap: S. Hislop, 19m 20.8s/117.01mph*

Senior (6 laps/226.38 miles)

1.	S. Hislop 1h 51m 59.6s/121.28	Norton
2.	C. Fogarty	Yamaha
3.	R. Dunlop	Norton
4.	N. Jefferies	Honda
5.	M. Farmer	Yamaha
6.	R. Holden	Yamaha
7.	I. Duffus	Kawasaki
8.	C. Gable	Honda
9.	D. Young	Honda
10.	J. Rea	Honda

Fastest lap: C. Fogarty, 18m 18.8s/123.61mph*

1993

Formula 1 (6 laps/226.38 miles)

1.	N. Jefferies 1h 54m 57.2s/118.15mph	Honda
2.	P. McCallen	Honda
3.	S. Ward	Honda
4.	J. Griffiths	Honda
5.	T. Nation	Yamaha
6.	J. Moodie	Honda
7.	S. Beck	Honda
8.	J. Rea	Yamaha
9.	R. Holden	Yamaha
10.	G. Radcliffe	Honda

Fastest lap: M. Farmer, 18m 46.4s/120.58mph

Sidecar Race A (3 laps/113.19 miles)

1.	D. Molyneux/K. Ellison 1h 05m 43.4s/103.33mph	Yamaha
2.	D. Saville/N. Roache	Yamaha
3.	E. Wright/P. Hill	Honda
4.	D. Hawes/E. Kiff	Yamaha
5.	R. Fisher/V. Butler	Yamaha
6.	R. Crossley/C. Hardman	Honda
7.	V. Biggs/J. Biggs	Yamaha
8.	A. Warner/S. Mace	Kawasaki
9.	P. Nuttall/R. Burns	Honda
10.	D. Kimberley/G. Vallance	Kawasaki

Fastest lap: D. Molyneux/K. Ellison, 21m 42.6s/104.27mph*

Supersport 400 (4 laps/150.92 miles)

1.	J. Moodie 1h 21m 15.4s/111.43	Yamaha
2.	I. Duffus	Yamaha
3.	S. Linsdell	Yamaha
4.	B. Reid	Yamaha
5.	D. Morris	Yamaha
6.	N. Jefferies	Honda
7.	J. Rea	Yamaha
8.	M. Baldwin	Kawasaki
9.	I. King	Honda
10.	P. Nicholls	Honda

Fastest lap: J. Moodie, 20m 8.4s/112.4mph*

Ultra-Lightweight 125cc (4 laps/150.92 miles)

1.	J. Dunlop 1h 24m 25.0s/107.26mph	Honda
2.	R. Dunlop	Honda
3.	B. Heath	Honda
4.	D. McCullough	Honda
5.	G. Bennett	Honda
6.	R. Parrott	Honda
7.	A. Caughey	Honda
8.	P. Ward	Honda
9.	A. Jackson	Honda
10.	I. Kirk	Honda

Fastest lap: J. Dunlop, 20m 51.2s/108.55mph

Sidecar Race B (3 laps/113.19 miles)

1.	D. Molyneux/K. Ellison	Yamaha
	1h 5m 50.0s/103.16mph	
2.	E. Wright/P. Hill	Honda
3.	R. Crosley/C. Hardman	Honda
4.	D. Hawes/E. Kiff	Yamaha
5.	R. Hanks/T. Hanks	Yamaha
6.	V. Biggs/J. Biggs	Yamaha
7.	K. Howles/R. Parker	Yamaha
8.	P. Gallagher/K. Ellard	Honda
9.	S. Sinnott/D. Corlett	Yamaha
10.	H. Langham/S. Langham	Yamaha

Fastest lap: D. Molyneux/K. Ellison, 21m 55s/103.29mph

Junior (4 laps/150.92 miles)

1.	B. Reid	Yamaha
	1h 18m 38.6s/115.14mph	
2.	J. Moodie	Honda
3.	J. Dunlop	Honda
4.	M. Baldwin	Yamaha
5.	L. Pullan	Yamaha
6.	D. Milling	Yamaha
7.	C. Fargher	Yamaha
8.	B. Jackson	Yamaha
9.	R. Coates	Yamaha
10.	R. Dunlop	Yamaha

Fastest lap: R. Dunlop, 19m 23.4s/116.75mph

Supersport 600 (4 laps/150.92 miles)

1.	J. Moodie	Honda
	1h 18m 41.8s/115.06mph	
2.	B. Jackson	Honda
3.	S. Beck	Honda
4.	I. Simpson	Honda
5.	M. Farmer	Yamaha
6.	N. Jefferies	Honda
7.	P. McCallen	Honda
8.	I. Duffus	Honda
9.	A. Batson	Honda
10.	D. Young	Honda

Fastest lap: J. Moodie, 19m 23.2s/116.77mph

Senior (6 laps/226.38 miles)

1.	P. McCallen	Honda
	1h 54m 47.8s/118.32mph	
2.	N. Jefferies	Honda
3.	S. Ward	Honda
4.	J. Griffiths	Honda
5.	I. Simpson	Kawasaki
6.	J. Rea	Yamaha
7.	A. Bennallick	Honda
8.	J. Barton	Kawasaki
9.	G. Radcliffe	Honda
10.	C. Day	Honda

Fastest lap: P. McCallen, 18m 45.8s/120.65mph

1994

Sidecar Race A (3 laps/113.19 miles)

1.	R. Fisher/M. Wynn	Yamaha
	1h 04m 14.6s/105.71mph	
2.	D. Molyneux/P. Hill	Yamaha
3.	M. Boddice Snr/D. Wells	Honda
4.	K. Howles/R. Parker	Yamaha
5.	G. Bell/N. Roache	Yamaha
6.	R. Hanks/T. Hanks	Yamaha
7.	D. Kimberley/T. Darby	Kawasaki
8.	E. Wright/R. Long	Yamaha
9.	V. Biggs/J. Biggs	Yamaha
10.	L. Schwartz/D. Jewell	Yamaha

Fastest lap: R. Fisher/M. Wynn, 21m 15.4s/106.49mph*

Formula 1 (6 laps/226.38 miles)

1.	S. Hislop	Honda
	1h 53m 37.s/119054mph	
2.	P. McCallen	Honda
3.	J. Dunlop	Honda
4.	G. Radcliffe	Honda
5.	I. Duffus	Yamaha
6.	N. Davies	Honda
7.	D. Young	Honda
8.	S. Linsdell	Yamaha
9.	C. Gable	Honda
10.	G. Williams	Honda

Fastest lap: P. McCallen, 18m 32.6s/122.08mph

Singles (4 laps/150.92 miles)

1.	J. Moodie	Yamaha
	1h 21m 21.60s/111.29mph	
2.	R. Holden	Ducati
3.	J. Griffiths	Yamaha
4.	G. Radcliffe	Yamaha
5.	M. Wood	Harris
6.	D. Young	Honda
7.	R. Price	Kawasaki
8.	M. Noblett	Gilera
9.	G. Sawyer	Yamaha
10.	J. Henderson	Kawasaki

Fastest lap: J. Moodie, 20m 05.4s/112.66mph*

Ultra-Lightweight 125 (4 laps/150.92 miles)

1.	J. Dunlop	Honda
	1h 25m 38.0s/105.74mph	
2.	D. McCullough	Honda
3.	C. Fargher	Yamaha
4.	N. Clegg	Honda
5.	G. English	Honda
6.	G. Dynes	Yamaha
7.	M. Watts	Honda
8.	A. Jackson	Honda
9.	A. Caughey	Honda
10.	I. Kirk	Honda

Fastest lap: J. Dunlop, 21m 04.6s/107.40mph

Supersport 600 (4 laps/150.92 miles)

1.	I. Duffus	Yamaha
	1h 18m 32.0s/115.30mph	
2.	I. Simpson	Yamaha
3.	S. Ward	Honda
4.	P. McCallen	Honda
5.	B. Jackson	Honda
6.	N. Jefferies	Honda
7.	J. Dunlop	Honda
8.	D. Young	Honda
9.	R. Holden	Yamaha
10.	M. Flynn	Honda

Fastest lap: J. Moodie, 19m 23.8s/116.71mph

Junior (4 laps/150.92 miles)

1.	J. Dunlop	Honda
	1h 18m 57.8s/114.67mph	
2.	B. Reid	Yamaha
3.	J. Griffiths	Yamaha
4.	I. Simpson	Honda
5.	I. Lougher	Honda
6.	G. Lee	Yamaha
7.	J. Courtney	Honda
8.	R. Coates	Yamaha
9.	S. Hazlett	Yamaha
10.	G. Dynes	Honda

Fastest lap: B. Reid, 19m 31.2s/115.97mph

Supersport 400 (4 laps/150.92 miles)

1.	J. Moodie	Yamaha
	1h 23m 41.2s/108.20mph	
2.	S. Linsdell	Yamaha
3.	D. Morris	Yamaha
4.	D. Young	Honda
5.	G. Long	Yamaha
6.	N. Piercy	Yamaha
7.	S. Trezise	Kawasaki
8.	P. Nicholls	Honda
9.	F. Finch	Yamaha
10.	D. Eaves	Yamaha

Fastest lap: J. Moodie, 20m 26.2s/110.77mph

Sidecar Race B (3 laps/113.19 miles)

1.	R. Fisher/M. Wynn	Yamaha
	1h 05m 41.0s/103.39mph	
2.	D. Molyneux/P. Hill	Yamaha
3.	M. Boddice Snr/D. Wells	Honda
4.	R. Hanks/T. Hanks	Yamaha
5.	G. Bell/N. Roache	Yamaha
6.	D. Kimberley/T. Darby	Kawasaki
7.	K. Howles/R. Parker	Yamaha
8.	P. Nuttall/R. Burns	Yamaha
9.	R. Bellas/G. Knight	Yamaha
10.	L. Schwartz/D. Jewell	Yamaha

Fastest lap: R. Fisher/M. Wynn, 21m 28.0s/105.45mph

Senior (6 laps/226.38 miles)

1.	S. Hislop	Honda
	1h 53m 53.8s/119.25mph	
2.	P. McCallen	Honda
3.	J. Dunlop	Honda
4.	N. Davies	Honda
5.	J. Griffiths	Kawasaki
6.	G. Radcliffe	Honda
7.	C. Day	Honda
8.	P. Hunt	Yamaha
9.	D. Goodley	Kawasaki
10.	D. Young	Honda

Fastest lap: S. Hislop, 18m 28.8s/122.5mph

1995

Formula 1 (6 laps/226.38 miles)

1.	P. McCallen	Honda
	1h 55m 15.8s/117.84mph	
2.	J. Dunlop	Honda
3.	S. Beck	Ducati
4.	N. Jefferies	Honda
5.	S. Ward	Honda

6.	S. Linsdell	Yamaha
7.	M. Flynn	Honda
8.	D. Leach	Yamaha
9.	P. Hunt	Yamaha
10.	G. Radcliffe	Honda

Fastest lap: P. McCallen, 18m 43.9s/120.85mph

Sidecar Race A (3 laps/113.19 miles)

1.	R. Fisher/B. Hutchinson 1h 03m 47.1s/106.47mph	Yamaha
2.	M. Boddice/D.Wells	Honda
3.	G. Bell/N. Roache	Yamaha
4.	R. Hanks/T. Hanks	Ireson
5.=	I. Bell/C. Hallam	Yamaha
5.=	K. Howles/S. Pointer	Yamaha
7.	V. Biggs/J. Biggs	Yamaha
8.	E. Wright/R. Long	Yamaha
9.	D. Wallis/T. Kirkham	Yamaha
10.	P. Nuttall/N. Crowe	Yamaha

Fastest lap: R. Fisher/B. Hutchinson, 21m 07.5s/107.16mph

Singles (4 laps/150.92 miles)

1.	R. Holden 1h 21m44.2s/110.78mph	Ducati
2.	D. Morris	BMW
3.	S. Linsdell	Yamaha
4.	B. Heath	Seeley
5.	R. Price	Kawasaki
6.	N. Davies	Yamaha
7.	M. Daynes	Tigcraft
8.	L. Pullan	Yamaha
9.	M. Jeffreys	Rotax
10.	D. Leach	KTM

Fastest lap: R. Holden, 20m 16.4s/111.66mph

Ultra-Lightweight 125 (4 laps/150.92 miles)

1.	M. Baldwin 1h 24m 30.8s/107.14mph	Honda
2.	M. Lofthouse	Yamaha
3.	J. Courtney	Honda
4.	D. McCullough	Honda
5.	N. Clegg	Honda
6.	G. English	Honda
7.	A. Jackson	Honda
8.	G. Bennett	Honda
9.	T. Ritchie	Honda
10.	M. Watts	Yamaha

Fastest lap: M. Baldwin, 20m 46.0s/109.01mph

Lightweight 250 (4 laps/150.92 miles)

1.	J. Dunlop 1h 18m 16.4s/111.68mph	Honda
2.	J. Courtney	Honda
3.	G. Lee	Yamaha
4.	P. McCallen	Honda
5.	S. Harris	Honda
6.	D. McCullough	Honda
7.	B. Jackson	Yamaha
8.	L. Pullan	Yamaha
9.	R. Coates	Yamaha
10.	M. Baldwin	Honda

Fastest lap: J. Dunlop, 19m 15.2s/117.5mph

Junior (4 laps/150.92 miles)

1.	I. Duffus 1h 17m 40.4s/116.58mph	Honda
2.	N. Jefferies	Honda
3.	C. Gable	Honda
4.	J. Dunlop	Honda
5.	S. Ward	Honda
6.	D. Leach	Kawasaki
7.	N. Davies	Honda
8.	M. Flynn	Yamaha
9.	L. Pullan	Honda
10.	I. Lougher	Honda

Fastest lap: I. Duffus, 19m 12.3s/117.87mph*

Sidecar Race B (3 laps/113.19 miles)

1.	R. Fisher/B. Hutchinson 1h 03m 07.5s/107.58mph	Yamaha
2.	D. Molyneux/P. Hill	Yamaha
3.	M. Boddice/D. Wells	Honda
4.	R. Hanks/T. Hanks	Ireson
5.	G. Bell/N. Roache	Yamaha
6.	I. Bell/C. Hallam	Yamaha
7.	M. Clark/D. Bilton	Yamaha
8.	D. Wallis/T. Kirkham	Yamaha
9.	G. Hayne/M. Craig	Special
10.	E. Wright/R. Long	Yamaha

Fastest lap: R. Fisher/B. Hutchinson, 21m 01.5s/107.67mph*

Senior (6 laps/226.38 miles)

1.	J. Dunlop 1h 54m 01.9s/119.11mph	Honda
2.	I. Duffus	Ducati
3.	S. Ward	Honda
4.	N. Jefferies	Honda
5.	D. Goodley	Kawasaki
6.	B. Jackson	Kawasaki
7.	C. Day	Kawasaki
8.	M. Rutter	Ducati
9.	S. Beck	Ducati
10.	D. Leach	Yamaha

Fastest lap: S. Ward, 18m 35.8s/121.73mph

1996

Formula 1 (6 laps/226.38 miles)

1.	P. McCallen 1h 56m 54.1s/116.18mph	Honda
2.	N. Jefferies	Honda
3.	M. Rutter	Ducati
4.	I. Duffus	Honda
5.	J. Griffiths	Honda
6.	M. Flynn	Kawasaki
7.	J. Dunlop	Honda
8.	J. Hodson	Kawasaki
9.	B. Jackson	Kawasaki
10.	S. Linsdell	Yamaha

Fastest lap: I. Duffus, 18m 44.0s/120.84mph

Sidecar Race A (3 laps/113.19 miles)

1.	D. Molyneux/P. Hill 1h 01m 34.8s/109.81mph	Yamaha
2.	R. Fisher/B. Hutchinson	Yamaha
3.	K. Howles/S. Pointer	Yamaha
4.	G. Bell/C.Hallam	Yamaha
5.	M. Boddice/D. Wells	Yamaha
6.	G. Hayne/M. Craig	Yamaha
7.	P. Nutall/N. Crowe	Yamaha
8.	J. Childs/S. Childs	Honda
9.	J. Holden/I.Watson	Jacobs
10.	V. Biggs/G. Biggs	Yamaha

Fastest lap: D. Molyneux/P. Hill, 20m 27.7s/110.63mph

Lightweight 250 (4 laps/150.92 miles)

1.	J. Dunlop 1h 18m 31.5s/115.31mph	Honda
2.	J. Moodie	Honda
3.	J. Griffiths	Honda
4.	P. McCallen	Honda
5.	N. Davies	Yamaha
6.	D. McCullough	Honda
7.	D. Young	Honda
8.	L. Pullan	Yamaha
9.	C. Gable	Yamaha
10.	N. Richardson	Yamaha

Fastest lap: P. McCallen, 19m 21.5s/116.94mph

Sidecar Race B (3 laps/113.19 miles)

1.	D. Molyneux/P. Hill 1h 01m 34.8s/110.28mph	Yamaha
2.	R. Fisher/B. Hutchinson	Yamaha
3.	K. Howles/S. Pointer	Yamaha
4.	G. Bell/C. Hallam	Yamaha
5.	R. Crossley/R. Long	Yamaha
6.	J. Childs/S. Childs	Honda
7.	I. Bell/N. Carpenter	Yamaha
8.	V. Biggs/V. Biggs	Yamaha
9.	J. Holden/I. Watson	Jacobs
10.	P. Nuttall/N. Crowe	Yamaha

Fastest lap: D. Molyneux/P. Hill, 20m 23.4s/111.02mph*

Singles (2 laps/75.46 miles)

1.	J. Moodie 41m 50.7s/108.19mph	Yamaha
2.	D. Morris	BMW
3.	B. Jackson	BRS
4.	J. Kehrer	MZ
5.	C. McLean	Ducati
6.	A. Bushell	Suzuki
7.	R. Price	Kawasaki
8.	D. Shimmin	Matchless
9.	R. Jerrfreys	Kawasaki
10.	M. Daynes	Suzuki

Fastest lap: D. Morris, 20m 45.5s/109.05mph

Ultra-Lightweight 125 (2 laps/75.46 miles)

1.	J. Dunlop 42m 34.6s/106.33mph	Honda
2.	G. Lee	Honda
3.	G. English	Honda
4.	I. Lougher	Aprilia
5.	B. Heath	Honda
6.	G. Dynes	Honda
7.	N. Clegg	Honda
8.	S. Rea	Honda
9.	G. Bennett	Honda
10.	C. McGahan	Honda

Fastest lap: J. Dunlop, 21m 02.1s/107.62mph

Junior (3 laps/113.19 miles)

1.	P. McCallen	Honda
	57m 43.4s/117.64mph	
2.	I. Duffus	Honda
3.	I. Simpson	Honda
4.	C. Gable	Honda
5.	J. Griffiths	Honda
6.	N. Davies	Kawasaki
7.	J. Moodie	Honda
8.	N. Jefferies	Honda
9.	B. Jackson	Honda
10.	L. Pullan	Honda

Fastest lap: P. McCallen, 19m 01.9s/118.94mph

Production 1000 (3 laps/113.19 miles)

1.	P. McCallen	Honda
	57m 53.1s/117.32mph	
2.	I. Duffus	Honda
3.	N. Davies	Yamaha
4.	C. Gable	Honda
5.	L. Pullan	Yamaha
6.	D. Young	Honda
7.	N. Jefferies	Honda
8.	A. Bennallick	Honda
9.	M. Flynn	Yamaha
10.	D. Jefferies	Honda

Fastest lap: P. McCallen, 19m 02.0s/118.93mph

Senior (6 laps/226.38 miles)

1.	P. McCallen	Honda
	1h 53m 24.8s/119.76mph	
2.	J. Dunlop	Honda
3.	N. Jefferies	Honda
4.	B. Jackson	Kawasaki
5.	L. Pullan	Yamaha
6.	D. Young	Honda
7.	J. Griffiths	Honda
8.	M. Flynn	Kawasaki
9.	N. Davies	Honda
10.	I. Simpson	Honda

Fastest lap: P. McCallen, 18m 32.0s/122.14mph

1997

Formula 1 (6 laps/226.38 miles)

1.	P. McCallen	Honda
	1h 53m 16.8s/119.90mph	
2.	M. Rutter	Honda
3.	B. Jackson	Kawasaki
4.	I. Simpson	Honda
5.	M. Flynn	Honda
6.	J. Dunlop	Honda
7.	A. Bennallick	Honda
8.	D. Goodley	Kawasaki
9.	S. Beck	Kawasaki
10.	P. Orritt	Yamaha

Fastest lap: P. McCallen, 18m 24.4s/122.98mph

Sidecar Race A (3 laps/113.19 miles)

1.	R. Hanks/P. Biggs	Ireson
	1h 03m 29.7s/106.95mph	
2.	V. Biggs/G. Biggs	Yamaha
3.	T. Hanks/S. Wilson	Yamaha
4.	J. Holden/I. Watson	Jacobs
5.	K. Howles/D. Jewell	Yamaha
6.	A. Schofield/A. Thornton	Yamaha
7.	G. Horspole/K. Leigh	Honda
8.	G. Bell/L. Farrington	Yamaha
9.	S. Norbury/A. Smith	Yamaha
10.	J. Martin/K. Harrington	Yamaha

Fastest lap: R. Fisher/R. Long, 20m 47.59s/109.23mph

Lightweight 250 (4 laps/150.92 miles)

1.	J. Dunlop	Honda
	1h 18m 20.1s/115.59mph	
2.	I. Lougher	Honda
3.	J. McGuinness	Aprilia
4.	S. Harris	Yamaha
5.	G. Dynes	Honda
6.	D. Young	Honda
7.	I. Simpson	Honda
8.	R. Coates	Yamaha
9.	J. Griffiths	Honda
10.	N. Richardson	Honda

Fastest lap: J. McGuinness, 19m 22.6s/116.83mph

Sidecar Race B (3 laps/113.19 miles)

1.	R. Fisher/R. Long	Baker
	1h 01m 47.8s/109.89mph	
2.	T. Hanks/S. Wilson	Yamaha
3.	I. Bell/N. Carpenter	Yamaha
4.	R. Hanks/P. Biggs	Ireson
5.	G. Horspole/K. Leigh	Honda
6.	J. Holden/I. Watson	Jacobs
7.	R. Cameron/P. Randall	Honda
8.	M. Boddice Snr/D. Wells	Honda
9.	G. Bell/L. Farrington	Yamaha
10.	S. Norbury/A. Smith	Yamaha

Fastest lap: R. Fisher/R. Long, 20m 29.7s/110.45mph

Singles (4 laps/150.92 miles)

1.	D. Morris	BMW
	1h 21m 58.2s/110.46mph	
2.	J. Barton	Ducati
3.	S. Linsdell	Yamaha
4.	J. Kehrer	MZ
5.	D. Shimmin	Matchless
6.	R. Hawkins	Rotax
7.	B. Jackson	Summerfield
8.	D. Trollope	Spondon
9.	M. Daynes	Suzuki
10.	K. Dixon	Seeley

Fastest lap: D. Morris, 20m 11.9s/112.07mph

Ultra-Lightweight 125 (4 laps/150.92 miles)

1.	I. Lougher	Honda
	1h 23m 55.4s/107.89mph	
2.	D. McCullough	Honda
3.	R. Dunlop	Honda
4.	G. English	Honda
5.	O. McNally	Honda
6.	G. Lee	Honda
7.	G. Dynes	Honda
8.	N. Clegg	Honda
9.	C. Richardson	Honda
10.	J. Dunlop	Honda

Fastest lap: I. Lougher, 20m 43.2s/109.25mph*

Junior (4 laps/150.92 miles)

1.	I. Simpson	Honda
	1h 16m 28.3s/118.41mph	
2.	P. McCallen	Honda
3.	M. Rutter	Honda
4.	D. Young	Honda
5.	J. Dunlop	Honda
6.	B. Jackson	Honda
7.	A. Archibald	Honda
8.	P. Dedman	Kawasaki
9.	S. Beck	Honda
10.	T. Montano	Honda

Fastest lap: I. Simpson, 18m 53.2s/119.86mph*

Production 1000 (2 laps/75.46 miles)

1.	P. McCallen	Honda
	38m 39.4s/117.12mph	
2.	I. Simpson	Ducati
3.	S. Beck	Honda
4.	M. Flynn	Suzuki
5.	J. Hodson	Yamaha
6.	D. Young	Honda
7.	A. Bennallick	Honda
8.	P. Hunt	Yamaha
9.	M. Rutter	Honda
10.	J. Moodie	Suzuki

Fastest lap: P. McCallen, 19m 15.6s/117.53mph

Senior (6 laps/226.38 miles)

1.	P. McCallen	Honda
	1h 53m 36.6s/119.55mph	
2.	J. Moodie	Honda
3.	I. Simpson	Honda
4.	B. Jackson	Kawasaki
5.	S. Beck	Kawasaki
6.	D. Young	Honda
7.	J. Dunlop	Honda
8.	D. Goodley	Kawasaki
9.	A. Bennallick	Honda
10.	C. Heath	Honda

Fastest lap: P. McCallen, 18m 31.3s/122.22mph

1998

Formula 1 (4 laps/150.92 miles)

1.	I. Simpson	Honda
	1h 16m 15.6s/118.74mph	
2.	M. Rutter	Honda
3.	J. Courtney	Honda
4.	S. Beck	Kawasaki
5.	J. Griffiths	Honda
6.	D. Norris	Ducati
7.	D. Winterbottom	Ducati
8.	D. Jefferies	Honda
9.	A. McDonald	Honda
10.	D. Lloyd	Honda

Fastest lap: I. Simpson, 18m 21.7s/123.28mph

Lightweight 250 (2 laps/75.46 miles)

1.	J. Dunlop	Honda
	46m 51.8s/96.61mph	
2.	B. Jackson	Yamaha
3.	J. McGuinness	Honda
4.	J. Courtney	Honda
5.	J. Griffiths	Honda

6.	G. Lee	Yamaha
7.	P. Williams	Honda
8.	G. Linham	Honda
9.	N. Piercy	Yamaha
10.	D. Kelly	Yamaha

Fastest lap: J. Dunlop, 22m 31.4s/100.50mph

* Note: Sidecar Race A was cancelled

Sidecar Race B (3 laps/113.19 miles)

1.	D. Molyneux/D. Jewell 1h 03m 45.1s/106.52mph	Honda
2.	K. Howles/N. Crowe	Yamaha
3.	G. Horspole/L. Leigh	Honda
4.	R. Hanks/P. Biggs	Yamaha
5.	J. Holden/I. Watson	Yamaha
6.	M. Boddice/I. Simons	Yamaha
7.	S. Norbury/A. Smith	Yamaha
8.	G. Lambert/D. Gale	Windle
9.	R. Cameron/P. Randall	Honda
10.	E. Wright/R. Pearce	Ireson

Fastest lap: D. Molyneux/D. Jewell, 20m 55.1s/108.22mph

Singles (3 laps/113.19 miles)

1.	D. Morris 1h 03m 11.2s/107.48mph	BMW
2.	J. Moodie	Honda
3.	M. Jeffreys	Rotax
4.	R. Prince	Kawasaki
5.	T. McGinty	Suzuki
6.	K. Dixon	Seeley
7.	A. Shortland	Rotax
8.	H. Chittka	Yamaha
9.	P. Shaw	Suzuki
10.	J. Robinson	Rotax

Fastest lap: D. Morris, 20m 38.4s/109.68mph

Ultra-Lightweight 125 (3 laps/113.19 miles)

1.	R. Dunlop 1h 0m 50.3s/106.38mph	Honda
2.	I. Lougher	Honda
3.	O. McNally	Honda
4.	G. Long	Honda
5.	G. Dynes	Honda
6.	G. Bennett	Honda
7.	B. Jackson	Honda
8.	T. Ritchie	Honda
9.	J. Dunlop	Honda
10.	T. Roebuck	Honda

Fastest lap: I. Lougher, 21m 03.1s/107.53mph

Junior (3 laps/113.19 miles)

1.	M. Rutter 59m 22.7s/114.37mph	Honda
2.	I. Simpson	Honda
3.	P. Dedman	Honda
4.	B. Jackson	Honda
5.	C. Heath	Honda
6.	J. Moodie	Honda
7.	M. Flynn	Suzuki
8.	D. Jefferies	Honda
9.	R. Britton	Honda
10.	A. Archibald	Honda

Fastest lap: J. Moodie, 19m 06.3s/118.49mph

Production 1000 (3 laps/113.19 miles)

1.	J. Moodie 56m 58.7s/119.19mph	Honda
2.	N. Davies	Kawasaki
3.	M. Rutter	Honda
4.	D. Jefferies	Yamaha
5.	B. Jackson	Yamaha
6.	P. Hunt	Yamaha
7.	I. Simpson	Honda
8.	M. Flynn	Suzuki
9.	J. Hodson	Kawasaki
10.	A. Archibald	Honda

Fastest lap: J. Moodie, 18m 45.3s/120.70mph

Senior (6 laps/226.38 miles)

1.	I. Simpson 1h 53m 23.1s/119.79mph	Honda
2.	B. Jackson	Kawasaki
3.	J. Courtney	Honda
4.	D. Jefferies	Yamaha
5.	J. Griffiths	Honda
6.	N. Davies	Yamaha
7.	P. Dedman	Honda
8.	S. Harris	Yamaha
9.	D. Winterbottom	Ducati
10.	A. Bennallick	Honda

Fastest lap: M. Rutter, 18m 23.9s/123.04mph

1999

Formula 1 (4 laps/150.92 miles)

1.	D. Jefferies 1h 14m 37.0s/121.35mph	Yamaha
2.	J. Dunlop	Honda
3.	I. Duffus	Yamaha
4.	J. Courtney	Ducati
5.	I. Lougher	Honda
6.	J. Griffiths	Yamaha
7.	N. Davies	Yamaha
8.	G. Dynes	Yamaha
9.	N. Jefferies	Kawasaki
10.	D. Winterbottom	Kawasaki

Fastest lap: D. Jefferies, 18m 21.9s/123.26mph

Sidecar Race A (3 laps/113.19 miles)

1.	D. Molyneux/C. Hallam 1h 00m 41.5s/111.90mph	Honda
2.	R. Fisher/R. Long	Honda
3.	T. Hanks/S. Wilson	Windle
4.	A. Schofield/I. Simons	Baker
5.	R. Hands/P. Biggs	Yamaha
6.	C. Lambert/L. Aubrey	Yamaha
7.	K. Howles/D. Jewell	Mistral
8.	M. Harvey/S. Thomas	Yamaha
9.	T. Baker/S. Parnell	Yamaha
10.	G. Bell/L. Farrington	Yamaha

Fastest lap: D. Molyneux/C. Hallam, 20m 04.5s/112.76mph*

Lightweight 250 (4 laps/150.92 miles)

1.	J. McGuinness 1h 17m 31.7s/116.79mph	Honda
2.	J. Griffiths	Yamaha
3.	G. Lee	Yamaha
4.	D. McCullough	Honda
5.	J. Dunlop	Honda
6.	G. Dynes	Honda
7.	B. Anstey	Yamaha
8.	R. Coates	Honda
9.	R. Richardson	Honda
10.	S. Brown	Honda

Fastest lap: J. McGuinness, 19m 08.2s/118.29mph*

Lightweight 400 (4 laps/150.92 miles)

1.	P. Williams 1h 23m 04.0s/109.01mph	Honda
2.	N. Piercy	Honda
3.	G. McMullan	Yamaha
4.	N. Jefferies	Yamaha
5.	B. Gardiner	Kawasaki
6.	D. Morris	Yamaha
7.	B. Degerholm	Kawasaki
8.	J. Vincent	Kawasaki
9.	P. Jarmann	Kawasaki
10.	B. Swallow	Honda

Fastest lap: P. Williams, 20m 25.9s/110.79mph

Sidecar Race B (3 laps/113.19 miles)

1.	R. Fisher/R. Long 1h 02m 26.3s/108.76mph	Honda
2.	I. Bell/N. Carpenter	Yamaha
3.	C. Lambert/L. Aubrey	Yamaha
4.	S. Norbury/A. Smith	Yamaha
5.	K. Howles/D. Jewell	Mistral
6.	M. Boddice Jnr/D. Wells	Honda
7.	R. Bellas/G. Knight	Yamaha
8.	M. Harvey/S. Thomas	Yamaha
9.	E. Wright/R. Pearce	Windle
10.	C. Harrison/M. Birdsell	Yamaha

Fastest lap: D. Molyneux/C. Hallam, 20m 08.3s/112.41mph

Ultra-Lightweight 125 (4 laps/150.92 miles)

1.	I. Lougher 1h 24m 17.3s/107.43mph	Honda
2.	O. McNally	Honda
3.	G. Dynes	Honda
4.	D. Lindsay	Honda
5.	R. Dunlop	Honda
6.	M. Wilcox	Honda
7.	T. Ritchie	Honda
8.	N. Richardson	Yamaha
9.	J. Crompton	Honda
10.	P. Harvey	Honda

Fastest lap: J. Dunlop, 20m 44.7s/109.12mph

Singles (4 laps/150.92 miles)

1.	D. Morris 1h 21m 54.0s/110.56mph	BMW
2.	B. Swallow	BRS
3.	R. Hawkins	Rotax
4.	D. Gallagher	Yamaha
5.	M. Jeffreys	Rotax
6.	D. Trollope	Yamaha
7.	A. Marsden	Yamaha
8.	H. Chittka	Yamaha
9.	A. Shortland	Rotax
10.	H. Robinson	Rotax

Fastest lap: J. Barton, 20m 10.4s/112.21mph

Junior (4 laps/150.92 miles)

Pos	Rider	Machine
1.	J. Moodie 1h 16m 39.8s/118.11mph	Honda
2.	D. Jefferies	Yamaha
3.	I. Duffus	Yamaha
4.	A. Archibald	Honda
5.	J. Dunlop	Honda
6.	J. Griffiths	Yamaha
7.	P. McCallen	Yamaha
8.	M. Rutter	Honda
9.	N. Davies	Yamaha
10.	B. Degerholm	Kawasaki

Fastest lap: D. Jefferies, 18m 53.6s/119.62mph

Production 1000 (3 laps/113.19 miles)

Pos	Rider	Machine
1.	D. Jefferies 56m 49.9s/119.50mph	Yamaha
2.	J. Griffiths	Yamaha
3.	P. McCallen	Yamaha
4.	A. Archibald	Honda
5.	G. Blackley	Kawasaki
6.	S. Smith	Yamaha
7.	N. Davies	Yamaha
8.	N. Jefferies	Yamaha
9.	R. Quayle	Kawasaki
10.	A. Bennallick	Yamaha

Fastest lap: I. Duffus, 18m 39.5s/121.32mph*

Senior (6 laps/226.38 miles)

Pos	Rider	Machine
1.	D. Jefferies 1h 51m 59.8s/121.27mph	Yamaha
2.	I. Duffus	Yamaha
3.	I. Lougher	Honda
4.	N. Davies	Yamaha
5.	J. Dunlop	Honda
6.	J. Griffiths	Yamaha
7.	J. McGuinness	Honda
8.	B. Degerholm	Kawasaki
9.	N. Jefferies	Kawasaki
10.	A. Bennallick	Honda

Fastest lap: J. Moodie, 18m 11.4s/124.45mph*

2000

Formula 1 (6 laps/226.38 miles)

Pos	Rider	Machine
1.	J. Dunlop 1h 52m 15.3s/120.99mph	Honda
2.	M. Rutter	Yamaha
3.	J. McGuinness	Honda
4.	I. Lougher	Yamaha
5.	J. Moodie	Honda
6.	J. Griffiths	Yamaha
7.	N. Davies	Yamaha
8.	C. Rennie	Kawasaki
9.	B. Gardiner	Honda
10.	J. Hodson	Kawasaki

Fastest lap: D. Jefferies, 18m 22.6s/123.18mph

Sidecar Race A (3 laps/113.19 miles)

Pos	Rider	Machine
1.	R. Fisher/R. Long 1h 01m 46.3s/109.94mph	Honda
2.	G. Horspole/K. Leigh	Honda
3.	S. Norbury/A. Smith	Honda
4.	R. Hanks/D. Wells	Yamaha
5.	B. Dixon/M. Lambert	Honda
6.	R. Baker/S. Parnell	Yamaha
7.	M. Cookson/C. Hibberd	Honda
8.	P. Dongworth/J. Leubke	Kawasaki
9.	C. Founds/P. Funds	Yamaha
10.	A. Laidlow/D. Hodgson	Yamaha

Fastest lap: R. Fisher/R. Long, 20m 26.8s/110.71mph

Lightweight 250 (3 laps/113.19 miles)

Pos	Rider	Machine
1.	J. Dunlop 58m 32.2s/116.01mph	Honda
2.	B. Anstey	Yamaha
3.	I. Lougher	Honda
4.	S. Harris	Honda
5.	J. Griffiths	Yamaha
6.	R. Quayle	Honda
7.	D. McCullough	Honda
8.	N. Richardson	Yamaha
9.	G. Dynes	Honda
10.	A. Jackson	Honda

Fastest lap: J. Dunlop, 19m 25.4s/116.55mph

Lightweight 400 (3 laps/113.19 miles)

Pos	Rider	Machine
1.	G. McMullan 1h 05m 17.9s/104.00mph	Yamaha
2.	B. Richmond	Honda
3.	B. Gardiner	Kawasaki
4.	R. Price	Yamaha
5.	J. Vincent	Kawasaki
6.	J. Barton	Yamaha
7.	P. Dobbs	Kawasaki
8.	P. McGee	Yamaha
9.	H. Chittka	Yamaha
10.	S. Barnett	Honda

Fastest lap: G. McMullan, 21m 20.4s/106.08mph

Sidecar Race B (3 laps/113.19 miles)

Pos	Rider	Machine
1.	R. Fisher/R. Long 1h 02m 52.2s/108.02mph	Honda
2.	S. Norbury/A. Smith	Honda
3.	G. Bell/C. Hallam	Yamaha
4.	G. Horspole/K. Leigh	Honda
5.	A. Schofield/I. Simons	Honda
6.	M. Harvey/S. Thomas	Yamaha
7.	B. Dixon/M. Lambert	Honda
8.	R. Baker/S. Parnell	Yamaha
9.	K. Howles/D. Jewell	Kawasaki
10.	S. Ramsden/P. Roberts	Jacobs

Fastest lap: G. Bell/C. Hallam, 20m 45.8s/109.02mph

Ultra-Lightweight 125 (4 laps/150.92 miles)

Pos	Rider	Machine
1.	J. Dunlop 1h 24m 30.8s/107.14mph	Honda
2.	D. McCullough	Honda
3.	R. Dunlop	Honda
4.	G. Dynes	Honda
5.	D. Lindsay	Honda
6.	I. Lougher	Honda
7.	M. Jackson	Honda
8.	C. Grose	Honda
9.	G. Bennett	Honda
10.	M. Wilcox	Honda

Fastest lap: J. Dunlop, 20m 51.1s/108.56mph

Singles (4 laps/150.92 miles)

Pos	Rider	Machine
1.	J. McGuinness 1h 22m 35.7s/109.63mph	AMDM
2.	J. Griffiths	AMDM
3.	J. Barton	Ducati
4.	R. A. Price	Yamaha
5.	E. Poole	Bimota
6.	P. Shaw	Suzuki
7.	M. Granie	Bimota
8.	K. Dixon	Seeley
9.	R. J. Price	Yamaha
10.	K. Wilkie	Seeley

Fastest lap: J. McGuinness, 20m 18.9s/111.43mph

Junior (4 laps/150.92 miles)

Pos	Rider	Machine
1.	D. Jefferies 1h 15m 52.8s/119.33	Yamaha
2.	A. Archibald	Honda
3.	I. Lougher	Yamaha
4.	J. Dunlop	Honda
5.	M. Rutter	Yamaha
6.	J. Moodie	Honda
7.	I. Duffus	Honda
8.	S. Harris	Yamaha
9.	B. Degerholm	Kawasaki
10.	R. Britton	Yamaha

Fastest lap: A. Archibald, 18m 41.1s/121.15mph*

Production 1000 (2 laps/75.46 miles)

Pos	Rider	Machine
1.	D. Jefferies 45m 55.6s/98.58mph	Yamaha
2.	R. Quayle	Honda
3.	M. Rutter	Yamaha
4.	R. Britton	Yamaha
5.	I. Duffus	Honda
6.	A. Archibald	Honda
7.	S. Harris	Suzuki
8.	J. Griffiths	Yamaha
9.	G. Blackley	Kawasaki
10.	J. Hodson	Kawasaki

Fastest lap: D. Jefferies, 22m 47.3s/99.34mph

Senior (6 laps/226.38 miles)

Pos	Rider	Machine
1.	D. Jefferies 1h 51m 22.8s/121.95mph	Yamaha
2.	M. Rutter	Yamaha
3.	J. Dunlop	Honda
4.	J. McGuinness	Honda
5.	A. Archibald	Honda
6.	J. Griffiths	Yamaha
7.	B. Degerholm	Kawasaki
8.	M. Davies	Yamaha
9.	G. Blackley	Kawasaki
10.	C. Rennie	Kawasaki

Fastest lap: D. Jefferies, 18m 00.6s/125.69mph*

2001

Note: The 2001 TT was cancelled due to the Foot and Mouth outbreak in the UK.

2002

Formula 1 (6 laps/226.38 miles)

1.	D. Jefferies	Suzuki
	1h 50m 05.10s/123.38mph	
2.	J. McGuinness	Honda
3.	J. Moodie	Yamaha
4.	I. Lougher	Suzuki
5.	R. Quayle	Suzuki
6.	J. Griffiths	Yamaha
7.	R. Britton	Suzuki
8.	R. Smith	Suzuki
9.	I. Duffus	Yamaha
10.	C. Heath	Yamaha

Fastest lap: D. Jefferies, 17m 52.2s/126.68mph*

Production 1000 (3 laps/113.19 miles)

1.	D. Jefferies	Suzuki
	55m 22.5s/122.64mph	
2.	I. Lougher	Suzuki
3.	B. Anstey	Suzuki
4.	J. Moodie	Yamaha
5.	I. Duffus	Suzuki
6.	J. McGuinness	Honda
7.	R. Britton	Suzuki
8.	R. Quayle	Suzuki
9.	A. Archibald	Honda
10.	J. Griffiths	Yamaha

Fastest lap: D. Jefferies, 18m 12.6s/124.31mph

Sidecar Race A (2 laps/75.46 miles)

1.	R. Fisher/R. Long	LMS
	1h 01m 25.9s/110.55mph	
2.	I. Bell/N. Carpenter	Yamaha
3.	G. Horspole/K. Leigh	Honda
4.	D. Molyneux/C. Hardman	Honda
5.	R. Hanks/D. Wells	Yamaha
6.	B. Dixon/M. Lambert	Honda
7.	P. Dongworth/S. Castles	Kawasaki
8.	S. Norbury/A. Smith	Yamaha
9.	M. Harvey.S. Thomas	Yamaha
10.	K. Howles/D. Jewell	Yamaha

Fastest lap: R. Fisher/R. Long, 20m 25.8s/110.80mph

Ultra-Lightweight 125 (4 laps/150.92 miles)

1.	I. Lougher	Honda
	1h 23m 20.4s/108.65mph	
2.	J. Crumpton	Honda
3.	R. Dunlop	Honda
4.	C. Palmer	Honda
5.	G. Bennett	Honda
6.	A. Jackson	Honda
7.	J. Vincent	Honda
8.	N. Bish	Honda
9.	N. Clegg	Honda
10.	B. Anstey	Yamaha

Fastest lap: I. Lougher, 20m 32.4s/110.21mph

Lightweight 400 (4 laps/150.92 miles)

1.	R. Quayle	Honda
	1h 22m 52.0s/109.27mph	
2.	J. Hodson	Yamaha
3.	R. Britton	Kawasaki
4.	N. Davies	Honda
5.	D. Madsen-Mygdal	Honda
6.	J. Barton	Yamaha
7.	J. McGuinness	Honda
8.	R. Farquhar	Kawasaki
9.	B. Gardiner	Kawasaki
10.	R. Price	Yamaha

Fastest lap: R. Quayle, 20m 28.4s/110.57mph

Production 600 (2 laps/75.46 miles)

1.	I. Lougher	Suzuki
	57m 08.4s/118.85mph	
2.	B. Anstey	Suzuki
3.	J. Moodie	Yamaha
4.	S. Harris	Suzuki
5.	A. Archibald	Honda
6.	R. Britton	Suzuki
7.	D. Jefferies	Suzuki
8.	G. Blackley	Honda
9.	R. Richardson	Suzuki
10.	J. McGuinness	Honda

Fastest lap: I. Lougher, 18m 49.5s/120.25mph

Senior (6 laps/226.38 miles)

1.	D. Jefferies	Suzuki
	1h 48m 53.1s/124.74mph	
2.	I. Lougher	Suzuki
3.	J. McGuinness	Honda
4.	R. Quayle	Suzuki
5.	R. Britton	Suzuki
6.	A. Archibald	Honda
7.	R. Farquhar	Yamaha
8.	C. Heath	Yamaha
9.	R. Smith	Suzuki
10.	S. Harris	Suzuki

Fastest lap: D. Jefferies, 17m 47.0s/127.29mph*

Sidecar Race B (3 laps/113.19 miles)

1.	R. Fisher/R. Long	Yamaha
	1h 01m 19.1s/110.75mph	
2.	D. Molyneux/C. Hardman	Honda
3.	I. Bell/N. Carpenter	Yamaha
4.	R. Hanks/D. Wells	Yamaha
5.	G. Horspole/K. Leigh	Honda
6.	P. Dongworth/S. Castles	Kawasaki
7.	K. Howles/D. Jewell	Yamaha
8.	T. Baker/S. Parnell	Yamaha
9.	B. Dixon/M. Lambert	Honda
10.	A. Laidlow/D. Dodgson	Yamaha

Fastest lap: R. Fisher/R. Long, 20m 17.3s/111.58mph

Lightweight 250 (4 laps/150.92 miles)

1.	B. Anstey	Yamaha
	1h 18m 31.1s/115.32mph	
2.	R. Smith	Honda
3.	R. Richardson	Honda
4.	R. Coates	Honda
5.	K. Shannon	Honda
6.	H. Voit	Honda
7.	P. Owen	Honda
8.	T. Keys	Honda
9.	D. Kelly	Yamaha
10.	H. Robinson	Honda

Fastest lap: B. Anstey, 19m 10.7s/118.03mph

Junior (4 laps/150.92 miles)

1.	J. Moodie	Yamaha
	1h 15m 56.9s/119.22mph	
2.	I. Lougher	Suzuki
3.	J. Griffiths	Yamaha
4.	R. Britton	Suzuki
5.	R. Farquhar	Kawasaki
6.	R. Quayle	Honda
7.	A. Archibald	Honda
8.	S. Harris	Suzuki
9.	B. Gardiner	Honda
10.	I. Duffus	Yamaha

Fastest lap: J. Moodie, 18m 45.9s/120.63mph

2003

Formula 1 (6 laps/226.38 miles)

1.	A. Archibald	Suzuki
	1h 50m 15.7s/123.18mph	
2.	I. Lougher	Honda
3.	J. McGuinness	Ducati
4.	J. Griffiths	Yamaha
5.	R. Farquhar	Suzuki
6.	S. Harris	Suzuki
7.	B. Blackley	Suzuki
8.	C. Heath	Suzuki
9.	P. Hunt	Suzuki
10.	G. Carswell	Suzuki

Fastest lap: A. Archibald, 18m 02.9s/125.43mph

Sidecar Race A (3 laps/113.19 miles)

1.	I. Bell/N. Carpenter	Yamaha
	1h 01m 39.0s/110.16mph	
2.	N. Crowe/D. Hope	Yamaha
3.	S. Norbury/A. Smith	Yamaha
4.	A. Laidlow/P. Farrance	Yamaha
5.	T. Baker/M. Hegarty	Yamaha
6.	A. Schofield/M. Cox	Jacobs
7.	G. Bell/J. Beckworth	Yamaha
8.	J. Holden/C. Hardman	Yamaha
9.	M. Harvey/S. Taylor	Shelbourne
10.	A. Brown/J. Dowling	Yamaha

Fastest lap: I. Bell/N. Carpenter, 20m 25.7s/110.81mph

Lightweight 400 (4 laps/150.92 miles)

1.	J. McGuinness	Honda
	1h 22m 40.97s/109.52mph	
2.	R. Britton	Honda
3.	R. Farquhar	Kawasaki
4.	D. Madsen-Mygdal	Honda
5.	R. J. Price	Yamaha
6.	A. Bennie	Yamaha
7.	C. McLean	Yamaha
8.	M. Hose	Kawasaki
9.	P. Jarmann	Kawasaki
10.	R. A. Price	Yamaha

Fastest lap: J. McGuinness, 20m 19.68s/111.36mph

Ultra-Lightweight 125 (4 laps/150.92 miles)

1.	C. Palmer	Honda
	1h 23m 20.57s/110.41mph	
2.	M. Wilcox	Honda
3.	I. Lougher	Honda
4.	R. Dunlop	Honda
5.	N. Beattie	Honda
6.	P. Owen	Honda
7.	T. Roebuck	Honda
8.	N. Moore	Honda

9.	M. Tyrrell	Honda
10.	M. Jackson	Honda

Fastest lap: C. Palmer, 20m 35.25s/110.41mph

Production 1000 (3 laps/113.19 miles)

1.	S. Harris	Suzuki
	55m 39.3s/122.02mph	
2.	B. Anstey	Suzuki
3.	R. Farquhar	Suzuki
4.	R. Britton	Suzuki
5.	C. Heath	Suzuki
6.	J. Griffiths	Yamaha
7.	P. Hunt	Suzuki
8.	A. Archibald	Suzuki
9.	M. Finnegan	Suzuki
10.	C. Breeze	Suzuki

Fastest lap: S. Harris, 18m 19.37s/123.55mph

Junior (4 laps/150.92 miles)

1.	B. Anstey	Triumph
	1h 15m 13.98s/120.36mph	
2.	I. Lougher	Honda
3.	A. Archibald	Suzuki
4.	R. Farquhar	Kawasaki
5.	S. Harris	Suzuki
6.	J. Griffiths	Yamaha
7.	R. Britton	Kawasaki
8.	G. Blackley	Honda
9.	J. Moodie	Triumph
10.	J. McGuinness	Triumph

Fastest lap: R. Farquhar, 18m 30.65s/122.30mph

Sidecar Race B (3 laps/113.19 miles)

1.	D. Molyneux/C. Hallam	Honda
	1h 04m 25.17s/105.42mph	
2.	N. Crowe/D. Hope	Ireson
3.	G. Lambert/D.Sayle	Molyneux
4.	B. Dixon/M. Lambert	Molyneux
5.	G. Bell/J. Beckworth	Yamaha
6.	J. Holden/C. Hardman	Yamaha
7.	A. Laidlow/P. Farrance	Yamaha
8.	R. Hanks/D. Wells	Molyneux
9.	A. Schofield/M. Cox	Jacobs
10.	A. Brown/J. Dowling	Yamaha

Fastest lap: D. Molyneux/C. Hallam, 20m 46.19s/108.99mph

Production 600 (2 laps/75.46 miles)

1.	S. Harris	Suzuki
	37m 49.79s/119.68mph	
2.	I. Lougher	Honda
3.	R. Farquhar	Kawasaki
4.	A. Archibald	Suzuki
5.	J. Griffiths	Yamaha
6.	R. Britton	Honda
7.	M. Finnegan	Honda
8.	B. Anstey	Triumph
9.	C. Heath	Yamaha
10.	R. Richardson	Kawasaki

Fastest lap: S. Harris, 18m 54.28s/119.75mph

Senior (4 laps/150.92 miles)

1.	A. Archibald	Suzuki
	1h 12m 42.91s/124.53mph	
2.	J. McGuinness	Ducati
3.	I. Lougher	Honda
4.	J. Griffiths	Yamaha
5.	R. Farquhar	Suzuki
6.	S. Harris	Suzuki
7.	B. Anstey	Suzuki
8.	R. Britton	Suzuki
9.	M. Parrett	Kawasaki
10.	G. Carswell	Suzuki

Fastest lap: A. Archibald, 17m 51.0s/126.78mph

2004

Formula 1 (4 laps/150.92 miles)

1.	J. McGuinness	Yamaha
	1h 12m 13.2s/125.38mph	
2.	A. Archibald	Suzuki
3.	B. Anstey	Suzuki
4.	J. Griffiths	Yamaha
5.	I. Lougher	Honda
6.	R. Britton	Suzuki
7.	M. Parrett	Yamaha
8.	C. Heath	Honda
9.	I. Armstrong	Yamaha
10.	I. Hutchinson	Suzuki

Fastest lap: J. McGuinness, 17m 43.8s/127.68mph*

Sidecar Race A (3 laps/113.19 miles)

1.	D. Molyneux/D. Sayle	Honda
	1h 01m 00.0s/111.33mph	
2.	N. Crowe/D. Hope	Honda
3.	S. Norbury/S. Parnell	Yamaha
4.	R. Hanks/D. Wells	Yamaha
5.	G. Lambert/I. Murray	Honda
6.	P. Dongworth/S. Castles	Kawasaki
7.	B. Dixon/M. Lambert	Honda
8.	G. Bryan/S. Hedison	Yamaha
9.	K. Howles/D. Jewell	Yamaha
10.	B. Currie/P. Bridge	Yamaha

Fastest lap: D. Molyneux/D. Sayle, 20m 06.1s/112.61mph

Lightweight 400 (4 laps/150.92 miles)

1.	J. McGuinness	Honda
	1h 22m 06.4s/110.28mph	
2.	S. Linsdell	Yamaha
3.	M. Parrett	Honda
5.	R. Richardson	Honda
5.	J. Barton	Yamaha
6.	D. Slous	Yamaha
7.	A. Bennie	Yamaha
8.	J. Hodson	Yamaha
9.	T. Montano	Yamaha
10.	R. Price	Yamaha

Fastest lap: J. McGuinness, 20m 12.3s/112.04mph

Ultra-Lightweight 125 (4 laps/150.92 miles)

1.	C. Palmer	Honda
	1h 23m 07.6s/108.93mph	
2.	R. Dunlop	Honda
3.	N. Beattie	Honda
4.	G. Bennett	Honda
5.	M. Jackson	Honda
6.	M. Tyrrell	Honda
7.	J. Vincent	Honda
8.	T. Roebuck	Honda
9.	T. Ritchie	Honda
10.	C. McGahan	Honda

Fastest lap: C. Palmer, 20m 28.9s/110.52mph

Production 1000 (3 laps/113.19 miles)

1.	B. Anstey	Suzuki
	54m 53.50s/123.72mph	
2.	J. McGuinness	Yamaha
3.	J. Griffiths	Yamaha
4.	I. Lougher	Honda
5.	A. Archibald	Suzuki
6.	R. Britton	Suzuki
7.	M. Parrett	Yamaha
8.	G. Carswell	Yamaha
9.	I. Armstrong	Yamaha
10.	N. Davies	Suzuki

Fastest lap: B. Anstey, 18m 05.7s/125.10mph

Junior (4 laps/150.92 miles)

1.	J. McGuinness	Yamaha
	1h 15m 06.0s/120.57mph	
2.	B. Anstey	Suzuki
3.	J. Griffiths	Yamaha
4.	R. Britton	Honda
5.	M. Parrett	Yamaha
6.	M. Finnegan	Yamaha
7.	G. Blackley	Honda
8.	R. Porter	Suzuki
9.	P. Hunt	Suzuki
10.	C. Heath	Yamaha

Fastest lap: J. McGuinness, 18m 25.4s/122.87mph*

Sidecar Race B (3 laps/113.19 miles)

1.	D. Molyneux/D. Sayle	Honda
	1h 01m 04.2s/111.20mph	
2.	N. Crowe/D. Hope	Honda
3.	S. Norbury/S. Parnell	Yamaha
4.	R. Hanks/D. Wells	Yamaha
5.	G. Bryan/S. Hedison	Yamaha
6.	G. Lambert/I. Murray	Honda
7.	J. Holden/J. Winn	Honda
8.	B. Dixon/M. Lambert	Honda
9.	A. Schofield/M. Cox	Equipe
10.	B. Currie/P. Bridge	Yamaha

Fastest lap: D. Molyneux/D. Sayle, 20m 00.2s/113.17mph

Production 600 (4 laps/150.92 miles)

1.	R. Farquhar	Kawasaki
	57m 46.1s/117.54mph	
2.	B. Anstey	Suzuki
3.	J. McGuinness	Yamaha
4.	J. Griffiths	Yamaha
5.	I. Lougher	Honda
6.	R. Porter	Suzuki
7.	C. Heath	Yamaha
8.	G. Blackley	Honda
9.	A. Archibald	Suzuki
10.	M. Parrett	Honda

Fastest lap: R. Farquhar, 19m 01.9s/118.94mph

Senior (4 laps/150.92 miles)

1.	A. Archibald	Suzuki
	1h 13m 08.1s/123.81mph	
2.	B. Anstey	Suzuki
3.	G. Carswell	Suzuki
4.	M. Parrett	Yamaha

5.	M. Finnegan	Yamaha
6.	C. Heath	Honda
7.	G. Martin	Suzuki
8.	G. Blackley	Honda
9.	D. Bell	Suzuki
10.	I. Armstrong	Yamaha

Fastest lap: J. McGuinness, 17m 49.9s/127.19mph

2005

Sidecar Race A (3 laps/113.19 miles)

1.	N. Crowe/D. Hope 1h 01m 49.3s/109.85mph	Honda
2.	S. Norbury/A. Smith	Shelbourne
3.	J. Holden/J. Winn	Honda
4.	P. Dongworth/S. Castle	Ireson
5.	S. Neary/S. Bond	Yamaha
6.	T. Baker/M. Hergarty	Yamaha
7.	B. Dixon/M. Lambert	Honda
8.	K. Klaffenbock/C. Parzer	Honda
9.	R. Stockton/P. Alton	Shelbourne
10.	B. Currie/K. Williams	Yamaha

Fastest lap: D. Molyneux/D. Sayle, 20m 12.8s/111.99mph

Superbike (6 laps/226.38 miles)

1.	J. McGuinness 1h 49m 25.74s/124.12mph	Yamaha
2.	A. Archibald	Suzuki
3.	M. Finnegan	Honda
4.	I. Lougher	Honda
5.	R. Porter	Yamaha
6.	G. Martin	Suzuki
7.	J. Griffiths	Yamaha
8.	C. Heath	Honda
9.	J. Maeda	Honda
10.	I. Armstrong	Yamaha

Fastest lap: J. McGuinness, 17m 50.53s/126.87mph

Superstock (3 laps/113.19 miles)

1.	B. Anstey 54m 39.74s/124.24mph	Suzuki
2.	I. Lougher	Honda
3.	R. Farquhar	Kawasaki
4.	J. Griffiths	Yamaha
5.	G. Martin	Suzuki
6.	P. Hunt	Suzuki
7.	M. Finnegan	Honda
8.	R. Britton	Honda
9.	I. Hutchinson	Honda
10.	C. Heath	Yamaha

Fastest lap: A. Archibald, 17m 52.54s/126.64mph

Supersport Junior A (4 laps/150.92 miles)

1.	I. Lougher 1h 14m 52.84s/120.92mph	Honda
2.	J. McGuinness	Yamaha
3.	J. Griffiths	Yamaha
4.	B. Anstey	Suzuki
5.	G. Martin	Honda
6.	R. Porter	Yamaha
7.	D. Lindsay	Honda
8.	A. Archibald	Suzuki
9.	J. Maeda	Honda
10.	N. Beattie	Yamaha

Fastest lap: R. Farquhar, 18m 27.54s/122.63mph

Supersport Junior B (4 laps/150.92 miles)

1.	R. Farquhar 1h 15m 01.42s/120.69mph	Kawasaki
2.	J. Griffiths	Yamaha
3.	R. Porter	Yamaha
4.	G. Martin	Honda
5.	M. Finnegan	Honda
6.	J. Maeda	Honda
7.	I. Hutchinson	Honda
8.	N. Beattie	Yamaha
9.	G. Carswell	Yamaha
10.	C. Palmer	Honda

Fastest lap: J. Griffiths, 18m 28.44s/122.54mph

Sidecar Race B (3 laps/113.19 miles)

1.	D. Molyneux/D. Sayle 59m 06.39s/114.90mph	Honda
2.	N. Crowe/D. Hope	Honda
3.	S. Norbury/A. Smith	Yamaha
4.	S. Neary/S. Bond	Yamaha
5.	R. Hanks/D. Wells	Molyneux-Rose
6.	B. Dixon/M. Lambert	Honda
7.	J. Holden/J. Winn	Honda
8.	T. Baker/M. Hegarty	Yamaha
9.	R. Stockton/P. Alton	Yamaha
10.	B. Currie/K. Williams	Yamaha

Fastest lap: D. Molyneux/D. Sayle, 19m 30.49/116.04mph

Senior (6 laps/226.38 miles)

1.	J. McGuinness 1h 49m 15.16s/124.32mph	Yamaha
2.	I. Lougher	Honda
3.	G. Martin	Suzuki
4.	M. Finnegan	Honda
5.	R. Britton	Honda
6.	J. Maeda	Honda
7.	J. Griffiths	Yamaha
8.	I. Hutchinson	Honda
9.	N. Beattie	Yamaha
10.	C. Palmer	Yamaha

Fastest lap: J. McGuinness, 17m 46.77s/127.32mph*

2006

Superbike (6 laps/226.38 miles)

1.	J. McGuinness 1h 48m 52.06s/124.76mph	Honda
2.	I. Lougher	Honda
3.	I. Hutchinson	Kawasaki
4.	M. Finnegan	Honda
5.	C. Donald	Honda
6.	J. Griffiths	Yamaha
7.	C. Rennie	Kawasaki
8.	P. Hunt	Yamaha
9.	D. Morgan	Honda
10.	R. Porter	Yamaha

Fastest lap: J. McGuinness, 17m 41.71s/127.93mph*

Superstock (4 laps/150.92 miles)

1.	B. Anstey 1h 12m 56.34s/124.14mph	Suzuki
2.	I. Hutchinson	Kawasaki
3.	J. Grifftihs	Yamaha
4.	G. Martin	Yamaha
5.	J. McGuinness	Honda
6.	I. Lougher	Honda
7.	M. Finnegan	Honda
8.	M. Parrett	Yamaha
9.	G. Carswell	Suzuki
10.	R. Frost	Honda

Fastest lap: B. Anstey, 17m 56.26s/126.20mph

Sidecar Race A (3 laps/113.19 miles)

1.	N. Crowe/D. Hope 1h 00m 27.15s/112.34mph	Honda
2.	S. Norton/S. Parnell	Yamaha
3.	J. Holden/A. Winkle	Honda
4.	R. Hanks/D. Wells	Yamaha
5.	G. Bryan/C. Hardman	Yamaha
6.	A. Laidlow/P. Farrance	Suzuki
7.	P. Dongworth/S. Castles	Yamaha
8.	T. Elmer/D. Marshall	Yamaha
9.	G. Jones/C. Lake	Honda
10.	D. Wallis/S. Wilson	Honda

Fastest lap: N. Crowe/D. Hope, 19m 55.97s/113.57mph

Supersport Junior 600 (4 laps/150.92 miles)

1.	J. McGuinness 1h 14m 03.73s/122.26mph	Honda
2.	I. Hutchinson	Kawasaki
3.	B. Anstey	Suzuki
4.	J. Griffiths	Yamaha
5.	I. Lougher	Honda
6.	C. Donald	Honda
7.	M. Finnegan	Honda
8.	N. Beattie	Yamaha
9.	D. Stewart	Yamaha
10.	M. Parrett	Yamaha

Fastest lap: J. McGuinness, 18m 15.61s/123.97mph

Sidecar Race B (3 laps/113.19 miles)

1.	N. Crowe/D. Hope 1h 00m 55.64s/111.46mph	Honda
2.	S. Norbury/S. Parbell	Yamaha
3.	R. Hanks/D. Wells	Yamaha
4.	B. Currie/M. Cox	Yamaha
5.	T. Baker/M. Hegarty	Yamaha
6.	C. Harrison/K. Hibberd	Honda
7.	R. Stockton/P.Alton	Yamaha
8.	K. Howles/D. Jewell	Suzuki
9.	J. Holden/A. Winkle	Honda
10.	N. Connole/J. Winn	Honda

Fastest lap: N. Crowe/D. Hope, 20m 09.35s/112.31mph

Senior (6 laps/226.38 miles)

1.	J. McGuinness 1h 47m 38.84s/126.17mph	Honda
2.	C. Donald	Honda
3.	B. Anstey	Suzuki
4.	I. Lougher	Honda
5.	G. Martin	Yamaha
6.	C. Rennie	Kawasaki
7.	D. Morgan	Honda
8.	R. Porter	Yamaha
9.	N. Beattie	Yamaha
10.	G. Carswell	Suzuki

Fastest lap: J. McGuinness, 17m 29.6s/129.45mph*

SELECT BIBLIOGRAPHY

Agostini, Giacomo and Delli Carri, Luca: *'Fifteen Times'*, Fucina, 2004.

Barker, Stuart: *'Barry Sheene 1950-2003: The Biography'*, Collins Willow, 2003.

Cade, Laurie: *'TT Thrills'*, Frederick Muller Ltd, 1957.

Crellin, Ralph: *'Japanese Riders in the Isle of Man'*, R&J Crellin Books, 1995.

Cringle, Terry: *'Manannan's Kingdom'*, Lily Publications Ltd, 2002.

Davison, G. S.: *'Racing Reminiscences'*, W.W. Curtis Ltd for The TT Special, 1948.

Davison, G. S.: *'The Story of the TT'*, W.W. Curtis Ltd for The TT Special, 1947.

Deane, Charles: *'Isle of Man TT'*, Patrick Stephens Limited, 1975.

Douglas, Andrew; Beighton, Peter; and Hislop, Steve: *'You Couldn't do it Now'*, Mannin Printing Limited, 1993.

Duke, Geoff: *'In Pursuit of Perfection'*, Osprey, 1988.

Fogarty, Carl and Bramwell, Neil: *'Foggy'*, Collins Willow, 2000.

Freudenberg, Matthew: *'The Isle of Man TT. An Illustrated History: 1907-80'*, Aston Publications, 1990.

Harris, Nick: *'Motocourse History of the TT Races: 1907-1989'*, Hazleton Securities Ltd, 1990.

Hilton, Christopher: *'A Man Called Mike'*, Motor Sport Publications Ltd, 1992.

Hislop, Steve and Barker, Stuart: *'Hizzy: The Autobiography of Steve Hislop'*, Collins Willow, 2003.

Kane, Gerard and Clark, Nigel (eds): *'Between the Hedges: History of the TT 1907-2000'*. Mortons Motorcycle Media Limited, 2000.

Kelly, Robert: *'How the TT Started'*, Island Development Co. (undated).

Kneale, Peter, and Kniveton, Gordon: *'The TT Experience'*, The Manx Experience, 1984.

Kneale, Peter and Snelling, Bill: *'Honda: The TT Winning Years'*, Amulree Publications, 1998.

Macauley, Ted: *'Mike: The Life and Times of Mike Hailwood'*, Buchan & Enright, 1984.

Marshall, Roger and Martin, Keith: *'Roger and Out'*, McKinnon Farmer Publishing Ltd, 1989.

McCallen, Phillip and Woods, Phil: *'Supermac'*, Aureus Publishing Ltd, 2000.

McDiarmid, Mac: *'Joey Dunlop: His Authorised Biography'*, Haynes Publishing, 2001.

McDiarmid, Mac: *'The Magic of the TT: A Century of Racing over the Mountain Circuit'*, Haynes Publishing, 2004.

Noyes, D; Scott, M; et al: *'Motocourse: 50 Years of Moto Grand Prix'*, Hazleton Publishing Ltd, 1999.

Peck, Alan: *'No Time to Lose: The Fast Moving World of Bill Ivy'*, Motor Racing Publications Ltd, 1972.

Pinchin, Gary: *'Isle of Man TT 1989 Review'*, McKinnon Farmer, 1989.

Pinchin, Gary: *'Isle of Man TT 1990 Review'*, McKinnon Farmer, 1990.

Read, Phil: *'Prince of Speed'*, Arthur Barker Limited, 1970.

Redman, Jim: *'Jim Redman: Six Times World Motorcycle Champion'*, Veloce Publishing Plc, 1998.

Redman, Jim: *'Wheels of Fortune'*, Stanley Paul, 1966.

Robb, Tommy: *'From TT to Tokyo'*, Courier-Herald Printers, 1974.

Savage, Mike: *'TT Heroes'*, Amulree Publications, 1997.

Snelling, Bill: *'The Tourist Trophy in Old Photographs'*, Alan Sutton Publishing Limited, 1994.

Surtees, John: *'Speed: John Surtees' Own Story'*, Arthur Barker Limited, 1963.

Walker, Mick: *'History of Motorcycles'*, Hamlyn, 1997.

Walker, Mick: *'Bob McIntyre: The Flying Scot'*, Breedon Books Publishing, 2006.

Walker, Mick: *'John Surtees: Motorcycle Maestro'*, Breedon Books Publishing, 2003.

Woollett, Mick: *'Mike Hailwood: A Motorcycle Racing Legend'*, Haynes Publishing, 2000.

Wright, David: *'TT Topics & Tales'*, Amulree Publications, 2006.

Mike Hailwood runs it wide at Governor's Bridge in his epic 1967 Senior battle with Giacomo Agostini. Both riders finished the race with scraped leathers from brushing stone walls and cottages.